EMILY DARE

CANADIAN HOSPITALITY LAW

LIABILITIES AND RISK

LONGCHAMPS • WRIGHT

D1294066

Emily DARE

Canadian Hospitality Law

Liabilities and Risk

Third Edition

Donald Longchamps
Algonquin College of Applied Arts
and Technology

Bradley H. Wright
The Wright Law Firm
Barrister & Solicitor

CANADIAN
HOSPITALITY
LAW

LIABILITIES AND RISK

LONGCHAMPS • WRIGHT

NELSON / EDUCATION

NELSON EDUCATION

Canadian Hospitality Law: Liabilities and Risk,
Third Edition

by Donald Longchamps and Bradley H. Wright

**Associate Vice-President,
Editorial Director:**
Evelyn Veitch

Marketing Manager:
Nigel Corish

Senior Developmental Editor:
Joanne Sutherland

Photo Researcher:
Kristiina Bowering

Permissions Coordinator:
Kristiina Bowering

Senior Production Editor:
Bob Kohlmeier

Copy Editor:
Erin Moore

Proofreader:
Carol J. Anderson

Indexer:
Dennis A. Mills

Production Coordinator:
Kathrine Pummell

Design Director:
Ken Phipps

Interior Design:
Fernanda Pisani

Cover Design:
Courtney Hellam

Cover Image:
Todd Pearson/Photodisc Red/
Getty Images

Compositor:
Integra

Printer:
Digital Print Center

COPYRIGHT © 2007 by
Nelson Education Ltd.

Printed and bound in Canada
10 11 12 13 17 16 15 14

For more information contact
Nelson Education Ltd.,
1120 Birchmount Road, Toronto,
Ontario, M1K 5G4. Or you
can visit our Internet site at
http://www.nelson.com

ALL RIGHTS RESERVED. No part of
this work covered by the copyright
herein may be reproduced,
transcribed, or used in any form or
by any means—graphic, electronic,
or mechanical, including
photocopying, recording, taping,
Web distribution, or information
storage and retrieval systems—
without the written permission of
the publisher.

For permission to use material
from this text or product,
submit all requests online at
www.cengage.com/permissions.
Further questions about
permissions can be emailed to
permissionrequest@cengage.com

Every effort has been made to
trace ownership of all copyrighted
material and to secure permission
from copyright holders. In the
event of any question arising as to
the use of any material, we will be
pleased to make the necessary
corrections in future printings.

**Library and Archives Canada
Cataloguing in Publication**

Longchamps, Donald, 1946–
Canadian hospitality law : liabilities
and risks / Donald Longchamps and
Bradley H. Wright. — 3rd ed.

Includes bibliographical refrences
and index.
ISBN 0-17-640721-9

1. Hospitality industry—Law and
legislation—Canada.
I. Wright, Bradley H. (Bradley
Herbert), 1952– II. Title.

KE1987.H65L66 2006
343.71'07864794   C2005-907210-5
KF2042.H6L66 2006

To my parents, Don and Agnes Longchamps,
and to Jane and Jessie Longchamps
for their assistance and encouragement

To my parents, Stuart and Joann Wright,
and to Susan, Brennan, Heather, and Emily
with my gratitude, love, and admiration

Brief Contents

Preface   xxvii
Acknowledgments   xxviii
About the Authors   xxix

Contents

Part 3   *Innkeepers and Guests*   *176*

Chapter 8   The Innkeeper–Guest Relationship   178

Chapter 9   Innkeepers   190

Part 4   *Management in the Hospitality Industry*   *238*

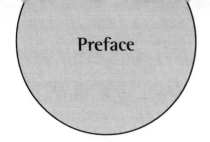

Preface

This book has been written for students and teachers of hospitality and travel law, and for lawyers, owners, managers, employees, and consumers in the hospitality industry. Readers of the book should gain valuable and practical insights into:

- the law applicable to hospitality businesses

- the nature of the relationships between innkeeper and guest, restaurateur and diner, travel agent and traveller, and private host and guest

- how to institute and maintain legal and management policies and practices that enhance a hospitality business

- how to prevent regulatory and other legal missteps concerning matters such as business licence requirements and employer–employee relations

- how to reduce the chances of negligence or of human rights liability to staff and the public

- how to read and use contracts, including conversing more knowledgeably with lawyers

- how to buy and operate a hospitality business

The authors still remember their student days, and we hope readers will find this book informative and interesting. We welcome your comments and suggestions.

Except for names in reported cases, all names used in the book are fictitious.

Donald Longchamps

Bradley H. Wright

Acknowledgments

The authors gratefully acknowledge the invaluable assistance of the people named below. Many others also helped but either did not wish to be acknowledged or were omitted by error. Our apologies to anyone we may have offended by the absence (or inclusion) of their names.

Donald Blakslee, *General Manager, Lord Elgin Hotel, Ottawa*

Lorraine Chaput, *Professor, Algonquin College of Applied Arts and Technology*

Enrico DeFrancesco, *Coordinator Bar Management, Algonquin College*

Robert Findlay, *Manager Retired, Embassy Hotel, Ottawa*

Rodger Johnston, *Professor, Algonquin College of Applied Arts and Technology*

Breda Kelly, *Algonquin College of Applied Arts and Technology*

Bob Kohlmeier, *Senior Production Editor, Thomson Nelson*

Jane Longchamps, *Chartered Accountant, Nortel Networks*

Moira McDonald, *Chateau Laurier Hotel, Ottawa*

Karen MacLaurin, *County of Carleton Law Library*

Joseph Mariani, *Professor, Algonquin College of Applied Arts and Technology*

Malcolm M. Mercer, *McCarthy Tétrault, Toronto*

Janine Miller, *Osgoode Hall Law Library, Toronto*

Erin Moore, *Copy Editor*

Mothers Against Drunk Driving

Kenneth J. Peacocke, *Legal Researcher*

Leanne Seel, *Parker Prins Seel, Chartered Accountants, Ottawa*

Ross Smiley, *Paragon Review & Consulting Inc., Ottawa*

Joanne Sutherland, *Senior Developmental Editor, Thomson Nelson*

Traffic Injury Research Foundation of Canada

Evelyn Veitch, *Associate Vice-President and Editorial Director, Thomson Nelson*

Stuart Wright, *Coté, Taschereau, Samson et Demers, Notaires, Quebec City*

We also express our appreciation to the following individuals who provided thoughtful reviews and useful suggestions, anonymously at the time, that helped improve this book.

David Butterton, *The Canadian Tourism College, Vancouver*

Bev Denyes, *Loyalist College of Applied Arts & Technology, Belleville*

Jim McCloy, *Red Deer College, Red Deer*

Gail McKay, *University College of the Cariboo, Kamloops*

Gail Muir, *University College of Cape Breton, Sydney*

Don Valeri, *Douglas College, New Westminster*

About the Authors

Donald P. Longchamps is a professor at Algonquin College of Applied Arts and Technology in Ottawa, Ontario, where he teaches courses in hotel and restaurant law, managerial accounting, and food and beverage control. He continues to consult in the hospitality field and has over 25 years' experience in the ownership and operation of hotels and restaurants in Canada and the United States. He is an advocate for the responsible use of alcohol and was a founding member of the Designated Driver Program for the former City of Nepean (now Ottawa). He has been recognized as an expert witness by The Superior Court of Justice in Ontario. Mr. Longchamps earned his Bachelor of Science in Hotel Administration at the University of Massachusetts, Amherst, his Diploma in Business Administration at the Eastern Ontario Institute of Technology, Ottawa, and his Certified Hospitality Instructor from the Education Institute in East Lansing, Michigan. He resides in Ottawa, Ontario. He may be reached as follows: Tel: 613-727-4723 x5416   Fax: 613-727-7670   E-mail: longchd@algonquincollege.com

Bradley H. Wright is a lawyer in private practice in Ottawa, Ontario, with over 23 years' experience in the fields of hospitality law, corporate and commercial law, real estate, and wills and estates. He earned his Bachelor of Arts and Bachelor of Law degrees at the University of Ottawa. He was called to the Bar in 1983. Since 1995, he has served as a bencher (governor) of the Law Society of Upper Canada, the body that regulates the legal profession in Ontario. He is a former trustee of the Law Foundation of Ontario, a charity that funds legal aid, public legal education, and research. He is a former Treasurer of CORDI, Carleton-Ottawa Residence for Disabled, Inc. He has taught several courses in business law and estate law at the community college level, guest-lectured at the university level, and has been a presenter at various continuing legal education seminars for fellow lawyers. He is the author of the book and libretto for *ROLES AWRY! Or The Cast That Ran Amok*, commissioned and performed by the Gilbert and Sullivan Society, Toronto Branch. Mr. Wright welcomes comments and feedback, and may be reached as follows: Tel: 613-825-8800   Fax: 613-825-9200   E-mail: wrightb@sympatico.ca

PART
ONE

The Legal Framework

1

Chapter One

The Canadian Legal System

Learning Outcomes

1. Define law.

2. Explain positive law, natural law, and legal realism.

3. List the purposes of law.

4. List the sources of law in Canada.

5. List the players in the Canadian legal system.

6. Explain the principles of common law.

7. Differentiate between divisions of law.

8. List the federal and provincial courts.

9. Describe the procedure in both civil and criminal matters.

Introduction

It is human nature to wait for problems, legal and non-legal, to arise before attending to them. Once they arise, they become more difficult and expensive to solve. For this reason, doctors make more money doing heart bypasses than they do advising their patients about healthy lifestyles. In law, as in health, an ounce of prevention is worth a pound of cure. Lawyers make more money addressing problems after they arise than they do preventing them. Those who would like to see a large number of lawyers put out of business should follow this simple rule: Do not enter into any agreement or relationship having legal consequences without first consulting a lawyer. For the players in the hospitality industry—owners, managers, employees, guests, and patrons—a defensive approach to the law pays dividends. In this book, we shall try to provide the players with the knowledge and skills that will enable them to better protect themselves and their businesses from negative legal experiences, which can be as mundane as licensing irregularities or as complex as multi-million-dollar personal injury lawsuits. As we navigate across the seamless web of **hospitality law**, we will be your travel agents. We will tour the legal system, drop in on human rights, enter into contracts, explore negligence, and send you to a wide variety of hotels and restaurants. We hope you enjoy the journey.

What Is the Law?

General Definitions

"**Law**" is an old Norse word imported to Great Britain by Viking invaders around the 7th century A.D. It means "layer" or "stratum," evoking a concept of laws that are laid down logically and strategically. Other legal words, such as "legal" itself, are not descended from law, but from *lex*, the Latin word for law.

The *Oxford English Dictionary* defines law broadly as "[t]he body of rules, whether formally enacted or customary, which a state or community recognizes as binding on its members or subjects." The problem with such a broad definition is that it applies as much to customary rules of etiquette in a community as it does to rules of law enacted by a state. While etiquette and law both govern human behaviour, the two terms are not synonymous. Other definitions incorporate the idea of enforcement. In *Introduction to English Law* (1989), Phillip James defines the law as "a set of rules which are generally obeyed and enforced within a politically organized society." By this definition, laws are societal rules that can be enforced by a political authority or by private citizens through the court system, police measures, and other means of enforcement. Social mores, by contrast, are enforced socially, not politically, and are not laws in this sense.

The rules of private clubs and the terms of private contracts are also not laws in James's sense because they are not enforced politically, at least at first instance, but by the consensus of the members of the club or the parties to the contract. However, these rules and terms may be enforced by resorting to laws. In an important sense, rules of etiquette, club rules, contract terms, and law may be regarded as part of a single continuum of mores and rules pertaining to human conduct and interaction. The farther along the continuum one travels, the more serious become the consequences of failing to abide by the rules. Although there is an increasingly severe set of sanctions for breaching the rules of etiquette, at some point the state steps in and begins imposing an increasingly severe set of sanctions of its own. Thus, it is legitimate to think of murder as the worst manners, but so bad that the state is compelled to step in and impose severe consequences for committing it. On the other hand, using the wrong fork is, most agree, beneath the interest of the state.

Of all the laws of the state, the vast majority are noncriminal. They are regulatory in nature and do not give rise to criminal penalties. With a few exceptions (e.g., the *Controlled Drugs and Substances Act* and *the Food and Drugs Act*), all the criminal laws in Canada fit into one book, the *Criminal Code of Canada*. Fortunately, human conduct is overwhelmingly legal. Even the worst criminals are law-abiding most of the time.

Positive and Natural Law

Positive law is defined as all the laws duly enacted by a body having the authority to enact and enforce them. Proponents of positive law argue that all persons under the jurisdiction of the enacting authority must obey all the laws of that authority, even if the laws are unjust. At the Nuremberg trials, German war criminals argued that they had merely obeyed the positive laws enacted by the Nazi government and therefore could not be found guilty of breaking the law.

Natural law is defined as those laws that are just and justifiable on moral, religious, or philosophical grounds regardless of whether or not the state has enacted or has failed to enact them. Proponents of natural law argue that there is an obligation to disobey unnatural laws, even if they have been duly enacted in the positive law sense. At Nuremberg, it was found that the positive laws passed by Hitler's government were so unnatural that everyone under that government's authority had a duty to disobey them. Natural law theory appeals to our sense of idealism; however, most, if not all, the positive laws of a state should be obeyed. Otherwise, it is likely that the society would descend into anarchy.

Civil disobedience is the act of refusing to abide by unjust positive or unnatural laws. Usually falling somewhere between treason and merely disturbing the peace, civil disobedience has a long and proud history. It has been the impetus for great advances in the law and in the evolution of our fundamental rights and freedoms. Taken too far, however, it leads to anarchy and the breakdown of the state. Civil disobedience should be reserved for important causes rather than indiscriminately applied to address every perceived injustice. Most injustices are better fought from within the system.

Legal Realism

The foregoing definitions and theories have characterized the law in fairly abstract terms. Many commentators have attempted to provide more concrete definitions. Some describe the law as a pyramid, with the sovereign or president at the top and then a spread down through parliaments or congresses, to provincial or state legislatures, to municipalities, to other governmentally empowered institutions, and, finally, to the people. Others describe the law as a jungle, impenetrably complex and treacherous; or as clouds, amorphous and imprecise, prone to tempests. Proponents of legal realism argue that the law is none of these things; rather, it is whatever the judges say it is. According to this theory, it does not matter whether the law was positively enacted or whether it is natural or unnatural. If the courts refuse to recognize it as a law, then it is not law; if they do recognize it, then it is law. Former prime minister Pierre Elliott Trudeau observed that the **Supreme Court of Canada** justices had, in making their judgment in the *Reference re Amendment of Constitution of Canada (Nos. 1, 2, 3), [1981] 1 S.C.R. 753* (known as the Patriation Reference), "blatantly manipulated the evidence before them to arrive at the desired result. They then wrote a judgment that tried to lend a fig-leaf of legality to their pre-conceived conclusion." Maybe so, but the Patriation Reference became the law of Canada.

Within some jurisdictional limits, elected representatives may enact whatever laws they please. However, it is the judicial interpretation of the law that tends to carry the day. The legislators may have had "red" in mind, but if the judge says "blue" without being overturned on appeal, then "blue" it is. Further, if the lower court judges agree that it is "red," but a majority of the judges on the final court of appeal say "blue," then "blue" triumphs. In a very real sense, then, the law is whatever the majority of the nine-member Supreme Court of Canada says it is, even if the other four agree with the three justices on the provincial court of appeal and the trial judge (thus, five justices can overrule eight). The Supreme Court's interpretation will govern until either the Court overrules itself or the government rewrites the legislation (as in *The Red Is Really Red and We Darn Well Mean It Act*).

Legal realism frustrates those who believe that judges should interpret law, not create it. However, the laws and the circumstances to which they apply are so varied and complex that it is impossible for legislation to cover every variation and complexity and thereby confine judicial activity to mere interpretation. The influence of the courts notwithstanding, Parliament and the provincial legislatures do retain the ultimate power to fashion the law. It is crucial that judges, who exercise the power of interpretation, be thoughtful, learned, incorruptible, and skilled in the arts of legal interpretation and judgment. Our legislators should be similarly qualified and at the same time more cognizant of broader socio-political considerations.

Based on our discussion thus far, the law may be defined as rules that are established by the state to govern human behaviour, that are enforced by the state or by bodies having authority derived from the state, and that are interpreted by the judiciary.

Purposes of Law

The law has a multitude of purposes. Some of the major ones are listed below.

1. To maintain the integrity of the state's boundaries.
2. To maintain law and order within the state.
3. To protect citizens from each other.
4. To provide a civilized forum for resolving disputes between citizens.
5. To protect citizens from illegal or oppressive government action.
6. To provide a civilized forum for resolving disputes between citizens and government.
7. To establish and enforce standards of education, professional qualifications, health care, and social programs.
8. To establish and enforce a wide range of standards, including those relating to working conditions, retailing practices, product safety, and advertising ethics.

Divisions of Law

There are two basic divisions of law. Public law is concerned mainly with government and the public interest, and encompasses such areas as constitutional law, criminal law, administrative law, and taxation. Private law is concerned mainly with interpersonal matters such as contract law, family law, property law, employment law, and tort law (negligence).

A distinction also exists between criminal law and civil law. Criminal laws are enacted to protect the political security of the state and the personal security of citizens. Civil laws are all the other laws. While penalties for breaches of criminal law include fines, jail terms, and capital punishment in some countries, civil law penalties typically consist of damages, orders, and **injunctions** that are awarded to the successful **litigant**. The term "civil law" also describes the noncriminal legal system in Quebec, as distinct from the British term "common law." In Canada as a whole, the term "civil rights" essentially means property rights, not human rights.

Figure 1-1 Divisions of Canadian Law

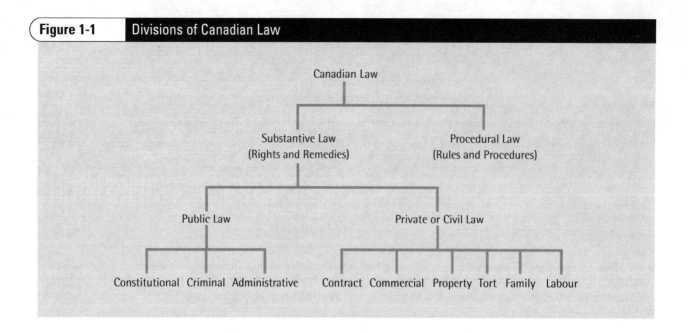

Laws are also divided into substantive laws, which consist of the rights and remedies available to everyone under the law; and procedural laws, which consist of the technical rules and procedures by which the substantive law rights are protected and the substantive law remedies are obtained and enforced. For example, the laws prohibiting discrimination are substantive. Procedural laws detail the form, timing, and filing requirements of an application to a court or a human rights tribunal made by those seeking redress for discrimination.

The Reach and Impact of the Law

The Seamless Web

The reach and impact of the law is impossible to calculate fully. Suffice it to say that a person cannot eat, sleep, walk, talk, work, buy, sell, trade, read, consult, drive, bicycle, marry, divorce, raise kids, be well, be ill, or even die without the law applying in some fashion. The law is often described as a seamless web in which each strand is connected, directly or indirectly, with every other strand. Regardless of the starting point, it is possible to weave legal scenarios that will lead to any other point on the web. A marital breakdown under family law often leads to division of property under real estate law. Property law has commercial law aspects. Commercial law touches on patents, shipping, taxation, litigation, and criminal law (e.g., fraud), while criminal law has a significant constitutional law component. The law is woven into every aspect of society. For most people, laws operate largely unnoticed in smoothing interpersonal and business relationships and regulating the activities of the state and its citizens.

Access to Justice

It is a truism that not only must justice be done, it must be seen to be done. The formal process of enacting laws is done in public in legislative assemblies. The formal process of interpreting and applying the laws is done, except in rare circumstances, in courts that are open to the public. The decisions of judges are rendered in open court or in readily available written form. With rare exceptions, the media are entitled to report and comment on the activities of government and the courts. Further, everyone can access the legislative acts of governments and the reported law cases by visiting law libraries or government bookstores.

Although the poor are not without access to the justice system, access is enhanced for those who can afford it. This may not be fair, but it is a fact of life that is unlikely ever to be eradicated. Given this reality, it is important that access to the justice system by the economically disadvantaged remain at or above an acceptable threshold. Of assistance in this regard are social programs such as legal aid, a strong sense of public duty among lawyers, and fair and sensible laws and rules that do not unnecessarily inhibit access to justice or add to the cost of seeking justice.

A Taste of History

From the dawn of civilization, humans have needed laws to govern their society. Until writing was invented, laws were oral and prone to wildly disparate interpretations. To foster certainty, various leaders over the centuries have tried to write them down and codify them. The earliest known written codification of law is attributed to Lipit-Ishtar of Isin (*c.*1868–*c.*1857 B.C.), who called himself a wise shepherd and wrote his laws in Sumerian on stone tablets. The best-known early written code of law is the *Code of Hammurabi*, who was king of the first dynasty of Babylon (*c.*1792–*c.*1750 B.C.). It was followed by the Pentateuch (the first five books of the Old Testament) around 1000 B.C. and later by the *Justinian Code* (A.D. 529). The *Justinian* (or *Roman*) *Code* was so successful that the next great attempt at writing one did not occur in the West for nearly 1300 years when the *Napoleonic Code*, later known as the *French Civil Code*, was introduced in 1804. The earliest known written Oriental codes date back to about 600 B.C.

The Hammurabian, Pentateuchal, and Justinian codes have greatly influenced the British legal tradition. In 1066, William the Conqueror brought to England the *Roman Code* and Norman French law, both of which were to supplant the pagan and Christian laws of the Celts, Anglo-Saxons, and Scandinavians. By the time Napoleon developed his *Code*, Britain's own laws were too entrenched to be overly influenced by it. Oriental, Indian, Islamic, and African codes have strongly influenced legal evolution elsewhere in the world. All the great legal systems are fundamentally similar.

The Canadian Governmental Hierarchy

In Canadian constitutional legal theory, the top rung in Canada's governmental hierarchy is occupied by the sovereign, currently Queen Elizabeth II. The sovereign appoints the governor general and the lieutenant governors, all of whom are nominees of the federal cabinet. In practice, the powers of the sovereign are subordinate to those of Parliament and the provincial legislatures. Except in very rare circumstances, the sovereign does not act except at the behest of Parliament or a legislature. The Canadian Parliament is composed of the House of Commons, whose members are elected, and the Senate, whose members are appointed by the federal cabinet through the governor general. The provinces have legislatures of elected members but no bodies equivalent to the Senate. The provinces create municipal governments that pass **bylaws** and issue work and compliance orders.

Federal legislation cannot become law until it is passed by both the House of Commons and the Senate and proclaimed into force by the governor general. The Senate may reject legislation sent to it by the House. Although such an event rarely occurs, the mere existence of this Senate power serves as a useful brake on excess on the part of legislators. Provincial legislation must be passed by the legislature and proclaimed by the lieutenant governor. Municipal bylaws must be passed by the municipal council.

Figure 1-2 The Canadian Governmental Hierarchy

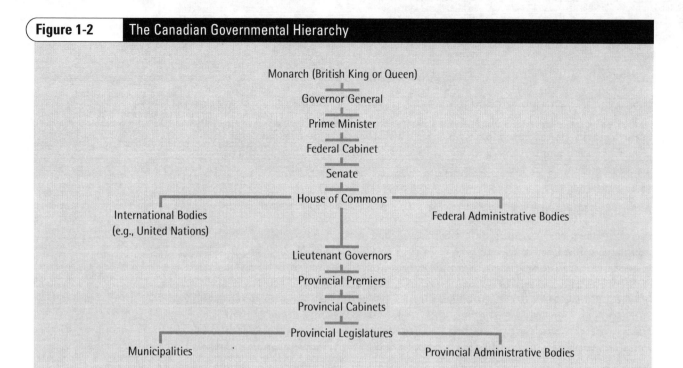

The governor general and lieutenant governors retain the power to dissolve Parliament or the legislature at will or to dismiss the sitting prime minister or premier. This power has been exercised only once each in the history of Canada and Australia. Sitting governments must nevertheless keep in mind that outrageous behaviour can lead to dismissal. In the United States, the only legal way to oust a president is through impeachment, a lengthy process. In Canada, a prime minister or premier who is clearly guilty of wrongdoing can be dismissed with much less delay and disruption.

The Players

Several essential groups participate in the dynamic workings of the law. At the top of the heap are the legislators and the judges, dancing and cavorting, but in different rooms and not always in unison. Below them come the lawyers, watching the dance and often trying to choreograph it, with varying degrees of success. Beside them sit the clients and the jurors, trying to follow the steps, unsure whether they are watching a waltz, a jitterbug, or a heart attack. Around them pace the police, fretting about their employers—their fellow citizens—and about what orders and impediments are about to be foisted on them by the legislators and the judiciary. Below them teem the mostly law-abiding masses.

Legislators

Pursuant to section 3 of the *Canadian Charter of Rights and Freedoms*, every citizen of Canada is qualified to run for membership in the House of Commons or a legislative assembly, either as a member of a political party or as an independent. Some legislators regard themselves as merely the conduit of the majority opinion of their constituents, but most subscribe to the view of Edmund Burke that they are elected to vote as their conscience dictates even if by doing so they are acting against the will of the majority of their constituents (he was right, but he lost the next election). The debate over capital punishment illustrates this point. While polls consistently show that a majority of Canadians favour capital punishment, a majority of the members of Parliament have consistently voted against reinstating it.

Judges

Federally appointed judges are addressed as "Mister or Madam Justice So-and-so," "Milord," or "Milady." Provincially appointed judges are addressed as "Your Honour" and justices of the peace as "Your Worship." Canadian judges wear robes (but not wigs) as symbols of their authority. As arbiters of community standards, judges must be participators in, and keen observers of, their communities. Most judges strive to make the best judgments they can.

Jurors

Canadian citizens who have not been convicted of an indictable criminal offence, who are between the ages of 18 and 70, and who do not have physical or mental disabilities that would impede the performance of their duty are qualified to serve as jurors. Parliamentarians, legislators, municipal councillors, firefighters, clergy, physicians, dentists, veterinarians, nurses, and coroners are ineligible because the uninterrupted performance of their work is in the public interest. Judges, lawyers, and law students are ineligible because of the influence they could exert on the rest of the panel. Newspaper editors, reporters, and publishers are ineligible because serving on a jury could compromise their independence and ability to report openly on the activities of the courts. Law-enforcement officers and prison guards (and their spouses), as well as salaried civil servants, are ineligible on the ground that they derive their income from the state, which is a party to the case, and thus are in a conflict of interest.

Criminal juries are composed of "12 persons good and true." No one knows how the number 12 was arrived at, although it may be related to the 12 Disciples of Christ or to the fact that, together with the judge, the jurors make 13, the number of people who served on a religious council in pagan England. The use of the number 13 came to be regarded as unlucky by the early Christians. For this reason, many high-rise hotels and office buildings skip floor 13 and disguise it as floor 14. Of course, no one should be superstitious; it's bad luck!

The jury system is fallible, unpredictable, inconvenient, unwieldy, vexing, and the best truth-seeking missile ever devised. Its flaws are human flaws and as such are unavoidable. Its negative traits can be reduced by a wise, learned, alert, and impartial judge.

Lawyers

A lawyer is merely someone with a law degree. Having a law degree does not entitle a person to practise law. One must first be called to the bar as a barrister and solicitor. In the United States, a lawyer admitted to the bar is called an attorney. In Canada, an attorney is an agent.

The practice of law is broken down into two broad categories: contentious and non-contentious. This division was imported into Britain by the Norman conquerors who brought two kinds of legal professionals: *les avocats*, from which is derived the word "advocate," and *les notaires*, who draft and notarize (certify) such documents as contracts, wills, and deeds. The British terms for these two groups are barristers and solicitors, respectively. Solicitors handle all the noncontentious legal matters for their clients, from real estate and marriage contracts, to company mergers, to international patent registrations. Barristers are lawyers who serve as advocates for their clients in court. Originally, barristers made their arguments while standing at a bar that separated them from the judge's bench area. British solicitors cannot appear in court to address contentious matters. For their part, British barristers cannot solicit clients, but have to wait for the solicitors to bring them briefs (summaries) of the contentious matters that have arisen among the solicitors' clients. Historically, barristers could not ask for payment. Instead, they turned their backs to their clients at the end of the trial; the client, in turn, dropped payment into a sack flung over the barrister's shoulder. Today, a patch of cloth sewn onto the back of lawyers' robes serves as a reminder of this quaint and obsolete custom.

When British lawyers first came to Canada, there was insufficient work to warrant maintaining the split in the professions. Thus, lawyers in Canada outside Quebec are both barristers and solicitors; as such, they can draft a mortgage in the morning and defend a murderer in the afternoon. In Quebec, notaries are lawyers equivalent to solicitors, but they cannot appear in court on contentious matters. Instead, lawyers handle the contentious courtroom work and some other matters. Outside Quebec, a notary is someone who certifies, but does not draft, documents. In British Columbia, notaries are also able to handle certain legal matters such as real estate conveyancing.

Before widespread schooling, about the only literate people were the clergy, scribes, doctors, and lawyers. "Clerk," signifying literacy, comes from the same root as "clergy." In the early days, lawyers were often paid by the word. Even today a document may begin, "I give, devise, bequeath, set over, transfer, convey, assign ... " Those words have different meanings in law and are included to cover all possible applications. "Devise" refers to a gift of real property, "bequeath" refers to a gift of personal property, and "transfer" and "assign" have different meanings. Good lawyers aim for plain English, but often the documents have to be lengthy and carefully worded in order to be clear and to cover numerous contingencies.

Clients

At some point during their lives, virtually everyone will need to consult a lawyer. Most of the consultations will be for noncontentious matters; some will result in litigation. Sir Robert Megarry once observed that the most important person in the courtroom is not the judge, a juror, a lawyer, the sergeant-at-arms, the court reporter, or even the winning litigant. The most important person is the losing litigant. If our system of justice is to be respected, open-minded losing litigants must believe the following: the evidence was presented fairly, their arguments were considered, they were represented competently, the outcome was not influenced by bribery, the judges were impartial, and the result was

Hi & Lois

arrived at in accordance with proper procedure and the law. Sometimes even winning litigants have mixed feelings. They are happy with the victory but annoyed at the process; a lawsuit is not generally a pleasant experience.

Police

In order to play their proper roles in the justice system, the police and other investigators need only obey the law, be competent and fair, remain open-minded, and avoid tunnel vision and a rush to judgment. Most police officers adhere to these guidelines.

Sources of Canadian Law

Citizens can research the law by reading legislative enactments, case reports, textbooks, and law journals; by accessing computerized search services; and by surfing appropriate sites on the Internet. However, anyone considering applying legal research without professional advice should keep in mind the familiar adage, "He who is his own lawyer has a fool for a client." There are four sources of Canadian law: royal prerogatives, legislative enactments, delegated lawmaking, and judge-made law.

Royal Prerogatives

Royal prerogatives are direct edicts from the sovereign, exercised through the governor general and the lieutenant governors. Although some royal prerogatives still exist in Canada, almost all have been eliminated. Once a royal prerogative has been removed, it cannot be revived. As a practical matter, royal prerogatives are no longer used except upon the express request of an elected government that is seeking, for example, to open or prorogue (terminate the current session of) Parliament.

Legislative Enactments

The Canadian Constitution

The *British North America Act (BNA Act)*, a statute enacted by the British Parliament in 1867, created a federation of Nova Scotia, New Brunswick, Lower Canada, and Upper Canada. The other provinces and territories joined later, with Newfoundland and Labrador the last to join in 1949. Section 91 of the *BNA Act* sets forth the powers of the federal government relating to such matters as the regulation of trade and commerce, taxation, national defence, banking, legal tender, bankruptcy, patents, marriage and divorce, criminal law, and anything else falling within the federal government's broad authority to make laws designed to promote the Peace, Order, and good Government (POGG) of the nation. Section 92 of the *BNA Act* sets forth the powers of the provincial governments relating to such matters as direct taxation, the issuance of licences, property and civil rights, and the administration of justice.

The *BNA Act* imported into Canada certain British constitutional principles such as those expressed in the Magna Carta and various unwritten (in the sense of not being statutory) conventions. For example, under British legal tradition, a person is free to do any act that is not prohibited by law. Under most other legal systems, individuals are prohibited from performing any acts that are not expressly authorized by law.

In 1982, the Canadian government patriated the constitution by means of the *Constitution Act (1982)*, which lists the statutes that constitute our written constitution and renames some of them. The *BNA Act* is now known as the *Constitution Act (1867)*.

Within their **jurisdictions**, Parliament and the legislatures may enact and repeal laws and regulations, and may overrule or modify judge-made case law. If a government passes a law that is constitutionally within the purview of the other level of government, the law is said to be *ultra vires* ("beyond the power") of the enacting government and hence of no effect. Many laws have been struck down for this reason. In the event of an overlap in jurisdiction or conflict of laws between Parliament and the legislatures, Parliament reigns supreme, a situation known as "**paramountcy**." Legislative bodies may give subordinate bodies various legal powers, such as the power to make and enforce bylaws and rulings. Municipalities, territorial assemblies, and administrative boards and tribunals are examples of subordinate bodies.

Except for the *Income Tax Act*, the *Excise Tax Act*, the *Criminal Code*, and a few other Acts, most of the laws that affect Canadians on a daily basis, including property rights, working conditions, business **licences**, highway traffic, and education, are within provincial jurisdiction.

Statutes, Regulations, and Orders-in-Council

Below the Constitution are the regular statutes. They come into force upon proclamation of a formal Act of Parliament or the legislature. Most statutes empower the government to pass regulations under the statute. Regulations relate mostly to practical matters and may be amended more easily than statutes. The broad policy issues remain within the purview of the statute. In addition to the statutes and regulations, the federal cabinet may bypass Parliament or the legislature and pass orders-in-council. Orders-in-council have the full force of law.

The *Quebec Civil Code*

When Quebec joined Confederation, it kept the *French Civil Code* for matters within provincial jurisdiction. For matters outside provincial jurisdiction, such as criminal law, the law in Quebec is the same as that in the rest of Canada. The new **Quebec Civil Code**, which came into force on January 1, 1994, is a brilliant descendent and adaptation of the *Roman Civil Code*, the *Napoleonic Code*, and the previous *Quebec Civil Code*.

Delegated Lawmaking

Municipalities

Through their municipal Acts, the provinces delegate to municipalities the authority to administer certain legal aspects for the territory within their jurisdiction. Municipal councils pass bylaws to regulate a wide variety of matters including property use and zoning, building permits, and licensing. Municipalities have various powers, such as issuing work orders against a property owner, to deal with violations of the bylaws. To raise revenue, municipalities may levy property and business taxes or charge licensing, permit, and other fees.

Administrative Boards

Through enabling legislation, the federal government and the provinces create boards, commissions, or tribunals (collectively known as "boards") that are empowered to administer specific matters. The boards, whose regulations and decisions constitute laws, also have various powers of enforcement such as refusing, suspending, or revoking a licence.

Judge-Made Law

Common Law

Until the reign of Henry II (1133–1189) of England, the king's subjects settled their disputes by fighting or by appealing to the local lord or sheriff. Their decisions were often suspect due to inattention, poor judgment, or corruption. To improve law and order, Henry II appointed judges to travel around the country and **adjudicate** local disputes. The royal judges tended to be less corrupt than local authorities and more capable, as a result of broader experience, of rendering sensible and fair judgments. To make justice more predictable and less arduous, the travelling judges soon began to follow each other's decisions. Slowly, their rulings became more regularized and commonly applied throughout Britain. The accumulation of judges' decisions became known as the **common law**.

Equity

Before long, the common law became so rigid that many unfair trial outcomes occurred. As a result, many litigants bypassed the common law courts and went directly to the king for justice. The kings delegated the task to their chancellors and vice-chancellors, who presided in what came to be known as the Court of Chancery. Originally, they were not bound by the rulings of the common law courts, but were free to dispense justice on **equitable** grounds, often on the basis of religious principles or matters of conscience. This body of law became known as equity. As it evolved alongside the common law, conflicts arose between the two systems. It was possible for a litigant to win under one system and lose under the other one. Choosing the most advantageous system became critical. Eventually, a statute was enacted to merge the equity and common law courts and to provide that, wherever a conflict arose between an equitable principle and a common law principle, the equitable principle would prevail.

Stare Decisis

Judges are bound by the principle of *stare decisis* ("it stands decided") to follow the precedents set by equivalent and higher courts, unless the precedents can be distinguished from the present case. In other words, if the facts of the present case are similar to the facts of a case previously decided by a higher or equivalent court, the judge is bound to follow the precedent of the previous decision. On the other hand, if the facts of the present case can be shown to be sufficiently different from those of the previous case, then the judge is not bound by the precedent. Lawyers earn a good living drawing subtle distinctions between cases.

The rationale for *stare decisis* is to make the law reasonably predictable and to avoid unnecessary appeals resulting from courts of equal or lower stature handing down inconsistent rulings. The principle applies primarily to appeal-level decisions and secondarily to decisions by courts of equal stature within the same jurisdiction. Decisions made by courts in other provinces or countries are persuasive to varying degrees, but not binding.

Decisions and Citations

When rendering decisions, judges typically set forth the facts, the legal issues, and the reasons. All oral decisions are recorded by the court reporter, and transcripts can be ordered. If the decision is too complex or important to render orally, the judge may prepare written reasons. If the case is of particular interest to the broader legal community, the decisions may be published in the report services, such as the *Dominion Law Reports*. For those engaged in legal research, it is essential that cases be fully and accurately documented. A text on proper research techniques and case citations should be consulted.

Figure 1-3 | Case Citations

CIVIL CITATION

Stanton	v.	Twack et al.	(1982),	14	A.C.W.S.	(2d)	447	(B.C.S.C.)
Plaintiff or Appellant	versus	Defendant or Respondent	year of report	volume number	title of report	edition	page number	name of court

Cases are either underlined or printed in italics. The abbreviation "et al." is short for "et alia," which is Latin for "and others." If the report uses the year as part of its name, the year is shown in square brackets and the comma appears before the year, e.g., Beauchamp v. Ayotte et al., [1971] 3 O.R. 21. The two case examples used above are real.

CRIMINAL CITATION

R.	v.	accused	(1998),	55	D.L.R.	(2d)	12	(S.C.C.)
Rex or Regina	versus	Defendant or Respondent	year of report	volume number	title of report	edition	page number	name of court

"R." is short for "Rex," which is Latin for "King"; "Regina" is Latin for "Queen." "R" stands for the "Crown," meaning the Canadian government. The case example used above is fictitious.

The Federal Courts

The Supreme Court of Canada

The Supreme Court of Canada ("SCC") is the highest court in Canada. It has nine federally appointed justices including the Chief Justice of Canada. Pursuant to the *Supreme Court Act*, three of the justices must come from Quebec; pursuant to convention, three come from Ontario, two from the western provinces, and one from Atlantic Canada. The decisions are always written. If the decision is not unanimous, a dissent is also written so that interested parties, including the Minister of Justice, can ponder the issues that bedevilled the Court. Sometimes dissenting judgments become the basis for new law. The SCC hears the following:

1. Criminal appeals from a provincial Court of Appeal sometimes as of right (where the permission of the Court is not needed) and sometimes with leave (where the permission of the Court is needed).

2. Civil appeals from a provincial Court of Appeal on matters of sufficient public or legal importance with leave.

3. Appeals from the Federal Court of Canada on matters of sufficient public or legal importance with leave.

4. References on constitutional matters at the request of the government.

One of three things can happen to a decision of a provincial Court of Appeal:

1. The losing side may abandon the matter, in which case the ruling of the provincial Court of Appeal will stand as the law in the province.

2. The SCC may deny leave to appeal (i.e., refuse to hear the case), thereby confirming the ruling of the court below.

3. The SCC may grant leave, and then may grant the appeal, confirm the ruling below but for its own reasons, dismiss the appeal, or send the matter back for a new trial.

The Federal Court of Canada

The Federal Court of Canada has a trial division and an appeal division. The trial division has exclusive first instance jurisdiction over federal–provincial or interprovincial disputes, maritime law, trademarks, copyrights, and patents; residual jurisdiction where no other court has jurisdiction; and concurrent jurisdiction with other courts over such matters as civil claims by or against the federal government and its servants, bills of exchange and promissory notes, aeronautics issues, and immigration issues excluding citizenship swearing-in ceremonies.

The appeal division hears appeals from the trial division; hears applications concerning decisions of federal boards, commissions, and other administrative tribunals; and adjudicates questions of law and appeals under various federal Acts other than the *Income Tax Act*, the *Estate Tax Act* and the *Citizenship Act*, all of which are dealt with by other courts.

Both the Supreme Court of Canada and the Federal Court of Canada are situated in the Supreme Court building on Wellington Street in Ottawa. While the Federal Court judges hold hearings across the country, the Supreme Court justices do not budge. Guarding the front entrance of the Supreme Court building are large bronze statues of two women, Veritas and Justitia (Truth and Justice). One holds a book, the other a sword. Neither is blindfolded.

Other Federal Courts

Other federal courts include the following:

1. The Tax Court of Canada, which hears appeals under the *Income Tax Act*, the *Excise Tax Act*, and the *Canada Pension Plan Act*.

2. The Court Martial Appeal Court of Canada, which hears appeals from the courts-martial in the military.

3. The Court of Canadian Citizenship, which holds citizenship swearing-in ceremonies under the *Citizenship Act*.

Federal Boards, Commissions, and Tribunals

Federal boards, commissions, and tribunals are quasi-judicial bodies that make determinations within their respective jurisdictions under applicable federal legislation. For example, the Immigration and Refugee Board hears claims relating to refugee status and matters of sponsorship, admissibility, and detention. Hearings before quasi-judicial bodies tend to be less formal than those held in the traditional courts. Appeals of decisions of federal boards, commissions, and tribunals are made to the Federal Court of Canada.

The Provincial Courts

While there are numerous small differences in the various provincial court systems, in all provinces the court system is divided into the superior courts whose judges are federally appointed and the lower courts whose judges are provincially appointed.

The Superior Provincial Courts

The superior provincial courts are composed of a trial division and an appeal division. The trial divisions hear a broad range of matters, some of which are listed below.

1. Cases involving serious indictable offences under the *Criminal Code*, including treason, murder, and conspiracy.

2. Cases involving offences under the *Criminal Code* that may proceed by election with or without a jury.

3. Civil cases involving sums over a set amount.

4. Family law matters (divorce, separation, custody, guardianship, etc.).

5. Administrative law applications concerning decisions of provincial boards, commissions, and tribunals (which are heard in Divisional Court in Ontario).

6. Appeals of summary conviction offences.

7. Appeals from small claims courts.

Other courts with specific mandates include Unified Family Court, which handles family law matters under both federal and provincial law; and Surrogate Court, which handles estate and competency matters. Both of these courts have the rank of a superior court trial division, which means that their decisions are appealable to the provincial Court of Appeal.

The provincial Courts of Appeal, in panels of three justices, hear appeals from the trial division and equivalent courts, applications for new trials, and references on issues of law.

| Figure 1-4 | The Canadian Court System (Simplified) |

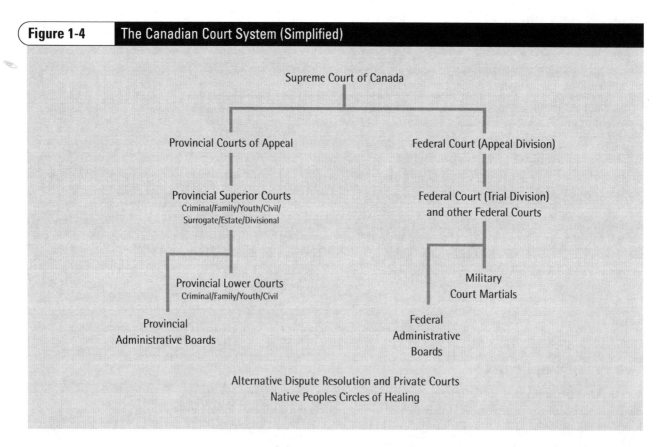

The Lower Provincial Courts

The lower provincial courts are very busy courts of first instance. They have little or no appeal jurisdiction and no juries, and usually include the following divisions:

1. Criminal division, which hears cases involving certain indictable *Criminal Code* offences, summary conviction offences, and offences under provincial statutes.

2. Family division, which hears some support and custody matters, matters affecting children (e.g., adoption), and some *Criminal Code* offences.

3. Youth division, which hears cases under child welfare legislation.

4. Small claims court, which hears mostly claims involving small sums of money.

Provincial Boards, Commissions, and Tribunals

Provincial boards, commissions, and tribunals are quasi-judicial bodies that make within their respective jurisdictions determinations pursuant to the applicable provincial legislation. Examples include liquor licence boards, which regulate the issuance and cancellation of liquor licences, and boards that hear appeals of decisions of municipal governments pertaining to such matters as zoning. Appeals of their decisions are generally made to a provincial superior court that has the rank of a trial division.

Civil Procedure

The Rules of Civil Procedure

Civil proceedings are typically private actions initiated by private persons. Criminal proceedings, in contrast, are typically initiated by the government. The primary responsibility for civil procedure lies with the provinces. The rules vary from province to province. The common term for a civil action is "lawsuit." In law, the word "person" refers to an individual, a corporation, or a trust. Any person is entitled to sue and be sued; exceptions are minors, the mentally incompetent, and the deceased, who must be represented by another person.

Civil procedure commences with the issuance of an originating process such as a statement of claim, notice of application, or petition for divorce. The court office places its seal on the document to signify that the process has started. Most civil proceedings begin with a statement of claim, which is a written statement by the plaintiff. A notice of application is used when the facts are not in dispute, when the only issue is the interpretation of a legal document, or when a statute authorizes commencement by application. Divorces are begun with a petition. Once the process has begun, it may be necessary to apply to the court for rulings on interim issues. This is done by way of a notice of motion. In some provinces, certain matters may be commenced by way of a notice of motion.

When the matter begins with a statement of claim, it is called an action; the person suing is the plaintiff and the person being sued is the defendant. When the matter commences with a notice of application, it is called an application, and the parties are the applicant and the respondent. When the matter begins by way of a petition, it is called a divorce, and the parties are the petitioner and the respondent. When there is an appeal, the person appealing is the appellant and the person whose victory below is being appealed is the respondent.

If a party satisfies the court that the subject matter of the dispute may disappear or deteriorate, the court may order the preservation of the matter pending the outcome of the trial.

Not all civil actions proceed under the general rules of civil procedure. For example, if a mortgagor (the person who borrowed the money) defaults (fails to pay) on the mortgage (the document offering up the real property of the mortgagor as security for the loan), the mortgagee (the person who lent the money) is entitled to recover the mortgage debt (the amount of the original loan plus interest and costs) by following the procedures relating to foreclosure (keeping the real property instead of chasing the money) or power of sale (selling the real property for the money) set forth in the provincial mortgage statute. A second example is the right of a commercial landlord to seize certain property of a defaulting commercial tenant. A third example is the right of an innkeeper to lien the luggage of a guest who has failed to pay the inn's bill (see Chapter 9).

The Stages of a Civil Action

Civil proceedings are divided into five stages: pleadings, discoveries, pretrial or mediation, trial, and appeals.

Pleadings

As noted above, the majority of civil proceedings begin with a statement of claim. The format is set forth in the rules. The **plaintiff** must plead enough facts to establish a valid claim. If the claim fails to give sufficient detail, the defendant may bring a motion for particulars. If the claim contains inappropriate **pleadings**, the **defendant** may move to have them struck out. Once the statement of claim has been prepared by the plaintiff and issued by the court office, it must be served personally on the defendant within a specified period of time. If the defendant cannot be served personally, the service may be effected by an allowable alternative such as a notice in the local newspaper or service on an adult at the defendant's residence. After being served, the defendant must file a statement of defence within a specified period of time. It is not sufficient simply to deny the allegations in the claim; the statement of defence must set forth reasonable grounds (even if they are later dismissed) on which to base a defence. The statement of defence may be served on, or mailed or faxed to, the plaintiff or the plaintiff's lawyer. The statement of defence admits the pleadings in the statement of claim that the defendant agrees with, and denies or asserts no knowledge of everything else. The defendant may also counterclaim against the plaintiff, crossclaim against a codefendant, or bring a third-party claim against a person who was not previously a party to the action. Upon receiving the statement of defence, the plaintiff may deliver a reply. If there is a counterclaim, the plaintiff (defendant by counterclaim) may deliver a statement of defence to the counterclaim.

Discoveries

Once the pleadings have closed, the **discovery** stage begins. The parties exchange **affidavits** listing all the documents relevant to the case. They must also provide the name and location of the possessor of any documents they no longer control. If more documents are found later, a supplementary affidavit must be delivered. Each party may examine the other party under oath. A certified reporter records the examination and prepares transcripts upon request. At the examination, all non-exempt documents must be produced for inspection. Exempt documents include solicitor–client communications and the lawyer's work product. Any physical property pertinent to the action may also be examined. If the claim includes damages for personal injuries or mental suffering, the claimant may have to undergo a medical examination. Misleading the other side is always improper but no more so than during discovery. The purpose of discovery is to place the issues, facts, and evidence on the table prior to the trial; the parties must also reveal the names of the witnesses, including experts, that they intend to call. Courtroom surprises, though common on television, are rare in real life.

Pretrial or Mediation Stage

Discovery enables both parties to appreciate the relative strengths and weaknesses of their cases. Not surprisingly, many disputes are resolved without a trial at the end of discovery. If a settlement is not reached after discovery, a trial date will be set. Prior to the trial, a pretrial is held at which the parties present their cases to a judge. Once a judge's opinion is heard, many cases settle. The judge at the pretrial is disqualified from presiding at the trial. In some jurisdictions, mediation is a mandatory step. The goal of pretrials and mediation is to avoid the trial or at least to reduce the number of issues to be addressed at **trial**.

When all else has failed, the parties head to trial. There are only two circumstances in which a case should reach trial. The first is when the plaintiff's lawyer is honestly convinced of the reasonableness of his or her position and the other side refuses to concur. The second is where the issues and laws are grey and the adjudication of a judge is required. Fewer than 5 percent of all litigation files reach trial. All the others conclude earlier somewhere along the bumpy, meandering road between the opening of the file and the door of the courtroom.

The Trial

If a civil trial by jury is selected, a six-member jury will be impanelled. Civil juries are fairly rare. They are most often employed when the plaintiff hopes to appeal to the compassion or outrage of a half-dozen amateurs (as opposed to one professional judge) in obtaining damages.

At the trial, the plaintiff makes the opening statement and presents the case. The plaintiff's witnesses are examined in chief by the plaintiff and may be cross-examined by the defendant. If the plaintiff has failed to present sufficient evidence to establish the claim, the defendant may move for a nonsuit. If the motion fails, the defendant presents the defence in chief subject to cross-examination by the plaintiff. The plaintiff may then present reply evidence. If the defendant presents no evidence, the plaintiff makes the closing address first. If the defendant does present evidence, the defendant makes the closing address first.

The burden of proof in a civil trial is not the same as in a criminal trial. In a criminal trial, the plaintiff must prove the case beyond a reasonable doubt. In a civil trial, the plaintiff must prove the case on a balance of probabilities. In other words, a civil party will win the case if the judge is 51 percent convinced of the correctness of that party's position. After weighing the evidence and listening to the arguments, the judge will render a decision, either orally immediately or in writing at a later date. If there is no jury, the judge decides the issues of both fact and law. If there is a jury, the jury decides the issues of fact, and the judge then decides the issues of law.

Appeals

The losing litigant may launch an **appeal** within a specified period of time. If the trial outcome was mixed, both litigants may appeal the aspects of the case that they lost. Civil appeals are not automatic. The appellant must first obtain leave to appeal from the provincial Court of Appeal. Appeals are limited to matters of law, not fact, unless the finding of fact by the court below was patently unreasonable. Losses on appeals can be further appealed until either leave to appeal is denied (which itself can be appealed) or the Supreme Court of Canada has rendered a decision. If the Supreme Court of Canada decision is unfavourable, the only recourse for the losing litigant is to convince Parliament or the legislature to change the law.

Offers to Settle and Costs

The rules of civil procedure encourage the parties to settle to reduce the strains on the court system. A party may serve an offer to settle on the other party. If the offer is reasonable, a party who refuses the offer may suffer adverse cost consequences even if the refuser wins the trial. For example, if the loser offered months earlier to settle the dispute for the same or more than the amount obtained in court, the court may punish

Figure 1-5 | The Civil Process

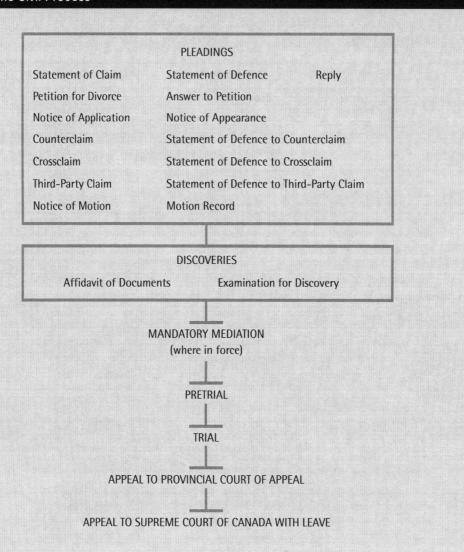

the winner by refusing to grant costs or even requiring the winner to pay the costs of the loser. A winner can lose more in court costs than the amount won under the claim. The message is: Be reasonable.

Usually, the successful party is granted costs. Standard "party and party" costs cover about 60 percent of the legal costs. If the judge is annoyed with the conduct of a party, she may award costs on a "solicitor and client" basis, which usually covers most of the expenses. If the judge is outraged by the conduct of a party, she may award costs "as between a solicitor and his or her own client," in which case the loser will pay every cent of the winner's expenses.

Alternative Dispute Resolution

A new trend in law is alternative dispute resolution (ADR). Private courts are used by litigants willing to bypass the regular courts to receive a speedier and less costly end to their disputes. Only reputable private courts should be engaged. Private court judges cannot issue contempt-of-court orders, and their decisions cannot be enforced except through the regular courts. The parties usually agree to abide by the decision of the private court. Such an agreement, if made with independent legal advice, is likely to be upheld by a regular court. Thus, the practical effect of a private court decision is usually the same as the decision of a regular court.

Enforcement of the Judgment

Once the plaintiff has obtained a judgment or an order, the defendant may comply without further ado. If not, the plaintiff may take steps to collect on the judgment or order, for example, by asking the sheriff to seize and sell the defendant's assets or to garnishee the defendant's wages. Collecting on a judgment depends on the creditworthiness and availability of the defendant. Obtaining the judgment may turn out to be an expensive and pointless exercise if the defendant is a stone from which blood cannot be extracted. Choose your debtors wisely.

Limitation Periods

All jurisdictions have limitation statutes that extinguish the right to sue after a specified time. The purpose is to end the permanent uncertainty defendants would otherwise face. For example, a motel wishing to collect an unpaid account from a guest must initiate court proceedings within six or 20 years, depending on the province, from the date on which the cause of action arose. Failure to do so will prevent the motel from using the court system to collect the debt. The only other legally available recourse would be moral persuasion. Without a limitation period, a defendant could be sued decades later, at which time witnesses might be unavailable, memories unreliable, and the evidence missing or compromised.

Criminal Procedure

Concepts

Criminal law is designed to protect society and its members from actions that threaten the security of the person or the state. It imposes penalties that are harsh enough to discourage all but the criminally determined, the foolish, or the mentally ill. While criminal law is not primarily designed to compensate the victim for the losses suffered, as a result of recent changes to the law the courts may now order restitution to the victim for economic losses arising from bodily injury or harm to property. Compensation for other damages, such as mental shock or defamation, can be obtained only in civil court.

Criminal law is the domain of the federal government pursuant to section 91 of the *Constitution Act (1867)*, and it applies in all provinces and territories in Canada. The provinces have enacted laws that carry such penalties as fines. The best known of these laws, which are called quasi-criminal laws, are the provincial highway traffic acts.

There are three types of criminal law: summary conviction offences for minor crimes; indictable offences for more serious crimes; and hybrid offences, which are offences that may proceed either summarily or by indictment at the election of the Crown. Indictable offences carry more severe penalties. The Crown can sometimes secure a guilty plea to a summary conviction simply by raising the spectre of proceeding by way of indictment.

In Canada and other jurisdictions that trace their legal heritage to British common law, a person charged with a criminal offence is presumed innocent until proven guilty. The prosecution has the burden to prove the person guilty beyond a reasonable doubt. Except in rare cases, the evidence must be presented in a public forum to enhance fairness and ensure justice will be seen to be done.

For all but a few offences, the Crown must establish both *actus reus* ("guilty act") and *mens rea* ("guilty mind"). If the accused is guilty of the act but did not have a guilty mind, then he or she is not guilty of a criminal offence. A person who did not or could not form the intent to commit the crime will not be found guilty of the crime. For example, a person who murders a victim while sleepwalking has committed the *actus reus* but has done so without *mens rea*. Another individual may have committed an *actus reus*, but be not guilty by reason of insanity; in essence, this means that the accused was suffering from a disease of the mind such that no true *mens rea* was present. It is far more common for there to be *mens rea* without *actus reus*. People who think about committing crimes without committing them far outnumber those who commit crimes without thinking about them. Merely thinking about a crime is not a crime (although plotting with others with intent is an act of conspiracy that is a crime).

An accused cannot escape culpability by claiming a lack of intent to commit the crime if he or she was willfully blind. For example, a person asked to be a mule by a drug smuggler cannot escape conviction by being willfully blind to the contents of the luggage. A person may also become criminally liable by aiding (assisting) or abetting (encouraging) the offender to commit the crime or by helping the offender to elude capture and thereby becoming an accessory after the fact.

Criminal law is governed by rules of procedure and evidence designed to make the process fair. The law and the rules are found largely in the *Criminal Code of Canada*, the *Canada Evidence Act*, the *Canadian Charter of Rights and Freedoms*, and in the case law. Under subsection 24(2) of the *Charter*, if a court concludes that evidence was obtained in a manner that infringed or denied any rights or freedoms guaranteed by the *Charter*, the evidence shall be excluded if the admission of it would bring the administration of justice into disrepute. Everyone is entitled to life, liberty, and security of the person, and to be left alone by the police unless the police have reasonable and probable grounds to believe that a crime has been, is being, or is about to be committed. Under paragraph 10(b) of the *Charter*, the police must inform any person they arrest or detain of the right to retain and instruct counsel without delay.

The Crown Attorney, or prosecutor, is the attorney (agent) of the Crown (government). Crown prosecutors are immune from liability for their actions unless they laid the charges without reasonable and probable grounds and with "malice in the form of deliberate and improper conduct" (*Nelles v. The Queen in Right of Ontario*, [1989] 2 S.C.R. 170). The Crown must disclose the essential elements of the evidence to the defence. The defence does not have the same broad obligation to disclose to the Crown; however, if the defendant intends to enter alibi evidence, the details must be disclosed so that the prosecution may investigate it.

For offences that can be tried only in a provincial superior court or for which the accused has an election and has elected to be tried in the superior court, the first step in the process is the preliminary inquiry in lower provincial court. Its purpose is to determine whether there is enough evidence to proceed to trial. The accused may waive the preliminary inquiry and proceed directly to trial. In rare cases, the Crown may bypass the preliminary inquiry and prefer (send) the indictment directly to the trial court and jury. For all other offences, the matter is remanded directly to trial in the lower provincial court.

If the Crown believes that the accused is a threat to the public or likely to abscond (run away), the Crown may show cause as to why the accused should be detained in custody or at least required to post bail. If the court finds that cause has not been shown, the accused must be released pending trial.

An accused is not required to submit to a polygraph (lie detector) test. The machines are not infallible. In 1980, when Robert Selkirk was a student at the University of Ottawa Law School, he was asked to be the guinea pig in a polygraph demonstration. Without preparation, and to the purple embarrassment of the technician, he proceeded to beat the machine. Fortunately for the justice system, Selkirk went on to a stellar career as a criminal law lawyer and judge. It is said that an innocent person should never take a polygraph test because of the possibility of a false reading, but that a guilty person should take the test for the same reason.

The Trial Process

The first step in the trial process is the **arraignment**. The accused appears in open court to hear the charges read and then pleads guilty or not guilty. If the plea is guilty, there is no trial and the matter proceeds to sentencing. If the plea is not guilty, the accused may, depending on the charge, choose trial by judge and jury or by judge alone.

In a jury trial, the judge begins by outlining the process to the jury. The judge then asks the jury to keep an open mind until all the evidence is heard and not to discuss the case with anyone. The Crown Attorney then presents the case for the prosecution by attempting to prove that the accused is guilty of the charges on the basis of direct or circumstantial evidence. Direct evidence has greater probative value than circumstantial evidence. An accused generally cannot be found guilty on the basis of circumstantial evidence alone unless it reaches the point of excluding any reasonable hypothesis of his or her innocence.

The Crown Attorney calls the prosecution's witnesses and examines them in chief. The defence counsel may cross-examine them in an effort to discredit their testimony. Physical evidence may also be introduced. For example, beer bottles found in a car may be introduced as evidence in a car accident case. The officer who found the bottles will testify as to the condition they were in and where they were (e.g., half-empty and sitting in the coffee-mug slot).

If the defence counsel believes that the Crown has not presented any evidence as to the essential elements of the case, she may ask for a directed verdict whereby the judge will direct that the proceedings be halted and the accused set free. If she is unable to obtain a directed verdict, she will present the case for the defence.

The defence counsel does not need to know (or even ask) whether the accused is guilty. It is up to the Crown to prove the case. Although the defence counsel must not knowingly present evidence that is false or misleading, she can poke as many holes as she legally can in the Crown's case and let the outcome unfold. For the Crown to succeed, the evidence must convince the 12 jurors—or judge if there is no jury—beyond a reasonable doubt, and on the basis of the facts and the law, that the accused is guilty as charged. The accused may well be guilty of the crime, but if the case is not proven, then the presumption of innocence applies, and the accused will not suffer the *Criminal Code* penalties.

Our judicial system is structured to ensure that guilty people who are not proven guilty remain free. If the system were not so structured, then no citizen would be immune from the unjust sanctions that could be imposed by the state. The resources of the accused are no match for the vast resources and powers of the state. The state has almost limitless funds, extensive investigatory powers, and ready access to forensic laboratories. For the most part, the accused has only the presumption of innocence and a hardworking lawyer. To minimize the tragic visiting of guilt upon the innocent and the annoying acquittal of the guilty, the rules of criminal procedure and evidence must be finely calibrated and constantly examined.

The accused cannot be compelled to testify and the Crown and judge cannot comment on the accused's failure to testify before the jury. Any witnesses called by the defence may be cross-examined by the Crown. A defence counsel who fears that the accused will make a bad impression on the stand may not call on him to testify, even if she is convinced of his innocence. As a rule, innocent clients should take the stand. Human nature being what it is, judges and juries cannot help but wonder why an accused has not testified. If the defence counsel is certain that the accused is guilty, she cannot call him as a witness if she believes that he will mislead the court. If he insists on testifying, all she can do is to ask him to state his name, sit down, and not assist him in any way. Such a display is, of course, highly prejudicial.

If the defence has adduced new evidence not previously addressed by the Crown, the Crown may adduce fresh evidence but only in reply to the new evidence of the defence. The defence counsel may cross-examine any reply witnesses.

After the evidence has been presented, the closing addresses are presented. The defence counsel emphasizes the evidence that proves innocence or casts reasonable doubt upon the Crown's case, while the Crown focuses on the evidence that tends to prove the case. The defence counsel addresses the jury last if the defence has called no evidence.

After the closing addresses, the judge charges the jury by reviewing the facts and evidence and by instructing them about the applicable law. The jury retires to the jury room to ponder the verdict. All 12 jurors must agree. If the verdict is not unanimous, the jurors will be discharged and a new trial will take place either before a new jury or before a judge alone.

Sentencing

I know not whether Laws be right or whether Laws be wrong.
All we know who lie in gaol is that the walls are strong.
And that each day is like a year—a year whose days are long.

—Anon

If the accused is found guilty, the judge must impose a sentence. Both the Crown and the defence may make submissions. Sometimes victim-impact statements are made. Imposing an appropriate sentence is often more difficult than finding guilt or innocence. Sentencing is as critical to our respect for law and order as the trial process itself. Sentences include discharges, suspensions, probation, community service orders, fines, restitution, deportation, and incarceration for terms up to life. The term can be indefinite if the convicted person is declared a dangerous offender. Capital punishment has been abolished for all offences under the *Criminal Code,* and in any event would likely not withstand a *Charter c*hallenge.

Some offences carry automatic sentences, leaving the judge no discretion to tailor the sentence to fit the crime and the criminal. First-degree murder carries an automatic life sentence with no parole for 25 years, while second-degree murder carries an automatic life sentence with no parole for 10 years. Of course, murder is wrong, but it seems odd to treat all killers of the same degree very similarly regardless of remorse and other factors. Spouse murderers are highly unlikely ever to kill again whereas contract killers will kill repeatedly until caught. It also seems odd to incarcerate mercy killers for as long as psychopathic killers. Respect for criminal law is enhanced when the principles of sentencing bear a reasonable relationship to the sanctioned conduct (i.e., the punishment should fit the crime). Judges should have wide discretion to tailor the sentences to the crime and to the criminal.

Sentencing has four purposes:

1. *Specific deterrence.* This is intended to deter a criminal from committing more crimes.

2. *General deterrence.* This is intended to deter everyone else from committing crimes.

3. *Rehabilitation*. This is intended to re-orient criminals to become law-abiding by choice.

4. *Protection of the public*. Until the court is satisfied that the criminal has been deterred or rehabilitated, the criminal must be incarcerated to ensure the protection of the public.

Sentences of less than two years are served in provincial reformatories; sentences of two years or more are served in federal penitentiaries. Jailed persons may apply for parole after completing a statutory minimum of their sentences. In cases where the sentence is two years or more, the National Parole Board decides whether the prisoner is worthy of parole.

A person with a criminal record may find it hard to be bonded (i.e., insured for honesty), and be disqualified from many jobs. He or she may apply for a pardon of a summary conviction five years after the full sentence has expired, or for a pardon of an indictable conviction three years after the full sentence has expired; thus, no one may receive a pardon for a life sentence. If pardoned, job applicants may state that they have no criminal record.

Appeals

A person found guilty may appeal the finding of guilt or the sentence or both. For some offences, the right to appeal the conviction is automatic; for others, leave to appeal must be obtained. The appeal judges will typically review only matters of law, not fact. With a few exceptions, the first appeal is to the provincial Court of Appeal. If the last appeal to the Supreme Court of Canada fails, the only recourse is ministerial intervention.

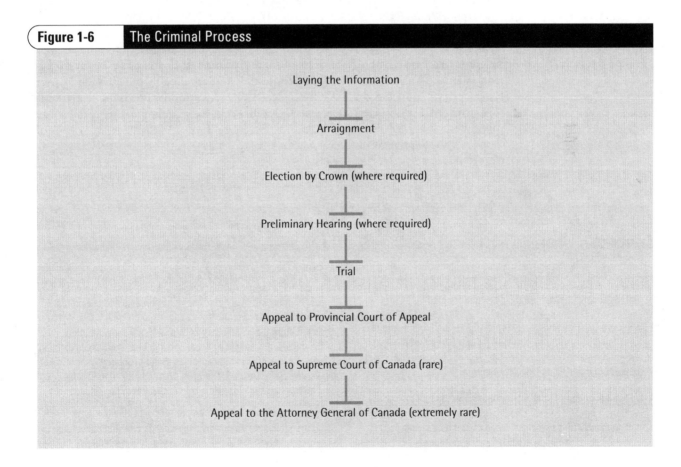

Figure 1-6   The Criminal Process

Laying the Information

Arraignment

Election by Crown (where required)

Preliminary Hearing (where required)

Trial

Appeal to Provincial Court of Appeal

Appeal to Supreme Court of Canada (rare)

Appeal to the Attorney General of Canada (extremely rare)

Summary

Law is difficult to define with precision. The most practical definition is that of legal realism, which holds that law is whatever the judges say it is. The main purposes of law are to maintain peace; to provide a civilized dispute-resolution mechanism between the state and persons, and between persons; and to provide a reliable system for regulating interpersonal and business relationships. The law touches upon virtually all aspects of human existence.

In Canada, supreme legal authority resides, in theory, in the monarch. In reality, it resides in Parliament and the provincial legislatures in their respective constitutional spheres. The federal and provincial levels of government delegate some authority to administrative boards, tribunals, and commissions; and, by provinces, to municipalities.

Sources of Canadian law include royal prerogatives, legislative enactments, decisions produced by delegated lawmakers, and the case law decisions of the judges. Canada's highest court is the Supreme Court of Canada. Other federal courts include the Federal Court of Canada and the Tax Court of Canada. The provinces have superior courts that comprise a trial division and an appeal division. The superior provincial court judges are appointed by the federal government. The provinces also have lower provincial courts that handle some criminal, family, youth, and civil matters. The judges in the lower courts are appointed by the provinces. Administrative boards, commissions, and tribunals tend to be less formal than courts and are empowered by statute to deal with narrow issues.

Civil actions are governed by highly technical rules of civil procedure. The rules attempt to ensure fairness to all parties and provide a mechanism for advancing the case to a conclusion. The rules encourage settlements in order to lessen the costs of involving the courts. The rules also specify how a judgment may be enforced and how collections may occur. Limitation periods restrict the time within which a plaintiff may commence an action.

Criminal law affects a small percentage of Canadians but is critical to maintaining law and order and, with constitutional law, to safeguarding the rights and freedoms of citizens against the tremendous power of the state. The rules of criminal procedure attempt to ensure that an accused person receives a fair trial. In practice, the vast majority of persons accused of a criminal offence either plead or are found guilty of either the offence as charged or an included offence (i.e., a lesser offence with the same basic elements as the main offence). Judges often consider sentencing to be as important if not more important than trials themselves. Given that mistakes do occur, there are rights of appeal. If the Supreme Court of Canada refuses to hear or dismisses the appeal, the only recourse is to the federal justice minister.

Discussion Questions

1. Is the law nothing more than what the judges say it is? Why or why not?

2. On what basis could both the federal and provincial governments claim jurisdiction over travel agencies?

3. Should DNA testing be mandatory? What should be done with samples that are obtained from a person who is later acquitted on a technicality? Can we be sure that the samples did not become contaminated?

4. Plea bargaining is the art of pleading guilty to a lesser offence in exchange for having more serious charges dropped. What are the advantages and disadvantages of the practice? Does it serve justice or subvert it?

5. You believe that the cashier of the restaurant that you manage has stolen $10,000 from the till over the past year. The witness is a pleasant waitress who has a criminal record for soft-drug possession. As the police are not collection agents, if the cashier is reported to the police, the restaurant may never recover the money. If the restaurant sues the cashier for return of the money, he might avoid a criminal record and hurt his next employer. Note that it is a crime to threaten criminal proceedings to collect a civil debt. Discuss the pros and cons of (a) suing the cashier and (b) reporting him to the police.

6. Natural Law may at times conflict with Positive Law. What current issues would give rise to this conflict? Does this conflict give rise to the validity of judge-made law?

Appendix: Sections 91 and 92 of the Constitution Act (1867)

Powers of the Parliament

91. It shall be lawful for the Queen, by and with the Advice and Consent of the Senate and House of Commons, to make Laws for the Peace, Order and good Government of Canada, in relation to all Matters not coming within the Classes of Subjects by this Act assigned exclusively to the Legislatures of the Provinces; and for greater Certainty, but not so as to restrict the Generality of the foregoing Terms of this Section, it is hereby declared that (notwithstanding anything in this Act) the exclusive Legislative Authority of the Parliament of Canada extends to all Matters coming within the Classes of Subjects next herein-after enumerated; that is to say,

    1. The amendment from time to time of the Constitution of Canada, except as regards matters coming within the classes of subjects by this Act assigned exclusively to the Legislatures of the Provinces, or as regards rights or privileges by this or any other Constitutional Act granted or secured to the Legislature or the Government of a Province, or to any class of persons with respect to schools or as regards the use of the English or the French language or as regards the requirements that there shall be a session of the Parliament of Canada at least once each year, and that no House of Commons shall continue for more than five years from the day of the return of the Writs for choosing the House: provided, however, that a House of Commons may in time of real or apprehended war, invasion or insurrection be continued by the Parliament of Canada if such continuation is not opposed by the votes of more than one-third of the members of such House.

    1A. The Public Debt and Property.

    2. The Regulation of Trade and Commerce.

    2A. Unemployment Insurance.

    3. The raising of Money by any Mode or System of Taxation.

    4. The borrowing of Money on the Public Credit.

    5. Postal Service.

    6. The Census and Statistics.

    7. Militia, Military and Naval Service, and Defence.

    8. The fixing of and providing for the Salaries and Allowances of Civil and other Officers of the Government of Canada.

    9. Beacons, Buoys, Lighthouses, and Sable Island.

    10. Navigation and Shipping.

    11. Quarantine and the Establishment and Maintenance of Marine Hospitals.

    12. Sea Coast and Inland Fisheries.

    13. Ferries between any Province and any British or Foreign Country or between Two Provinces.

    14. Currency and Coinage.

    15. Banking, Incorporation of Banks, and the Issue of Paper Money.

    16. Savings Banks.

    17. Weights and Measures.

    18. Bills of Exchange and Promissory Notes.

Chapter 1 / The Canadian Legal System

19. Interest.

20. Legal Tender.

21. Bankruptcy and Insolvency.

22. Patents of Invention and Discovery.

23. Copyrights.

24. Indians, and Lands reserved for the Indians.

25. Naturalization and Aliens.

26. Marriage and Divorce.

27. The Criminal Law, except the Constitution of Courts of Criminal Jurisdiction, but including the Procedure in Criminal Matters.

28. The Establishment, Maintenance, and Management of Penitentiaries.

29. Such Classes of Subjects as are expressly excepted in the Enumeration of the Classes of Subjects by this Act assigned exclusively to the Legislatures of the Provinces.

And any Matter coming within any of the Classes of Subjects enumerated in this Section shall not be deemed to come within the Class of Matters of a local or private Nature comprised in the Enumeration of the Classes of Subjects by this Act assigned exclusively to the Legislatures of the Provinces.

Exclusive Powers of Provincial Legislatures

92. In each Province the Legislature may exclusively make Laws in relation to Matters coming within the Classes of Subject next herein-after enumerated; that is to say,

1. The Amendment from Time to Time, notwithstanding anything in this Act, of the Constitution of the Province except as regards the Office of Lieutenant Governor.

2. Direct Taxation within the Province in order to the raising of a Revenue for Provincial Purposes.

3. The borrowing of Money on the sole Credit of the Province.

4. The Establishment and Tenure of Provincial Offices and the Appointment and Payment of Provincial Officers.

5. The Management and Sale of the Public Lands belonging to the Province and of the Timber and Wood thereon.

6. The Establishment, Maintenance, and Management of Public and Reformatory Prisons in and for the Province.

7. The Establishment, Maintenance, and Management of Hospitals, Asylums, Charities, and Eleemosynary Institutions in and for the Province, other than Marine Hospitals.

8. Municipal Institutions in the Province.

9. Shop, Saloon, Tavern, Auctioneer, and other Licences in order to the raising of a Revenue for Provincial, Local, or Municipal Purposes.

10. Local Works and Undertakings other than such as are of the following Classes:

    (a) Lines of Steam or other Ships, Railways, Canals, Telegraphs, and other Works and Undertakings connecting the Province with any other or others of the Provinces, or extending beyond the Limits of the Province;

    (b) Lines of Steam Ships between the Province and any British or Foreign Country;

(c) Such Works as, although wholly situate within the Province, are before or after their Execution declared by the Parliament of Canada to be for the general Advantage of Canada or for the Advantage of Two or more of the Provinces.

11. The Incorporation of Companies with Provincial Objects.

12. The Solemnization of Marriage in the Province.

13. Property and Civil Rights in the Province.

14. The Administration of Justice in the Province, including the Constitution, Maintenance, and Organization of Provincial Courts, both of Civil and of Criminal Jurisdiction, and including Procedure in Civil Matters in those Courts.

15. The Imposition of Punishment by Fine, Penalty, or Imprisonment for enforcing any Law of the Province made in relation to any Matter coming within any of the Classes of Subjects enumerated in this Section.

16. Generally all Matters of a merely local or private Nature in the Province.

Chapter Two

Human Rights in Canada

Learning Outcomes

1. Analyze the evolution of human rights legislation in Canada.

2. Comply with current employment and human rights legislation.

Introduction

Fundamental rights relating to the dignity, security, and integrity of the person are collectively termed **"human rights" in Canada** and "civil rights" in the United States. Throughout history, extracting them from the governing authority has often been accomplished only at great cost to life, limb, and land. In the distant mists of our legal heritage, human rights held little sway. The sovereign often ruled with an arbitrary disregard for the rights of his subjects. The turning point in British legal culture was King John's signing of the Magna Carta at Runnymede in June 1215. Magna Carta, whose terms were extracted from the king by a group of armed and determined barons, contained only limited rights and was designed to protect the nobility, not the peasantry, but it was a start. By the time of Confederation in 1867, many of the battles for fundamental, political human rights had already been fought and won in Britain and Europe. Other battles were still to come, such as full equality for women and other groups.

Today, most Canadians take human rights for granted. When we do think about them, it is often with a sense that they have always existed and always will. To avoid complacency, we need only recall the treatment, during the Second World War, of Canadian citizens whose only "crime" was to be of Japanese descent; the virtual ban on Chinese immigration between 1923 and 1947; and much of the treatment of Native people throughout our history.

There are also examples from the hospitality industry. In 1936, Fred Christie entered the York Tavern in Montreal and ordered a beer. He was refused service because he was black. He sued on the ground that he had a right to be served in a licensed and public establishment. The case reached the Supreme Court of Canada, which ruled in the tavern's favour, its main argument being that the case had to do with freedom of contract and commerce, not human rights. In 1912, Saskatchewan had a law that forbade Chinese men from hiring white women. Quong Wing had hired two white women to work in his restaurant in Moose Jaw. Although the women testified that he was a good employer and a gentleman, he was fined five dollars for employing them. He appealed to the Supreme Court of Canada. Upon losing that appeal, he had to fire two employees who liked working for him and did not want to lose their jobs. A third example is the fact that, at one time, white members of Canadian Football League teams stayed in whites-only hotels while their black teammates were relegated to hotels that accepted blacks.

While societal attitudes have undergone a shift since those Supreme Court cases, infringements of human rights still occur distressingly often. To appreciate how fragile our fundamental freedoms are, we need only consider the conduct of the police and prosecutors in the Guy Paul Morin case. They were so zealous to convict him of the rape and murder of his nine-year-old neighbour, Christine Jessop, that they were prepared to ignore human rights and legal safeguards, fabricate evidence, perjure themselves, pressure witnesses into perjuring themselves, and unfairly present the evidence before the court. One of the key elements in the conviction was the testimony of Christine's mother and brother. During the initial investigation, they had told the police that they had returned home at a certain time, but if that were correct, then Morin could not have been the abductor. Over several months, the police persuaded them that they must have been mistaken about the time, and that if they did not change their evidence, their daughter and sister's murderer would escape punishment. The Jessops changed their evidence before the trial, affording Morin the time he would have needed to abduct Christine. Although there were no witnesses and no physical evidence placing him at the scene (semen was found in Christine's underwear, but the specimen was too small to be analyzed at that time), Morin was convicted. Following advances in DNA testing, an inquiry was held into the conviction. The new tests proved that the semen was not his. Just as important, the Jessops testified as to what they had originally told the investigators. The skewed evidence as to the timing collapsed and Morin was exonerated.

Investigators and prosecutors bear a heavy responsibility to ensure that charges are laid only in accordance with lawful evidence gathering and legal procedure and to consider fully and fairly any evidence that tends to exonerate a suspect. They must also be prepared to admit error. In our criminal justice system, we have findings of "Guilty" or "Not Guilty." We have no finding of "Innocent." The Morin inquiry established that he was not only not guilty, but innocent. One of the most disturbing postscripts to his exoneration was the statement by one of the investigators that, "It may not have been his semen on her underwear, but that doesn't prove it wasn't his hands around her neck." Such tunnel vision, such inability to admit error even in the face of proven innocence, is antithetical to justice and a threat to the human rights of everyone. In the United States, since the advent of reliable DNA testing, over 100 inmates on death row have been shown to be innocent of the crime for which they were convicted and sentenced to die. How should such a statistic affect the debate on capital punishment?

Investigators and prosecutors are, for the most part, good people who do a fine job in difficult circumstances. They do not usually set out deliberately to procure a wrongful conviction. The errors usually occur in good faith. As Barbara Gardner said as she was being led to the gallows, "Good people are always so sure they are right." The problems have to do with human nature, which is immutable, and our adversarial legal system, which is the worst system except for every other system. Although it is often said that the prosecution never wins or loses because justice is served whatever the outcome, prosecutors and investigators do not lay charges against someone they think is innocent. Their desire to win, coupled with their belief that the suspect they have targeted is guilty, may sometimes colour their perceptions and cause them to highlight or exclude evidence on the basis of a predetermined theory. Without high levels of personal integrity and open-mindedness on the part of prosecutors and investigators, and careful attention to human rights and criminal procedure, systemic abuses would multiply. Competence in the handling of forensic evidence is also vitally important. Mishandled forensic evidence can lead to wrongful convictions of the innocent, and also to failures to convict the guilty. Tainted forensics was the basis on which O.J. Simpson was found not guilty in his criminal trial.

In any society, there are opposing drives toward anarchy and tyranny. The ideal midpoint between the two extremes is a fair and respected system of law and order. The safeguard against anarchy is the enforcement of law and order. The safeguard against tyranny is respect for human rights. Authority and liberty are interdependent. Too little or too much of one hurts the other. Our society is governed by the rule of law, which requires that the law be applied fairly and not arbitrarily. There is, however, a central dilemma posed by the rule of law. If the people creating the laws have an evil intent, then the laws will be evil. In a truly just society, laws must be just in themselves before they can be justly applied.

Canadian Human Rights Legislation

Canada is bound in international law by the 1948 Universal Declaration of Human Rights, which was co-authored by a Canadian, John Humphrey, and which recognized human dignity as the foundation of freedom, justice, and peace. In Canada, the *Canadian Charter of Rights and Freedoms* and provincial human rights codes have played crucial roles in the evolution of Canadian human rights legislation.

The *Canadian Bill of Rights*

While legislation affecting human rights has been in force in Canada since the founding of the country, the first formal national codification occurred when John Diefenbaker's Conservative government enacted the *Canadian Bill of Rights* in 1960.

While a salutary undertaking, the **Bill of Rights** was seriously flawed in that it applied only to matters under federal jurisdiction and, further, did not negate any existing statutes with which it conflicted.

The *Canadian Charter of Rights and Freedoms*

With the passage of *The Constitution Act (1982)*, Pierre Elliot Trudeau's Liberal government patriated residual technical constitutional authority from Britain. In the process, the government enacted the **Canadian Charter of Rights and Freedoms**, which is the only charter of rights entrenched in the Canadian constitution. As such, it overrides any federal or provincial laws that are inconsistent with it. While the *Charter* has its admirers, some critics have suggested that hardened criminals are escaping deserved incarceration as a result of *Charter* loopholes. Putting aside debate over the *Charter*'s relative worth, it can be predicted with certainty that it will not be the final stage in the evolution of Canada's human rights law.

Section 2 of the *Charter* guarantees the following fundamental freedoms:

(a) freedom of conscience and religion;

(b) freedom of thought, belief, opinion and expression, including freedom of the press and other media of communications;

(c) freedom of peaceful assembly; and

(d) freedom of association.

The *Charter* guarantees the following rights (notice the difference between "citizens" and "everyone"):

1. Democratic rights for citizens, such as the right to vote and to run for election to the House of Commons or a legislative assembly (section 3)

2. Mobility rights for citizens to enter, remain in, or leave Canada, and to move to and work in another province (section 6)

3. Legal rights for everyone, such as the right to life, liberty, and security of the person (section 7); the right, on arrest or detention, to retain and instruct counsel without delay and to be informed of that right (section 10); and to be presumed innocent until proven guilty (paragraph 11(d))

4. Equality rights for everyone, such as equal protection and equal benefit of the law without discrimination and, in particular, without discrimination based on race, national or ethnic origin, colour, religion, sex, age, or mental or physical disability, subject to allowable affirmative action programs (section 15)

5. Rights for everyone pertaining to French and English, the official languages of Canada (section 16)

6. French or English minority language and educational rights for citizens (section 23)

7. Rights pertaining to enforcement, which include the right to seek legal remedy when rights or freedoms guaranteed by the Charter are infringed or denied (section 24)

8. Existing Aboriginal and treaty rights that pertain to the Aboriginal peoples of Canada (section 25)

9. Any other rights or freedoms that exist in Canada (section 26)

Section 33, the controversial notwithstanding clause, provides for a legislative override in stating that "Parliament or the legislature of a province may expressly declare in an Act of Parliament or of the legislature ... that the Act or a provision thereof shall operate notwithstanding a provision included in section 2 or sections 7 to 15 of this *Charter*." However, the declaration shall cease to have effect no later than five years after it was made.

Under the *Charter*, the police must have reasonable and probable grounds to make an arrest. The *Charter* right "to be secure against unreasonable search or seizure" (section 8) is derived from the old common law concept of *habeas corpus* ("you shall have the body"), which was a judicial writ requiring the prosecutor to bring the detainee before a court rather than arbitrarily holding him. Provided they have reasonable and probable grounds for making the arrest, the police may search the detainee (including body cavities). In order to search the residence or place of business of a detainee, the police must obtain a search warrant; some exceptions to this requirement are noted in the *Criminal Code* and the *Controlled Drugs and Substances Act*.

The *Charter* binds the federal and provincial governments, their agencies, and departments. It does not, as the following case shows, bind individuals or private corporations.

Re Blainey and Ontario Hockey Association et al. (1986), 54 O.R. (2d) 513 (C.A.), leave to appeal to the Supreme Court of Canada refused (1986), 58 O.R. (2d) 274

The appellant, an outstanding 12-year-old girl hockey player, fully accepted by her coaches and teammates, was prevented from continuing to play on a boys' hockey team by the regulations of the Ontario Hockey Association and the Canadian Amateur Hockey Association. At the time, section 19(2) of Ontario's Human Rights Code allowed discrimination where participation in an athletic activity was restricted to persons of the same sex. The Court of Appeal held that section 19(2) was void for infringing the right to equal treatment and equal benefit without discrimination based on sex under section 15(1) of the Charter. However, as the Charter does not bind private parties, the court could not order her reinstatement. The appellant then brought her complaint to the Ontario Human Rights Commission where a Board of Inquiry upheld her right to play on the boys' team. Interestingly, the Board also held women's hockey was an allowable special program under the Ontario Human Rights Code such that it would not be an infringement to discriminate against males wishing to join a women's hockey team.

Provincial Human Rights Legislation

Partly because the *Charter* does not bind individuals or private corporations, and partly because much social and commercial activity falls under provincial jurisdiction, the provinces have passed their own human rights legislation to regulate conduct involving individuals and private corporations. Ontario's *Human Rights Code* is an example. It was enacted in 1962 and has been amended several times. Of particular relevance are the following sections:

1. Every person has a right to equal treatment with respect to services, goods and facilities, without discrimination because of race, ancestry, place of origin, colour, ethnic origin, citizenship, creed, sex, sexual orientation, age, record of offences, marital status, family status or handicap.

2.(1) Every person has a right to equal treatment with respect to the occupancy of accommodation, without discrimination because of race, ancestry, place of origin, colour, ethnic origin, citizenship, creed, sex, sexual orientation, age, record of offences, marital status, family status, handicap or the receipt of public assistance.

5.(1) Every person has a right to equal treatment with respect to employment without discrimination because of race, ancestry, place of origin, colour, ethnic origin, citizenship, creed, sex, sexual orientation, age, record of offences, marital status, family status or handicap.

5.(2) Every person who is an employee has a right to freedom from harassment in the workplace by the employer or agent of the employer or by another employee because of race, ancestry, place of origin, colour, ethnic origin, citizenship, creed, sex, sexual orientation, age, record of offences, marital status, family status or handicap.

7.(3) Every person has a right to be free from (a) a sexual solicitation or advance made by a person in a position to confer, grant or deny a benefit or advancement to the person where the person making the solicitation or advance knows or ought reasonably to know that it is unwelcome; or (b) a reprisal or a threat of reprisal for the rejection of the sexual solicitation or advance ...

9. No person shall infringe or do, directly or indirectly, anything that infringes a right (in the Code).

Human Rights in the Hospitality Industry

Background

The hospitality industry is among Canada's top revenue-producing industries. It is often referred to as "the people industry" because of the vast number of people it employs and serves. Thus, it is no surprise that it is featured in many human rights cases. The majority of the cases stem from improper hiring and firing, poor employment practices, and sexual harassment in the workplace. Most establishments are owned, managed, and staffed by people who are aware of their legal and moral obligations, and strive to make themselves and their businesses models of appropriate behaviour. Unfortunately, there are a few who do not make sufficient effort to do so. Employers may be held liable for any contraventions of human rights legislation or other misbehaviour. As we shall see in Chapter 4, employers may also be held liable for improper acts of their employees and agents through a doctrine known as vicarious liability. As a society, we are becoming less and less tolerant of discrimination, although what constitutes discrimination is sometimes difficult to discern. As it has in the past, the case law will continue to reflect our improving understanding of what constitutes discrimination.

Discrimination

The term "**discrimination**" has been used to describe everything from benign **nepotism** to virulent racism. Discrimination is often employed to guard political, socio-economic, or religious turf. It is human nature to prefer the interests of oneself, one's family, one's community, and so forth over the interests of others. Within those groups, it is human nature to prefer one's own sex, co-religionists, friends, and so on. Only when discrimination becomes contrary to the legitimate interests of society as a whole do enlightened laws and social mores apply appropriate reinforcements and sanctions against the adverse consequences of discrimination. On the other hand, discrimination based on merit serves the legitimate interests of society and is allowed and even encouraged. Furthermore, the law does not prevent discrimination based on matters that do not have a meaningful impact on the legitimate interests of society. For example, provided there are no human rights violations, an employer can hire one applicant over others because the employer and successful applicant discover they share a hobby such as volunteering at a hospital even though the hobby has nothing to do with the job description. An unsuccessful applicant could not sue on the basis that his hobby is just as interesting. Furthermore, several types of discrimination, such as affirmative action programs, are expressly allowed under human rights legislation. They are discussed under "Exceptions," page 47.

In Canada, Aboriginal people and all immigrant groups, including English-speaking whites, have faced discrimination at one time or another. In the early 1900s, some businesses posted in their windows signs that read, "Help Wanted. The Irish need not apply." This often comes as a surprise to those who have not realized that white, Christian English-speakers have discriminated against white, Christian English-speakers. The fact that Canadians of Irish descent have since become members of the establishment causes people to forget that they had to fight their way in. Today, people of many backgrounds stand at the centre of Canadian culture, influence, and power, and Canada is very much the richer for it. Having to fight one's way into positions of power and influence is a common societal dynamic. No profession is without its challenges and hurdles. Success in academia requires scholarship. Success in business requires good ideas and superior products or services. Success in democratic politics requires an ability to appeal to voters. When the criterion of success is merit, there is no quarrel with the process. However, when the criteria are based on race, sex, creed, and other fundamentally irrelevant considerations, laws and social mores step in to disallow them. One of the strategies various groups use to fight their way in is to push for the adoption and proper application of human rights laws. An advantage to this is that everyone benefits in the long run.

Various laws address various kinds of discrimination. Benign nepotism is discouraged by laws that prevent politicians and senior bureaucrats from using their positions to obtain jobs for their close relatives, while virulent racism is held in check by laws banning, for example, racially motivated hate mail. Sometimes the law must walk a fine line between prohibiting discriminatory conduct and infringing basic freedoms. Nevertheless, we should never forget that discrimination is both insidious and ubiquitous, and that constant personal and societal vigilance is required to keep it at bay. The onus is on our political system to enact and uphold just laws. The onus is on each individual to formulate and abide by just codes of conduct.

Racism

While **racism** is a problem that arises in every ethnic group in the world, racists constitute only a small minority of any ethnic group. Racism is not only morally repugnant, it is also bad for business. Given that racists are in the minority, it is counterproductive to alienate the majority of one's customers—the non-racists from all backgrounds. Following are examples of cases involving racism that have occurred within the context of the hospitality industry.

Garnet Angeconeb v. 517152 Ontario Ltd. and Ruby Cullen (1993), 19 C.H.R.R. D/452 (Ont. Bd. Inq.)

Angeconeb, an Ojibway Indian, made a reservation to stay at the Red Dog Inn. Upon arrival, he was given a room that was filthy, reeked of alcohol and cigarette smoke, and lacked a safety chain. The inn's records showed that certain rooms were clearly set aside for Native persons. Other guests who were not of obvious Native heritage received rooms of superior quality. A police officer offered evidence that he had telephoned the inn on behalf of persons who needed accommodation and was asked by the clerk whether they were Natives "because all the 'Native rooms' were occupied." The Board of Inquiry found that the room assignment policy was discriminatory based on race and ancestry, and awarded Angeconeb $2500.

McNab v. Calyniuk Restaurants Inc. (1995), 24 C.H.R.R. D/22

Ms. McNab is of Cree ancestry. She went to Ryly's with several friends at about 10 p.m. on October 5, 1992. Shane McKay and Krista Spratt, who are white, entered first and were admitted after paying the cover charge. They were not asked for identification. Ms. McNab was asked for identification. She produced three pieces of photo identification which showed she was over the legal drinking age. However, the doorman said that she could not be admitted unless she had Saskatchewan Government Insurance identification. When Ms. McNab could not produce this, she was refused entry to Ryly's.

When her friends learned that Ms. McNab would not be admitted, they decided to leave, and Krista Spratt said to the doorman on her way out "Kiss my ass." He rejoined "Not if it is as brown as hers," referring to Ms. McNab.

The Board of Inquiry found that Calyniuk Restaurants Inc. had provided no non-discriminatory reason for refusing entry to Ms. McNab. In 1991 the Liquor Licensing Commission of Saskatchewan advised restaurant owners who sell alcohol that they should rely primarily on S.G.I. photo identification for proof of age. However, the doormen at Ryly's testified that they did accept other identification. The Board of Inquiry found that Calyniuk Restaurants Inc. did not have a standard policy that S.G.I. photo identification was required in all circumstances.

The Board of Inquiry concluded that Ms. McNab was treated differently because of her race and ancestry.

The Board also accepted Ms. McNab's evidence that she was hurt and humiliated by the experience, experienced a loss of confidence, and felt like a second-class citizen. She no longer felt comfortable with white people.

The Board of Inquiry ordered Calyniuk Restaurants Inc. to pay Ms. McNab $1,500 compensation.

Ram v. McDonald's Restaurant of Canada Ltd. (1991), 16 C.H.R.R. D10

Atish Ram, of Fijian ancestry, had lived in Canada most of his life. In 1983 he applied for a management training position with McDonald's. He worked in a number of locations over the following five years. In all of these locations, Mr. Ram was called racially derogatory names by supervisors and other employees. These names included "Chocolate," "Black Man," "Buckwheat," "Toby," and "Boop" (short for Bhupinder, a common name from India). Some of these names were taken from TV programs; all of them refer to colour and have a derogatory meaning.

In 1986 Mr. Ram became ill with severe stomach pains. In October he had his appendix removed. Subsequently, he suffered from stress, migraines, and dizziness. He went on short-term disability leave twice, was transferred to a location which was considered less stressful. When he became too ill to work again he was told that his employment would be terminated and he could apply for long-term disability benefits. Mr. Ram filled out an application form for the long-term benefits, but he did not submit the medical reports necessary to complete the application. Mr. Ram testified that he did not submit the reports because a McDonald's official said to him that "all you little Hindus want is insurance money." Mr. Ram alleged that his illness was caused by the racial harassment he experienced, and that his employment was terminated because of a disability.

> The council found that Mr. Ram was discriminated against because of his race, but did not find a causal connection between the racial harassment and his illness. The Council found that the employer had taken steps to accommodate Mr. Ram by transferring him to a less stressful location and offering him long-term disability benefits.
>
> The Council upheld the complaint of race discrimination but dismissed the complaint based on physical disability. The Council awarded Mr. Ram $2,000 compensation.

In Chapter 9 we will see that hotels have the right to assign rooms. There is no conflict between these two propositions. The hotelier can place the guest into any room in the hotel as long as there is no illegal discrimination behind the assignment.

Shepherd v. Bama Artisans Inc. (1988), 9 C.H.R.R. D/5049 (Ont. Bd. of Inq.)

A black man stood in line to gain entrance to a club. White people behind him were allowed first. When he finally reached the door, he was charged twice the normal cover charge. After some time, the manager cleared the dance floor and re-admitted only white patrons. The Board of Inquiry found this a blatant disregard for human rights.

Re M. (July 29, 1988, Ont. H.R.C.)

A white motel owner refused accommodation to a white woman when he learned that her husband was black. The Human Rights Commission ordered the owner to pay a fine, write an apology, and post the *Human Rights Code* in his motel. Although the fine was small and the apology cost little, the commission desired to send a clear message to the owner and the public by requiring the operator to post the *Human Rights Code*. The commission desired that the operator, and others who might read the posted *Code*, become informed and learn what is and is not expected of people in Canada.

Human rights legislation prohibits employers, their employees and agents from discriminating against employees or members of the public because of race.

The Recruitment of Personnel

An example of legislation pertaining to the recruitment of personnel is found in section 23 of Ontario's *Human Rights Code*, which reads as follows:

23.(1) The right under section 5 to equal treatment with respect to employment is infringed where an invitation to apply for employment or an advertisement in connection with employment is published or displayed that directly or indirectly classifies or indicates qualifications by a prohibited ground of discrimination.

23.(2) The right under section 5 to equal treatment with respect to employment is infringed where a form of application for employment is used or a written or oral inquiry is made of an applicant that directly or indirectly classifies or indicates qualifications by a prohibited ground of discrimination.

23.(3) Nothing in sub-section (2) precludes the asking of questions at a personal employment interview concerning a prohibited ground of discrimination where discrimination on such ground is permitted under this Act.

23.(4) The right under section 5 to equal treat-ment with respect to employment is infringed where an employment agency discriminates

Merit is the most important consideration when hiring.

against a person because of a prohibited ground of discrimination in receiving, classifying, dis-posing of or otherwise acting upon applications for its services or in referring an applicant or applicants to an employer or agent of an employer.

Section 23 of Ontario's *Human Rights Code* assigns a dual liability for an advertisement for employment that contravenes the section. The print or broadcast medium that carries the ad and the person who placed it are jointly and severally liable. Under the former Ontario *Human Rights Code*, employers who qualified for exceptions under the Code could place information in the advertisement indicating the nature and existence of the exception and that only qualifying applicants should apply. Section 23 of the current Code requires that this screening take place at the interview stage, not the advertising stage. Critics say that this requirement obliges employers and nonqualifying applicants to go through a wasteful charade; others regard the provision as an attempt to avoid abuses, to foster tolerance, and to minimize the publication of permitted discrimination.

Subsection 23(2) of the Code is an attempt to prohibit employers from screening out applicants sight unseen. Questions relating to sex, race, religion, or marital status, and indirect questions that are seen as an attempt to obtain the same information, are all con-trary to the Code. Subsection 23(4) prohibits employment agencies from discriminating against potential employees. This prevents employers from using outside employment agencies to circumvent the Code. For further discussion of the job application and inter-view processes, see Chapter 14.

Sex Discrimination

Discrimination on the basis of sex, except in limited commonsensical instances, is contrary to the *Charter of Rights and Freedoms* and to provincial human rights legislation. As the fol-lowing case shows, ignorance does not leave an employer any less guilty of discrimination.

Krohn v. United Enterprises Ltd. (May 16, 1994, Sask. Bd. of Inq.)

A female bartender was removed from tending the bar and told to wait tables. The manager believed that the customers preferred to have women wait on them. The Board of Inquiry found that this was sex discrimination, even though the manager believed that his views were complimentary to the women and that he was taking a commercially reasonable approach to the desires of his customers.

Women may also experience discrimination because they are (or may become) pregnant or, as the following case shows, because an employer holds biased views concerning a woman's family status.

Hurley v. Mustoe, [1981] 1 R.L.R. 208 (Employment Appeal Tribunal)

Hurley was fired from her job when her employer discovered that she had four young children. The children were being cared for by their father while she was at work. The employer said it was his policy not to hire women with young children because the mothers could not be relied upon to arrive at work on time and stay for the whole shift. He did not have a similar policy for men with young children. The Employment Appeal Tribunal held this was discrimination on the basis of sex.

Although there have been cases in which men have been discriminated against on the basis of sex, sex discrimination affects many more women than men. Another prohibited ground of sex discrimination is sexual orientation.

Sexual Harassment

Sexual harassment is defined in the Ontario Restaurant Association Compliance Guide as "a course of **vexatious** conduct or comment that is known or ought reasonably to be known to be unwelcome." Under subsection 7(3) of Ontario's *Human Rights Code*, "every person has a right to be free from a sexual solicitation or advance made by a person in a position to confer, grant or deny a benefit or advancement to the person where the person making the solicitation or advance knows or ought reasonably to know that it is unwelcome; and to be free from a reprisal or a threat of reprisal for the rejection of the sexual solicitation or advance." Sexual harassment includes not only direct sexual advances but also unwelcome sexual flirtations, sexually suggestive or obscene comments or jokes, leering, and displays of sexually offensive materials. Harassment may be found even where the behaviour is not intentional, although lack of intention to harass may mitigate the penalty.

The hospitality industry is vulnerable to sexual harassment cases largely because many businesses use sex in some fashion to attract customers. These businesses are not limited to strip clubs, but include any restaurants, bars, clubs, and hotels that require female (and some male) employees to wear skimpy, revealing, or simply alluring clothing. These businesses are also selling intoxicating beverages that may influence the way people think. Such employees may be subject to harassment from managers, co-workers, owners, or customers. Managers have an obligation to protect their employees from such treatment.

Janzen v. Platy Enterprises, [1989] 1 S.C.R. 1252

The plaintiffs were two waitresses employed by the defendant. Another employee, a cook, continuously touched and made unwanted sexual advances toward them. The cook falsely told them that he had the power to fire them. The waitresses brought their concerns to management, but management did nothing. One of the complainants quit and the other was fired. The Human Rights Commission awarded one waitress $3500 in damages and $480 in lost wages, and the other $3000 in damages and $3000 in lost wages. The verdict was upheld on appeal by the Supreme Court of Canada which took the opportunity to define sexual harassment non-exhaustively and broadly as "unwelcome conduct of a sexual nature that detrimentally affects the work environment or leads to adverse job-related consequences for the victims of the harassment." Thus, sexual harassment in the workplace constitutes sanctionable discrimination.

Another ground for seeking a remedy for discrimination is breach of fiduciary duty. A fiduciary relationship exists when one person, the fiduciary, has the power to affect another person's property or legal interests such that the other person is vulnerable to the power of the fiduciary. Employers and supervisors often have this sort of influence over employees. Thus, sexual harassment may amount to a breach of fiduciary duty giving rise to legal remedies.

Simpson v. Consumers' Association of Canada et al. (2002), 57 O.R. (3d) 351 (C.A.)

S was dismissed from his position as executive director of the appellant association in Ottawa for sexually harassing female employees in several incidents. (1) S had told his first secretary that she could enjoy opportunities for advancement if she had a sexual relationship with him. She refused. S became unpleasant toward her and she resigned. (2) Following a business meeting in Montreal, S tricked the appellant's in-house counsel into visiting a strip club, engaged her in a sexual discussion, and paid for a table dancer. (3) S invited his new secretary (with whom he was having an open affair and unfairly mentoring), the in-house counsel, and another man to S's cottage to discuss business matters, after which S and the new secretary went skinny-dipping in view of the others. (4) During a business trip in Quebec City, S undressed and entered a hot tub in the hotel suite in view of other employees. The new secretary was bare-breasted in the tub. (5) In a hospitality suite in Banff, S grabbed the buttocks of G, the appellant's bookkeeper. The incident was seen by H who complained to other staff members such that the workplace became "abuzz with unrestrained gossip" over that and the other incidents. S apologized to G and fired H. After an internal hearing, the appellant fired S.

S brought an action for wrongful dismissal and was successful. The trial judge found that the incidents had taken place, but outside the workplace and consensually among friends and, therefore, were not employment-related. He disbelieved some of the complainants' testimony. With respect to incident (1), he found that S had merely been "testing the waters," had accepted her rebuff and had not pressed the issue further. The judge also found that the other events such as the resignations and the discomfort in the office were unrelated to S's behaviour. The trial judge noted that the bookkeeper had not treated the matter involving her as serious and had been upset when others used the incident for their own purposes without her knowledge and consent. The judge also noted that the Association had had no sexual harassment policy in place and that the incidents had occurred prior to the heightening of societal consciousness concerning sexual harassment in the workplace. The Association appealed.

The Court of Appeal found no grounds on which to disbelieve the complainants, and found that the lack of a formal sexual harassment policy did not amount to condonation by the employer, did not excuse S's behaviour, and did not entitle S to benefit from its absence. Indeed, the Court found that, as executive director, it was part of S's duties to ensure that workplace harassment did not occur.

The Court held that the trial judge had erred in finding that S's sexual conduct had occurred outside the workplace. Although many of the incidents had taken place in social settings, the social settings had arisen in the context of business meetings or retreats at hotels. The same analysis applied to the incident at the cottage. It would be artificial and contrary to the purpose of controlling sexual harassment in the workplace to say that after-hours interaction between a supervisor and other employees cannot constitute the workplace for the purpose of the application of the law regarding employment-related sexual harassment.

The Court held that the trial judge had erred in finding that there had been consensual conduct among friends. When there is a power imbalance between a supervisor and an employee, the employee may feel restrained from objecting for fear of adverse employment-related consequences.

The Court found that S's offer to his first secretary of opportunities of advancement in exchange for sexual favours had been an abuse of power and a breach of duty to his employer, who is obliged to offer advancement fairly and equally on the basis of merit.

The *Simpson* case in part illustrates that the absence of a sexual harassment policy will not help an employee who is otherwise shown to have engaged in sexual harassment. The absence of a policy may, however, leave an employer open to a charge by a sexually harassed employee that the employer has not taken reasonable steps to control sexual harassment in the workplace. Employers have a duty to monitor the actions of their employees to ensure that actionable discrimination and other improper conduct does not occur. Indeed, in many circumstances, employers must do more than merely monitor and respond; they must take active steps, such as establishing education programs and a written sexual harassment policy, to prevent the improper conduct from occurring in the first place. Once improper conduct is brought to the attention of the employer, the employer must address the matter in a fashion that is both timely and in accordance with an employer's responsibilities under the law.

Burridge v. Katsiris (1989), 11 C.H.R.R. D/427 (Sask. Bd. of Inq.)

Burridge, a waitress at the defendant's restaurant, charged that her employer had harassed her by pinching her bottom and placing his hands down her shirt. She stated that while discussing a promotion, he made comments about her personal relationships. The Board of Inquiry concluded that it was reasonable for her to believe that she would only continue to be employed and promoted if she accepted the harassment. Both the individual and the corporate defendants were found guilty of sexual harassment. The individual defendant was found to be the "directing mind" behind the corporation. Burridge was awarded $4000 in lost wages and $1000 for hurt feelings.

Clark v. Canada (1994), 3 C.C.E.L. (2d) 172 (Fed. T.D.)

Clark, a female RCMP officer, was subjected to repeated sexual harassment by fellow officers. She was forced to resign because of the stress and depression she suffered. She sued the Crown. The Crown was vicariously liable because the conduct took place on the job and the supervising officers had done nothing to end the harassment. In fact, the employer, through the apathy of its officers, was a major part of the problem. Clark received $5000 for pain and suffering and $88,000 for lost income.

In a case outside the hospitality industry, an employee sued Canada Post Corporation because her workplace was bedecked with Playboy calendars and other sexually explicit pictures. Her case was heard by the Canadian Human Rights Tribunal, which awarded her $5,700 in damages. Hospitality business owners and managers should be on the lookout for any sexually offensive material on their premises. Misuse of e-mail and the Internet may also give rise to charges of harassment.

While strip clubs appear to be dens of blatant discrimination, the strippers do not often complain, no doubt because they recognize and accept that minimal clothing is a requirement of the job. Of course, exotic dancers are free to sue any employer they believe has intolerably infringed their rights. Lap dancing is sometimes shown to be an act of prostitution. In such a case, lap dancing constitutes an infringement of the rights of exotic dancers because it requires them to engage in acts the solicitation of which is a criminal offence. In Toronto, the demise of lap dancing resulted not from an application to a human rights tribunal or a criminal prosecution, but from a municipal bylaw that regulated the conduct very strictly.

Ballantyne v. Molly 'N' Me Tavern (1983), 4 C.H.R.R. D/1191 (Ont. Bd. of Inq.)

Ballantyne was offered employment as a waitress on the condition that she perform the job naked from the waist up. Male waiters were not subject to the same conditions of employment. The Board of Inquiry concluded that where male and female employees occupy the same position of employment and are subjected to qualitatively different dress requirements, a clear infringement of the *Code* is established.

Many eating establishments appear to be staffed almost exclusively by servers of one sex. For example, many formal dining rooms are staffed by men while many lounges and roadhouses are staffed by women. Where there is not some underlying justification unique to the establishment or where the employees are not being treated as equals, then it may be that the employment practices that produce such results are flawed and improper.

Doherty and Meehan v. Lodger's International Ltd. (1981), 3 C.H.R.R. D/628 (N.B. Bd. of Inq.)

Two waitresses employed in the defendant's bar were fired because they refused to wear a uniform that consisted of a tuxedo-style jacket, shorts, and high-heeled shoes. Male employees at the same bar in the same job were not required to wear a uniform. The waitresses argued that the uniforms were "hideous" and made them feel "exploited, humiliated and degraded." The Board of Inquiry found that by requiring the waitresses but not the waiters to wear revealing uniforms, the employer had engaged in discrimination on the basis of sex. The board went on to say that an employer must be prepared to demonstrate comparable treatment of both male and female employees.

Chapter 2 / Human Rights in Canada

Hospitality business owners and managers are responsible for protecting employees from harassment. In some cases, the offender is an owner or manager of the business. In other cases, the offender is another staff member, in which instance the business may still be vicariously liable if it does nothing to stop such behaviour. In still other cases, as the following case illustrates, the offender is a customer.

Nixon v. Greensides, [1993] 11 Sask. R. 75 (Q.B.)

A waitress was continuously being harassed by a customer named Duncalfe. Other female employees had been harassed by the same customer. The staff brought their concerns to the attention of the manager at a staff meeting. Two weeks later, the manager brought the concerns to the attention of Duncalfe. He apologized to the staff, but persisted in his behaviour thereafter. Criminal charges were eventually laid against him, and a hearing was held as to the conduct of the business. The Saskatchewan Human Rights Commission found that the business did not act fast enough and that the action taken was not strong enough to prevent the impugned behaviour. The commission found that the two-week delay was "incomprehensible" and that Duncalfe should have been barred from the establishment long before.

This case demonstrates that management's responsibility to protect staff from harassment extends to harassment from customers. Contrary to the old saw, customers are not always right, and their behaviour must be monitored. Many employers have adopted a policy of zero tolerance when it comes to sexual harassment. Employers who have not established clear and effective anti-harassment policies should seriously consider doing so.

Although most sexual harassment is male to female, the reverse does occur as does male to male and female to female. Sexual harassment can occur without there being a demand for sex—for example, an employer timed the amount of time one of his female staff was spending on washroom breaks, and then criticized her for it. Because he had not timed the men, he was found guilty of harassment.

Physical Disability

Section 5 of Ontario's *Human Rights Code* prohibits discrimination against employees on the basis of handicap. Employment-related medical exams are prohibited during the job-application process. Thereafter, testing may be done only on reasonable grounds and for reasonable purposes.

R. v. S.R.L. (April 29, 1991, Ont. H.R. Bd. of Inq.)

The plaintiff, a bartender for the defendant, was terminated after having an epileptic seizure on the job. He caused no injury or damage during the seizure. The employer informed him that he was a good employee, but that he was no longer suitable for their needs. The employer even gave him a letter to this effect to assist him with his claim for unemployment. The Board of Inquiry considered section 5(1) of Ontario's *Human Rights Code*, which states that every person has a right to equal treatment with respect to employment without discrimination because of race, ancestry, place of origin, colour, ethnic origin, citizenship, creed, sex, age, record of offences, marital status, family status, or handicap. Handicap is expressly defined to include epilepsy. The board noted that had the epilepsy posed a risk to the employee or to others, then the job may have been deemed unsuitable for epileptics. However, the board ruled that the bartender was no risk to anyone, that he was capable of performing the tasks, and that the employer had terminated him solely on the basis of a nonmalicious prejudice. This was a case of discrimination on the basis of handicap. The board further noted that the bartender was under no obligation to inform his employer or future employers of his handicap.

D. v. H.H.L. (May 12, 1989, B.C.H.R.C.)

D, a waitress in the defendant's restaurant, was transferred out of public view because of her acne. Customers and staff had commented to management about her skin, and as a result management moved her into a position with no face-to-face contact with customers. D took her concern to the British Columbia Human Rights Council. The council found that her acne was a physical disability and that it was because of her disability that she had lost her position. The argument that her removal was desired by the customers provided no defence. The restaurant was ordered to reinstate her.

D. v. H.H.L. expands the definition of what most people would regard as a disability.

P. v. G. (May 15, 1990, Sask. Bd. of Inq.)

The plaintiff went to a restaurant with her seeing-eye dog. The manager claimed he refused her entry because she did not have a reservation. The Board of Inquiry concluded that the most likely reason was her disability and dog. The manager testified that he did not know that seeing-eye dogs are allowed in public restaurants. The failure of the restaurant to be aware of the law respecting seeing-eye dogs was not acceptable. Ignorance of the law is no excuse. The plaintiff was awarded $250 for mental suffering.

In *P. v. H., [1988] 3 W.W.R. 119 (Man. Q.B.)*, it was held that a blind person does not have to provide proof of blindness in order to enter the premises with a seeing-eye dog. The court also stated that such dogs are essential guides and that by not allowing the plaintiff's dog to enter, access to the restaurant was effectively denied.

In recent years, the hospitality industry has offered enhanced access and services for customers with physical challenges; however, there is always room for improvement. A business may be found liable for discrimination if it is not wheelchair accessible. Many hotels and restaurants have built access ramps, enlarged entrances, and installed appropriate bathroom facilities to better serve customers with physical disabilities. While the renovation costs can make extensive upgrades impractical, hospitality operators should be mindful of the needs of the physically challenged and address them wherever practical.

Drugs and Alcohol

Drug or alcohol dependency is considered a handicap; therefore, testing for it is prohibited during the job-application process. Tests may be conducted after a written offer of employment has been submitted to the employee provided the testing is in relation to the employee's ability to perform the essential duties of the job. Reasonable accommodation must be granted to an applicant who fails the test. During the course of employment, employers may not discriminate against employees on the basis of drug or alcohol dependency unless the employer has strong grounds for believing that the dependency (1) is seriously and adversely affecting the employee's behaviour; (2) has caused the employee repeatedly either to miss or be late for work; or (3) has jeopardized the safety of the employee, other employees, and/or the public.

Only qualified professionals may perform drug tests. Knowledge of the results, including the reasons for the tests, should be restricted to the doctor or the employer's medical department. The information should not be stored in the employee's personnel file. If the employee suffers from an alcohol or drug dependency, the employer must make reasonable efforts to accommodate the employee by, for example, providing time off for treatment, counselling, and transportation. Where hiring or assisting an employee would constitute undue hardship for the employer, the employer may refuse to hire or may dismiss the employee.

Age

Section 5 of Ontario's *Human Rights Code* prohibits discrimination against employees on the basis of age. Some hospitality managers believe that having elderly people serve meals is bad for business. While the rights of the elderly may never be perfectly protected, age discrimination contravenes all human rights codes in Canada.

Creed

The term "creed" refers to political and religious beliefs and affiliations. Under human rights law, a person cannot be discriminated against for being, for example, a Communist and/or a Presbyterian. When setting an employee's individual work schedule, an employer must take into account holidays particular to that individual's religion, whether or not they have been sanctioned as statutory holidays.

Record of Offences

Persons may not be discriminated against on the basis of their conviction for an offence for which a valid pardon has been granted and not revoked, or for an offence in respect of a provincial enactment. Thus, an employer may discriminate against (e.g., not hire) a person convicted of a *Criminal Code* offence for which no valid pardon has been granted. In some circumstances, such as employment requiring bonding, an employer may fire an employee who has lied about the existence of a criminal record. Such a firing would be for cause, which means that the employee would lose the ability to seek common law redress.

The Duty to Accommodate

An employer is required to make an effort to accommodate the protected needs of employees. For example, an employee may refuse to work on a day of religious significance, such as Sunday for Christians and Saturday for Seventh Day Adventists and Jews. The refusal cannot be used not to hire or to fire the employee. Instead, the employer must accommodate the employee, perhaps by having the Sunday worshippers work on Saturdays and the Saturday worshippers work on Sundays. A job advertisement or description cannot make working on a worship day a requirement of the position. Where reasonable, an employer must accommodate an employee who suffers from a drug or alcohol dependency. The duty to accommodate does not apply if to do so would constitute an undue hardship for the employer.

Exceptions

Ontario's *Human Rights Code* has several exceptions to its application, including the following:

1. Affirmative action programs designed to relieve hardship that have as their object the achievement of equal opportunity or the elimination of the infringement of rights under Part I (section 14)

2. Preferential treatment for persons aged 65 or more (section 15)

3. Canadian citizenship, lawful admittance to Canada, and domicile in Canada. These are permitted job preferences in some circumstances (section 16)

4. Handicap exceptions where the person is incapable of performing or fulfilling the essential duties of the task and cannot otherwise be accommodated without undue hardship (section 17)

5. Allowable special-interest organizations, such as religious, philanthropic, educational, fraternal, or social organizations (sections 18 and 19)

6. Restrictions to persons of the same sex on grounds of public decency, restrictions on drinking age, and certain restrictions and preferences of recreational clubs (section 20)

7. Restrictions relating to accommodation shared with the owner or owner's family where the kitchen or bathroom is shared, or restrictions relating to the accommodation of persons of the same sex (section 21)

8. Bona fide restrictions in insurance contracts relating to age, sex, marital or family status, or handicap (section 22)

9. Special employment considerations, such as where a prohibited ground of discrimination is a reasonable and bona fide employment or advancement qualification because of the nature of the employment, and where the employment or advancement may be granted or withheld by reason of the person being the spouse, child, or parent of the employer or employee (section 24)

10. Bona fide considerations as to participation in pension and disability plans (section 25).

In addition, there are aspects of human interaction that do not fall under human rights legislation. It is permissible to discriminate on grounds that are not prohibited in the Code. For example, an employer may discriminate against a smoker in favour of a nonsmoker.

The Road to Redress

Any person who believes that there has been a breach of rights and freedoms under the *Charter* or a provincial human rights code may seek remedies through the employer's internal process, if any, the regular courts, or human rights tribunals. A *Charter* application to a court can result in a law being declared unconstitutional and thus invalid and of no force. If a complaint is made to a human rights commission, the matter will first be investigated by an officer of the commission. The officer may visit the premises, review the relevant documents, interview witnesses, and make recommendations. If the complaint is not resolved, the matter will be referred to a full hearing by the commission. Upon finding an infringement, the commission may make any order necessary to remedy the infringement, such as the payment of financial compensation to the victim, reinstatement of the victim, fines, or the application of workplace policies and educational programs. If complainants wish to recover more than commissions grant, they may sue in the regular courts under a claim for wrongful dismissal, a breach of fiduciary duty, or vicarious liability. As with any litigation system, the process is often long and frustrating, and cases have been known to drag on for years. Whether the fight is worth it is difficult to assess until the process has come to an end.

Employers may avoid problems by seeking legal advice, by asking their human rights commission whether or not a proposed course of action would infringe the legislation, and by implementing and enforcing anti-discrimination policies in the work environment.

Summary

One of the purposes of law is to protect members of the public from improper conduct on the part of governments or other members of the public. This objective is particularly evident in human rights law, an area that is continually evolving. As novel situations arise, novel remedies must be found. Employers should strive to avoid having their human rights conflicts aired publicly. Such conflicts have a negative impact on goodwill and the working atmosphere of the business. Unfair though it is, wrongly accused employers tend to suffer even if they are ultimately vindicated. The time and energy spent resolving conflicts is more productively spent producing revenue. Management should be on the alert for anything that may give rise to conflict. Once areas of conflict are identified, a concerted effort should be made to remedy them. As stressed in the previous chapter, an ounce of prevention is worth a pound of cure.

Discussion Questions

1. Harvard law professor Alan Dershowitz once said, "No one wants justice." What do you think he meant by this statement? Discuss with reference to lawyers and judges, the media, victims and their families, and accused persons.

2. Why was the *Bill of Rights* largely ineffective as a piece of human rights legislation?

3. Do you think Canadians are better protected under the *Charter of Rights and Freedoms* than they were before its proclamation? Why or why not?

4. If one accepts the premise that only the guilty have something to hide, why should a detained person have the right to remain silent?

5. The owner of a restaurant has hired his father to be the bookkeeper. The owner had advertised the position and one of the applicants was a chartered accountant who uses a wheelchair. While the owner's father is a competent bookkeeper, the accountant is more qualified in terms of skills and experience. Under Ontario's *Human Rights Code*, would the accountant have reasonable grounds for bringing a discrimination case against the owner? Why or why not?

6. Discuss examples of sexual discrimination without sexual overtones.

Appendix: Canadian Charter of Rights and Freedoms

(Part 1)

Whereas Canada is founded upon principles that recognize the supremacy of God and the rule of Law:

Guarantee of Rights and Freedoms

1. The Canadian Charter of Rights and Freedoms guarantees the rights and freedoms set out in it subject only to such reasonable limits prescribed by law as can be demonstrably justified in a free and democratic society.

Fundamental Freedoms

2. Everyone has the following fundamental freedoms:

    (a) freedom of conscience and religion;
    (b) freedom of thought, belief, opinion and expression, including freedom of the press and other media of communications;
    (c) freedom of peaceful assembly; and
    (d) freedom of association.

Democratic Rights

3. Every citizen of Canada has the right to vote in an election of members of the House of Commons or of a legislative assembly and to be qualified for membership therein.

4. (1) No House of Commons and no legislative assembly shall continue for longer than five years from the date fixed for the return of the writs at a general election of its members.

    (2) In time of real or apprehended war, invasion or insurrection, a House of Commons may be continued by Parliament and a legislative assembly may be continued by the legislature beyond five years if such continuation is not opposed by the votes of more than one-third of the members of the House of Commons or the legislative assembly, as the case may be.

5. There shall be a sitting of Parliament and of each legislature at least once every twelve months.

Mobility Rights

6. (1) Every citizen of Canada has the right to enter, remain in and leave Canada.

    (2) Every citizen of Canada and every person who has the status of a permanent resident of Canada has the right:

    (a) to move to and take up residence in any province; and
    (b) to pursue the gaining of a livelihood in any province.

    (3) The rights specified in subsection (2) are subject to

    (a) any laws or practices of general application in force in a province other than those that discriminate among persons primarily on the basis of province of present or previous residence; and
    (b) any laws providing for reasonable residency requirements as a qualification for the receipt of publicly provided social services.

(4) Subsections (2) and (3) do not preclude any law, program or activity that has as its object the amelioration in a province of conditions of individuals in the province who are socially or economically disadvantaged if the rate of employment in that province is below the rate of employment in Canada.

Legal Rights

7. Everyone has the right to life, liberty and security of the person and the right not to be deprived thereof except in accordance with the principles of fundamental justice.

8. Everyone has the right to secure against unreasonable search or seizure.

9. Everyone has the right not to be arbitrarily detained or imprisoned.

10. Everyone has the right on arrest or detention

    (a) to be informed promptly of the reasons therefor;
    (b) to retain and instruct counsel without delay and to be informed of that right; and
    (c) to have the validity of the detention determined by way of habeas corpus and to be released if the detention is not lawful.

11. Any person charged with an offence has the right

    (a) to be informed without unreasonable delay of the specific offence;
    (b) to be tried within a reasonable time;
    (c) not to be compelled to be a witness in proceedings against that person in respect of the offence;
    (d) to be presumed innocent until proven guilty according to law in a fair and public hearing by an independent and impartial tribunal;
    (e) not to be denied reasonable bail without just cause;
    (f) except in the case of an offence under military law tried before a military tribunal, to the benefit of trial by jury where the maximum punishment for the offence is imprisonment for five years or a more severe punishment;
    (g) not to be found guilty on account of any act or omission unless, at the time of the act or omission, it constituted an offence under Canadian or international law or was criminal according to the general principles or law recognized by the community of nations;
    (h) if finally acquitted of the offence, not to be tried for it again and, if finally found guilty and punished for the offence, not to be tried or punished for it again; and
    (i) if found guilty of the offence and if the punishment for the offence has been varied between the time of commission and the time of sentencing, to the benefit of the lesser punishment.

12. Everyone has the right not to be subjected to any cruel and unusual treatment or punishment.

13. A witness who testifies in any proceedings has the right not to have any incriminating evidence so given used to incriminate that witness in any other proceedings, except in a prosecution for perjury or for the giving of contradictory evidence.

14. A party or witness in any proceedings who does not understand or speak the language in which the proceedings are conducted or who is deaf has the right to the assistance of an interpreter.

Equality Rights

15. (1) Every individual is equal before and under the law and has the right to the equal protection and equal benefit of the law without discrimination and, in particular, without discrimination based on race, national or ethnic origin, colour, religion, sex, age or mental or physical disability.

    (2) Subsection (1) does not preclude any law, program or activity that has as its object the amelioration of conditions of disadvantaged individuals or groups including those that are disadvantaged because of race, national or ethnic origin, colour, religion, sex, age or mental or physical disability.

Official Languages of Canada

16. (1) English and French are the official languages of Canada and have equality of status and equal rights and privileges as to their use in all institutions of the Parliament and government of Canada.

    (2) English and French are the official languages of New Brunswick and have equality of status and equal rights and privileges as to their use in all institutions of the legislature and government of New Brunswick.

    (3) Nothing in this Charter limits the authority of Parliament or a legislature to advance the equality of status or use of English and French.

17. (1) Everyone has the right to use English or French in any debates and other proceedings of Parliament.

    (2) Everyone has the right to use English and French in any debates and other proceedings of the legislature of New Brunswick.

18. (1) The statutes, records and journals of Parliament shall be printed and published in English and French and both language versions are equally authoritative.

    (2) The statutes, records and journals of the legislature of New Brunswick shall be printed and published in English and French and both language versions are equally authoritative.

19. (1) Either English or French may be used by any person in, or in any pleading in or process issuing from, any court established by Parliament.

    (2) Either English or French may be used by any person in, or in any pleading in or process issuing from, any court in New Brunswick.

20. (1) Any member of the public in Canada has the right to communicate with, and to receive available services from, any head or central office of an institution of the Parliament or government of Canada in English or French, and has the same right with respect to any such institution where

    (a) there is a significant demand for communications with and services from that office in such language; or

    (b) due to the nature of the office, it is reasonable that communications with services from that office be available in both English and French.

    (2) Any member of the public in New Brunswick has the right to communicate with, and to receive available services from, any office of an institution of the legislature or government of New Brunswick in English or French.

21. Nothing in sections 16 to 20 abrogates or derogates from any right, privilege or obligation with respect to the English and French languages, or either of them, that exists or is continued by virtue of any other provision of the Constitution of Canada.

22. Nothing in sections 16 to 20 abrogates or derogates from any legal or customary right or privilege acquired or enjoyed either before or after the coming into force of this Charter with respect to any language that is not French or English.

Minority Language Educational Rights

23. (1) Citizens of Canada

   (a) whose first language learned and still understood is that of the English and French linguistic minority population of the province in which they reside, or

   (b) who have received their primary school instruction in Canada in English or French and reside in a province where the language in which they received that instruction is the language of the English or French linguistic minority population of the province, have the right to have their children receive primary and secondary school instruction in that language in that province.

   (2) Citizens of Canada of whom any child has received or is receiving primary or secondary school instruction in English or French in Canada have the right to have all their children receive primary and secondary school instruction in the same language.

   (3) The right of citizens of Canada under subsections (1) and (2) to have their children receive primary and secondary school instruction in the language of the English or French linguistic minority population of a province

   (a) applies wherever in the province the number of children of citizens who have such a right is sufficient to warrant the provision to them out of public funds of minority language instruction; and

   (b) includes, where the number of those children so warrants, the right to have them receive that instruction in minority language educational facilities provided out of public funds.

Enforcement

24. (1) Anyone whose rights or freedoms, as guaranteed by this Charter, have been infringed or denied may apply to a court of competent jurisdiction to obtain such remedy as the court considers appropriate and just in the circumstances.

   (2) Where, in proceedings under subsection (1), a court concludes that evidence was obtained in a manner that infringed or denied any rights or freedoms guaranteed by this Charter, the evidence shall be excluded if it is established that, having regard to all the circumstances, the admission of it in the proceedings would bring the administration of justice into disrepute.

General

25. The guarantee in this Charter of certain rights and freedoms shall not be construed so as to abrogate or derogate from any aboriginal, treaty or other rights and freedoms that pertain to the aboriginal peoples of Canada including

(a) any rights or freedoms that have been recognized by the Royal Proclamation of October 7, 1763; and

(b) any rights or freedoms that may be acquired by the aboriginal peoples of Canada by way of land claims settlement.

26. The guarantee in this Charter of certain rights and freedoms shall not be construed as denying the existence of any other rights or freedoms that exist in Canada.

27. This Charter shall be interpreted in a manner consistent with the preservation and enhancement of the multicultural heritage of Canadians.

28. Notwithstanding anything in this Charter, the rights and freedoms referred to in it are guaranteed equally to male and female persons.

29. Nothing in this Charter abrogates or derogates from any rights or privileges guaranteed by or under the Constitution of Canada in respect of denominational, separate or dissentient schools.

30. A reference in this Charter to a province or to the legislative assembly or legislature of a province shall be deemed to include a reference to the Yukon Territory and Northwest Territories or to the appropriate legislative authority thereof, as the case may be.

31. Nothing in this Charter extends the legislative powers of any body or authority.

Application of Charter

32. (1) This Charter applies

    (a) to the Parliament and Government of Canada in respect of all matters within the authority of Parliament including all matters relating to the Yukon Territory and Northwest Territories; and

    (b) to the legislature and government of each province in respect of all matters within the authority of the legislature of each province.

    (2) Notwithstanding subsection (1), section 15 shall not have effect until three years after this section comes into force.

33. (1) Parliament or the legislature of a province may expressly declare in an Act of Parliament or of the legislature, as the case may be, that the Act or a provision thereof shall operate notwithstanding a provision included in section 2 or sections 7 to 15 of this Charter.

    (2) An Act or a provision of an Act in respect of which a declaration made under this section is in effect shall have such operation as it would have but for the provision of this Charter referred to in the declaration.

    (3) A declaration made under subsection (1) shall cease to have effect five years after it comes into force or on such earlier date as may be specified in the declaration.

    (4) Parliament or the legislature of a province may re-enact a declaration made under subsection (1).

    (5) Subsection (3) applies in respect of a re-enactment made under subsection (4).

34. This Part may be cited as the Canadian Charter of Rights and Freedoms.

Rights of the Aboriginal Peoples of Canada (Part 2)

35. (1) The existing aboriginal and treaty rights of the aboriginal peoples of Canada are hereby recognized and affirmed.

  (2) In this Act, "aboriginal peoples of Canada" include the Indian, Inuit, and Métis peoples of Canada.

3

Chapter Three
The Law of Contracts

Learning Outcomes

1. Define contract.

2. Explain the role of contracts in commercial and other relationships.

3. Explain the six elements in the formation of a contract.

4. Explain the consequences of breaching a contract.

5. Illustrate some common contract usage in the hospitality and business fields.

Introduction

A **contract** is a written or oral (or partly written and partly oral) promise exchanged for another promise or for a performance that the law will enforce. If the law will not enforce it, then it is not a legally binding contract. Contracts are indispensable tools of business and other human interactions. They lend a degree of predictability to matters that would otherwise be fraught with uncertainty. Even the relatively simple economic activity of barter involves the six essential elements of the formation of a contract: offer, acceptance, consideration, intention, capacity, and legality. For those in business, an understanding of the legal requirements and the effects of contracts is critical. Without such knowledge, a businessperson runs a high risk of forfeiting benefits bargained for and of being liable for unexpected obligations.

Unilateral and Bilateral Contracts

In a unilateral contract, one party provides a promise and the other party provides a performance. The **promissee** fulfills the bargain simply by supplying the performance requested. There is no need to notify the promissor in advance. For example, a hotel manager might place a notice in the hotel's front window announcing that the hotel will pay $1,000 to anyone who climbs the flagpole and rescues the hotel's resident cat. Would-be rescuers need not notify the manager of their intention to perform; they need only perform. Upon delivery of the cat to the manager, the intrepid climber becomes entitled to the money as promised.

> **Carlill v. Carbolic Smoke Ball Company, [1892] 2 Q.B. 484**
>
> Carbolic placed an advertisement promising to pay £100 (a large sum in the 1890s) to anyone who caught the flu despite using the company's smoke balls in the manner prescribed. Carlill used the smoke balls as specified and still caught the flu. She successfully sued Carbolic on the basis that she had performed her part of the bargain and that advance notice of her performance was not necessary.

Unilateral (one-way) contracts feature an exchange of a promise for a performance. Bilateral (two-way) contracts feature an exchange of a promise for a promise. Of course, the bilateral promises still have to be performed, but the exchange of the bilateral promises brings into existence the contract that the parties then perform. With bilateral contracts, the exchange of promises brings the contract into being before the performance (which may not occur for months); with unilateral contracts, the performance itself brings the contract into being. Until the performance occurs in a unilateral contract, there is no contract. Whether the contract is unilateral or bilateral, once the performance is completed, the performer is entitled to fulfillment of the balance of the contract (i.e., receipt of the benefit of the originating promise). Most contracts are bilateral. Multilateral contracts follow the rules pertaining to bilateral contracts.

Invitations to Treat

The phrase "**invitation to treat**" means that one person is inviting other persons to make an offer. The invitation to treat is not an offer, but merely an invitation to someone else to make an offer. For example, a restaurant invites customers to treat by presenting a menu. The offer is made when the customer offers money for food. The offer is accepted when the restaurateur agrees to supply the food. The payment terms are usually tactily understood to be the amount shown on the menu; however, nothing in law stops the customer from offering to buy the item for less than the price on the menu. Equally, nothing stops the restaurant from refusing the low offer.

Advertisements that are not the originating component of unilateral contracts are not offers, but are invitations to interested persons to make an offer. When a bistro advertises its meatloaf at a special price, the bistro is not promising to supply every possible reader of the ad with a meatloaf at that price. It is understood that only a limited number of meatloafs are available at the special price. Similarly, hotels often advertise a range of room rates, but have only a limited number of rooms in each range. The first guests to claim the rooms receive them at the advertised rate. Guests who have not made reservations may find that all the specially priced rooms have been taken. Such advertisements are not misleading because it is understood that no hotel has an unlimited number of rooms for an unlimited number of potential guests. The advertisement would be misleading only if the lower-priced rooms were never available, or if it referred to "rooms" when only one lower-priced room was available.

Although it is often present, an invitation to treat is not an essential element of a contract. A consumer who does not see a menu or a list of room rates may nevertheless make an offer to buy the goods or services without first having been invited to make an offer.

The Six Essential Elements of a Contract

Offers

The first of the six essential elements of a contract is the offer. An offer is tentative until it is accepted. A tentative offer is made when a potential guest informs the desk clerk that he or she is interested in renting a room.

An offer may be conditional. The offer is binding during the conditional period. If the conditions are met or waived, the contract becomes firm. If the conditions are not met or waived prior to the expiry date of the conditions, the offer is no longer binding. Most offers stipulate that if there is a failure to meet conditions that the **offeror** will not waive, then the offer will be null and void and any deposit moneys will be returned with (or without) interest.

Lapse

An offer does not remain open indefinitely. It either lapses or is **revoked** if it is not first rejected, accepted, or countered pursuant to law. An offer lapses when:

1. the **offeree** fails to accept the offer by a deadline;
2. the offeree fails to accept the offer within a reasonable time if there is no deadline; or
3. a party dies, becomes mentally incompetent, or otherwise loses the capacity to make contracts prior to acceptance.

The first instance of lapse is clear. If an offer sets a deadline for acceptance and none is received by that time, the offer lapses. The second instance of lapse is not so clear. If the offer sets no deadline for acceptance, the offer will be good only for a reasonable time. The definition of "reasonable" depends on the subject matter of the contract and the expectations of the parties. An offer to buy a shipment of bananas will have a shorter term than an offer to buy 400 mattresses because the former item (a consumable product) has a shorter life span than the latter item (a durable product). The third instance may also present difficulties. It is not always easy to determine whether a party has lost the mental capacity to make a contract.

Registration is a contractual agreement.

Revocation

An offer may be revoked any time prior to acceptance. Offers may contain a clause making them **irrevocable** for a certain time. Real estate offers and offers to purchase businesses are almost always irrevocable for a few days to give the vendor time to consider whether to reject, accept, or counter the offer from the purchaser.

Options

An **option** is an agreement by the offeror not to revoke the offer for a given period. Until the option expires, the offeror cannot revoke the offer and must not compromise the offeree's option rights. An option provides time to deliver the offer to the offeree, as well as reassurance to the offeree that the offer will not be revoked prior to the option deadline.

Acceptance, Rejection, and Counteroffer

Acceptance is the second essential element of a contract. Upon being presented with an offer, an offeree may either accept, reject, or counter the offer. Until the offer has been accepted, there is no contract. Acceptance is made by taking a positive and unambiguous step, either verbally or with an act. Acceptance may be effected by performance. A travel agent who wants her office painted may say to a painter, "If you want the job, be here Monday and start painting." If the offeree appears on Monday and starts painting, this establishes his acceptance of the offer. Silence by the offeree cannot constitute a binding acceptance unless the offeree has previously indicated that silence would be a method of acceptance. **Rejection** may be effected by positive communication as well as by silence. Rejection terminates the offer, and any further dealings between the parties must involve a fresh offer.

If an offeror amends a term prior to acceptance, the change revokes the offer and the new proposal becomes a new offer. On the other hand, if an offeree amends a term but otherwise accepts the offer, the offeree has not accepted or rejected the offer, but has made a **counteroffer**. The offeror is now the counterofferee, and must decide whether to accept, reject, or counter the counteroffer. The counterofferee may amend the amendment and return the document to the counterofferor, who then becomes the counter-counterofferee. The contract will be binding (subject to conditions) once the parties have executed the document without further amendments or, in the case of an oral agreement, have agreed to the final terms.

Communication, Timing, and Locality

The offeror chooses the manner of communicating the offer and lives with the consequences of the choice. Consider an offeror who mails the offer and then, prior to receiving the acceptance, revokes the offer. If the acceptance is in the mail postmarked prior to the date of the revocation, then the acceptance is complete and the revocation

is invalid. On the other hand, if the offeree accepts an offer using a method of communication that is slower than the manner in which the offer was conveyed, then the offeree must live with the consequences. Consider an offeree who responds by mail to a faxed offer from the offeror. If the offeror revokes the offer by fax prior to the arrival of the acceptance in the mail, the revocation will stand. Under common law, an offeree may accept by the fastest method available regardless of how the offer was conveyed. Thus, an offer delivered by mail may be accepted by fax. Unless the contract provides otherwise, the following rules of delivery of acceptance apply:

1. For mail and telegrams, acceptance occurs when and where the acceptance is put in the post or delivered to the telegraph office. The parties will be bound even if the letter or telegram goes missing provided the offeree is able to prove that, within the time for acceptance, the letter was posted or the telegram was delivered to the telegraph office.

2. For instantaneous communications, such as telephone, fax, and e-mail (see "E-Commerce Considerations," page 67), the acceptance occurs when and where it is received by the offeror.

3. The law applicable to the contract is the law of the place where the acceptance occurs.

Although most offers and acceptances are communicated in writing or verbally, there are instances where neither a written nor verbal method is used. For example, on stock market floors, traders use hand signals to buy and sell stocks. Similarly, auctioneers and buyers use signals to enter into purchase and sale contracts.

Consideration, Gratuitous Promises, and Seals

Consideration

Consideration, and seals that stand in place of consideration, constitute the third essential element of a contract. The price a party pays for the promise of the other party is called consideration. While the term "price" suggests a monetary payment, the consideration need not be monetary in nature. The courts require consideration or a seal but, except in the limited circumstances discussed below, are not concerned whether the deal is fair. In the business world, people are generally assumed to know what they are doing, and if they make a bad bargain, they must live with the result. If Tony offers to sell Carol his car for consideration of $100 (or her stereo) and she accepts, an enforceable oral contract is created. If he later learns that the car is worth much more and wishes to renege, she can enforce the original promise (unless she brought about his error in assessing the value).

Gratuitous Promises

Promises made without consideration are **gratuitous**, and the failure to perform them generally has no remedy in law. In such a case, there is no contract, and any agreement purporting to be a contract on those terms is void. If Tony promises to give Carol his car next week without seeking anything in return, the promise is gratuitous. Since Tony is not receiving consideration, Carol would have no legal grounds upon which to sue if he later failed to honour his promise.

The gratuitous reduction of a debt is another example of an unenforceable contract. Suppose Tony owes Carol $100 and the due date has passed. If Carol asks Tony for $75 stating that she will forgive the $25, she can still sue for the $25 once she has the $75 because there was no consideration given by Tony, or received by Carol, for the debt reduction. There are circumstances in debt reduction in which consideration does arise. If Carol agrees to accept a lesser amount provided she is paid now rather than when the debt is due (say, next month), she is receiving consideration in the form of advanced payment of part of the debt. She may be happy to forgo some debt to recover most of it immediately. Such an arrangement is enforceable, and she would be precluded from pursuing the balance. Forbearing from suing for the balance of a debt is good consideration, and is the basis of many lawsuit settlements.

Under common law, if the promise is gratuitous and a person relies on it to his or her detriment, there is no legal recourse. Thus, if Carol relies on Tony's **gratuitous promise** to give her his car and buys seat covers for it in anticipation, she will not be able to recover the cost of the covers if he reneges on the promise. However, the courts may supersede the common law rule by applying the equitable remedies of injurious reliance or **promissory** estoppel to bind gratuitous promissors to their promises in cases where the promissees, acting reasonably and to their detriment, have been induced to rely on the gratuitous promises. The courts examine whether the promissee reasonably and injuriously relied upon the promise, or whether the promissor is estopped by equitable principles from denying the obligations arising out of his or her promise. In either case, the promissor is bound and the promissee recovers.

Seals

Promises made under the promissor's seal are binding even in the absence of consideration. The seal is a device of document execution dating from the days when only the clergy, lawyers, and scribes were literate. The illiterate (who included kings and queens) pressed their signets onto warm wax to indicate their willingness to be bound by the contents of the document. Consideration is not required because the solemn act of sealing proves the promissor's intention to be bound. This is what was originally meant by the phrase "to seal the deal." Seals are still often employed, but without signets and wax. Today, it is sufficient to write the word "seal" or to affix a red gummed wafer next to one's signature or mark.

Unconscionable Transactions

Courts are concerned with the value of the consideration only when the judge's conscience is scandalized by the transaction. When, by virtue of lopsided bargaining powers, abuse of authority, or breach of **fiduciary** duty, a person manipulates another into a very bad bargain, the courts may set aside the contract as an unconscionable transaction. To be set aside, the transaction must be more than just unfair; it must be unconscionable.

Intention to Create a Legal Relationship

Intention to create a legal relationship is the fourth essential element of a contract. Unless the parties intend to make a contract, there is no contract. The contract may state that the parties intend to be legally bound or the intention may be inferred from the conduct of the parties. Usually, the execution of the contract provides the necessary evidence of intention. Execution occurs when a party places his or her signature or mark on the document, or when a signing officer of a corporation signs on behalf of the corporation. Unless required by statute, witnesses are not necessary, but may be helpful if an issue as to execution later arises.

An enforceable contract is formed when a hostess hires a caterer to cater a party. The agreement between them is intended to bind them legally, thereby giving rise to remedies in law in the event of breach. On the other hand, there is no contract between the hostess and the guests she has invited for dinner. If the caterer fails to supply the dinners to the hostess, the hostess can sue the caterer, but if the hostess fails to supply the dinners to her guests, her guests cannot sue her. The relationship between the hostess and her guests may be based on a written invitation and a sincere intention to feed and be fed, but the hostess and her guests did not intend to create a legally binding relationship. Similarly, two parties who promise to travel together on a holiday do not normally intend to create a legally binding relationship.

Capacity of the Parties

The fifth essential element of a contract is the **capacity** of the parties to enter the contract. If one of the parties lacks the legal capacity to enter into the contract, then the contract may be void or voidable depending on the circumstances and the type of incapacity.

Mental Illness, Substance Abuse, and Senility

Persons who can prove that at the time of making the contract they were incapacitated due to mental illness, substance intoxication, or senility, and that the other party was aware of the incapacity, may **repudiate** or enforce the contract at their option. Upon regaining capacity, the person must repudiate promptly or risk being bound.

Minors

Under common law, a minor is a person under the age of 21. Many provinces have lowered the age of majority by statute. Generally, contracts made by minors are enforceable or voidable at the option of the minor, but not at the option of the other party. However, there are cases where a contract made by a minor is enforceable by the other party. Contracts of employment or apprenticeship that are beneficial to the minor bind the minor. Further, contracts for a necessity of life are enforceable after delivery of the necessity to the minor. If a minor contracts for a room and a meal in a budget hotel when stranded there, the contract is enforceable. The lodging and food are necessities, not extravagances. Other necessities include legal advice, medical treatment, clothing, and reasonable transportation arrangements.

These principles are designed to protect minors, but not to place weapons in their hands. If a minor enters into a contract for a non-necessity and has made some payments, he or she may still void the contract, but will likely not recover money already paid. Upon voiding the contract, the minor will have to return any unused portion of the goods or services remaining in his or her control. Upon reaching the age of majority, an otherwise nonbinding contract that is of an ongoing or continuing nature may become binding on the ex-minor unless he or she repudiates it promptly. If the contract is not of an ongoing or continuing nature, the ex-minor must ratify it promptly. If the contract was void in the first place, it cannot be ratified.

Renting a suite for a school graduation party is not a contract for a necessity. The hotel may prefer to make the contract with the minor's parents, although minors honour their contracts as often as adults do (i.e., almost always).

Agents and Principals

An agent is a person authorized by a principal to enter into contractual relations with other parties on behalf of the principal. If the agent has acted in accordance with the real or apparent authority given to him by the principal, the agent will not be liable to the other party, but the principal will be. If the agent has acted outside the scope of his authority, he will be liable to the principal. If the agent leads the other party to believe that he is acting as a principal and not as an agent, the agent and not the principal will be bound by the contract. If the agent does not inform the other party as to whether he is an agent or a principal, the other party, upon learning that the contract is with an undisclosed principal, may pursue either the agent or the principal. Agency law is discussed in detail in Chapter 15.

Powers of Attorney

A power of attorney is a special form of agency whereby the donor, in writing, grants power to an attorney to act on his or her behalf. Attorney means agent, not lawyer. The donor must be at least 18, mentally competent, and must understand the powers granted. The power may be restricted and may cover property, personal care, and medical treatment. An attorney must act in the best interests of the donor, and is liable to the donor for losses resulting from unreasonable conduct or bad faith. Persons who have not named an attorney run the risk that their affairs will be managed improperly or by a person not of their choosing. Powers of attorney avoid complications, needless legal and other expenses, and government meddling.

Spouses and Cohabitants

Married or not, men and women who cohabit may contract in their own names. As a rule, they are regarded as separate parties with respect to property and liability. In some circumstances, if one spouse conveys property to the other spouse in order to avoid creditors, the property is deemed not truly separate and the conveyance may be set aside.

Business Partners

Partners may bind, and be bound by, other partners. Unless the partner's conduct is outside the scope of a partner's authority to the knowledge of the affected third party, the contractual and tortious conduct of a partner binds the other partners. Unless a former partner has properly retired from the partnership, he or she may continue to be liable. Methods of proper retirement include novation of contracts between the remaining partners and their creditors, and registration of a notice of dissolution of partnership pursuant to provincial regulation.

Corporations

Corporations cannot act except through their authorized officers. It is not necessary to verify whether the officer has proper authority; the officer need only appear to have authority. The officer binds the corporation by signing and affixing the corporate seal to the document or by adding below the signature the sentence "I have authority to bind the Corporation." The use of the seal here is for the purpose of executing the document, not for the purpose of dispensing with consideration (unless that is also the parties' intention).

Native People

Reserve lands cannot be used as security for debts. A disposition of reserve land to anyone lacking reserve rights is void unless it is approved by the federal government. Native persons who reside off the reservations have the same contractual capacity as any other citizens.

Diplomatic Immunity

In general, diplomats posted to Canada are beyond the jurisdiction of Canadian courts. An embassy that fails to pay for the use of a convention hall cannot be forced by Canadian courts to honour its contract. In the rare circumstance in which a foreign government refuses to honour its undertakings, negative publicity may result in the payment being produced. Of course, the implications of such publicity would have to be considered in advance.

Enemy Aliens

In peacetime, aliens (defined by residency, not citizenship) have the same contractual rights as residents of Canada. During hostilities, aliens lose their capacity to contract unless the contract is of clear benefit to Canada or is pursuant to government licence. Contracts with enemy aliens that are against the public interest are void.

Bankrupts

The capacity to contract is reduced for undischarged bankrupts until they are discharged. An insolvent person is not necessarily bankrupt and may continue to contract; however, he runs the risk of punitive court awards against him if further losses are unfairly sustained by others.

Legality

The sixth essential element of a contract is **legality**. Absent legality, there is no contract. The purpose of a contract must not be to break the law or run counter to public policy. If it is, the contract will be either void or illegal and unenforceable. If the contract is void, no contract ever existed, and the courts will try to return the parties to their pre-contract condition. If the contract is illegal, the court will not assist anyone who has entered into it, and the parties' losses will fall where they may, a result that will not necessarily be in the interests of justice. A contract to import banned foodstuffs is illegal. If a party has paid money but the payee has failed to deliver the goods, the payor will not be able to use the courts to seek a remedy.

Other Elements of Contract Formation

Other issues that affect the formation of contracts include the requirement of writing (for some contracts), part performance, the privity rule, exceptions to the privity rule, and risk.

The Requirement of Writing

Except for certain types of contract discussed below, it is not a legal necessity that the contract be in writing. Contracts are binding whether written or oral, or partly written and partly oral. If the oral terms of a contract can be ascertained, then the oral contract is as enforceable as a written one. The main difficulty with oral contracts is proving the terms. Many a friendship and partnership have foundered on innocent (and sometimes not so innocent) misunderstandings about the exact terms of an oral contract. The closer the friendship or partnership is, the more indignant the victim is. Every lawyer has heard the sad cry, "I can't believe they could do that to me." Commonly, both parties make the same lament to their respective lawyers.

Pursuant to the *Statute of Frauds*, the *Sale of Goods Act* and similar provincial statutes, certain contracts are so fraught with potential conflicts over terms that they are not enforceable unless they are in writing. For practical purposes, there are eight types of contracts that must be in writing to be enforceable:

1. Agreements involving an interest in land, such as agreements of purchase and sale, mortgages, and long-term leases

2. Domestic contracts, including marriage contracts, cohabitation agreements, separation agreements, and promises made in consideration of marriage

3. A guarantee of another's debt where the guarantor is not a primary surety of the debt

4. A promise by an estate trustee to pay out of his or her own pocket without reimbursement the debts of the deceased's estate

5. Certain agreements involving minors that must be ratified in writing upon the minor reaching the age of majority

6. Agreements that expressly state that they are not to be performed within one year. If the contract does not expressly so state, it is considered to be for an indefinite term, and need not be in writing under this rule. British Columbia, Manitoba, and Ontario have abolished the requirement that these contracts be in writing.

7. Under sale of goods legislation, agreements for the purchase and sale of goods (not services) having a value exceeding a minimum amount. The minimum varies from jurisdiction to jurisdiction but is in the $30 to $50 range. When several goods are purchased at once, the aggregate price is used to determine whether the legislation applies. The requirement of writing is waived where the value of the goods is below the minimum, and also where (a) the buyer actually receives the goods and either makes a statement or commits an act that signifies the buyer's acceptance of the existence of the oral contract; or (b) the buyer gives part or full payment (by money or in kind) to the seller for the goods, and the seller accepts it. In both cases, the conduct of the parties establishes the existence of the oral contract and renders it enforceable as to the balance of its terms, including payment. Where the contract is for both goods and services, the requirement of writing under the sale of goods legislation does not apply.

8. Under consumer protection legislation, agreements that provide that delivery of the goods and/or services, or payment for them, is to occur at a future time. Typically, such legislation protects only the buyer, not the seller, and is designed to reduce the problems surrounding high-pressure sales tactics where the goods and/or services are not delivered at the moment of sale.

Part Performance

In the case of interests in land, the courts have softened some aspects of the rule that the agreement must be in writing. If pursuant to an oral contract to acquire land the plaintiff takes possession of and makes improvements to the land with the acquiescence of the owner such that it would be an injustice to the plaintiff if the owner were not held to the oral contract, the courts may enforce the contract if the part performance by the plaintiff is unequivocal evidence of the existence of the contract. If the performance is equally or more applicable to a different transaction, such as a contract to maintain the property, then the plaintiff's claim will fail.

The Privity Rule

Generally, the obligations and benefits arising under a contract are confined to the parties to the contract. Persons who are not parties to the contract are called nonparties, strangers or, sometimes confusingly, third parties. Under the common law rule of privity, a contract does not impose any obligation nor confer any benefit upon a nonparty. A plaintiff suing under a contract must prove privity (i.e., that he and the defendant are the parties to the contract being sued upon). If Bill contracts with a travel agency to buy Ann a plane ticket to Athens, Ann has no privity with the travel agency and cannot sue the agency if it breaches the contract. Only Bill has **privity of contract** on which to base a lawsuit.

Exceptions to the Privity Rule

In the case of *Fraser River Pile & Dredge Ltd. v. Can-Dive Services Ltd.*, *[1999] 3 S.C.R. 108*, the Supreme Court of Canada held that the doctrine of privity should evolve in light of modern commercial reality and be relaxed where:

a) the parties to the contract intended to extend the benefit to the nonparty seeking to rely on the contract; and

b) the activities performed by the nonparty must be the very activities contemplated as coming within the scope of the contract.

It remains to be seen how far this case will extend. In the meantime, to mitigate the often harsh consequences of the privity rule, the law recognizes ten exceptions where enforceable rights and liabilities may be enjoyed or suffered by non- or substituted parties. Set forth below are the ten exceptions. The first eight arise in hospitality law. The last two are included for completeness.

The Tort Law Bypass

As we shall see in Chapter 4, under the law of negligence (also known as tort law), persons who are not privy to a contract may recover damages for the injurious consequences of a contract by suing in negligence instead of suing in contract. For example, if a hotel caters a reception contracted for by a host, and a guest of the host suffers food poisoning, the stricken guest cannot sue the hotel in contract because there is no privity between the guest and the hotel. However, the guest can bypass that roadblock by suing in negligence.

Principals of Agents

As we shall see in Chapter 15, where an agent makes a contract on behalf of a principal, the principal becomes entitled to the benefits and subject to the obligations under the contract.

Vicarious Liability

Employers are vicariously liable when their employees harm a third party with whom the employer has no contract. Vicarious liability also arises under tort law. An employer may escape liability if the employee acted wholly outside the scope of his or her employment.

Corporation Formed by an Amalgamation

Where two or more corporations amalgamate, the new corporation is bound by any contracts previously entered into by any of the amalgamating corporations.

Collateral Warranties

If a contract features a collateral warranty provided by a stranger to the contract, an injured party to the main contract may sue the collateral warrantor. For example, a store may sell an oven to a restaurant with a manufacturer's warranty. If the restaurant suffers damage from a defective oven, the restaurant may sue the manufacturer directly. Collateral warranty is the contract law side of the coin; negligent misrepresentation (see Chapter 4) is the tort law side.

Assignment of Liabilities (Novation)

A promissor may assign his liabilities under a contract to another party, if the promissee consents. If promissors could assign liabilities without the consent, no one would ever have to repay a debt because a promissor could simply assign the liability to a deadbeat. (Assignment of liabilities is sometimes called "novation," but that term should be limited to when two parties tear up their first contract and enter into a new one. Novation is not really an exception to the privity rule; it is a new contract.)

Interests in Land

An assignment of liabilities may occur without the promissee's consent where the subject matter of the contract involves an interest in land (mainly mortgages and leases). Because the land secures the debt, the lender (mortgagee) is unaffected by the assignment and may sue both the original debtor (mortgagor) and the new one if the mortgage goes into default. Similarly, a subtenant under a sublease is subject to the terms of the original lease, and the landlord may pursue both the original tenant and the subtenant in the event of default.

Assignment of Rights

Generally, a party may assign her rights (as distinct from liabilities) under a contract. For example, a lender is free to assign to anyone her right to receive repayment of the loan. The assignee enjoys the same rights and is subject to the same obligations as the assignor.

Trusts

The settlor creates the trust, the trustee manages the trust, and the beneficiary benefits from the trust. The trust contract is between just the settlor and the trustee, but the interests of the beneficiary are so great that the law allows the beneficiary to enforce the terms of the trust.

Life Insurance Policies

A beneficiary named in a life insurance policy between an insured and an insurer may force the insurer to pay the insurance proceeds to the beneficiary upon the death of the insured.

Allocation of Risk

Generally, risk under a contract follows ownership or title to the subject matter. The parties are free to re-allocate responsibility for the risk. Hotels and restaurants often order supplies. The parties may determine whether the buyer or the seller shall bear the risk during transit. For cash-on-delivery (COD) contracts, the seller retains title and the risk until the goods are delivered to and paid for by the buyer. For free-on-board (FOB) contracts, the buyer acquires title to the goods and assumes the risk the moment the seller delivers the goods to the carrier. For cost-insurance-freight (CIF) contracts, the buyer acquires title to the goods before delivery, but the seller is responsible for the costs and risks of delivery to the buyer's location.

If there is no COD, FOB, CIF, or similar contract, title and risk may be determined by a bill of lading. A bill of lading is a receipt given to the seller by the carrier who is handling the consignment. The consignor on the bill is the seller. The consignee has the right to determine the delivery. If the buyer is the consignee, the seller loses control over the goods and the risk passes to the buyer. If the seller is the consignee, the seller retains control over the goods and bears the risk until delivery to the destination that the seller has designated on the bill.

E-Commerce Considerations

The traditional precepts of contract law continue to apply to electronic commerce. For example, Web-based advertisements are regarded as invitations to treat, not offers. However, an advertisement containing the number of units in stock could be considered an offer.

The *Uniform Electronic Commerce Act* allows acceptance to be made electronically. Acceptance occurs as with other forms of instantaneous communication at the place of acceptance unless the parties agree otherwise. As the globe shrinks and business is conducted in countries around the world, the place of contract acceptance can be important and problematic. A Canadian accepting an offer in Quebec City will normally enjoy the application of Quebec and Canadian law, as applicable, to the contract. A contract featuring parties in multiple countries poses interesting questions of applicable law especially if the rules of contract acceptance are different. Some countries do not follow our Western legal traditions.

In 1996, the United Nations adopted the Model Law on Electronic Commerce drafted by the United Nations Commission on International Trade Law. Its utility will depend on how many nations adopt it. Until there is international consensus, countries must enter into a series of bilateral trading partner agreements.

In Canada, the Uniform Conference of Canada has adopted the *Uniform Electronic Commerce Act*, which is based on the Model Law established by the United Nations. The *Uniform Electronic Commerce Act* is intended to harmonize federal and provincial legislation. The UECA has three parts to it.

Part 1. Provision and Retention of Information.

Part 1 gives legal recognition to electronic contracts, sets the conditions to meet requirements of the *Uniform Electronic Commerce Act*, the requirements for information to be in writing, recognition of electronic signatures, and the requirement to present and retain a document in original form.

Part 2. Communication of Electronic Documents

Part 2 provides that all matters of a contract can be expressed by means of an electronic document, permits the involvement of electronic agents, and establishes the time and place of sending and receiving of electronic documents.

Part 3. Carriage of Goods

Part 3 applies to actions related to contracts of carriage of goods.

All provinces and territories have enacted legislation for electronic commerce. In 2000, Ontario became the first province to enact e-commerce legislation—the *Electronic Commerce Act*, S.O. 2000, c.17. Among other things, it provides, with some exceptions, for legal recognition of electronic information and documents. It provides that electronic information or forms cannot be used, provided, or accepted without a person's consent; however, consent may be implied by conduct except for public bodies, which are not bound unless they give their express consent. Information in electronic form is deemed to be in writing if it is accessible for subsequent reference and capable of being retained by the accessing person. Mere access, such as to a website, is insufficient. There must also usually be reliable assurance as to the integrity of the information in the electronic format. A legal requirement for a signature is satisfied by the provision of a prescribed, reliable electronic signature—typically an encrypted password. Electronic information is presumed to have been received by the addressee,

a) if the addressee has designated or uses an information system for receiving information of the type sent, when it enters that information system and becomes capable of being retrieved and processed by the addressee; or

b) if the addressee has not designated or does not use an information system for receiving information of the type sent, when the addressee becomes aware of the information in the addressee's information system and it becomes capable of being retrieved and processed by the addressee.

Regardless of the physical location of the addressee's information retrieval system, the electronic information is deemed to have been received at the addressee's place of business. If the addressee has more than one place of business, the receipt is deemed to occur at the place of business having the closest relationship to the underlying transaction or, if there is no underlying transaction, the addressee's principal place of business or, if there is no principal place of business, the addressee's habitual residence. The Act does not apply to wills, codicils, testamentary trusts, powers of attorney, documents that create or transfer interests in land and require registration to be effective against third parties, negotiable instruments (such as bills of exchange), and, except for contracts for carriage of goods, title documents.

Void and Voidable Contracts

A contract that is defective or that has been breached may be void or voidable. If the contract is void, it has no legal effect. Judges are reluctant to find that a contract is void, and generally only do so if it is for an illegal purpose or if one or more of the six essential elements of a contract are missing. If the contract is void, the parties are returned to their pre-contract positions. If it is determined that the contract was for an illegal purpose, the courts will not return the parties to their pre-contract positions, and the losses will fall where they may.

A contract that is voidable is a contract in which the offending party has done something that allows the innocent party the option to rescind the contract or insist on performance. The innocent party may lose the option to rescind if:

1. he or she affirms the contract;

2. he or she takes some benefit under the contract;

3. he or she fails to rescind the contract within a reasonable time such that the position of the other party is adversely affected by the delay; or

4. an innocent third party acquires some rights under the contract prior to the attempt to rescind.

If the subject matter of the contract has passed to an innocent third party who has supplied value in exchange for the subject matter, the original owner may recover the subject matter only if the contract is void *ab initio* and was not for an illegal purpose. If the contract is merely voidable, the subsequent bona fide purchaser for value will be entitled to keep the subject matter, and the original owner may pursue only the person with whom the voidable contact was made, even if that person cannot be found or is **judgment-proof**. While void contracts may still be honoured by a party who feels a moral obligation to do so, the honouring is not pursuant to contract, but is merely a gratuitous charitable gesture or good deed.

Interpretation of Contracts

Rules of Interpretation

Once the contract has been formed, it must be interpreted. Most disputes revolve around not whether the contract exists but what the terms mean. Language being what it is, it is not unusual for reasonable people to disagree about the meaning of a contract, a term in the contract, or even the implications of the placement of a comma in a sentence. The devils, as is sometimes said, are in the details. While many contractual terms are expressly set forth in the contract, others are implied. Implied terms are commonsense matters arising out of the nature of the enterprise or transaction, or matters that would likely have been made explicit if the parties had thought of them in time to add them. As a rule, courts will imply reasonable terms to give effect to the intentions of the parties, but will not go so far as to draft a new contract.

Interpreting contracts is often difficult due to bad drafting, bad grammar, or misuse of vocabulary. The courts use two approaches to contract interpretation: strict and liberal. The strict approach concerns itself with the plain or dictionary meanings of the words and holds the parties to an objective reading of the contract. The more subjective liberal approach assesses the overall purpose of the contract and intention of the parties. The judges generally use whatever approach best allows them to do justice in the case. The rules of evidence apply, sometimes in combination with the *contra proferentum* and parol evidence rules (see below).

The *Contra Proferentum* Rule

A contract that has been drafted by one party and foisted on the other party, who therefore lacks a real opportunity to negotiate, will be interpreted strictly against the drafting party. Thus, the courts will interpret a standard form contract such as an insurance policy or airline ticket in favour of the consumer with respect to any loopholes or ambiguities in the wording.

The Parol Evidence Rule

Before a contract is entered into, the parties negotiate the terms orally or in writing. Many written contracts have a clause which states that the contract constitutes the entire agreement between the parties and that there are no terms outside the contract. If after entering into a written contract a party finds that a term is missing, he or she will be held to the contract as written. Where the other party does not consent to an amendment, the parol ("outside") evidence rule prevents a term, previously agreed upon but not included in the final version, from being added to the written contract. Nothing stops the parties from making a contract that is partly written and partly oral; however, once the written part is executed, the **parol evidence rule** prevents one party from altering it without the consent of the other party. To the extent the terms are ascertainable, the oral part of the hybrid contract will continue to apply to the parties.

The parol evidence rule has many exceptions. It does not apply to evidence concerning the formation of the contract (e.g., legality, capacity, duress, mistake), or to evidence concerning any conditions precedent to the formation of the written contract. The rule does not apply to oral contracts made after the written contract. Extrinsic evidence as to the later oral contract, even concerning how the oral contract amended the written contract, is admissible.

H. v. K. (July 15, 1996, Doc. No. C954322, Vancouver, Lowry J. (B.C.))

H operated a business that consisted of a small eight-seat café in leased premises in an old building. In 1992, she approached the city for a licence to increase the café to 25 seats. The city gave her a temporary licence conditional on her remaining the occupant of the premises. H wrote the city confirming that she would abide by the requirement and would neither advertise nor sell the business as a 25-seat operation. Naturally, in a selfless gesture to give students a case to consider, she did otherwise. In 1994, she listed the business for sale as a 25-seat restaurant. K and S offered to buy the business assuming that it was licensed for 25 seats. The offer was accepted along with a deposit. The balance of the price was to be paid on closing. K and S began operating the business pending the closing. When K applied for a transfer of the licence from H to K and S, the city informed K that no licence would be issued for a 25-seat restaurant. H, K, and S then agreed to add the following **addendum** to the agreement:

> Completion date is extended to 96 hours after the vendor has received a business licence approval for a 25-seat restaurant. In the event that approval for 25 seats is not received prior to June 30, 1995, then, at the purchaser's option, all deposit monies will be returned and the contract shall be null and void.

H contacted the city's Planning Department, which inspected the property. The Department made numerous recommendations for upgrades to the premises, which were financially impractical given the age of the building. As a result, H made no application for a 25-seat licence. She did receive a written confirmation that she could continue to use the space as a restaurant as long as there were no further alterations and she remained the operator. K and S closed the business and left the premises. H resumed possession and reopened the restaurant. Several months after June 30, 1995, she obtained the licence approval that K and S had requested. H then took the position that she had met the requirements under the addendum and claimed that K and S had orally agreed to extend the deadline.

H sued for damages, and K and S countersued for their deposit. The issue was whether H had received the approval for the licence change in accordance with the terms of the contract and its addendum. The court held that H had not received the licence for a 25-seat restaurant by June 30, 1995, and that the parol evidence rule precluded the inclusion of an oral term extending the deadline. H was ordered to return the deposit and pay K and S's legal costs.

Certainty of Terms

The essential terms of a contract must be precise enough to allow for a sensible interpretation. In some instances, custom and trade usage will make a seemingly vague agreement precise. For example, a contract for the purchase of nitrogenized marl may be incomprehensible to a layperson, but very clear to a person in the agriculture industry. The essential terms must also be complete and not subject to uncertainties. Terms may be complete even though they are conditional provided the condition is capable of certainty. For example, a condition as to time should specify a date and not simply refer to "within a reasonable time." Consideration is an essential term but it may be conditional on a future certain event. For example, the interest to be charged from time to time for default under a contract may be expressed as the prime rate of the Bank of Canada plus 3 percent. At the time of signing the contract, no one knows what the effective rate will be, but it is certain to be known at the necessary time.

Warranties and Conditions

Regrettably, the words "warranty" and "condition" are often used interchangeably and inconsistently. The word "warranty" should be used only to describe any term in a contract the breach of which gives rise to various remedies but none so drastic as the termination of the contract. The word "condition" should be used only to describe any term the breach of which is so serious and fundamental that the remedies include termination of the contract.

Waivers and Disclaimers

A party may waive his or her rights under a contract, but the language used must be clear. A waiver is effective only as to the terms waived. A party cannot impose a waiver on another party. The waiver must be the voluntary act of the waiving party.

Parties often attempt to minimize or eliminate some aspects of their contractual liability through the use of disclaimers. Here are two examples:

> In the event of fire, theft, flood, lightning, war, destruction, strike, lockout, sabotage, plague, famine, pestilence, or act of God, Bombs Away Inc. disclaims all responsibility for any losses whatsoever howsoever, wheresoever and whensoever occasioned.

> We express no opinion as to the accuracy of the information contained in this book.

Disclaimers are interpreted strictly against the party relying on them (*contra proferentum*). The more blanket the disclaimer, the less likely it will stand; the more limited the disclaimer, the more likely it will stand. The courts also look for fairness on the part of the person attempting to benefit from the disclaimer. If there was no reasonable opportunity to examine the terms or if they were not brought to the attention of the injured party, the disclaimer will be of little or no assistance to the party relying on it. Further, a disclaimer will generally not assist a party who is in fundamental breach of the contract because it would be unfair to allow a party to a contract to blithely breach the contract in outrageous ways and then rely on the disclaimer to avoid responsibility. (See also Chapter 4.)

Standard Form Contracts

Many businesses make use of standard form contracts. Examples include automobile leasing or sales agreements, insurance policies, and travel and event tickets. Standard form contracts are a convenience, but they remove any real opportunity to negotiate the terms. The offeree must take it or leave it. If he signs it, the courts will generally deem him to have read it and bind him to the terms. If he later wishes to bring a breach-of-contract suit, the courts will apply the usual rules of contract interpretation and liability. In the case of standard form contracts that are not signed, such as travel or event tickets and parking or cloakroom receipts, the courts examine additional matters. A promissor benefiting from an unsigned standard form contract must act reasonably and must bring the essential terms of the contract to the attention of the promissee. The promissee will not be bound if the print was too fine to be legible, or if the risks were not brought sensibly to the notice of the promissee. Two examples of such notices are the signs in cloakrooms stating that "The management is not responsible for lost or damaged items," and general posted warnings stating "Use at your own risk."

The Importance of Good Grammar

Proper vocabulary and good grammar are critical to drafting and interpreting contracts. While it is never too late to acquire vocabulary and learn good grammar, vigilance and alertness are required. There is no one perfect code of grammar. There are many issues about which reasonable grammarians disagree, such as splitting infinitives and ending sentences with prepositions. Grammatical rules change over time, although not nearly as much as vocabulary, whether through the coining of new words (e.g., "hypermedia") or through changes in meaning.

If there is no perfect grammar code, how can one ever be sure that one's writings and utterances are acceptable? Those who say that the most important thing is to be understood are partly right. Those who insist that strict rules of grammar must be followed are also partly right. The fact is that clarity of expression is most easily accomplished by applying sensible rules of grammar and by using appropriate vocabulary. Proper punctuation is also important. For example, the insertion of commas can radically change the meaning of the same sentence. There is a world of difference between "Woman without her man is nothing" and "Woman, without her, man is nothing." Mastering the basic rules of grammar is not difficult, and is worth the effort. Good grammar makes our communications more intelligible and our arguments more persuasive—"bad grammar do opposite."

Termination of Contracts

So far, we have reviewed the six essential elements of contract formation and other matters such as enforcement and interpretation. Now, we turn our attention to how contracts may be discharged, impeached, breached, and remedied.

Discharge of Contracts

To discharge a contract is "to cancel or unloose the obligations of a contract" (*Black's Law Dictionary*, 4th edition). Contracts are discharged in four ways.

By Performance
Discharge occurs when the parties to the contract have completed their respective parts of the bargain—that is, the performance expected of them.

By Agreement
If both parties have not yet finished their contractually required performances, they may agree not to complete the contract. The promise by each party not to insist on performance by the other is the consideration for the agreement not to complete. If one party has completed his or her performance and one has not, the discharge by agreement must be under seal unless there is fresh consideration.

By Frustration
A contract is frustrated when, through no fault of the performing party, a supervening event renders the contract impossible to perform. A contract to book three floors of the Tinderbox Lodge for a convention will be frustrated if the lodge burns down prior

to the start of the convention. The contract will not be frustrated if the promissor himself burns the lodge down as a means of escaping the booking. Self-induced frustration is breach of contract because of the presence of fault. Where the contract has been partly performed but then frustrated, the parties may be held to an accounting. Where the goods are obtainable elsewhere on the market, the loss of the goods will not necessarily frustrate the contract. If a restaurant orders 30 tablecloths, the supplier cannot plead frustration if the delivery truck is stolen because he can easily supply 30 more tablecloths. A party may contract out of the defence of frustration and remain liable despite an incident of frustration. Commercial leases, for example, may provide that the rent will continue even if the premises are destroyed. This forces the tenant to have insurance and protects the landlord against an interruption of revenue.

By Operation of Law

A bankrupt is absolved from liability upon an order for discharge. An undischarged bankrupt remains liable, through the trustee, for the realizable portion of his or her debts. A deceased is discharged on death from the performance of personal service contracts. Upon attaining majority, a minor is discharged from an unratified noncontinuing contract. Limitation Acts are statutes that limit the time within which a plaintiff may commence an action. They do not discharge contracts, but bar enforcement actions if the plaintiff fails to issue the claim prior to the end of the limitation period. If that happens, the defendant is for all practical purposes discharged from the contractual obligations.

Impeachment of Contracts

Contracts may be impeached by the victim of offending behaviour. The victim has recourse to many remedies, discussed in detail below, depending on the nature of the offending behaviour.

Duress

A party who is coerced into an agreement may, at his option, declare the contract void or insist on its performance. Duress includes extortion or the threat of extortion and violence or the threat of violence to the victim or the victim's parent, spouse, or child. It also occurs where the offender takes wrongful or deceitful advantage of the victim by, for example, refusing to honour the contract unless the victim sweetens the terms beyond the original contract.

Undue Influence

A party who is unduly influenced into entering into a contract may, at her option (exercised promptly once the undue influence has ended), either declare the contract void or insist on its performance. Undue influence most commonly arises when there is a special relationship between the influencer and the influencee in which the influencer has a special power or knowledge over the influencee. (Where an influencer exerts undue influence on an influencee, the influencee may catch influenza.) Examples of such relationships include lawyer/client, doctor/patient, and trustee/beneficiary. To remove any taint of undue influence, the dominant party should insist that the other party receive independent legal advice.

Mistake

Parties to a contract sometimes find that they have made a mistake, such that the contract differs in some respect from what they intended. The courts restrict the meaning of the word "mistake" in contract law. The lay definition of "mistake" would effectively negate the usefulness of contracts as a business tool because there would never be certainty or reliability. The law recognizes three types of mistake: common, mutual, and unilateral.

A common mistake occurs when there is no disagreement between the parties about the nature of the mistake. For example, if a travel agent books a room in a hotel that both the agent and the customer believe is open but that is in fact out of business, the contract is void, and the parties are returned to their original positions.

A mutual mistake occurs when, unbeknownst to each other, the two parties have a different understanding of what a term means. The courts will not void the contract, but will rule on which of the two understandings is more reasonable. Suppose a travel agent thought that the booking was for the airport Hilton and the customer thought that it was for the downtown Hilton. If the airport Hilton is closed, the court may suppose that a reservation at a Hilton in the destination city was to be booked and therefore uphold the contract.

A unilateral mistake occurs when one party is mistaken about a term in the contract and the other party is aware of the misunderstanding. The contract is enforceable, and the party who is aware of the other's mistake is under no obligation to make the mistaken party aware of his or her mistake. On the other hand, if a party brought about the mistake by misrepresenting, however innocently, a fact that induced the other party to enter into the contract, then it is incumbent upon the former to inform the latter upon learning of the mistake.

Misrepresentation

There are three kinds of misrepresentation: innocent, negligent, and fraudulent. If the misrepresentation was innocent, the plaintiff can sue for **rescission** but not for damages. If the misrepresentation was made recklessly or carelessly, it is negligent; if made knowingly, it is fraudulent. Upon proving negligent or fraudulent misrepresentation, the plaintiff may terminate the contract and sue in contract and tort for damages. In all cases of misrepresentation, the victim may insist on performance by the offender rather than rescission or damages. (In tort law, there are only two kinds of misrepresentation: negligent and fraudulent, also known as **deceit**.)

Under common law, a misrepresentation of mere opinion is insufficient to found an action in contract; it must be a misrepresentation of a fact. The inflated statements of sellers regarding their products—"This is the best car you can buy" and "My motel is worth at least $200,000"—are not misrepresentations of fact and thus are not actionable under common law. However, statements such as "This car has only 27 000 kilometres on it" when the car has 127 000 kilometres on it, and "I have an offer for $190,000" when no such offer has been made, are misrepresentations of fact and actionable as such. The statement "My motel is worth at least $200,000" is not a misrepresentation of fact because the price is dependent on what a given buyer will pay. There are no ceilings on price, only floors. In this regard, it is wise to remember that price and value are very different concepts.

It is not always easy to determine whether a statement is fact or opinion. Legislation prohibiting unfair business or trade practices has extended the common law remedies of rescission or damages in certain circumstances to cover losses resulting from inaccurate or dishonoured statements of mixed fact and opinion or in situations in which it is difficult to determine whether the statement is fact or opinion.

Many cases of misrepresentation in the hospitality industry deal with misleading financial and other information in the purchase of the business, including misrepresentation as to government permits and licences, the condition of the physical plant, the potability of the water, the historical profitability of the business, and an endless list of other conditions of sale.

B. v. 7 Ont. Ltd. (January 20, 1995, Doc. No. 27421/91, E. MacDonald J. (Ont. Gen. Div.))

The vendor of a restaurant had his accountant prepare a second set of books that gave an enhanced aroma to the economic feasibility of the restaurant. A purchaser, seduced by the succulence of the cooked books, bought the business. He later obtained the correct information and proved that the books were nothing more than a soufflé of deceit. The court found the vendor guilty of fraudulent misrepresentation and awarded the plaintiff $340,000 in general damages and $20,000 in punitive **damages**.

Contracts of Utmost Good Faith

Sometimes information critical to the contract is known by only one of the parties. If the contract requires a high level of trust between the parties, the knowledgeable party must disclose the information to the other party. For example, a hotelier must disclose to an insurer whether or not the hotel has suffered a previous fire and the location of the nearest fire hydrant. If the utmost good faith is not demonstrated by the hotelier, the insurer need not honour the insurance policy. This doctrine, indiscriminately applied, would render commercial relationships quite uncertain. The mere withholding of special knowledge is not enough to invoke an impeachment remedy; the withholding must occur within a contract that the courts have imbued with a duty of utmost good faith.

Non Est Factum

Generally, the courts will bind a person to her bargain on the assumption that she read and understood the contract before signing it. If she can satisfy the court that the contract she signed was qualitatively different from the contract she thought she was signing, then the document may be set aside on the basis of *non est factum* ("It is not my deed"). This defence was more common when more people were illiterate. Today, this defence rarely succeeds.

Breach of Contract

A party is usually considered to have met his or her obligations under a contract if the obligations have been substantially performed. What constitutes substantial performance depends on the contract and the circumstances surrounding the performance. Generally, if the contract has been substantially performed, then it has not been breached. Thus, a minor breach will not normally free the parties to a contract from performance. The breach must be of the whole contract or a fundamental condition. A contract is breached when repudiation, failure to perform, or sabotage occurs.

Repudiation

A party may declare that he will not commence or complete the performance required by the contract and thereby repudiate the contract. If the repudiation occurs before the time for commencement of the performance, the innocent party may anticipate the breach, rearrange her affairs accordingly, and sue for any damages.

Failure to Perform

One party may fail to perform fully as required in the contract. There is no express repudiation, but the performance is less than contracted for. There are degrees of failure to perform, ranging from partial to complete. The remedy may take into account any partial performance.

Karalekas v. Canada Trustco (unreported, 1998), Ottawa Small Claims Court

In 1997, a Canada Trust branch made a reservation at the Steak and Caesar Restaurant in Ottawa for 30 people for the Saturday before Christmas. In effect, the bank promised to send 30 paying diners and the restaurant promised to feed them. No one called to cancel and no one showed up. Unable to obtain an explanation or an apology, the restaurateur, Paul Karalekas, sued the bank for breach of contract in Small Claims Court and won. The court found that a bilateral contract had been brought into being by virtue of the exchanged promises and awarded the restaurant $1,765.

Not every broken dinner reservation will result in damages for breach of contract. As we will see below, a plaintiff must demonstrate damages and that may be difficult if a couple breaks their reservation but the restaurant nevertheless does good business that day. Here, a large part of the restaurant had been set aside for the large number of diners expected and it was not available for other patrons until it was too late.

Sabotage

One party may perform a willful act that is in contradiction to the agreement or that renders the contract incapable of being performed. In the case of a magician contracted to appear at a resort, a willful act can be anything from releasing the rabbits into the wild to refusing to pay for the transportation necessary to reach the resort.

Remedies

Breach of contract does not necessarily mean that the contract is terminated. The innocent party may forgive the breach and continue to regard the contract as legally binding. If the innocent party terminates the contract, however, various remedies become available.

Limitation Periods

An aggrieved party must commence the action before the end of the statutory limitation period; otherwise, the claim is barred. Limitation periods across Canada range from six to 20 years.

Necessity of Loss

Under contract law and civil law generally, except where nominal or **punitive damages** are claimed and assessed, one cannot successfully sue unless one can demonstrate a loss.

Duty to Mitigate

Under contract law and civil law generally, an injured party has a responsibility to **mitigate** or contain the damages as much as is reasonably possible. For example, although statutes now provide minimum severances for many employees, under common law a person who has been wrongfully dismissed must honestly look for a new job in order to minimize the damages claimed above the statutory minimum. The plaintiff may not take advantage of the situation by running up unnecessary expenses, thereby inflating the claim.

W.E.M.L. v. M.R.C.L. (December 4, 1995, Alta. C.A.)

P signed a long-term lease for a restaurant in a mall. The space was L-shaped and had little frontage. The venture was unprofitable. P closed the restaurant and moved his inventory out. P continued to pay rent, but ultimately the landlord served a termination notice. Although the lease terminated, P remained liable for the rent under a liquidated-damages clause in the lease. Eventually, P stopped paying the rent. In doing so, he claimed that the landlord had not mitigated and thereby released him from his obligation to pay rent as damages. The landlord contended that he was unable to relet the property because of a slow market. P argued that the difficulty in reletting was a direct result of the shape of the shop: if the landlord allocated more frontage, the shop could be relet. The court ruled that while there had been no failure to mitigate up to the time of the trial, there had been a failure to mitigate continuing from the time of the trial. The landlord was ordered to repay the rent (with interest) from that point forward.

Rectification

In some circumstances, the courts will rectify a written contract that contains a clear error for which there is ample evidence. The most common are typographical errors and mistakes in copying information from source documents. The party asserting the error must convince the court that it is necessary to correct the error in order to give effect to the clear intentions of the parties. The courts will not rectify the contract if to do so would in essence rewrite the contract for the parties. The remedy is available only to correct a written document so that it corresponds to the intention of the parties. Rectification cases rarely reach a courtroom. Most often when there is such an error, the parties execute an amendment to the original contract to correct the error. A claim for rectification may require a judge's intervention if one of the parties has taken an assignment of the contract and is unsure whether a mistake occurred.

Rescission

If the parties can be returned to their pre-contract state, an innocent party may opt to rescind the contract instead of continuing to enforce it. In that event, the innocent party cannot seek damages: the party has been returned to his or her original state and therefore has suffered no damages.

Injunctions

An innocent party may wish to restrain an offender from acting inconsistently with the contract. For example, if a diner has an exclusive contract with a supplier for papayas, the diner may **enjoin** the supplier from supplying the papayas to a competitor for the duration of the contract. Interim injunctions may be obtained until the matter can be dealt with more completely by the courts. If the subject matter of the contract is perishable or susceptible to swift disappearance such that awaiting trial would render the dispute moot, an applicant may obtain a preservation order, which preserves the subject matter until the dispute can be dealt with more fully.

Specific Performance

In some cases, the innocent party wishes to have the original benefit of the contract, not a monetary compensation. An award of damages may be inadequate compensation if the subject matter of the breached contract is rare or unique, such as land or art. In such cases, the innocent party may seek a court order that requires the breacher to perform the contract as originally contemplated. Courts will not order specific performance if supervision of the performance by the court would be required. For example, a travel guide will not be ordered to act as a guide if he or she refuses to honour a contract.

Quantum Meruit

Some contracts, particularly oral ones, make no mention of the price to be paid for the provision of the goods or services. Applying the principle of *quantum meruit* ("the amount he merits"), the courts may award the reasonable worth of the goods delivered or services rendered. A person cannot merit an amount by unilaterally supplying a good or service, or we would all be fabulously wealthy (at least until someone turned the tables on us). The provision of the goods or services must come at the request of the person who is to be liable to pay the merited amount. The doctrine of *quantum meruit*, which concerns goods and services, is first cousin to the doctrine of part performance, which concerns interests in real property.

Damages

Damage awards are intended to put innocent parties in the position they would have been in if the contract had been completed. This is accomplished by providing fair compensation for the reasonably foreseeable losses resulting from the breach of contract. The compensation is for damages that were reasonably foreseeable at the time the contract was made, not at the time of the breach. Parties should be held liable only for matters that were within or ought to have been within their contemplation at the time they entered into the agreement.

Nominal Damages
Sometimes a party wishes redress on principle even though there are minimal or no losses. A court may award nominal damages of typically one dollar. However, to discourage the uneconomic pursuit of mere principles through the court system, judges may also chastise the winning party with an unfavourable award of legal costs.

Liquidated Damages
The parties may by contract predetermine the amount of the damages in the event of a breach. If the amount is a genuine pre-estimate, the courts will usually allow the **liquidated** damages to stand. If the amount is too high, the courts may strike it as a penalty. If it is too low, the courts may strike it as a disguised exemption clause. Courts tend to uphold exemption clauses if the breach is of a nonfundamental term, and to strike them if the breach is of a fundamental term.

Expenses and Loss of Profits
The innocent party may recover expenses and reasonably anticipated profits lost as a result of the breach if the expenses or loss of profits were contemplated by the parties at the time of making the contract. The innocent party may also recover losses that flow naturally from the breach even if they were not overtly in the contemplation of the parties, provided they were reasonably foreseeable had the parties turned their minds to the issue at the time.

General Damages
Some nonmonetary losses, such as mental distress, are difficult to quantify. Such losses are tort law concepts. A court must estimate the monetary compensation, known as general damages, for nonmonetary losses. Mental distress can occur when, for example, a holiday is ruined by a breach of contract, or when an employee is wrongfully dismissed.

Punitive and Exemplary Damages

Punitive and **exemplary damages** are awards above compensatory damages. Punitive damages are imposed to punish the offender for malicious or wanton behaviour such as an unconscionable breach of contract. Exemplary damages are imposed to make an example of the offender, not necessarily to punish, though the payor may find the distinction rather subtle.

> **B.C. Ltd. v. G. Holdings Ltd. (May 31, 1996, B.C.S.C., Doc. No. C930387, Melnick J., Vancouver)**
>
> When negotiating to buy a hotel, P had doubts about the financial statements but closed anyway. Pursuant to the contract, D was required, on closing, to deliver to P the assets required for the normal running of the business and to have maintained those assets until the closing. The building was also warranted to be in sound condition. After taking possession, P found that some of the equipment included in the agreement was missing and that the building was not in a state of good repair. P brought an action against the defendant for breach of contract, claiming that he had been fraudulently misled. Evidence at trial established that D had removed many items of inventory. Members of the hotel staff testified that, at the time the agreement was executed, the roof and boilers were in a poor state of repair and the roof had serious leaks. The court awarded P damages of approximately $218,000 for breach of contract. In addition, the court found that D had made many fraudulent misrepresentations, and awarded a further $198,400 as punitive damages. The punitive award might have been higher, but P was found to have been contributorily negligent in that he failed to take advantage of his opportunities to be more diligent in inspecting the statements, inventory, and premises.

This case demonstrates the need for a vendor to ensure that a purchaser is not misled, and the need for a purchaser to carry out all sensible pre-closing inspections and analyses. At a minimum, most purchasers should consult professionals with expertise in law, financial statements, and building inspections.

Enforcement of Remedies

Once the plaintiff has obtained a judgment or an order against the defendant, the defendant may comply without further ado. If not, the plaintiff may seek the assistance of the sheriff's office to seize and sell the defendant's assets or garnishee the defendant's wages. Failure by the defendant to abide by an injunction or order for specific performance may trigger contempt of court proceedings. As a practical matter, remedies are only as good as the credit of the defendant. Choose your debtors wisely.

Contracts in the Hospitality Industry

A myriad of the interactions between hospitality providers and the public are contractual, such as reserving a room at a hotel, ordering a meal at a restaurant, booking a holiday through a travel agent, hiring and firing staff, ordering supplies, buying or leasing equipment, buying or leasing premises, buying business and other insurance, entering into a franchise agreement, engaging renovators and repair technicians, and retaining professionals for advice.

Reservation Contracts

The room-reservation contract is central to the operation of a hotel. Everyday hotels handle hundreds of thousands of these contracts. Potential guests can make reservations by telephone or through the Internet. Many hotel chains have reservation centres that handle large numbers of reservations on a daily basis for all their properties and associates.

A room reservation is a contract between an innkeeper and a guest. To be enforceable, it must have the six essential elements of a contract. Failing to honour a reservation is a breach of contract. An innkeeper who dishonours a reservation may be liable for the guest's costs. A guest who does not cancel a reservation in the manner agreed upon in the reservation contract may be liable for the price of the room. Many hotels require that all guaranteed reservations must be cancelled prior to 6:00 p.m. A "no-show" is a reservation contract that has been breached by a guest. Unless the reservation has been guaranteed by the guest and the hotel has obtained a credit card number, no-shows are a largely uncollectable expense. The guest may have a plausible but unverifiable excuse, such as having cancelled the reservation through a staff member whose name is unknown.

Hotels should have a clear cancellation policy indicating the time by which a guest may cancel without penalty. Cancellation numbers or time and date codes given to the guest and recorded by the hotel can put the hotel in a strong position when pursuing a guest for breach of a reservation contract. Whether the hotel should do so, particularly when the guest is a long-time and valued client, is a business decision that calls for discretion and a sense of public relations. In the case of large bookings and resort and cruise ship reservations, the contract should indicate the deadline for cancellations without penalty, and set forth any partial payment and administrative charge policies. When reservations are cancelled on time, advance payments or deposits (minus allowable administration charges) should be returned without delay with a letter expressing the hope that the hotel may be of service in the future.

Guests may guarantee their reservations by forwarding a deposit or by providing a billing address, but usually do so by credit card number. A guaranteed reservation is advisable when a hotel is busy or when the guest is planning to arrive after 6:00 p.m. Some hotels confuse the issue by advertising that they guarantee all reservations. This may be nothing more than a promise that, as long as the guest arrives before the agreed-upon time, a room will be available. Hotels using such marketing ploys should word them carefully.

Overbooking

A hotel room is a most perishable commodity—if a room is not sold on a particular day, that room's revenue is lost forever. Experience shows that a percentage of guests with reservations will not arrive. In order to maximize revenues, innkeepers regularly overbook. Provided they do not overestimate the no-shows, no harm results. However, most hotels have at one time or another failed to honour room reservations.

A hotel should have a standard operating procedure to guide their staff's actions when overbooking and **walking the guests**. This policy should include a guideline as to how many extra reservations can be taken. In such a case, a manager should deal with the guest. The manager should acknowledge forthrightly that the hotel is holding the reservation, apologize for being unable to honour it, minimize the inconvenience to the guest by promptly arranging for a comparable room in another hotel and by covering the guest's reasonable expenses such as telephone calls, taxi fare to the new hotel, and any tips already given to the porter. If the guest must commute back and forth—as would be the case if the first hotel were hosting a convention attended by the guest—the additional expenses should also be covered. If such procedures are followed, then the walked guest will likely not incur damages and therefore have little grounds to seek legal retribution.

Some guests will be very understanding and, if well treated, may return to the first hotel. The airlines offer special incentives for people willing to offer up their seat. There may be some opportunity for hotels to look at such programs.

Appendix 3 contains a sample room Reservation Contract Reply Form. It provides evidence of the existence of a reservation contract by providing evidence of the offer, the acceptance, the consideration, and mutual intent of the two parties. Any concerns the reservations representative of the hotel may have concerning the capacity of the guest to enter into the reservation contract may be indicated in the "Remarks" section of the Reply Form; otherwise, capacity is assumed. Legality is also assumed. Note that assumptions may be rebutted when appropriate. Not all accommodation providers use a Reply Form to confirm a reservation contract, particularly with repeat guests. Instead, they rely on the reservation contract typically made over the phone or on the Internet and usually guaranteed by a credit card number.

Conventions and Business Meetings

Success in the convention, meeting, banquet, and catering field depends on the attention paid to the details of the guest's requests. These functions are planned far in advance. The planners of the event are often not present at the time of performance. Sales staff for the property will meet with the guest and draw up the contract for the event. It is imperative that the service staff is informed of all requirements.

Conventions usually involve large numbers of attendees and overnight accommodation. Business meetings may involve smaller numbers of people using meeting rooms but not overnight accommodation. Listed below are some of the issues that should be addressed in a convention or business meeting contract, as applicable:

1. Whether to offer a mass check-in option to the convention organizers. If the organizers or the hotel prefer to register each guest individually, the hotel should be in a position to do so quickly and efficiently.

2. Whether special equipment such as overhead projectors, flipcharts, movie screens, faxes, modem outlets, and secretarial services are to be supplied. If they are, the contract should specify the number, type, charges, time limits, and damage policies.

3. Whether the walls of the rooms or public areas may be used to post information or hang products and, if so, the responsibility for damage repair.

4. Whether signs can be erected and, if so, the size, type, and location of the signs, and the responsibility for their removal.

5. Whether coffee and meals are included and, if so, the quality and quantity, and the timing, charges, and clean-up responsibilities.

6. Whether public relations, media management, public access, privacy measures, and security services are to be provided and, if so, the nature and cost of them.

7. Responsibility for insurance coverage and the amount and types of coverage.

8. The number, type, location, and layout of meeting rooms reserved for the participants.

9. The number, type, and location of bedrooms the hotel reserved for the participants.

10. The number and type of any meals to be included (banquet/catering contract checklist).

11. Cancellation policies, guarantee dates, deposits, notice provisions, warranties, and other such administrative matters.

Successful special events, such as this banquet, are the result of careful and detailed planning.

Banquets and Catering

Banquets are held on-site at the hotel or restaurant. Catered functions are held off-site but make use of the establishment's wherewithal. The staff may attend and prepare the meals off-site, or prepare the meals in-house and transport them to the site. Listed below are some of the issues that should be addressed in a banquet/catering contract, as applicable:

1. The names and addresses of all the parties to the agreement.

2. The dates when the minimum and final numbers of participants must be known.

3. The charge policies for additional participants and no-shows.

4. The date and time of the function.

5. The location of the function—on-site or off-site. If the site is in the client's home or place of business, whose kitchen facilities will be used and when will they be available?

6. The size and type of rooms. Many establishments offer different rooms for different purposes. A politician will be annoyed if she is given a room so large that it looks like she has little support. A groom will be annoyed if his relatives are exiled to the corridor.

7. Whether rooms adjacent to the function room are included. A host with an open bar is not interested in supplying drinks to the party next door. Brides and grooms often require change rooms. What is the cost and who shall pay?

8. Whether the lobby or other public areas may be used for picture-taking or displays. Double-booking of these areas should be avoided.

9. The floor plan for the tables and dance floor, and whether the dance area will be clear for the whole event or cleared after dinner.

10. The type (china, paper, plastic) of place settings (dishes, cutlery, and napery) required. If the site is in the client's home or place of business, whose settings will be used?

11. The style of service (buffet or served) for the meal and any hors d'oeuvres.

12. The full menu including all charges, changes, extras, and substitutions.

13. Whether a late-evening snack before the end of the banquet is included.

14. Whether the bar service is open (prepaid by the host) or cash (paid by the participants), as well as the hours of service and the supply of bartenders.

15. The type and quantity of alcohol to be served.

16. Staffing, security, and any other services expected from the hotel relating to public relations and media/public access and control.

17. The supply and format of any entertainment, including any restrictions.

18. The number of nondining guests who may be joining the party before or after the meal.

19. Cancellation policies for both parties, including circumstances beyond the control of one or both parties (e.g., fire, accidents, labour strife, acts of God).

20. The advance-deposit policy.

21. The payment policy. Label tips and taxes as either included or extra.

22. The gratuity policy.

23. Repayment policies.

24. Amendment policies.

25. Disclaimers.

26. Responsibility for insurance and the amount and types of coverage.

27. Any other goods or services for the event, such as decorations and entertainment.

28. Any disturbances caused by setting up and taking down temporary buffets.

Establishments may cater in-house or they may hire outside caterers. All responsibilities should be clearly specified. Any changes should be revealed in a timely fashion. If the guests are expecting in-house catering and an outside service has been retained, it is necessary to advise them without delay. If a caterer is providing service to a location he does not own or control (e.g., a private home or a rented hall), it is imperative to address such issues as the supply of cutlery and linens, and the condition of the location, before and after the banquet.

Summary

Well-constructed contracts are essential to the smooth functioning of business relationships. The hospitality industry uses a myriad of contracts on a daily basis. Contracts should be carefully negotiated and reviewed by legal counsel to enhance their effectiveness, cover contingencies, and avoid unwanted consequences and problems of misinterpretation. Although many contracts are equally binding whether they are written or verbal, other contracts, such as agreements of purchase and sales of real estate, must be in writing to be enforceable. In law as in medicine, preventing a problem is far more cost-effective than treating it. Individuals should seek legal assistance before entering into any material agreement or relationship that has legal consequences. Appendix 3 has many sample hospitality contracts.

Discussion Questions

1. How does a unilateral contract differ from a bilateral contract? Give an example of each.

2. What is the difference between an invitation to treat and an offer? Give examples.

3. What are the six essential elements of a contract? Can a valid contract be formed in the absence of any one of the elements? Why or why not?

4. Draw up the standard operating procedure for walking a guest.

5. Analyze a business meeting or banquet contract to determine whether all the elements of contract formation are present, whether the language used is clear, and whether all parties have been well protected.

6. Under what circumstances can a minor be held responsible for using a hotel's facilities? Give examples of instances when a minor may not be liable.

7. Harvey, the owner of a small corporation, booked a business meeting room on behalf of the corporation. The room was at the Cliffhanger Lodge and the reservation was for the next weekend. The night before the meeting was to start, Harvey entered the hospital with chest pains. He cancelled the booking. It was too late for the lodge to accept another booking for the room. Is the lodge without recourse? Why or why not?

8. With legal advice, Claude, the new manager of a hotel and convention complex, signed an employment contract which provided that should he be terminated for any reason, he could not work for any hotel and convention complex in Canada until 10 years had elapsed. The hotel fell on hard times and dismissed Claude, paying him a reasonable severance. Claude moved to a new province and was immediately hired to manage a convention complex of comparable size to his previous employer. His previous employer went to court to prevent him from working for the new complex and to recover monetary damages. Assess the strengths and weaknesses of Claude's defence.

9. Protagoras (c. 490–421 B.C.), a Greek philosopher, posed the following conundrum: A law professor made a contract with a student, which provided that the professor would not be paid until the student had won his first case as a lawyer. At the end of the course of study, the professor demanded payment, but the student refused to pay on the basis that he had not yet won a case. The professor sued the student, believing that he could not lose. If he won the case, he would have an enforceable judgment against the student. If he lost, the student would have his first victory as a lawyer and would have to pay. As the trial began, the student moved for a nonsuit, believing that he could not lose. If he won the motion for the nonsuit, he would not have to pay his professor. If he lost the motion, he would not have won his first case and would still not have to pay. Who should win and why?

4

Chapter Four

The Law of Negligence

Learning Outcomes

1. Define tort law.

2. List the elements of negligence.

3. Analyze a case using the appropriate elements required for various torts.

4. Assess the hospitality industry's duties to guest, invitee, licensee, and trespasser.

5. Assess the liability when the plaintiff takes on risk voluntarily.

6. Assess whether a waiver or disclaimer precludes a plaintiff seeking a remedy.

7. Describe the obligation to help a person in distress.

8. Describe the obligations of manufacturers of food and beverages.

Introduction

Every year, thousands of hospitality business operators must defend court claims brought by injured plaintiffs alleging that the operators are responsible for the injuries. In some cases, the operators may be fully or partially liable. In other cases, they may prove that they were not responsible for the injuries. Preventing negligence claims is preferable to curing them.

Common Law

The law of **negligence** evolved, and continues to evolve, out of the plethora of judge-made assessments of fault in the conduct of individuals and businesses. Negligence consists of a breach of a duty of care wherein the breach proximally causes an injury to a party to whom the duty is owed. The degree of duty varies depending on, for example, the nature of the relationship between the injurer and the injured. Although the distinctions are narrowing and blurring, an innkeeper owes a different duty to a guest than to a **trespasser**. One of the highest duties of care required of anyone is the duty owed by innkeepers to their guests.

The four main elements of negligence are:

1. Existence of a duty of care

2. Breach of the duty

3. Injury resulting from the breach

4. Proximate cause of the injury by the breach

There are two types of negligence (intentional and unintentional) and two kinds of liability (conditional and strict). They are described later in the chapter.

Legislative Amendment

Some injuries are so catastrophic that the injurer is financially devastated and the injured is inadequately compensated. High insurance premiums give insureds an incentive to avoid negligent conduct even though the damage awards are defrayed by large pools of premium payers. For some conduct and injuries, insurance has proven to be an inadequate regulatory and compensatory mechanism. Governments have enacted laws to codify the standard of care and to impose liabilities for breaches thereof. Occupiers' liability acts and innkeepers' acts are just two examples. Some legislation has heightened the standard, while other legislation has capped liability. Still other legislation has disposed of the notion of fault, no-fault automobile insurance being an obvious example. There are winners and losers as a result of the changes, but the legislators believe that the competing interests have been fairly balanced.

Principles of Negligence

The Duty of Care

Everyone has a duty to take reasonable care to avoid causing injury to those to whom the duty is owed. The injury may be to the mind, the body, the property, or the pocketbook of the victim. The definitions and degrees of the duties, and the consequences of breaching them, constitute the laws of negligence, also known as the law of torts, an old French term meaning "wrongs." The torts may occur intentionally, or unintentionally through recklessness, carelessness, or bad luck. The duty may be imposed for acts of commission or omission, and imposed even when the **tortfeasor** (the person committing the tort) took every precaution to avoid the injury.

At one time, **tort** damages were not recoverable if the plaintiff lacked a contractual relationship with the tortfeasor. The British case that expanded the class of plaintiffs is *Donoghue v. Stevenson, [1932] A.C. 562 (H.L.)*. The plaintiff drank a bottle of ginger beer—purchased and given to her by a friend—only to discover the corpse of a snail inside. She sued the manufacturer even though she had no contractual link to the vendor. The House of Lords invoked a broad concept of "neighbour" to define persons to whom a duty of care is owed, and found that a duty was owed to the plaintiff. Lord Atkin expressed the concept as follows:

> [A]cts or omissions which any moral code could censure cannot in a practical world be treated so as to give a right to every person injured by them to demand relief. In this way rules of law arise which limit the range of complaint and the extent of their remedy. The rule that you are to love your neighbour becomes in law, you must not injure your neighbour; and the lawyer's question, "Who is my neighbour?" receives a restricted reply. You must take reasonable care to avoid acts or omissions which you can reasonably foresee would be likely to injure your neighbour. Who, then, in law, is my neighbour? The answer seems to be persons who are so closely and directly affected by my act that I ought reasonably to have them in contemplation as being so affected when I am directing my mind to the acts or omissions which are called in question.

The House of Lords was of the opinion that, even when there exists no privity of contract, a manufacturer owes a duty of care to its neighbours (broadly defined) for whom injuries can be reasonably foreseen.

The Reasonable Person

The concept of the **reasonable person** is a useful judicial resource with which to examine and test human conduct. The concept supplies a measuring stick by which to judge objectively whether the alleged tortfeasor behaved unreasonably or whether the victim brought about his or her own injury. The reasonable person uses careful and thoughtful behaviour, has at least some commonsense, and is entitled to expect reasonable conduct from others. The reasonable person avoids endangering others, shies away from foolishness, and is entitled to assume that ginger beer is not seasoned with snails. The standard of the reasonable person is not one of perfection, but the standard does rise as the severity of the consequences rises.

The standard is not used when judging the mentally ill or children. Children are allowed to be childish. An obligation rests with the adults to look after them. The standard is a sliding scale: a growing child is increasingly expected to recognize dangers and act accordingly. Children are rightly regarded as a vital resource, and most communities have strict regulations to protect them. A requirement that all outdoor swimming pools be enclosed with an appropriate fence is one example. Dangerous situations hold a special attraction for many children. Pools, discarded refrigerators and freezers, unattended machinery, snow and sand piles that can collapse on a tunneller, and fast-moving water in storm ditches are just a few.

The reasonable-person test also does not apply when the assessment of liability does not depend on concepts of intention or fault, but is strictly imposed regardless of conduct. **Strict liability** means that the tortfeasor will be held liable even if his conduct was reasonable. What constitutes reasonable behaviour is not always left to the courts and individuals to decide; it may be prescribed by statute. Thus, if a person engages in conduct contrary to the statute, the conduct may be negligent and a breach of the duty to act reasonably.

The Purposes of Tort Law

There are six primary purposes of tort law:

1. Regulation
2. Deterrence

3. Compensation

4. Dispute resolution

5. Education

6. Prevention

Tort law hovers over almost all interpersonal, professional, and business relationships. By imposing sanctions on those who stray beyond the boundaries of reasonable or regulated noncriminal behaviour, tort law deters people from activities that are a risk to others. We live in a free society, but the freedom to swing your arm ends short of your neighbour's nose. By providing a means of redress to the aggrieved, tort law helps to minimize or defuse conflict. It is a social safety valve of incalculable utility. As principles of negligence become established, refined, and incorporated into community knowledge, tort law serves as a valuable educative and preventative tool. Tort law keeps people on their toes (and off yours).

For the victims of tortious conduct, tort law provides a method of seeking compensation. Tort compensation is meant to place the victim in the position she would have been in but for the tort. Special damages are awarded for identifiable past, present, and future expenses. General damages are awarded for aspects that are not easily quantifiable in financial terms, such as mental suffering and loss of companionship. As a rule, tort compensation should not provide windfalls, although there have been cases emanating from the United States that suggest that a plaintiff can win millions of dollars, at least at the trial level, that are out of proportion to the injury. In Canada, a trilogy of cases (including *Andrews v. Grand & Toy Alberta Ltd., [1978] 2 S.C.R. 229*) decided by the Supreme Court of Canada has effectively capped Canadian general damage awards at $100,000 in 1978 dollars. The amounts awarded today are adjusted for inflation.

Punitive (to punish the tortfeasor) or exemplary (to make an example of the tortfeasor) damages may be awarded when the court wishes to express its outrage over grossly negligent, quasi-criminal, or high-handed conduct on the part of the tortfeasor. Punitive or exemplary damages more than compensate the victim, and send a strong message that such conduct will not be tolerated by the courts.

Intentional Torts

The Eight Intentional Torts

Because the acts or omissions that constitute negligence rarely involve criminal intent, the remedies are found in civil rather than criminal court. That said, in those cases in which the wrong involves the intentional infliction of harm, tort law approaches criminal law. There are eight intentional torts:

1. Assault

2. Battery

3. Trespass

4. Conversion

5. False imprisonment

6. Intentional infliction of mental suffering

7. Deceit (also known as fraudulent misrepresentation)

8. Intentional interference with contract (more remote from criminal law)

Assault (the threat of a serious unwanted touching) and battery (the act of a serious unwanted touching) are both torts and crimes. Assault is the threat of punching someone in the nose whether by statement or body language; battery is the actual punch. Depending on the circumstances and severity, remedies may be pursued in the criminal and/or civil courts.

Conduct is intentional when the result of the action is intended by the tortfeasor, and unintentional when it may be presumed that a reasonable person would not have intended the result. If one throws a snowball intending to hit the barn door, intention to inflict harm is not established if the snowball happens to hit a passerby. Liability may still be found if the snowball was carelessly or recklessly (negligently) thrown. Although cases of intentional torts in the hospitality industry are relatively rare, the following examples illustrate how they may occur.

- Trespass may occur when a person enters a motel room without a valid reason or authority. Opening a guest's mail without proper authority is a trespass to property.

- Assault and battery may occur when a bar bouncer bodily ejects a patron onto the parking lot. Owners and operators may be tortiously liable for assault and battery to the victim, and criminally liable to the state if criminal intent is proven. Under criminal law, the prosecution must prove its case beyond a reasonable doubt, which, for the sake of argument, we define as 98 percent certainty; under civil law, the burden is a balance of probabilities, which we define as 51 percent certainty. If a judge or jury is 66 percent certain that the evidence is sufficient to find against the defendant, then a criminal defendant will be acquitted and a civil defendant will be held liable. The different outcomes of the O.J. Simpson criminal and civil trials are well-known illustrations of this distinction.

- Conversion occurs when a person, without lawful authority, intentionally exercises control over another person's chattel in a manner inconsistent with the owner's title, either by wrongfully taking it, rightfully taking it but wrongfully retaining it, or (without taking or retaining it) wrongly disposing of it by such means as sale or destruction. Conversion occurs when the owner of a restaurant sells without consent the bathrobes and towels of a separately owned adjacent motel as part of a promotion. The line between conversion and the criminal act of theft can be very fine.

- False imprisonment may arise when an operator believes that a patron is leaving the premises without paying, and confines the patron to an area from which he or she may not safely leave. If it is discovered that the patron had paid, the operator may be found liable for false imprisonment.

- A travel agent who knows that his customer is heading for a long-awaited, badly needed skiing holiday may be liable for intentionally inflicting mental suffering if he deliberately plots, perhaps by booking the customer into substandard accommodation far from the ski hills, to make the holiday miserable.

- Deceit, or the fraudulent misleading of another person, is established if the maker of the statement knew it was false or did not care whether it was true or false. A hotel vendor who knowingly and falsely tells the purchaser that the boiler in the basement is capable of twice its actual capacity is liable for deceit.

- A club owner who urges a popular singer, dancer, or other stage performer to break her binding contract with a competitor club in order to hurt the competitor's business commits the tort of intentional interference with contract.

Defences to the Intentional Torts

A defendant may escape liability upon establishing one or more of the following defences:

1. Consent
2. Self-defence
3. Defence of property
4. Defence of a third person
5. Necessity
6. Legal authority
7. Lack of intention

Consent

A person who gives an informed consent to an action may not recover (through a judgment or an order) damages unless they go beyond the reasonable scope of the consent. For example, participants hurt in the ordinary course of a sport cannot recover for assault and battery. On the other hand, a boxer does not expect to be attacked by his opponent in the hallway after the bout. Such an attack would be outside the consent and would likely be an actionable tort.

Self-Defence/Defence of Property/Defence of a Third Person

A defendant will normally not be found liable if her actions were in defence of herself, her property, or a third person she wished to protect.

Necessity

If an act of trespass is necessary (e.g., landing a plane in a farmer's field due to lack of fuel), no intentional tort has occurred. However, the trespasser may be found liable for any damage he or she causes during the necessary trespass.

Legal Authority

A defendant who has the legal authority to commit the act in question will generally not be found liable. If a patron leaves a bar with no intention to pay and is detained, the owner will not be found to have falsely imprisoned him.

Lack of Intention

The aforementioned club owner would not be found liable for intentional interference with contract if it were proven that he did not intend to harm the competitor. There can also be no interference when the contract between the performer and the competitor has been repudiated or breached by the competitor.

In all such cases, the defences will be examined for reasonableness. A defendant will not escape liability if a theoretically proper defence was unreasonably or excessively effected.

Negligence (Unintentional Torts)

Confusingly, the word "negligence" is used to describe the whole field of tort law as well as this main branch of it. Unintentional negligence is found when the tortfeasor is presumed not to have intended the resulting injury. Like any accident, negligence can occur in the twinkling of an eye and be perpetrated by the most well-intentioned people. The following case illustrates the four main elements of negligence identified at the outset of this chapter.

Menow v. Jordan House Hotel Ltd. and Honsberger, [1974] S.C.R. 239

Menow, a regular at the Jordan House Hotel, was known to drink to excess and become obnoxious. The hotel finally banned him from the premises, but some time later offered to serve Menow again on condition that he be accompanied by a responsible adult. One night, Menow entered the hotel with a friend who intended to stay with him. Toward the end of the evening, the friend suggested they leave the premises. Menow ignored the suggestion, which the friend repeated several times. Eventually, the friend, tired of chaperoning Menow, left without him. The staff at the hotel saw that Menow was on his own, but continued to serve him. As was his custom, Menow became bothersome to everyone in the bar, and the staff ejected him. He left the premises in such a drunken state that he was unable to negotiate his way along a roadside. He was hit by a car driven by Honsberger, and suffered serious injuries as a result. Menow sued the hotel and Honsberger claiming that they were responsible for his injuries.

The Supreme Court of Canada found that the Jordan House employees had violated two duties they owed Menow—namely, the duty imposed on them by the provincial liquor licensing regulations not to serve someone who is intoxicated, and the duty to protect him when they ejected him knowing that he was unlikely to reach home safely. The Supreme Court determined that the Jordan House Hotel could have given Menow a room, called the police, or arranged for safe transportation home.

All four elements of negligence are evident here. First, the hotel had a duty of care to Menow (not to serve alcohol to an already intoxicated person). Second, the hotel breached the duty. Third, Menow suffered injury. And fourth, the breach of the duty was a proximate cause of the injury. The driver, Honsberger, was also held liable; the Court found that he had a duty to Menow, which was not to drive negligently. The case was one of unintentional negligence because none of the defendants had intended to cause Menow, or anyone, any injuries.

Murphy v. Little Memphis Cabaret Inc., [1996] O.J. No. 4600 (Q.L.) (December 9, 1996, Doc. No. 94-GD-28654, Windsor, Zuber J. (Ont. Gen. Div.))

Murphy and C arrived at the Little Memphis Cabaret around midnight. Present were four other patrons who had been in the bar since approximately 9:00 p.m. Their identity was never learned. There was no evidence that the four patrons or Murphy and C were intoxicated. There was no sign of trouble until last call was announced. At that time, one of the four men shouted, "Are you calling me a queer?" Another of the four patrons punched C. The bouncer and other patrons ushered the four men out the back door. The manager then escorted Murphy and C out the front door to wait for a cab. Shortly after, witnesses noticed that at least one of the four men had made his way to the front of the tavern and was beating Murphy. Murphy suffered a fractured skull and extensive damage to his facial bones, which required surgery and the insertion of plates. He suffered from severe headaches and balance problems for some time after the attack.

> The court found that the tavern had failed in its duty to protect Murphy from
> dangers that had originated within the premises. The court held that no inordinate
> burden would have been placed on the tavern keeper had he allowed Murphy and
> C to stay inside until the four belligerent patrons had departed; called a taxi for
> Murphy and C, or allowed them to call one; or summoned the police. The court
> stated that "the failure to do any one of these simple things ... constitutes a
> breach of the duty owed to the plaintiff." The tavern was liable to Murphy for his
> injuries and to his wife for the loss of his companionship.

Like the *Menow* case, this case illustrates the four elements of negligence, all of which must be present in order for a defendant to be found liable.

Causation and the Burden of Proof

Foreseeability and Proximate Cause

When strict liability rules do not apply, liability is conditional. The general rule is that a person is liable for negligence only if the consequences of the act were reasonably foreseeable. It would be unreasonable to saddle a person with liability for consequences that are not foreseeable. On the other hand, failing to assign liability for reasonably foreseeable consequences would destroy the concept of a duty of care.

To succeed in a lawsuit for negligence, a plaintiff must prove on a balance of probabilities that the defendant's act, or failure to act, was the proximate cause of the injury. The plaintiff's case will fail if the defendant's act or failure to act was too remote a cause. In other words, liability will be found if the injuries were reasonably foreseeable even if the injuries occurred in a way that was not readily foreseeable. Put another way, for liability to attach, the tortfeasor need only foresee that damages are likely to occur without knowing exactly how they will occur. In *R. v. Coté (1974), 51 D.L.R. (3d) 244, 252*, Mr. Justice Dickson of the Supreme Court of Canada stated that, "It is not necessary that one foresee 'the precise concatenation of the events'; it is enough to fix liability if one can foresee in a general way the class or character of injury which occurred."

Findings of causation depend on the facts of each case. Injuries always have causes, but not every injury is the proximate result of negligence on the part of the defendant. Where to draw the line is a vexing question. It can be very difficult deciding whether or not a particular consequence was reasonably foreseeable.

> S. v. E.P. Ltd. (November 21, 1996, Doc. No. 4340, St. John's
> (Nfld. S.C. Trial Div.))
>
> On a Sunday in 1993, ten members of the S family dined at the E restaurant,
> which had a wishing well. The children entertained themselves by gathering pen-
> nies and throwing them into the well. On a return visit to the well, the children
> brushed against a divider causing it to fall on S. S sued E for breaching the duty of
> care. S's husband also sued for consequential loss. The court found that the E
> owed a duty of care to its invitees to prevent damage resulting from unusual dan-
> gers. However, the court concluded that the divider was not an unusual danger or
> even a danger at all as it had existed for years without mishap. The injury to S was

the result of an accident that her own children had caused by unbalancing a fairly sturdy divider. Since the divider was not inherently dangerous, no further duty was owed. Negligence could not be proven because there was no breach of duty on the part of the owner; his conduct had been reasonable.

The Thin Skull Rule

The thin skull rule deems it unnecessary that the full extent of all the damages be reasonably foreseen for liability to attach. A tortfeasor may have anticipated that damages would flow from his or her act, but be astonished at the seemingly unreasonable quantity of them. It is of no matter; the tortfeasor will generally be liable for all of the injuries provided some injury was reasonably foreseeable. In the case of *Dulieu v. White and Sons, [1901] 2 K.B. 669, p. 679*, the Court stated: "If a man is ... negligently injured in his body, it is no answer to the sufferer's claim for damage that he would have suffered less injury, or no injury at all, if he had not had an unusually thin skull or an unusually weak heart."

Res Ipsa Loquitur ("The Thing Speaks for Itself")

If the plaintiff establishes that the injury could not have happened but for some negligence, then the thing speaks for itself, and the defendant has some explaining to do. The legal burden of proving negligence remains with the plaintiff; however, under this doctrine, the evidentiary burden regarding the alleged negligence shifts from the plaintiff to the defendant. The elements of *res ipsa loquitur* are as follows:

1. The injury was caused by misadventure that would not normally occur without negligence.
2. The thing causing the injury was within the absolute control of the defendant.
3. The plaintiff did nothing to provoke the accident.
4. The plaintiff had no prior knowledge of the danger.

If a pedestrian walking past a hotel is struck by a piece of the ventilation system falling from the roof, it might not be possible to prove all the elements of negligence. If there were no witnesses on the roof, he might not be able to prove how the duty of care was breached; however, it is self-evident that some form of negligence must have existed for an object such as a piece of a ventilation system to fall from the roof of a hotel: the thing speaks for itself.

S. v. J.M.I. (1992), 106 Sask. R. 71 (Prov. Ct.)

A family suffered food poisoning after eating a pizza prepared at the defendant's restaurant. The cause was staphylococcus aureus, a common bacterial contaminant in processed meat and an ingredient of the pizza. After examining the application of the doctrine of *res ipsa loquitur*, the court observed:

> In an action for negligence, the plaintiff has the legal burden of proving that the accident was caused by the defendant's negligence. This legal burden of proof does not shift. At the conclusion of the evidence, the court must be satisfied that, on a balance of probabilities, the accident was caused by the negligence of the

defendant. If not, the plaintiff's action fails. However, in the course of the trial, the application of the doctrine of *res ipsa loquitur* may raise a prima facie inference against the defendant, and unless he introduces some evidence to rebut this inference, he will lose.... The defendant can satisfy the evidential burden by introducing a reasonable explanation of the happening of the accident that is consistent with the proven facts, and is as consistent with there being no negligence on his part as with the inference that there was negligence.... The ordinary principles of circumstantial evidence point to the conclusion that the illness arose from the pizza. The doctor's report confirms the symptoms were consistent with eating contaminated processed meat—an ingredient of the Hawaiian pizza. I conclude that the plaintiffs have established a prima facie case on a balance of probabilities. ... The defendant has not introduced a reasonable explanation of the happening of the plaintiffs' illness that is as consistent with there being no negligence.

The plaintiffs in the above case did not have to establish all the details of the negligence. They did establish that they became ill, likely from eating pizza prepared by the defendant, and that they had not brought about their own illness by mishandling the pizza. They established a prima facie case of negligence and, on the basis of *res ipsa loquitur*, shifted the evidentiary burden onto the defendant.

In some cases, the requirement that the plaintiff should have no prior knowledge of the danger assists the defendant. Consider a situation where a plaintiff trips on a step on a return visit. Based on the plaintiff's previous visit to the site, she may be found to have been aware of the danger, in which case *res ipsa loquitur* would not shift the evidentiary burden.

Negligence Per Se

Failure to meet the requirements of a government law may constitute negligence per se. For example, the federal *Hazardous Products Act* restricts some products and controls the importation, manufacture, and sale of others. If the Act is breached, the manufacturer or vendor may be liable on the basis of negligence per se. Further, throughout Canada, there exist stringent pool operation and fire safety codes. A hotel must have an adequate fire alarm system. If the alarm system fails for any reason, the hotel may be liable on the basis that the failure to abide by the fire code was negligence per se.

Hamm Estate v. Wellington Hotels Ltd. (1990), 65 Man. R. (2d) 133 (Q.B.)

The family of a drowned hotel guest sued the hotel for damages. H was swimming alone when he experienced trouble, began thrashing, and sank. A witness summoned help. The pool was so murky that H could not be seen. The first rescuer had to dive in twice to locate H. After he was forced to return to the surface, a second rescuer dived in and pulled H to the surface. H died without regaining consciousness. In their negligence suit, H's family accused the hotel of (1) failing to provide adequate supervision; (2) failing to provide adequate safeguards such as oxygen and other resuscitation equipment; and (3) failing to maintain proper clarity of the water.

It was determined that the hotel was not required to provide a lifeguard (there was a sign to that effect), and that the hotel did nothing to lead H to believe that his swimming would be supervised. Further, the hotel had on its premises all the equipment required under the regulations of Manitoba's *Public Health Act.* Thus there was no liability on the basis of claims (1) and (2). The key issue was the murkiness of the water. In Manitoba, there is a regulation that states, "No person shall operate a swimming pool unless the pool water is of a clarity to permit a black disc 15 cm in diameter on a white background located on the bottom of the pool at its deepest point to be clearly visible from any point on the deck of the pool or to a distance of 9 m away from this disc." Had the water in the swimming pool been as clear as the regulation required, the rescue would have been effected quicker. However, the court found that there was no causal connection between the murkiness of the water and H's death; there was no evidence that the delay had made any material difference in the death. The action was dismissed.

The hotel was fortunate not to be liable. Pool owners would be wise not to count on such a ruling in the future.

Gutek v. Sunshine Village Corp. (1990), 65 D.L.R. (4th) 406 (Alta. Q.B.)

The defendant was successfully sued by a skier who was injured by the defendant's ski lift, which had recently been inspected by a government employee. The court held that with respect to inspections the government has no obligation to a business operator.

This case upholds the proposition that operators cannot rely on government inspections, but must take all reasonable steps themselves to ensure that the goods that are the subject of the inspection are of merchantable quality and reasonably fit for the purpose.

Exceeding Regulatory Minimums

Negligence per se is a justifiable concept because everyone ought to abide by government regulations. However, government regulations set forth only minimum requirements, and they may be insufficient to meet the court-imposed standard of care. The courts point out that a hotel is different from individuals and many other businesses. Hotels deal with many more people than individuals and most businesses, and are therefore often required by the courts to go beyond minimum requirements. Swimming pools are a good example. An innkeeper who operates a pool may decide that a higher degree of care than mere adherence to regulatory minimums is required, and take the appropriate precautions. The key is to meet or exceed the standard of care as it continues to evolve in the courts. The judicial trend throughout this century has been to set ever higher standards of care for ever wider classes of neighbours.

Conditional and Strict Liability

Generally, a finding of liability for negligence is conditional on whether the tortfeasor intended the injury or, if he did not intend the injury, whether he breached a duty of care in an unreasonable way for which he should be faulted. On the other hand, **strict liability** does not rest on intent or fault. It may be imposed regardless of how innocent the tortfeasor was or of how much care was taken to avoid causing the injury. Strict or absolute liability is imposed upon anyone who uses land and buildings in an unnatural way or who is involved in particularly hazardous activities, such as the storage of dynamite, the manufacture of natural gas valves, and the delivery of chlorine. If damage results from the nature or use of inherently dangerous products, liability may follow

Chapter 4 / The Law of Negligence

even though all reasonable precautions were taken and the defendant's conduct was faultless. Manufacturers and vendors of hazardous products have a duty to make their products safe, warn of the dangers, and provide sufficient and understandable information as to the proper handling of the products. If a label does not contain a sufficient warning, an injured party may sue both the vendor and the manufacturer.

Lambert v. Lastoplex Chemicals Ltd. (1972), 25 D.L.R. (3d) 121 (S.C.C.)

The manufacturer of a lacquer sealer placed on the container three warnings that read: "Caution. Inflammable. Keep away from open flame!"; "Keep away from fire, heat, and open-flame lights!"; and "Caution. Inflammable. Do not use near open flame or while smoking." The plaintiff read the warnings before using the sealer on his basement floor. He turned down the thermostat so that his furnace would not start, but did not turn off the pilot light. The pilot light set fire to the fumes, causing an explosion. The Supreme Court of Canada held that the cautions were insufficient because they did not warn against sparks or against leaving pilot lights on near the use area. The court applied the doctrine of strict liability, found for the plaintiff, and stated:

> Where manufactured products are put on the market for ultimate purchase and use by the general public and carry danger (in this case by reason of high inflammability), although put to the use for which they are intended, the manufacturer, knowing of their hazardous nature, has a duty to specify the attendant dangers, which it must be taken to appreciate in a detail not known to the ordinary consumer or user. A general warning, as for example, that the product is inflammable, will not suffice where the likelihood of fire may be increased according to the surroundings in which it may reasonably be expected that the product will be used. The required explicitness of the warning will, of course, vary with the danger likely to be encountered in the ordinary use of the product.

Based on the Supreme Court of Canada ruling in *Rivtow Marine Ltd. v. Washington Iron Works (1940), 40 D.L.R. (3d) 530 (S.C.C.)*, the duty upon manufacturers to warn of dangers may extend to dangers they discover even after the product has been sold and distributed. Hospitality business operators should not rely on manufacturers' warnings, but should exercise the utmost care and caution at all times.

Newfoundland and Labrador, Ontario, Manitoba, Alberta, and British Columbia have passed legislation making dog owners strictly liable for the attacks perpetrated by their dogs. Wild animals kept as pets also tend to attract strict liability.

The liability imposed on servers of alcohol is close to being absolute. The serving establishment may feel that it was not negligent and that its staff did what could be done. In the view of many courts, however, establishments should be held liable for any injuries caused by drunken customers if the staff were in a position to know of a customer's level of drunkenness, yet failed to respond appropriately. The courts appear increasingly to regard the service of alcohol as a hazardous activity, a reasonable stance in light of the fact that more North Americans have died in alcohol-related car accidents than in the Second World War.

The Plaintiff's Own Conduct

The principles discussed above give injured parties a method for determining liability. Each of the doctrines has requirements that the plaintiff must meet. If the requirements are not met, the plaintiff will fail to assign liability to another person. The principles discussed below are invoked by defendants to demonstrate that they are not responsible, in whole or in part, for the injuries. Thus, in addition to the four elements required to establish negligence, there is a fifth element that bears upon whether, and to what extent, the plaintiff will recover damages. In some instances, it may be determined that the fault lies proportionately with several of the parties.

Contributory Negligence

If a plaintiff has been injured but the injury was wholly the result of his own negligence, he will fail in his lawsuit and the case will be dismissed.

Alchimowicz v. City of Windsor et al. (January 6, 1997, Doc. No. 93-GD-23952, Windsor, Quinn J. (Ont. Gen. Div.))

Alchimowicz attended a birthday party for P. The party was held at P's in-laws' home. The host and guests were mostly co-workers at the F restaurant. The plaintiff arrived at approximately 9:00 p.m. and drank heavily until about 1:00 a.m. Some staff of F who worked that night did not arrive until after 1:30 a.m. The guests who arrived late included the defendants, Pa and T. At about 3:00 a.m., P announced that the party was over and that it was time for everyone to leave. A number of guests gathered outside the house and decided to go to a nearby beach. Alchimowicz and the restaurant workers who had arrived late drove to the beach. Alchimowicz was the only person in the group who had been drinking excessively. When the group arrived at the beach, Alchimowicz was asleep in the back of the car. The group left him there and walked to the beach. Before they reached the water, Alchimowicz ran past them, stripped to his shorts, and jumped in. He played in the water for a while before joining the others where they had gathered at the end of a dock. When Alchimowicz had nearly reached the defendants, he knocked a pair of sandals into the water. He said that he would retrieve them. T and Pa told him not to bother, but Alchimowicz climbed onto the railing, ignored a shouted warning, and dived. The water was four feet deep. He slammed into the bottom and was rendered a quadriplegic. His blood alcohol level at the time of the accident was between 250 and 300 mg per 100 mL of blood—a considerable amount.

Alchimowicz brought an action against the city (the owner of the dock), the host, each of the partyers at the beach, and the restaurant they worked for. None of the defendants knew how much Alchimowicz had drunk over the course of the evening. In the reasonable view of the defendants who had been present, he had drunk a controlled amount. Alchimowicz contended that his friends owed him a duty not to take him to such a dangerous place given his state of inebriation. The court determined that no such duty was owed by the defendants. If the duty was owed, Alchimowicz would have had to prove that the defendants knew of the extent of his intoxication. The defendants had not witnessed excessive drinking, had not supplied him with any alcohol, had not made him drive, and had not made him dive. The court also found that P, the host, had not served alcohol to Alchimowicz, and had not been in a position to monitor or control his actions. When Alchimowicz left the party, he was safely in a car and not driving. He was with people who were not drunk and were capable of taking care of him. The court ruled that any duty owed by P terminated when Alchimowicz left P's premises. The court ruled that Alchimowicz's damages and injuries were not caused or contributed to by the acts or omissions of any of the defendants. Alchimowicz was the sole cause of his damages, and his case was dismissed.

Chapter 4 / The Law of Negligence

The plaintiff's own negligence need not be inconsistent with a finding of negligence on the part of the defendant. If there is negligence on the part of both plaintiff and defendant, the damages are apportioned in accordance with the respective liabilities of the parties.

Nieto v. Bison Properties Ltd. (1995), 56 B.C.C.A. 303, 92 W.A.C.S. 303 (C.A.)

On her first visit to the defendant hotel, Nieto was injured while exiting the front door. An unusual step was hidden by the door. A sign warned of the step, but it was very discreet and not at eye level. There were no other indications of the step, such as a handrail or bright paint strip. The court found that the step was an unusual danger and that the sign was insufficient to satisfy the hotel's duty to warn of such dangers. The court awarded Nieto 75 percent damages, but held her 25 percent liable on the ground that she had already used the doorstep on her way into the hotel. Although the plaintiff was negligent in having forgotten the step, the majority of the blame rested with the hotel. The hotel had been warned of the danger and had done little to remedy it.

Voluntary Assumption of Risk

A person who participates in an activity knowing that injury could result is said to have voluntarily assumed a risk—for example, attending a hockey game knowing that being hit by a stray puck is a possibility. To limit liability, tickets to professional hockey games often carry a warning on the back. The defence is not available when the injuries are derived from a breach of a statutory duty. To benefit from the doctrine, the defendant must establish the following:

1. The plaintiff knew about the risk.
2. The plaintiff understood the risk.
3. The plaintiff had a choice to avoid the risk.
4. The plaintiff voluntarily assumed the risk.
5. The defendant was not in breach of a statutory duty from which the injuries flowed.

To be considered a **voluntary assumption of risk**, the plaintiff must understand the nature and accept the degree of the risk. If she could not appreciate the nature or degree of the risk, the defence will fail. Alcohol is known to affect judgment. If the plaintiff was intoxicated at the time it is alleged that she assumed the risk, the courts will find that she did not do so voluntarily in the sense required to sustain the defence.

Buehl Estate v. Polar Star Enterprises Inc. (1989), 72 O.R. (2d) 573 (H.C.J.)

The resort owner warned the plaintiff about a potential danger. The plaintiff later became intoxicated, ignored the warning, and was injured. The court found that the plaintiff had not voluntarily assumed the risk and held the resort partially liable.

S. v. F.S.H.L. (December 13, 1994, Doc. No. 282T/93, Platana J. (Ont. Gen. Div.))

S was a 53-year-old man visiting the M.L. resort. He went to the beach to inquire about a fishing expedition. The employee in charge was on the dock. To reach the dock, S had to walk along two sets of two 2' by 8' planks lying end to end from the shore to the dock. The midpoint of the makeshift bridge rested on a floating log. S reached the dock, but on the return trip he fell, suffering severe back and neck strains. He sued the resort. The resort contended that S had voluntarily assumed the risk because when he ventured out to the dock, the planks and the terrain and water under them were clearly observable. The court did not agree that S should have fully appreciated the danger, found the resort liable, and awarded S $36,000 in general damages.

Beauchamp v. Ayotte et al., [1971] 3 O.R. 21

The plaintiff's husband, Lorenzo Beauchamp, had been drinking all afternoon at the Standard House Hotel owned by Ayotte. Beauchamp's drinking partner, Latour, testified that Beauchamp had not been walking straight. The first waiter testified that he had served Beauchamp four beers and that Beauchamp may have drunk some of Latour's beer. The second waiter, whose shift began at 4:00 p.m., testified that he had served Beauchamp one beer and that Beauchamp had no difficulty walking and did not look drunk when he left at about 5:00 p.m. Beauchamp and Latour went to Beauchamp's house for supper. Mrs. Beauchamp testified that her husband was not intoxicated at that time. Beauchamp and Latour returned to the Standard House Hotel and had two or three more beers. Beauchamp met another friend, Massicotte, and had two more beers in less than fifteen minutes. They then decided to go upstairs to the ladies' beverage room. Beauchamp had trouble with the first step of a steep staircase. After arriving, he ordered one beer. There was an argument and Beauchamp left the room before finishing the beer. On the same staircase he had climbed earlier, he fell, fatally injuring himself. The waiter in the ladies' beverage room testified that because Beauchamp had not looked intoxicated, he had seen no reason not to serve the beer. Another patron confirmed the waiter's testimony that Beauchamp had not been stumbling or weaving.

The staircase was not ideal. One section had treads and risers of uneven dimensions. Another section lacked a handrail. A landing was cramped and had a door that opened inward. The staircase was narrow and had a steepness of 45 degrees compared with an industry standard of 30 degrees. There were no signs warning users of the condition of the staircase. As a patron of the Standard House for many years, Mr. Beauchamp had been quite familiar with the staircase. The employees had been using the staircase for many years, carrying full trays of glasses without a recorded mishap. The court held that the staircase was hazardous even for sober patrons and that it was reasonable to assume that the employees had learned to minimize the dangers of a staircase they used every day. The defendant was found to have breached its duty of care.

It was not alleged in the statement of claim that the defendant had served the deceased to or beyond the point of intoxication. The court found that the deceased had not reached the stage of dangerous intoxication as contemplated by the statute sufficient to make the waiters apprehensive about serving him further. The deceased was a regular customer who had never been known to drink to excess.

Nevertheless, the court did find contributory negligence. Beauchamp had drunk a considerable amount of beer between lunch and the time of the accident. He should have taken extra precautions in negotiating a perilous stairway. The court held that, although it could not be said that the deceased had voluntarily assumed the risk with full knowledge of the risk, he had nevertheless some knowledge of the risk and had failed to exercise sufficient caution. The court held the deceased 40 percent liable and the defendant hotel 60 percent liable.

Harwood v. Westview Holding Ltd. (1991), 61 B.C.L.R. (2d) 115 (C.A.), affirmed (July 13, 1989), Doc. Powell River 86 060 (B.C. Co. Ct.)

A former employee of the establishment fell down a dimly lit staircase that the public had used for years without mishap. The plaintiff was found to have accepted the risk of using the staircase, and the establishment escaped liability.

Campbell v. Spoke Tavern, [1987] O.J. No. 1524 (Q.L.)

The plaintiff, who attempted to re-enter the premises after having been ejected twice, was found to have voluntarily assumed the risk of injury.

The Last Clear Chance Exception

When injuries to plaintiffs are solely the result of their own actions, they have no one to blame but themselves. However, there is an instance in which liability can be assessed against another party even though the plaintiff brought the injuries upon himself. This rule, known as the last clear chance, applies in the following circumstances:

1. The plaintiff is negligent.
2. As a result of the negligence, the plaintiff finds himself in a dangerous position.
3. The defendant is aware of the danger the plaintiff is in.
4. The defendant has a last and clear opportunity to avoid the injury by exercising his own ordinary care, but fails to do so.

At the end of a rainy workday, P, an avid motorcyclist, decides to ride his bike home. En route he has difficulty controlling the vehicle. D, driving behind P, recognizes the problems that P is having. Rather than following at a safe distance, D comments to his wife what a fool P is, and tries to pass him. P crashes to the pavement and D runs over P's leg. P sues. The court finds that P brought about his own injuries by voluntarily assuming the risk of biking on a slick road. For his part, D recognized the danger P was in, but nevertheless decided to pass rather than keep a safe distance and avoid an accident. The last act leading to the tragedy could have been avoided by D; thus, D is liable under the doctrine of last clear chance.

The last clear chance rule is rarely applied. The courts prefer to apply other, less cluttered doctrines such as **contributory negligence** and assumption of risk.

Waivers and Disclaimers

Waivers and disclaimers are contracts in which one party agrees that he understands the risks, agrees to proceed notwithstanding the risks, and (usually) agrees not to hold the other party liable in the event of injury. If the plaintiff knows and understands the limitation of liability in the waiver or disclaimer, then the plaintiff may be precluded from a tort or contractual remedy.

Hotels that offer exercise facilities may require guests to sign a waiver before they are allowed to use the equipment.

A waiver is a separate contract in which one party agrees to give up a right. Disclaimers, which often take the form of warnings placed in documents that are not intended to be signed (e.g., tickets and packaging), are an attempt to impose unilaterally the disclaimer terms upon the other party. Disclaimers may also appear in contracts that are negotiated in detail. In some contracts, the terms of the disclaimer are vital and carefully negotiated terms.

In today's world, the hospitality and recreation fields increasingly overlap. Resorts seeking a competitive edge are adding adventure attractions such as bungee jumping. Many operators feel they can reduce the risk of liability by placing disclaimers on their tickets or by having the participants sign waivers. While there is some truth in this, providing disclaimers and requiring signed waivers usually do not preclude the injured person from bringing a civil action against the operator for gross negligence or fundamental breach of contract.

Over the years, the courts have curtailed the usefulness of waivers. One such curtailment is the duress the person may be under when asked to sign a waiver. A waiver produced just seconds before the start of a white-water rafting trip gives rafters, who are anxious to leave, little time to think about the potentially negative consequences of signing the waiver. Another curtailment is a failure to bring the disclaiming words sufficiently to the patron's attention (e.g., using print that is too fine or by obscuring a sign with plants).

Special Applications of Negligence Law

Vicarious Liability

The doctrine of **vicarious liability** makes employers responsible for the actions of their employees while they are on the job. The employee is an agent of the employer. Given that the employer benefits from the labour of the employees, it is fair that the employer be liable for the torts committed by the employees in the performance of their duties. The doctrine makes it imperative that employers carefully screen job applicants. An employer seeking to hire a bouncer should take precautions to ensure that the candidate does not have a criminal record for assault. Employers should also be on the lookout for any signs of racist or sexist behaviour.

Smart v. McCarty (1980), 33 N.B.R. (2d) 27 (Q.B.)

In this New Brunswick case, a waiter struck a patron after being insulted by the patron. The court recognized that waiters in taverns routinely suffer some abuse by patrons, but held that the waiter was using an improper mode in performing his duty, as opposed to acting outside the scope of his employment. The employer was found vicariously liable.

While employers are vicariously liable for tortious acts, they may also find themselves responsible for a tortious failure to act (nonfeasance) on the part of their employees.

McCarthy v. Pupus Enterprises Ltd., [1996] B.C.J. No. 967 (Q.L.)

McCarthy and two friends entered the defendant nightclub between 12:30 a.m. and 1:00 a.m. They were greeted by John Doe, a heavy-set, leather-clad biker sporting a ponytail and "rings" that could best be described as "brass knuckles." McCarthy shook John Doe's hand, but then apologized, saying that he must have mistaken Mr. Doe for someone else. McCarthy wished him a good evening and went on his way. Several people witnessed John Doe, but no one could (or would) identify him.

McCarthy and his friends had a round of drinks and then lingered by the dance floor. McCarthy and one friend went to the shooter bar while another friend went to the washroom. Suddenly, McCarthy was attacked from behind by Mr. Doe, who struck him repeatedly on his face and head. McCarthy's friend tried to intervene but was grabbed by another biker and thrown out a back door that locked behind him. The bar's disc jockey noticed the commotion and ran down from his booth to intervene. Two more staff members appeared and escorted McCarthy out the front door. McCarthy sustained a fractured nose, cuts needing numerous stitches, two broken teeth, and injuries to his neck and shoulders. The court found that the attack upon McCarthy was unprovoked and held John Doe liable for the damages McCarthy sustained in the assault. The court also had to decide whether a duty was owed to McCarthy by the nightclub. The owners and operators of the club confirmed that they had a policy of checking customers for weapons. One of the owners, who had been managing the club that night, testified that nothing unusual had occurred and that he had not seen any weapons. He also failed to see McCarthy being beaten or the ambulance that took him away. The court ruled that the nightclub had a duty of care to protect its patrons, and had breached its duty. The doorman should have enforced the no-weapons policy. The brass knuckles had been clearly visible to everyone and should never have escaped the attention of someone charged with the responsibility of watching for weapons. The court also found that the club's staff had been slow to intervene. The court assessed general damages at $35,000 and loss of income at $20,000. While the club and Doe were found jointly liable, Doe had disappeared and so the club was obliged to pay the entire award.

This case demonstrates that an employer must answer for the failures of its employees. Under corporate law, a corporation is treated as a separate person from its shareholders, directors, officers, and employees. The risk exposure of the shareholder is thus protected behind the veil of the corporation and his risk exposure is generally limited to the amount of his financial investment. Generally, if a corporation or one of its employees acts negligently, the plaintiff sues the corporation and the employee, but not the shareholders (assuming the shareholder is not also the employee, which is frequently the case in smaller companies).

Shareholder liability was a key question in the following case.

D. v. 5 Ont. Ltd. (Jan. 28, 1991, Gibson J. (Ont. Gen. Div.))

A patron was ejected from a cabaret for indecently assaulting a dancer. The bouncer threw him into the parking lot and beat him severely. Although the patron made no effort to defend himself as he lay on the pavement, the bouncer continued to kick him. The patron suffered permanent brain damage. The court found the cabaret, its shareholders, and the bouncer liable for the damages sustained by the patron. Massive general and special damages were awarded together with punitive damages of $50,000.

Here, the shareholders were directly involved in running the cabaret. In hiring the bouncer, they failed to check his references, which would have revealed that he had used undue force in the past. The court also found that the owners had failed to properly train, instruct, or supervise the bouncer. The award of punitive damages conveys a strong message that such failures will be taken very seriously by the courts. It is incumbent upon corporate officers to ensure that rigorous screening is practised during the hiring process and that employees are properly trained before they come in contact with the public.

The scope for vicarious liability can be quite broad. In *R. v. Levy Bros. Co., [1961] S.C.R. 189*, the Supreme Court of Canada held that an employer may be vicariously liable for the torts of an employee committed in the course of employment even if the employer "did not authorize, or justify, or participate in, or, indeed, know of such misconduct, or even if he forbade the acts, or disapproved of them."

An employer may escape liability if the employee was on a frolic of his own—that is, acting wholly outside the scope of his employment. If an employer has a contract to supply pineapples, and the employer's driver employee negligently runs into a pedestrian while making the delivery, the driver will be personally liable and his employer vicariously liable. If the driver steals his employer's fruit truck, hightails it out of town, and hits someone, the driver will still be liable, but the employer may not be liable if it is shown that the employee was acting wholly outside the context of his employment. The employer may be liable, however, if he knew that the driver had a history of erratic, criminal behaviour.

An owner may also be found vicariously liable for torts committed by a person who has become an agent of the owner, even if only briefly. If a bouncer enlists the assistance of a patron in ejecting another patron, the owner of the bar may be liable if the assisting patron uses excessive force. The assisting patron may be the agent of the owner for only the few seconds or minutes that it takes to evict the offending patron, but those few seconds or minutes are enough to saddle the owner with liability for injuries to the offending patron.

Montgomery v. Black, [1989] B.C.J. No. 1800 (Q.L.)

The plaintiff pinched an employee of a bar. Her boyfriend forcibly evicted the plaintiff from the premises and beat him severely once outside. The staff of the bar knew that the boyfriend had worked as a bouncer at other bars, knew of the circumstances of the eviction, and acquiesced in the boyfriend's conduct. The boyfriend had become an agent of the bar. The court held the bar partially liable for the plaintiff's injuries.

Robertson v. Marleau, [1989] B.C.J. No. 1915 (Q.L.)

In another case, the plaintiff suffered injuries at the hands of another patron who assisted the hotel staff in removing the plaintiff from the premises. The court held that the patron had become the agent of the hotel, but found that no excessive force had been used inside the premises, that the staff were prohibited from leaving the hotel to pursue an eviction, that the assault occurred outside the premises, and that the staff had not participated or acquiesced in the assault. The hotel was not liable.

Failure to correct a problem within a reasonable time frame can be another ground for a finding of vicarious liability. An employer who learns that an employee is incompetent or a danger to other employees and customers, and who does not address the problem in a timely fashion, may be vicariously liable for any torts committed by the employee.

Negligent Misrepresentation

While most tort cases involve an act or a failure to act, a person may also be liable for making a negligent statement. Liability may follow if a person negligently gives advice or information knowing the recipient intends to rely on it, and the recipient does rely on it reasonably to his or her detriment. For many years, liability attached only if the statements were fraudulent (the tort of deceit) or if there was a contractual or fiduciary relationship between the parties; but not if the negligent statement caused only economic loss as opposed to personal or property injury. The British case of *Hedley, Byrne & Co. Ltd. v. Heller & Partners Ltd., [1963] 2 All E.R. 575, [1964] A.C. 465 (H. of L.)* extended tort recovery to economic losses, proximately caused by the negligent statements, suffered by reasonable relyers. A banker gave negligent advice about a business to a potential investor who was not a client of the bank, or even known to the bank at the time the advice was given. In finding liability, the House of Lords stated: "[I]f someone possessed of a special skill undertakes, quite irrespective of contract, to apply that skill for the assistance of another person who relies on such skill, a duty of care arises."

As the following case shows, liability may also follow if there is a failure to give all the necessary information or advice to a person who is reasonably relying on the adviser's skill.

Reibl v. Hughes (1980), 114 D.L.R. (3d) 1 (S.C.C.)

The plaintiff had a partially blocked artery in his neck. The defendant doctor advised him that he had an ongoing 10 percent chance of a stroke if the blockage remained untreated and a good prognosis with surgery. However, the doctor failed to advise him that the surgery had a 4 percent risk of death and a 10 percent risk of stroke during the postoperative recovery period, and that there was no need to rush to operate. Had the plaintiff delayed the surgery for 18 months, his pension would have vested. The surgery was performed properly, but during the recovery period the plaintiff suffered a massive stroke that left him partially paralyzed.

He lost his job and benefits. The Supreme Court of Canada upheld the trial judge's award of $225,000 and stated, "Even if a certain risk is only a mere possibility that ordinarily need not be disclosed, if its occurrence carries serious consequences it should be regarded as a material risk and the patient informed of it."

No liability will flow if the advice-giver makes an appropriate and timely disclaimer to, or receives an informed consent from, his audience as to his accountability or the reliability of the advice. Further, no liability will flow if the recipient of the advice does not rely on the advice or relies unreasonably on it. Professionals such as lawyers, doctors, and accountants are particularly vulnerable to charges of **negligent misrepresentation**, but others, including hospitality industry personnel, are susceptible as well. Suppose a travel agent is informed by a professional singer that if she does not arrive in a distant city by a certain time, she will lose a lucrative contract. If the travel agent carelessly advises her to take a plane that makes several lengthy stopovers and does not land at the singer's destination until after the deadline, he may be liable for the loss of profit flowing from the negligent statement. On the other hand, if the agent is not aware of the urgency, he will be liable only for objectively foreseeable damages.

Passing Off

It is tortious for businesses and persons to pass off their goods or services in such a way that reasonable members of the public would be misled into thinking they were dealing with another business or person who offers the same or similar goods or services. The victim of such conduct may bring a passing-off action (1) for an injunction preventing the continuation of the passing off and (2) for damages. McDonald's is a name that has become synonymous with fast food. A business known as McDonald's Chinese Food would likely be liable for **passing off**. Even though McDonald's does not (at the moment) sell Chinese food, it would not be unreasonable for patrons of McDonald's Chinese Food to assume that they were dining at part of the better-known business chain rather than at a small local business that may not have the same quality controls, price ranges, and services. On the other hand, McDonald's Cruise Ship Propeller Parts and Repair would not give rise to any such false assumptions.

Defamation

It is tortious to publicize false statements about a person that lower his or her existing reputation in the community. Slanders are spoken defamations, while libels are written ones. Publication is essential; thus, there is no tort if the communication is to no one other than the subject of the **defamation**. Defences to an action for defamation include the following:

1. The statement is true.
2. The statement was made with the consent or at the invitation of the plaintiff.
3. The statement enjoys absolute privilege (e.g., statements made by parliamentarians in Parliament or by participants in, and in respect of, judicial and quasi-judicial matters).
4. The statement enjoys a qualified privilege—provided it was made honestly, in good faith, and without malice—in situations where the interest invoked by the utterer is objectively more important than the reputation of the victim.
5. The statement is fair comment—that is, a subjective opinion (as opposed to a statement of fact) on matters or persons of public interest.

If the statement was made maliciously, the protection of some of the above defences may be lost. In a business setting, deliberately or negligently making untrue statements about former employees can expose the maker and his or her employer to an action for defamation.

Injurious Falsehood

The term "defamation" is reserved for the tort of defamation against a person. "**Injurious falsehood**" is the term used for the tort of defaming a business, product, or property. Defamation damages the reputation of the individual; injurious falsehood damages the reputation of someone's business, product, or property. Spreading a false rumour that the owner of a competing eatery is a thief is defamation. Spreading a false rumour that the competing eatery was recently cited for unsanitary premises is injurious falsehood.

Private and Public Nuisances

Private nuisance is a continuing and unreasonable, i.e., tortious, interference with the beneficial use of another person's land. A flashing neon sign outside a bar may constitute a private nuisance to a neighbour, but the noise generated at another neighbour's party may not. A public nuisance is something that affects people in general (e.g., a polluted water supply). A belching smokestack may be either a public nuisance or—to people who demonstrate a greater injury than the general public—a private nuisance.

The need to strike a balance between the rights of individuals and the right of society as a whole to benefit from various activities has led to certain exemptions. For example, airport noise, within reason, is exempted from nuisance liability. Sometimes something that was not previously considered a nuisance may become one as a result of a change in the use of neighbouring land. One Nova Scotia case concerned farmers who had kept pigs without incident long before the suburbs of the town expanded out to the country. The expansion introduced into the area suburbanites who were unsettled by the odour of pig manure emanating from the farm. They brought a claim of nuisance, which was upheld by the court.

Helping People in Distress

Apart from the moral obligation and excluding legal obligations owed to persons in one's care or by reason of being an occupier (see "Occupiers' Liability" below), there is no legal obligation to help people in distress if you have not caused the distress. This is an evolving area of law and bears close watching.

Horsley v. MacLaren (1972), 22 D.L.R. (3d) 545 (S.C.C.)

M owned and operated a cabin cruiser. One of his passengers fell into the water in circumstances that were not the result of any negligence on the part of M. M put the cruiser into reverse in an attempt to rescue the passenger. Another passenger, H, dived overboard in a rescue attempt and was drowned. The Supreme Court of Canada held that M's actions did not constitute negligence and did not induce H to dive overboard.

Manufacture and Service of Food

On the basis of common law and statutes such as the federal *Food and Drugs Act* and provincial sale of goods legislation, a food service operator may be found liable for preparing or serving contaminated food.

Heimler v. Calvert Caterers Ltd. (1974), 4 O.R. (2d) 667 (H.C.J.), affirmed (1975), 8 O.R. (2d) 1 (C.A.)

An employee who was a typhoid carrier was the source of infection for seven people attending a wedding. The judge noted that a very high standard of care is demanded of those in the food-handling business. Section 4 of the *Food and Drugs Act* provides:

4. No person shall sell an article of food that:

    (a) has in or on it any poisonous or harmful substance;

    (b) is unfit for human consumption;

    (c) consists in whole or in part of any filthy, putrid, disgusting, rotten, decomposed animal or vegetable substance;

    (d) is adulterated; or

    (e) was manufactured, prepared, preserved, packaged or stored under unsanitary conditions.

The court ruled that it was immaterial whether or not the owner had taken all reasonable precautions to ensure the good health of employees coming in direct or indirect contact with the public: the *Food and Drugs Act* had created a strict liability for food manufacturers and therefore the defendant was liable.

Sale of Goods Legislation

Tort liability may also flow from provincial sale of goods legislation, which provides for the existence of the following implied warranties:

1. The vendor owns the goods and has the right to sell them.

2. The goods reasonably correspond to their description or samples.

3. The goods are of merchantable quality.

4. The goods are reasonably fit for their intended purpose.

In cases where the parties have forgotten to include a price as a term in their contract, the legislation provides that the price shall be reasonable.

Similar provisions are found in the *Quebec Civil Code*. Sale of goods legislation applies only to written contracts in which goods are exchanged for an amount above a financial threshold depending on the jurisdiction. Included in these contracts are outright sales and conditional sales contracts in which possession of the goods is transferred initially and title is transferred upon final payment. The legislation does not apply to oral contracts, to written contracts falling below the financial threshold, or to exchanges of goods for goods, services for services, money for services, or loan security agreements in which there is no intention to transfer title. The definition of goods excludes real property (but includes crops on the land), intangible property such as stocks and bonds and money itself, and intangible rights such as the right to sue. If a lodge retains an artist to create a wall hanging, the contract is for a service and is not subject to the sale of goods legislation. Once the wall hanging has been delivered, the lodge can resell it pursuant to a contract that is subject to the legislation.

The parties may contract out of the statute; thus, it is permissible for one party to purchase goods that are not of merchantable quality with a view to restoring them to merchantability for use of resale. The legislation simply imports its requirements into any contract of money for goods that is silent on the statutory issues. In the event that there is a contract between the parties and a breach of warranty under the legislation, the aggrieved party has the option of suing for breach of contract or in tort.

C. v. R.H.M. (1974), 14 N.S.R. (2d) 252 (T.D.)

A flour manufacturer was found liable for damages suffered when the plaintiff discovered a partially decomposed mouse in a bag of flour. The rotting mouse had rendered the flour of unmerchantable quality and not reasonably fit for its intended purpose as a cooking ingredient. The court ruled that there was a burden on the defendant to adduce evidence that, during the bagging process, procedures were in place to ensure that mice could not enter the bags.

Occupiers' Liability

Occupiers' Liability Legislation

The following discussion relates to the traditional common law distinctions between invitees, licensees, and trespassers. In many jurisdictions, statutes and some common law decisions have blurred the distinctions. Prince Edward Island, Ontario, Manitoba, Alberta, and British Columbia have passed **occupiers' liability** legislation that erases the distinction between invitees and licensees by extending to licensees the duty of care owed to invitees. Nevertheless, an understanding of the traditional divisions is useful when it comes to assessing and predicting judicial interpretation of the statutes.

Premises are broadly defined to include land, buildings, other structures, water, houseboats and other vessels on water, portable structures used for business or shelter, and planes, trains, automobiles, and other vehicles.

An **occupier** is any person having possession of, control over, or responsibility for the premises. There may be more one occupier, and the definition is not limited to owners or residential and commercial tenants. Control includes determining who may enter upon the premises and regulating what they may do once there. Responsibility includes being responsible for the care and condition of the premises. A person who began not as an occupier may become an occupier upon acquiring or exercising a sufficient degree of possession, control, or responsibility. Occupiers owe a reasonable duty of care to persons who enter upon the premises, or who are merely in the vicinity of the premises, to protect them from any foreseeable dangers arising or emanating from the premises. In determining what is rea-

Invitees, licensees, and trespassers are all owed a duty of care.

sonable, occupiers must bear in mind the diversity of the people who are likely to enter, including the boisterous, the young, the elderly, and the physically challenged. Businesses catering to virtually everyone, such as hotels and restaurants, must be especially attentive in this regard. Failure to abide by regulatory requirements usually results in a finding of liability under negligence per se unless the failure did not cause the injury; however, merely meeting the regulatory requirements will not necessarily save an occupier from a finding of liability.

Duty Owed to Invitees

Under common law, an **invitee** is someone who enters upon the occupier's premises while having with the occupier a common interest of mutual advantage, usually but not always financial. Hotel guests, restaurant patrons, store customers, moviegoers, employees, deliverers, maintenance personnel, students on campus, and hospital patients are all examples of invitees. An innkeeper's invitees include not only those who rent the rooms but also the visitors of the invitees. The invitees of a restaurant or bar include not only the patrons who purchase meals and beverages but also the friends who accompany them. Sometimes a distinction is drawn between a contractual entrant (i.e., a person who is on the premises pursuant to a contract, such as a hotel guest) and other invitees whose financial contribution to the occupier is discretionary (e.g., shoppers). The distinction is rather artificial. Whether they are hotel guests or browsers in a mall, invitees are persons who have entered upon the occupier's premises with intentions of mutual benefit.

The occupier has a duty to invitees to inspect the premises for dangerous conditions and to exercise reasonable care to prevent damage arising from them. The occupier is also liable to an invitee for any damages from unusual dangers that the occupier knew or ought to have known about. Under common law, an occupier owes invitees a duty

1. not to willfully create a danger or wantonly injure the invitee;

2. to remove or warn the invitee of existing or unusual dangers that the occupier is aware of; and

3. to remove or warn the invitee of existing or unusual dangers that the occupier ought to have been aware of.

B. v. T & C Inn Ltd. (April 10, 1996, Doc. No. 131, Schwartz J. (Nfld. S.C. Trial Div.))

The plaintiff (B), her husband, and son were customers of the T & C lounge one winter afternoon. They had one cocktail each and after about half an hour left by the same door they had entered. On the way out, B fell on the steps and broke her wrist. She brought an action against the lounge for damages. On the day of the accident, the parking lot was covered in snow. The owner of the lounge testified that a man had been hired to clear the snow after every snowfall. The maintenance man was not called as a witness, but the owner testified that he had looked at the steps immediately after the accident and had noted that they did not appear slippery. The court found B to be an invitee and considered four questions in determining liability:

1. Was there an unusual danger?

2. If so, was it one which the defendant knew about or ought to have known about?

3. If so, did the defendant use reasonable care to prevent damages arising from the unusual danger?

4. Did the plaintiff take reasonable care to ensure her own safety?

The word "unusual" in this context means "not usually found in these circumstances," not "unexpected." The court found that ice and snow are not unusual winter conditions in Canada and that denizens are expected to exercise appropriate care to ensure their own safety. The court found that B was familiar with the usual weather conditions in the area and that she was aware of the conditions around the entrance to the lounge. B had had no difficulty entering the lounge and there was no evidence to suggest that the conditions had changed during her stay. Other witnesses, including B's husband and son, testified that there had been no unusual build-up of ice or snow. The court concluded that the conditions at the time of the fall were not unusual, that B was fully aware of them, and that the management of the lounge had exercised reasonable care.

This case illustrates some limits on the duty an occupier owes an invitee. The defendant was aware of its responsibilities concerning the snow and steps, and was found to have met them in the circumstances. The reader may compare this case to *Nieto v. Bison Properties Ltd., supra*. Though the discrepancy may seem puzzling, it may be helpful to know that, in the paraphrase of one British law lord, it is possible, except in the plainest of cases, for a judge to decide the case on either side of the issue with reasonable legal justification. The decisions as to whether there was contributory negligence, a last clear chance, or comparative negligence in a given case is often reduced to one thing: the judge's personal judgment. In litigation, the addition or subtraction of just one factor (among many) can radically change the outcome of the case. The law can be used to support the conclusion that is derived from the finding of fact.

Duty Owed to Licensees

Under common law, a licensee is someone who is on the premises with the express or implied permission of the occupier, but who, unlike the invitee, is not necessarily on the premises for reasons in common with the occupier. A job applicant is considered a licensee. The applicant is not yet a source of revenue either as an employee or as a consumer, but is nevertheless on the premises with the implied permission of the manager or owner. Under common law, an occupier owes licensees a duty:

1. not to willfully create a danger or wantonly injure the licensee; and
2. to remove or warn the licensee of existing dangers that the occupier is aware of.

The major difference between the duties owed to an invitee and owed to a licensee is that, for the former, the inviter/innkeeper must inspect for and warn of potential dangers, not just existing ones. The duty of inspection is not owed to a licensee, as the following example illustrates. A job applicant plans to pick up an application form at the front desk of a hotel. The main lobby floor is being washed, and the innkeeper has roped off the area and placed a sign at the entrance to warn of the danger. In so doing, the innkeeper has met the obligation to a licensee. If, unbeknownst to the innkeeper, the floor in the lobby is still slippery, the innkeeper is under no obligation to a licensee to inspect. Such a duty is, however, owed to an invitee.

Duty Owed to Trespassers

Under common law, a trespasser is someone who is on the premises without any permission, express or implied, of the owner. Trespassers are not expressly afforded the duty of care in the occupiers' liability legislation; thus, the common law likely still has application. Nevertheless, the standard of care owed to trespassers has risen in modern times. Under common law, an occupier owes trespassers a duty:

1. not to willfully create a danger or wantonly injure the trespasser.

The duty owed to trespassers was the key issue in a case involving a shop owner in Miami whose store was repeatedly burgled. After alarms and window bars were installed, the intruders entered through roofing vents. The owner placed an electrical plate below the vents. One day, a trespasser dropped from the ceiling, landed on the plate, and was electrocuted. The plate was held to be too extreme a measure, amounting to a willful or wanton injury to the trespassing intruder, and the shopkeeper was found guilty of criminal negligence.

In *Veinot v. Kerr-Addison Mines Ltd., [1975] 2 S.C.R. 311*, the Supreme Court extended the common law by requiring occupiers to treat trespassers with common humanity if the occupier had actual knowledge of the trespasser or knew of facts that would make it likely that trespassers would enter the premises. Thus, occupiers are liable to trespassers for reasonably foreseeable injuries (1) if they know that their premises are being, or will be, used as a passage to another destination; or (2) if their premises have features that may allure children.

Many rural property and resort owners have little affection for snowmobilers who tear across their fields with no regard for others. They may be tempted to string wires four feet above the ground across a well-travelled route. In the middle of winter, the wire would be at the right height to injure a snowmobiler. A court would find such a trap to be a tortiously extreme method of curbing trespassers. Indeed, it would likely result in a charge of criminal negligence.

Prevention of Negligence Claims

The costs of liability for negligence include higher legal and insurance costs, lower revenues, damaged goodwill, fewer patrons, loss of business opportunities, problems with landlords or tenants, and unwanted governmental intervention such as regulatory impediments or criminal sanctions. Fortunately, there are many steps that can be taken to reduce liability. As with virtually all legal matters, prevention is the best policy. While acting in accordance with law and commonsense cannot guarantee freedom from liability, acting on a contrary basis is almost certain to attract it. Wise hospitality owners and managers fashion, implement, and enforce sensible standard operating procedures, and require and encourage their staff to follow them. In addition, they perform regular inspections, exercise constant vigilance, anticipate problems, seek good advice, make adjustments as needed, and obtain insurance just in case.

Risk cannot be eliminated, but it can be reduced. Proven methods of risk reduction include standard operating procedures, staff training, regulatory adherence, record keeping, waivers and disclaimers, releases, and insurance. If an accident does occur, it is crucial to preserve the scene so that a comprehensive and accurate investigation may be conducted. The scene should be disturbed only insofar as may be necessary to prevent further injury or death. Methods of risk reduction are explored in greater depth in Part 2 (Liability and Risk in the Hospitality Industry) and Chapter 12 (Regulatory Requirements).

Standard Operating Procedures

Standard operating procedures (STOPS) are vital to businesses. In their absence, there is too much uncertainty and blurring of responsibility, to the detriment of a business.

Templates are available from a number of sources. For example, liquor licence boards publish booklets covering a variety of concerns such as pricing the drinks, dealing with intoxicated patrons, and satisfying the regulatory requirements.

Staff Training

STOPS are effective only if they are followed. Thanks to vicarious liability, an owner cannot delegate ultimate responsibility to anyone. Staff and hands-on owners should receive adequate training. Once staff are trained, their skills should be upgraded or at least maintained. Training programs run by regulatory bodies or the hospitality industry itself are available across Canada. In-house training from the veterans of a business is also invaluable.

Regulatory Adherence

It can sometimes appear that government laws and regulations are a meddlesome hindrance to entrepreneurial activity, but they are there for a reason and have usually been considered over a considerable period of time by well-intentioned and competent people. The courts have underscored this by developing the theory of negligence per se. The countless regulations businesses must follow pertain to matters as diverse as specifications for load-bearing walls, swimming pool chemicals, workers' compensation programs, airplane embarkation rules, fees and taxation. Knowing and abiding by the laws and regulations is good entrepreneurship.

Record Keeping

The keeping of some business records is a legal requirement. Although they are not mandated by law, records of activity in a business are very useful should claims later be made. Pursuant to statutes of limitation, some claims may be brought years after the events in question.

Waivers and Disclaimers

As discussed earlier in the chapter, waivers and disclaimers are attempts to limit liability by having the patron agree to or accept their terms. The tendency of the courts to curtail their application limits their utility, but this does not mean they should not be employed. Waivers and disclaimers that are clearly worded and fairly communicated will offer stronger resistance to legal challenges than their poorly communicated counterparts.

Releases

Releases are signed after the injury has arisen and are part of a settlement. They are used to prevent the claimant from accepting a settlement and then reviving the claim or bringing a fresh one based on the same facts.

Insurance

When all else fails, adequate insurance can cushion the blow and save the business from ruin. A detailed discussion of insurance is provided in Chapter 13.

Summary

Every year, thousands of hospitality businesses face lawsuits of varying degrees of legitimacy. The principles of negligence are used to determine and apportion liability. The party advancing the principle has the burden of proving, on a balance of probabilities, the elements relied upon. Hospitality operators should review periodically the duties arising by the nature of their business, property, and guests, and determine how best to meet those duties. The task may be complicated, especially given the sometimes inconsistent findings of the courts. For example, some courts have found rate-paying guests to be invitees and social guests to be licensees, while other courts have found all guests to be invitees. The lines are blurry (consider a company party with nonemployee spouses in attendance), and much depends on the facts of each case. Different duties are owed to different people depending on their legal status. Invitees are owed higher duties of care, while licensees and trespassers are owed successively lower duties. A still higher degree of care is owed to an invitee who is also a child.

Discussion Questions

1. What are the four elements of negligence?

2. What do you think is the most difficult element to prove? Why?

3. Using two examples relating to the hospitality or travel industries, describe how *res ipsa loquitur* might assist a plaintiff in proving negligence.

4. In defending a claim for negligence, what might a defendant assert with respect to the plaintiff's own behaviour? How might a plaintiff respond to the assertion?

5. Discuss how the age of a person can be a contributing factor to liability.

6. If a person goes out for a night on the town, consumes a vast amount of alcohol, and has an accident, is he or she guilty of voluntary assumption of risk? Why or why not?

7. Following an automobile accident caused by an intoxicated driver, who else other than the driver might the innocent, injured party look to for redress?

8. If a plaintiff is attempting to establish the liability of a defendant by using the doctrine of vicarious liability, what defences might the defendant use?

PART
TWO

Liability and Risk in the Hospitality Industry

Chapter Five

The Accommodation Sector

Learning Outcomes

1. Assess the liability and impact of negligence on the accommodation sector.

2. Analyze an accommodation case study and identify culpability under the law of torts.

3. Demonstrate how fire and other emergency procedures are implemented.

4. Create the standard operating procedures that would reduce the chance of culpability for a hospitality property from the liabilities associated with negligence.

Introduction

Chapter 4 explored the general principles of negligence law. Part 2 examines negligence law in relation to the hospitality industry, and how hospitality businesses can take steps to avoid or at least minimize conduct and situations for which they could be found liable for negligence. While Part 2 has been organized into three sections—accommodation, food, and alcohol—there is a great deal of overlap. The word "establishment" will be used to refer to all accommodation and food- and alcohol-service businesses.

It might appear from the previous chapter that as soon as a person becomes a guest or customer of a hospitality business, he or she enjoys an immediate blanket insurance policy such that the business will be liable for virtually any mishap. This is not quite the case, however. Hospitality businesses are not perfect insurers of guests or customers, but certainly owe them a wide-ranging duty of care, and, in some circumstances, the liability is strict.

Much of the law applicable to negligence in the accommodation sector is derived from **occupiers' liability** cases. The best way to protect a business from liability is to fulfill the duties and obligations owed by an occupier to invitees, licensees, and even trespassers. Proper training of staff, proper maintenance and regular inspections of the physical plant, commonsense, and good legal and practical advice are the keys to minimizing liability dangers. Daily or regular inspections, which should be part of standard operating procedures, help to ensure that the premises are safe, that staff members are performing their jobs properly, and that the duties owed to the public are being met. Job descriptions should include the obligation to follow the standard operating procedures and to make the relevant inspections.

Maintenance

Employees and Contractors

The hospitality industry employs a vast number of cleaners and maintenance workers. Many businesses have on staff, or ready access to, a person who is responsible for the upkeep and maintenance of the entire property, including the equipment and building systems. In smaller establishments particularly, the owner may fill this role. While many general maintenance workers are quite proficient in a wide variety of tasks including painting and basic repairs, they may lack the skills to maintain or repair sophisticated pieces of equipment and technological systems. Almost any maintenance person with basic training can clear a blocked drain. Greater expertise is required to repair an elevator or calibrate a hot-water booster. Some work can be undertaken only by specially trained and licensed workers such as electricians. The qualifications, training, and skills of both in-house and contracted maintenance personnel should be checked and should withstand scrutiny in a court of law. Some work is subject to a building permit and inspections by a municipal or provincial inspector. Failure to abide by the municipal and provincial regulations can lead to increased tort liability if the work is defective.

Maintenance Records

Ongoing maintenance records for the building, equipment, and mechanical systems such as elevators, heating, and fire alarms should be kept. The records will show the responsible efforts of management to keep everything in excellent running order, and may help to establish that a failure occurred shortly after an outside contractor made a repair. A third-party claim against the contractor may prevent the hospitality business from incurring a large insurance headache. When using outside contractors, innkeepers should require that both the work and the maintenance schedule be recorded in writing by the contractor and given to the innkeeper.

General Maintenance

The only constant is change. No sooner is a physical asset built or installed than it begins to deteriorate. The variable is the rate of deterioration, which in turn varies according to the quality of the material, the workmanship, the maintenance, and the degree of use and exposure to which the asset is subjected. The severe weather changes in Canada's four seasons present serious challenges to the physical plant, increasing the need for continuous maintenance and repair, especially for surfaces exposed to the elements.

The House and Grounds

Hotels are divided into the "front of the house" and the "back of the house." These terms do not mean that the **hotel** is physically divided into two sections, front and back; rather, the "front" and "back" denote the public and nonpublic areas of the hotel. These areas are not wholly separate but are intertwined like the circulatory and lymphatic systems of the body, with some crossover. The back of the house includes the kitchen, housekeeping closets, freight elevators, service stairwells, loading docks, offices, boiler rooms, electrical rooms, and service tunnels. The front of the house includes fully public areas, semi-public areas, and guest areas.

Fully public areas include the sidewalks, parking lots, entrances, lobbies, stairwells, retail areas, mezzanines, display corridors, restaurants, bars, and banquet halls. The public areas of a hotel handle all the guests of the hotel in addition to all the people who frequent the hotel or its retail areas for any other reason. Proprietors must exercise all due reasonable care to save the public, including **nonguests**, from harm arising from negligence.

Semi-public areas include swimming pools, fitness rooms, and rooftop running tracks. Such areas are normally accessible only to registered guests, the guests of registered guests, and other invitees and licensees; however, other people often gain access to semi-public areas, usually with the consent, tacit or express, of the innkeeper.

Guest areas include the guest rooms, guest floor hallways, ice and vending rooms, executive lounges, and other rooms reserved for the use of the guests.

The Grounds

The grounds of any hotel or resort, including the lawns, tennis courts, paths, and municipal sidewalks, must always be safe for use by the guests. Any part of the grounds that are being repaired or that are in need of repair should be effectively closed to the public—and perhaps even to the staff—until the repairs are completed. Informal walkways or shortcuts should be inspected for dangers. Railroad ties or gardening fences that surround planted areas or trees might be difficult to see and present a risk to guests taking shortcuts from the parking lot to the hotel. It is not enough for the innkeeper to provide well-marked and well-lit walkways. He or she must also ensure that access to other areas is barred or that the other areas are also safe.

Sidewalks

Sidewalks between the building and the street are typically owned by the municipality, which has the responsibility to repair and maintain them. The responsibility for keeping the sidewalks safe from the temporary effects of the weather usually lies with the building owner. Owners are required by legislation and bylaws to shovel snow off the sidewalk, and to spread sand or salt on icy surfaces. Failure to do so can leave the owner, not the municipality, liable for damages.

Steps and Ramps

The steps and ramps leading from the sidewalk to the entrance are owned by the business. As with parking lots, the maintenance and weather challenges are the responsibility of the owner. Steps should be marked with a sign or obvious change of colour or material, and feature a sturdy handrail. Sudden changes in elevation should be clearly marked. Regular inspections are essential. Clear step markings deteriorate over a winter due to shovelling, scraping, and ice-removal chemicals. *Nieto v. Bison Properties Ltd. (1995), 56 B.C.C.A. 303, 92 W.A.C.S. 303 (C.A.), supra* is a case in point. In order to assist persons who use wheelchairs or who otherwise find steps challenging, an increasing number of owners are building ramps. Railings and automatic doors are also very useful. Given the slant, it is important to ensure that they do not become ski slopes, regardless of the season.

Outdoor Staircases

Outdoor staircases must be in top condition, clearly visible, well lit with light-sensitive lights, and devoid of snow, ice, and debris. Regular inspections are essential.

Harwood v. Westview Holding Ltd. (1991), 61 B.C.L.R. (2d) 115 (C.A.), affirmed (July 13, 1989), Doc. Powell River 86060 (B.C. Co. Ct.)

H suffered an ankle injury when she fell at the foot of an outside staircase beside a hotel. The poorly lit staircase went down a steep slope; at the base was a concrete slab. H had previously worked at the hotel and had used the staircase without incident at least 25 times. The staircase had been used extensively by the public for more than eight years without incident. The trial judge found that H had failed to take proper care to ensure her own safety. Her action and subsequent appeal were dismissed. Neither the accident-free history of the staircase nor the defendant's ignorance of the hazard was necessarily a determining factor. However, there was ample evidence to support the trial judge's conclusion that H had accepted the risk.

Ouelette v. Kinsmen Club of Ladysmith (March 20, 1990), Doc. No. V00885 (B.C.C.A.), affirming (October 18, 1988), Doc. No. Nanaimo CC7451 (B.C.S.C.)

Upon leaving the club, O, who weighed about 225 pounds, descended wooden stairs that were 10 feet wide with treads nailed across three stringers. One of the boards broke, causing her to fall. At trial, the evidence established that the stairs were built by volunteer labour with donated lumber and did not conform to the building code that specified one stringer for every two feet of span. The evidence also established that the accident would not have happened had the building code been followed. The club's appeal was dismissed. The trial judge did not apply too high a standard; he did not err in finding that the club had acted imprudently in not following the building code.

Outdoor Lighting

All walkways that the guest should or might use should be well lit, preferably with light sensors so that the lights will be on during dark periods in the daytime.

Parking Lots and Garages

Hotels have a duty to protect guests and the public. Parking areas should:

1. be well lit, in good repair, and demarked from the neighbourhood, perhaps by fences;

2. be safe and secure and feature staff who can escort guests to and from their cars;

3. be free of bushes, pillars, and alcoves that can hide attackers;

4. be located near the hotel entrance, particularly for guests, such as those with disabilities, who may require proximity to the door;

5. feature notices advising of emergency phones and surveillance cameras; and

6. feature notices that trespassers and miscreants will be prosecuted.

Parking garages suffer more salt damage than outdoor lots because the air temperature inside is usually above freezing, causing the snow and ice to melt and mix more readily with the salt thereby increasing the rate of corrosive oxidation. Stale air should be adequately vented. If the hotel offers valet parking, the valets should be trustworthy, preferably bonded, and hold valid driver's licences. The insurance policy should cover malfeasance by a valet.

Outdoor Recreation Areas

Many hotels and resorts offer tennis courts, lawn bowling, golf courses, and so on. The greater the grassy area, the more likely the groundhog damage. Groundhog holes can cause painful injuries. Tennis court surfaces are often tarmac. Such surfaces must be maintained like parking lots. Tennis courts should be surrounded by fences high enough to stop stray tennis balls from hitting passersby. Balls hit high over the fence are less likely to cause much damage. The net winch should be kept in good condition. A spinning handle can break a wrist.

Garbage and Storage Areas

Dumpsters should have sturdy sides and lids to keep out children and wild animals. Sheds should have secure windows and locks.

Fully Public Areas

Entrances

Entrances create a first and lasting impression on customers. Whether the establishment is a grand hotel or a greasy spoon, entrances should be as safe, clean, and attractive as possible.

The Canadian climate requires that doors be substantial enough to keep out sometimes very inclement weather. A wide variety of doors are available. The clear glass door, a staple of the industry, is attractive in most settings. The door allows a person on one side to see if someone else is approaching from the other, and thus prevents collisions from being instigated by either party. The major drawback to this style of door is that, if the door is kept clean, it becomes invisible to users (particularly distracted ones). Like birds smashing into glass towers, people have been known to crash into—and sometimes through—clear glass doors. One solution to the problem is to place markings on the glass, such as notice stickers or horizontal bars with reflective strips. Harvey's, the Canadian fast-food chain, places across the width of all glass, at about waist level, a strip of orange tape. The orange tape, which is colour-coordinated with the chain's logo, makes the glass noticeable to customers. One of the first things the Sheraton Hotel chain does when it takes on a franchisee is to have the operator place stickers of the company logo on all doors to the hotel. In addition to warning of the presence of the glass doors, the stickers serve as a constant reminder of the name of the chain. If logos or stickers are not available, a push bar can be used. The bars can also complement the door cosmetically. The best solution is to use a combination of techniques.

Brennan v. Sahara Nights Restaurant Ltd. (1986), 52 Sask. R. 48 (Q.B.)

On exiting the defendant's premises while looking backward over his shoulder, the plaintiff pushed the glass portion rather than the handle of the door. The glass broke, causing him to sustain a cut on the wrist. The court held that the plaintiff, by not looking where he was going, had failed to exercise reasonable care to ensure his own safety.

Pajot v. Commonwealth Holiday Inns of Canada Ltd. (1978), 20 O.R. (2d) 76 (H.C.), 86 D.L.R. (3d) 729 (H.C.)

The plaintiff guest was injured when he fell through a poorly marked glass door. The court found that the plaintiff had exercised reasonable care, but that the hotel had failed to exercise reasonable care to prevent injuries to an invitee from an unusual danger of which it was, or ought to have been, aware. There was an implied warranty that the premises were as safe as the exercise of reasonable care and skill could make them.

Revolving doors reduce expenses by acting as a seal. The "wings" of the revolving door seal in the heated or air-conditioned hotel air and seal out the winter cold or summer heat. Children are sometimes tempted to play in a revolving door, causing it to rotate at high speed. A person who absent-mindedly enters the spinning door can be hit with enough force to cause injury. Revolving doors should be supervised. Innkeepers should also be on the lookout for large groups attempting to use the door at the same time. Unfortunate crushes and pinches can occur. In one case, a large crowd that had attended a Notre Dame football game attempted to use a hotel's revolving door. The result was injuries to other users. The hotel was found liable by the court for failing to monitor and control the situation.

Automatic doors are a convenience; however, they are often quite heavy. They tend to operate with minimal maintenance; thus, it is possible not to notice minute changes in their force and speed. Continuous small changes over time might amount to a large and dangerous change. The speed and force with which automatic doors open or close should be monitored regularly. The inspection should include a measurement of the time it takes for the door to swing open and the force with which the door closes. If the guests include a significant number of seniors or children, the door should be adjusted to a suitable speed setting.

Double doors should be far enough apart so that the operation of one of the doors will not interfere with the operation of the other.

Most commercial doors are constructed of metal hardware and glass components. Under normal conditions, the hardware components are long-lasting, but they should be checked for wear, stress, and, if applicable, lubrication. Even strengthened glass can be damaged through collisions with luggage and repeated use. The glass in doors should be checked to ensure that it is secure, and any damaged glass should be replaced immediately. A heavy pane that is damaged but left in service is a hazard. As glass ages, it becomes brittle; thus, any glass that shows signs of stress should be replaced without delay.

Lobbies and Vestibules

Of the interior public areas, hotel lobbies and restaurant vestibules handle the greatest amount of traffic and are particularly vulnerable to Canadian weather conditions. This is particularly hard on floor materials, leading to premature deterioration and dirty, slippery surfaces. The selection of the lobby floor covering can do much to increase or reduce the risk of liability. A hard, smooth surface such as wood, vinyl, or marble does not absorb wet, sloppy messes. Slippery lobby floors present a substantial risk, and require almost continuous attention from staff during bad weather. Carpeting is a popular alternative because it is less slippery. The drawback is that carpets are harder to clean than a hard-surface floor. They can become extremely soiled, necessitating regular deep cleaning. One solution is to place over the heavy-traffic areas runners that can be replaced and cleaned.

Whenever floors are being cleaned or maintained, barriers should be placed around the area. Substandard cleaning materials or practices and a failure to inspect may also lead to liability. Proper products should be used, and the work should be inspected before the barriers are removed. If the floor is excessively polished or not quite dry, serious falls can result. Electrical cords running to or from an outlet outside the barrier may become frayed and mix with water elsewhere on the floor, giving new meaning to the phrase "tripping the light fantastic." Cords should be secured to the floor with tape, and warning signs should be posted.

Maintenance equipment and materials may be an attraction to children and should never be unattended. Proper storage is essential. Luggage and items that are left on the floor by staff, guests, and others also present potential risks. Constant vigilance is required. Nothing should block the approaches to doorways, staircases, escalators, and elevators.

Because a lobby is such a high-traffic area, it is important to keep it dry, clean, and attractive.

Stairwells and Mezzanines

Falls on staircases and mezzanines are potentially more deadly than a fall on a floor. Staircase carpet rods may become loose and increase the chance of someone hooking a heel and falling. Loose threads, tears, and separated seams also greatly increase the chances of an accident. Stairwells must conform to the building code even after years of use. Worn steps must be replaced or resurfaced. Banisters should be inspected regularly to ensure that they have not become loose. When maintenance is being performed, barriers and signs should be erected.

Crowd Control

The layout of the public areas and the materials employed in their decoration must be examined for crowd-control and security purposes. The hotel has to anticipate the potential size of the crowds that may gather as well as other special situations that may arise.

Public Elevators

In *Blackhawk Hotel v. Bonfoey, 227 F. (2d) 232 (Minn., 1955)*, the court ruled that hotels have a "nondelegable duty when it comes to elevators." This means that the owner's duties to maintain elevators and to exercise reasonable care cannot be delegated to any other person. Elevators present two major concerns: (1) whether they are mechanically sound; and (2) whether they are stopping properly, flush with the floor of destination. The latter concern is the more prevalent. Elevators have an excellent record for mechanical soundness.

A valid provincial **licence** is required by those wishing to own and operate an elevator. The licence must be posted inside the elevator. Elevators should be maintained and repaired only by licensed personnel. All personnel operating operator-assisted elevators should be properly trained in the use of the machine and in emergency procedures.

> **Sawler v. Franklyn Enterprises Ltd. (1992), 117 N.S.R. (2d) 316, 324 A.P.R. 316 (T.D.)**
>
> P was employed by the defendant hotel's tenant. The elevators in the hotel were installed by O. They were serviced twice a month and repaired as required. When P entered the elevator, a steel plate weighing nineteen ounces fell off the floor indicator located above the door, injuring her on the head and shoulders. She sued both the hotel and O for damages. The court dismissed the action against the hotel and found O solely liable, partly on the basis of *res ipsa loquitur*. The hotel was not liable because its employees had not worked on or near the elevator. O was liable because it had control over the maintenance of the elevator, and had been negligent in failing to re-install the indicator plate properly after it was removed during a maintenance visit. The danger posed by an improperly installed indicator plate was an unusual danger known to O.

All elevators have weight restrictions. As with other public areas, crowd control is important. Alert supervision or warning bells may be required to enforce the weight restrictions.

If the cable snaps, most elevators have brakes to slow and halt the fall. Unless there is no choice, passengers and staff should not attempt to open the door of an elevator that is stuck between floors. Forcing open the door can trigger further movement, with disastrous consequences. The repair company or the fire department should be called. If the brakes fail, there is nothing to be gained by jumping with the expectation that you will be in midair when the elevator hits bottom. You will still be travelling at the rate of the fall, and will slam into the floor a millisecond later at that speed. The best course of action is to lie flat so that the force of the impact will be spread as evenly over your body as possible.

Indoor Lighting

Proper lighting reduces negligence claims. Halls and rooms that are purposely left dark to create atmosphere increase the risk to guests who may not see steps, changes in floor coverings, or obstacles placed in the aisles. In rooms such as bars and lounges, discrete floor-level lighting and lighting around danger zones such as doorways should be installed. As the population ages, proper lighting will increase in importance.

Black Lion Inn Ltd. v. Johnson (April 18, 1991), Doc. No. CA010634 (B.C.C.A.)

The plaintiff, aged 71, entered the defendant pub. She safely negotiated the one step leading up to a booth and sat down. When she rose to leave a few moments later, she fell and injured herself when she failed to negotiate the step. The trial judge found the defendant 75 percent at fault. The defendant's appeal was dismissed. The subdued lighting in the pub and the proximity of the step to the seat created an unusual hazard that imposed a duty on the defendant to alert patrons of the change in floor level.

Furniture

All furniture should be in good condition and regularly inspected for such hazards as loose legs or fasteners. Furniture in poor condition should be immediately removed for repair. Defective chairs placed to the side of the room have a way of finding their way back into circulation. The furniture must be able to withstand use by large guests, and be solid or tethered enough to be safe for children. Some pieces of furniture are more dangerous than others because of their design. Even sober guests are more likely to fall off bar stools than sofas. Cribs should meet government safety standards, and staff should be trained in their proper assembly.

Howells v. Southland Canada, Inc. (February 28, 1995), Doc. New Westminster S013266 (B.C.S.C.)

H bought a cup of coffee and decided to drink it in the store at one of the tables provided. As he sat down, the plastic chair broke, injuring him. He sued the owner and operator of the store for damages. The action was dismissed. Although the defendant owed a common law duty to use reasonable care, there was no evidence in this case that the chairs were inherently unsafe, and the reason the chair broke could not be established. H could not rely on the *res ipsa loquitur* doctrine because there was a possible explanation for the accident that did not involve negligence on the part of the defendant.

Wall Hangings

Wall hangings such as mirrors, pictures, and tapestries are often misleadingly heavy. The hardware used to hang them should be carefully chosen to ensure that it can easily hold the weight of the hanging. The hanging should be secure enough to withstand more than the occasional brush against it. Special framing and hardware may be needed to hold the item in place. The plaster and drywall used in commercial settings are no more solid than those used in homes; therefore, heavy objects may pull away from the wall, sending the object down onto passersby. If a hanging has come loose, new holes may be needed to hang it securely the second time. Care should be exercised when hanging chandeliers and other fixtures from the ceiling. To reduce the risk of injury caused by a falling object, the cleaning of a chandelier should be done only when the area beneath it is closed to traffic.

Retail Shops

Many hotels offer retail outlets for the convenience of guests and to attract other customers who are not staying in the hotel. The outlets are typically clothing boutiques, hair salons, travel agencies, ticket agencies, lottery booths, automatic tellers, or therapeutic massage centres. The hotels do not generally own the retail outlets, but lease floor space to them. The hotel as landlord (lessor) should enter into a proper commercial lease with the outlet setting forth the terms that the tenant (lessee) must follow. For example, although the hotel will have its own insurance, the lessee should have its own insurance as well. The lease should also provide that, should the insurance lapse, the landlord may pay the premiums and add them to the rent, and that failure to maintain the insurance constitutes an act of default under the lease, entitling the landlord to terminate the lease. Evicting tenants is unpleasant. Proper screening of tenants and sound leases minimize such difficulties. The lease should also limit the commercial activities of, and the equipment used by, the lessees, thereby preventing them from subsequently offering services that would increase the danger to the hotel or place the hotel in possible breach of an exclusive-use provision given to another lessee.

Semi-Public Areas

Dining Rooms, Bars, and Banquet Halls

Some eating and drinking areas such as semi-private executive lounges are open only to the executive-level guests and their guests and not to the general public. Other areas such as ground-floor dining rooms and bars welcome everyone. Eating and drinking areas are subject to much traffic and should be in top condition at all times. The same concerns for floor coverings discussed with respect to lobbies apply with equal force to eating and drinking areas. These areas receive plenty of guest and staff traffic. Those who have ever been within earshot of a collision between a busboy and a waiter will appreciate the fact that swinging kitchen doors—even the ones with the portholes—are crash magnets. The best solution is to have one door for entry and another for exit. The layout of the dining room should discourage patrons from passing too close to the swinging doors.

When a staff member spills something, it must be removed or cleaned without delay. If this is not possible, the staff member should flag the spill (perhaps with a table napkin or a chair) or stand guard until it can be removed or cleaned. If the spill is caused by a customer or someone other than a staff member, the duty to clean or barricade it arises after the spill has been noticed or should have been noticed. A reasonable time is allowed to elapse.

Rees v. B.C. Place Ltd. (November 25, 1986) (B.C.S.C.), 3 A.C.W.S. (3d) 313

The staff failed to clean spilled beer within a reasonable time. Judgment for the plaintiff.

McPhail v. T & L Club (Brantford), [1968] 2 O.R. 840, 1 D.L.R. (3d) 43 (C.A.)

M slipped on a small piece of cheese on a dance club floor. Cheese and crackers were provided at the tables, and the defendant employed two workers to pick up the debris. The trial judge found the defendant liable. At the appeal, however, it was determined that although the defendant was subject to a high duty to maintain the premises in a safe condition for dancing, that duty did not entail constant inspection to prevent possible injury from bits of fallen food. The defendant was not an absolute insurer, and M had not been exposed to unreasonable risk.

Young v. Hubbards Food Services Ltd. (1995), 145 N.S.R. (2d) 13, 418 A.P.R. 13 (S.C.), additional reasons at (1995) 41 C.P.C. (3d) 349, 146 N.S.R. (2d) 70, 442 A.P.R. 70 (S.C.)

The plaintiff attended a bridal shower that was held at the defendant's dance hall. She paid an admission fee and sat at a table chosen by her friends. She left the table to get some snacks. On her return, she slipped on the linoleum dance floor. She had remarked to her friends that the dance floor was slippery, but had not complained to the defendant's staff. She adduced expert evidence of two engineers to demonstrate that she had fallen because the dance floor had a lower slip coefficient than required. She argued that the defendant had breached its duty to her as a contractual entrant to the premises. The action was dismissed. The duty owed to her by the defendant was not absolute, but one of reasonable care. The evidence did not establish, on a balance of probabilities, any negligence or breach of contract on the part of the defendant. There was no evidence that on the night of the mishap (as opposed to when the experts tested it) the slip coefficient of the dance floor was less than required. Even if it had been, there was no evidence that the condition of the dance floor had caused the plaintiff to fall. The cleaning and maintenance procedures followed by the defendant were appropriate. The premises were reasonably fit for the purpose intended. Further, the defendant was not required to post signs warning that the dance floor might be slippery.

Patrons should never be served alcohol if they show signs of intoxication. Inebriated guests can be escorted to their rooms. Other customers pose more difficult problems. Depending on the circumstances, they can be sent home by taxi or given a room for the night, even if the hotel does not expect to be paid for the room. Granting free use of a perhaps otherwise unoccupied room may prove far less costly than a lawsuit for injuries sustained subsequent to the departure of the impaired patron from the establishment.

Edwards v. Tracy Starr's Shows (Edmonton) Ltd. (1984), 33 Alta. L.R. (2d) 115, 56 A.R. 285, 13 D.L.R. (4th) 129 (Q.B.), varied (1987), 61 Alta. L.R. (2d) 233 (C.A.)

The plaintiff was invited to a strip club. While walking down an aisle, he tripped over an obstacle. He testified that he had not noticed the obstacle because he had been distracted by the antics on the stage. The defendant was liable for failing to remove the obstacle. The plaintiff was not contributorily negligent for allowing the stripper to distract him because the defendant had intended the show to be distracting.

Flambés

Flambé cooking involves fire and flammables, and can be dangerous to the guests and staff. The server faces the diner with a sizzling pan and the makings of a Molotov cocktail. The server should never pour liquor from an open bottle unless a special pouring spout has been inserted; otherwise, the flame can travel up the stream causing the bottle to explode. The location of the service table that the waiter uses should be such that no other diner or staff member can bump into the waiter or the table. Flambé cooking should be performed in an area that is visible to the guests but protected from traffic. The distance between the service table and the patron should be great enough that if a flame bursts momentarily out of control, it will not reach the patron, the tablecloth, or other flammable objects.

Aisles

Safe and adequate aisles are essential. Provincial legislation sets forth maximum seating and thus minimum aisle space requirements. Aisles should remain passable at all times, including for people who use walkers and wheelchairs, even if it means taking out some seating.

Fehr v. O.T. Karz Kafe Ltd. (1993), 110 Sask. R. 207 (Q.B.)

The plaintiff attempted to seat herself in the defendant's restaurant. The table and chairs were jammed into a corner close to the bar, forcing her to squeeze into her chair while pushing the others apart. She struck the back of her head against the overhang of a bar structure located behind her. The court held that the combination of the bar overhang and the proximity of the table and chairs to each other constituted an unusual danger, and that the plaintiff had taken all reasonable care in the circumstances.

Public Washrooms

Public washrooms should be inspected and cleaned often. Along with kitchens, washrooms are high-density condominiums of germs. Opinions about the quality of a hospitality business are often drawn from the cleanliness of the washrooms. They should be in top running order and very sanitary. Any needed repairs should be done immediately. Hand dryers should be located well away from water sources, soap should be available at the sinks, and bathroom tissue should never be allowed to run out. The need to keep floor coverings dry is especially true of washrooms, which often contain slippery flooring. Washrooms are often a site of choice for undesirable activities. Security personnel may be required to monitor washrooms for anti-social behaviour or criminal activities such as drug dealing. In the event of a difficult or dangerous situation, the best course is to call the police and warn other people not to enter.

McChesnie v. Tourond (1995), 99 Man. R. (2d) 209 (Q.B.)

A guest was sexually assaulted and robbed in a hotel washroom. Another guest was sexually assaulted in the same washroom three weeks later. The hotel had 30 floors, 272 guests, and one security officer who did two complete patrols per shift.

The guest sued on the ground that the hotel had failed to keep the premises safe. The security officer and his company were added as third parties. The action was dismissed. Although a hotel is not an absolute insurer of the safety of its guests, there is an implied warranty that a hotel will make its premises reasonably safe for them. In this case, the security officer and the patrol system constituted a reasonable standard of safety.

Some restaurants that cater to the trucking industry offer additional bathroom services such as showers and hygiene stations. As service is increased, so are the risks. Showers increase the chance of a customer falling or being scalded. Control devices should regulate the hot water supply, and the flooring in the shower area should be nonslip to reduce the chance of falls. Housekeeping standards should be as exacting in truckstop facilities as they are in hotels.

Swimming Pools and Saunas

Swimming pools are common features in hotels. As innkeepers are not absolute insurers, they are generally liable only if they fail to exercise reasonable care, which includes using commonsense and implementing applicable governmental regulations. Most jurisdictions include in their public health legislation pool regulations that address such items as depth markers, allowable slope of the pool floor, diving boards, lighting, steps, supervision, security, water quality, and germicides. The operator must comply with the public health legislation; failure to comply may result in liability for negligence per se. Regular monitoring and full periodic inspections are essential to the process. Like any other structure, pools change over time. For example, a diving board may have been added, the liner may have cracked, or tiles may have raised. Many jurisdictions have inspection requirements that must be followed.

Pool equipment such as diving boards and water slides are engineered for particular purposes. Pool operators should ensure that the equipment is appropriate for their pool. To meet safety regulations, an Olympic diving board requires a specific water depth. Failure to provide such a depth is likely to plunge the hotel into litigious hot water.

Tests for water quality and clarity are very important. The filtration system and the chlorine or bromine content in the pool must be maintained and monitored at least daily. The person conducting the tests must be trained to perform this task to the standard required. If the chlorine or bromine level drops below the standard, infectious germs will multiply in the water, resulting in ear infections and possibly other unpleasant conditions. The pool should be closed immediately if the test results are outside the appropriate limits.

Daily maintenance of a pool requires use of equipment such as vacuums and brushes. The

It is essential to maintain a clean and safe pool area.

equipment presents a risk to guests if left in the deck area. The pool is like any other area of the hotel. When staff are cleaning or performing maintenance work, the pool should be closed to the public. Many operators let the weather and the demands of guests dictate when the pool is opened. Pools should remain closed until conditions warrant opening them.

Few establishments that provide pools also provide lifeguards. Large, clear signs must inform patrons that there is no supervision and that use of the facilities is at the risk of the patron. Despite the disclaimer signs, the owner has a responsibility to ensure that the facilities are in good working order and that there are no hidden dangers. The disclaimer will not protect the hotel against claims for gross negligence or failure to abide by government regulations.

House rules, including hours of operation, should be posted and enforced to improve safety and reduce liability. The rules can cover running, playing, alcohol, and a host of other topics. Glass is especially dangerous around the pool because it is an area in which people often walk barefoot. All drinks should be served in plastic or paper cups.

Whirlpools and hot tubs must also be monitored regularly. Guests with high blood pressure or heart conditions perhaps should not use them. Children should not use them unless accompanied by an adult. Water quality should be tested on a daily basis. Alcohol and temperature-control equipment also present serious dangers.

The heating mechanism in the sauna must never malfunction. Saunas can be dangerous. Air temperatures of 90 degrees Celsius stress the heart muscle. The world's leading users of saunas, the Finns, have one of the world's highest incidences of heart disease. Whirlpools, which typically feature water temperatures of about 38 degrees Celsius, are much easier on the heart, but require large amounts of chlorine. For both saunas and whirlpools, signs should warn users against staying in them too long, and give reasons. A member of the Hockey Hall of Fame who was drinking alcohol in a sauna fell and broke his ankle. Rules prominently posted and a ban on alcohol go a long way toward reducing accidents.

Innkeepers are deemed to have more knowledge of statutory and regulatory safety requirements than homeowners, and must take corrective action more expeditiously. When a regulation is breached, the innkeeper's superior knowledge may result in greater liability than would be imposed on a homeowner. Further, if a hotel is aware that meeting the regulation is not sufficient to eliminate a danger, the hotel must exceed the requirements of the regulation. Statutory provisions are minimums, not maximums, and they may even be inadequate.

Cempel v. Harrison Hot Springs Hotel Ltd. (March 18, 1996), Doc. Vancouver C936351 (B.C.S.C.)

C, age 16, went with friends in the middle of the night to swim in the source pool from which the defendant hotel obtained the water for its swimming pools. The hotel admitted that it was the occupier of the source pool and was responsible for its upkeep, maintenance, and design. The hotel was aware that young people swam in the source pool at night fairly regularly. The source pool often contained steaming water, with a temperature of about 60 degrees Celsius. On the night of the accident, the source pool was not lighted, and there were no signs posted. Surrounding the pool was a wire fence on top of a low wall. C climbed onto the fence, intending to climb down into the pool, which she thought was a hot tub that was closed for the night. The top of the fence was 4.6 metres above the walkway. The fence was rusted and the stanchions were detached from the upper beam. A portion of the beam gave way, resulting in C's partial immersion in the pool. She sustained serious burns requiring multiple skin grafts over 21 percent of her body. After spending 51 days in the hospital, she wore compression garments for eight months. She was left with extensive scarring, difficulties in walking and standing, and emotional problems. The court held that the source pool was an unusual danger, requiring a high standard of care to ensure that visitors were reasonably safe in using the premises. It was foreseeable that young people would try to climb into the pool, and reasonable steps should have been taken to prevent such an occurrence. The wall at the point at which C had climbed in was not high enough to meet the standard of reasonable care. The hotel had also breached its duty of care in failing to ensure that the fence was in proper condition. The changes the hotel made to the enclosure since the accident showed that the hotel could have made the structure safer earlier. C's own actions, however, had been foolhardy, and she had failed to take reasonable care for her own safety. She was found 75 percent liable and the hotel was found 25 percent liable. C received 25 percent of her nonpecuniary damages, lost wages, loss of earning capacity, cost of future care, cost of vocational counselling, and special damages.

Fitness Rooms and Running Tracks

Fitness rooms may have a wide variety of exercise machines. Many hotels have found that they increase room sales and bring in additional revenue from local fitness buffs. The equipment must be inspected on a regular basis to ensure that it is working properly and is safe. If a pulley snaps, there could be a serious injury. Serious weight trainers tend to be conscientious about returning the weights to the racks, but periodic checks should still be done to ensure that the floor is not strewn with obstacles. Most of the users are not experts, and few have their doctor's approval. A weight room attendant who gives advice on the use of the equipment must be knowledgeable. If not, the guest may think that the advice is from an expert, follow it, and suffer an injury. In *Robinson v. Madison (November 9, 1987) (B.C.S.C.), 7 A.C.W.S. (3d) 166*, the plaintiff fell from a backswing machine at a gymnastics club. The principle of *res ipsa loquitur* was held to apply to fitness equipment, and the club was liable.

Running tracks should be inspected for wet, frayed, uneven, or weakened surfaces. Rooftop running tracks should be surrounded by fences high enough to contain exuberant athletes. *Drodge v. St. John's Young Men's and Young Women's Christian Association (1987), 67 Nfld. & P.E.I.R. 57 (Nfld. T.D.)* was a case in which water on a gymnasium floor was found to be an unusual danger for which the defendant was liable. The principle underlying this finding would also apply to indoor running tracks, but not to rooftop running tracks.

Guest Areas Outside the Guest Rooms

Corridors

Guest-floor corridors and their floor surfaces must be in excellent condition. Today, the covering of choice is carpeting. The seams and runs should be taut and flat enough that the risk of tripping is eliminated. Any changes of elevation should be clearly indicated with a sign, special lighting, or a change in floor colour. Hallways should be kept clear at all times. Room-attendant carts, cleaning equipment, plants, vacuum cords, room service trays, and luggage are all potential hazards that could cause a guest to fall and create a liability for the hotel.

Lighting is another important consideration. To create atmosphere, some hotels keep the hallways dimly lit. This may compromise the safety of the guests by reducing their ability to see obstacles and hazards. Atmosphere is best obtained in a less problematic way. Poorly lit hallways may also give unwanted persons the opportunity to lie in wait for a guest. The innkeeper has a duty to protect guests from intruders. The entire hotel should be policed in order to keep uninvited persons away from the guest floors.

Unless their backgrounds are known to the innkeeper, deliverers should not be allowed on the guest floors. Sexual predators have been known to pass themselves off as deliverers. Delivery people such as pizza drivers should be required to leave their wares at the front desk. A staff member may deliver them to the guest's room or the guest may be called to fetch them.

Ice and Vending Machines

Ice and vending machines on the guest floors are a convenience to guests, but carry the risk that the floor area around the machines can become wet. The hotel has a duty to monitor the areas and to remove the danger within a reasonable time after becoming aware of it.

Housekeeping Closets

Housekeeping closets on the guest floors are handy repositories for cleaning supplies and equipment. Dangerous substances should not be kept in housekeeping closets, but rather returned to a central and secure storage area. Arsonists have been known to find their fuel in housekeeping closets. The doors should be kept locked as much as possible. Young guests and family pets could be seriously injured from ingesting or touching cleaning solutions.

Rolling Stock

Service carts, laundry hampers, and meal trolleys should not be placed in aisles and doorways where they may block entrances and passageways and become a hazard to guests, particularly those who are absent-minded or in a hurry.

Emergency and Fire Doors

Provincial fire codes require that a door capable of retarding fire be located between the hallways and the fire escape staircases. The doors can be opened only in one direction. They may also help to stop intruders from gaining access to the guest floors. If the doors are left or held open, they cannot perform their function. All staff should be instructed to close and secure open fire doors, and never to leave them ajar in order to ease the performance of their jobs.

Inside Guest Rooms

Security and Safety

The responsibility to provide the guest with a secure room has been part of the common law since the case of *Re Calye, 77 Eng. Rep. 520, 521 (K.B. 1584)* (see Chapter 8). Metal keys can be copied and are prone to theft. Keyless entry systems, usually disposable strips of plastic with temporary codes or hole patterns, have reduced thefts and wrongful entries. The key locking technique, along with the fire escape plan and other legal notices, should be posted on the back of the guest room door. The mechanism on the door should be inspected regularly to ensure that it is in good working order.

A high percentage of all accidents happen in the home. The guest room is the guest's home away from home. A high standard of care is owed for safety and cleanliness. In the American case of *Nelson v. Ritz Carleton Restaurant and Hotel Co., 157A 133 (N. J. 1931)*, a guest stepped on a pin in his room and was awarded, in today's dollars, over $100,000.

Guests often lie in bed to watch television, a practice that can result in empty drinking glasses being on the floor beside the bed. If the housekeepers do not find the glasses when cleaning the room, the next guest may suffer a serious cut. Housekeepers and room inspectors should be instructed to check under the bed and in other nooks and crannies.

Ashtrays should be provided even in smoke-free rooms in case a nonsmoker invites a smoker to the room. Wastepaper baskets should be made of fire-retardant material.

Many hotels in operation today were built generations ago. The demand for electricity by the guests has increased dramatically since then. Today's travellers pack hairdryers, stereo systems, laptop computers, and a host of other gadgets. Innkeepers should ensure that the room's electrical capacity can meet the needs of guests. Rooms should not be equipped with multi-outlets and extension cords; they are menaces when overloaded.

Murphy beds (no relation to the lawgiver) and day beds can cause injuries when being opened or stowed. Rooms with such beds are often rented by senior citizens in a tour group. The hotel should arrange for a staff member to lower, extract, or stow the bed.

Lighting

Proper lighting reduces the risk of falls in a hotel room. Strategically placed light switches are essential. The most important switch is the one located at the entrance to the room. It ensures that a guest need never enter and cross a dark room. A light switch should also be located near the bed for use during the night.

Ceilings

Ceilings take a surprising amount of abuse. Some guests bounce objects off them; others shower them with champagne. Ceilings should be repaired without delay because it is often difficult to determine the amount of damage they have sustained and how close they are to collapse. Once repaired, ceilings should be monitored for further signs of decay.

Window Treatments

Many hotel rooms come with three pairs of curtains: sheers, decorative curtains, and blackout curtains. If they are hung from the drywall like pictures, the plaster may not support the weight for long. Valances and curtain rods should be secured to the structure of the building, not just the drywall. Window treatments are easy to inspect. It is usually apparent if the drapes are not hanging straight or the rods are sagging. Room attendants should adjust the drapes every morning to ensure that they are secure and moving properly.

Patio Doors and Screens

Patio doors allow intruders relatively easy access to guest rooms. It is important to ensure that locking mechanisms work. Window screens present special problems in the guest rooms. The hardware for window screens should be checked to ensure that there is no possibility of the screens becoming flying objects that could damage people or automobiles below. A window screen should be strong enough to resist a child who might fall or push against it.

Balconies

Fewer hotels today have balconies, partly because air conditioning has lessened their utility and partly because of the increased risk associated with them, especially to children. Balcony furniture should not present a means for a child to climb over the railings. Balconies have also been used by intruders. Warnings and locking instructions should be clearly visible to guests.

Gordon v. Blakely, [1931] 2 W.W.R. 902 (B.C.S.C.)

The plaintiff, a guest in the defendant's hotel, was told by the defendant's staff that she could use a balcony to dry her bathing suit. She was not warned of a 30-centimetre drop separating the room floor from the balcony floor, and she did not notice it because of the inadequate lighting. The court found that most balcony floors are level with the room floors, and that the depression in the floor was an unusual hazard known to the defendant and unknown to the plaintiff. The defendant had failed in its duty to warn her.

Buehl Estate v. Polar Star Enterprises Inc. (1989), 72 O.R. (2d) 573 (H.C.J.)

The deceased, who was intoxicated at the time of his death, was fatally injured in a fall that took place at a rented unit in a lodge. He had stepped through the second-floor patio door and, because there was no balcony on the other side of the door, fallen to his death. The lodge owner had made all the occupants of the room, including the deceased, aware of the danger. The estate of the deceased brought an action for damages. The court held that it was reasonably foreseeable that an occupant might open the door for ventilation, and might have consumed alcohol, impairing judgment and memory. Thus, the lodge owner owed a duty to barricade the door. However, the deceased was found to have been 65 percent contributorily negligent.

Child-Proofing

Every room in an establishment should be inspected for potential hazards to children. Furniture should safely accommodate climbing children and never be placed within dangerous proximity of an unsecure window. It may be advisable to consult an expert in child-proofing techniques.

Telephones

While hotels are not legally required to supply a telephone in each guest room, it is hard to find a room that does not have one. The telephone should be conveniently located by the bedside. If the cost is not too prohibitive, there should be a phone in the bathroom as well. Front-desk staff should be trained to recognize a call for help. Any guest who calls the front desk regarding a problem, be it health- or safety-related, is owed a prompt and competent response. Special training helps to ensure that situations are handled swiftly, tactfully, and properly.

Bathrooms

In both hotels and homes, more accidents occur in the bathroom than in any other room. Wet floors are the most common hazard. Bathtubs and shower stalls should have slip-free surfaces. The taps should be conveniently located. Anything in a bathtub or stall that a guest might grab onto for support, even if not intended for such a use, should be secure enough not to pull away from the wall. If a bathroom fixture is in need of repair, the room should be put out of order until the repair is completed. The location of electrical appliances in a bathroom should be such that if they fall, they will not land in the bathtub. If the bathroom counter is too small to comfortably accommodate the appliances, they should be mounted securely on the wall.

Guests can be scalded as a result of water-temperature fluctuations. Many hotels set the temperature of the hot water well below scalding thresholds and use special protective valves. Care should be taken to ensure that the boosters employed in the dishwashing rooms to raise the temperature of the water used to sanitize pots and pans are not inadvertently attached to the pipelines supplying hot water to the guest rooms. Water hot enough to sanitize pots can cause serious injury. The water temperature of the guest bath can be tested when the housekeeping staff cleans the tub area. By cleansing the tub with the hottest water and rinsing it with the coldest water, the room attendant can check the water temperature for suitability.

Joyce v. Canadian Pacific Hotels Corp. (1994), 26 Alta. L.R. (3d) 72, 161 A.R. 53 (Q.B.)

While staying at the defendant hotel, J slipped in the bathtub, which had a manufactured nonslip surface. The action succeeded. An occupier's obligation is to take such care as is reasonable in all the circumstances to ensure that the visitor is reasonably safe in using the premises. The failure of a visitor to take reasonable care is merely an issue of contributory negligence. The hotel had discharged some of its obligations by installing nonslip surfaces in its bathtubs. However, the installation did not completely discharge the occupier's duty. The hotel also had a duty to maintain and repair the bathtubs, to perform ongoing inspections, and to rectify deficiencies or problems. The hotel did not have reasonable procedures in place for these purposes. Accordingly, the hotel had not taken such care as was reasonable in all the circumstances to ensure that visitors would be reasonably safe in using the premises. J had not done anything abnormal or exceptional in getting out of the bathtub, and was not contributorily negligent for his fall.

The Back of the House

Back-of-the-house areas are generally out of bounds to the public. Unless invited, the public should not enter them. They should be clearly marked to discourage wanderers but the duty of care to the public continues to apply. Commonsense and reasonable foresight are required. If inherently dangerous materials are stored on site, perfect foresight may be required, for the liability would be strict in the event of an accident.

Repushka v. Perentes Enterprises Ltd. (1996), 140 Sask. R. 55 (Q.B.), additional reasons at [1996] 9 W.W.R. 734 (Sask. Q.B.)

R was a frequent customer at the defendant restaurant. He received permission to use the telephone in the kitchen. After making his call, he went down a back hall that was illuminated by a light in the kitchen. At the end of the hall was a stairway to the basement. He fell down the stairway and suffered injuries. When he was discovered, it was noticed that his pants were unzipped and resting at mid-thigh. He did not explain why he had gone down the back hall rather than using the restroom located on an adjacent hall. He sued the defendant in negligence. The action was dismissed. There was nothing unusual in encountering, at ground level, a stairwell leading to the basement level of a building. The location of the stairwell was exactly where it might be anticipated to be. There was nothing unusual about either the stairwell or the stairway, nor did they show evidence of any defect. While the hallway was somewhat cluttered, there was no evidence that any of the objects present had caused the plaintiff to fall.

Service Stairwells and Freight Elevators

Guests should not be allowed to use the service stairwells or freight elevators. The back of the house is rarely as safe as the front. Nevertheless, service stairwells and freight elevators are sometimes used by guests for convenience or during emergencies. The hotel must foresee these uses and plan accordingly. Freight elevators sometimes do not receive adequate attention. Some of the doors are the kind that open from the top and bottom simultaneously with the use of a strap. The straps and hinges do wear out. A worn strap or weakened hinge can result in someone being hit on the head with the door. Freight elevators are used primarily to transport staff and cleaning and other materials; therefore, spills are an additional risk.

Kitchens, Ovens, and Walk-in Freezers

Kitchens and walk-in freezers are out-of-bounds to the public, but are of concern with respect to employees and service personnel. Notwithstanding their portrayal as death traps in gangster movies, real-life walk-in freezers are equipped with inside escape bars. Grills and ovens are dangerous, especially during busy, stressful times when safety issues might be overlooked.

Safety Features and Security Measures

A hotel owes its guest a reasonable measure of security. A hotel will be liable if there is legal causation between its negligence and the guest's injury. If adequate security has been provided, an injured guest will be less able to prove negligence. Common measures include periodic tours by staff, surveillance cameras, and alarm systems. Security requirements within a hotel may vary depending on the season, the event, and the guests. As a rule, employees should be consulted at the ends of their shifts. No employee should disappear at the end of a shift without first communicating with a supervisor.

Safety Equipment

Building codes and licences mandate certain safety equipment and notices. The purpose of the equipment and notices is to reduce danger and save lives. Innkeepers should be fully aware of the operational and maintenance requirements of their emergency equipment.

Fire Prevention

As the following excerpt from the Ontario *Hotel Fire Safety Act* illustrates, provincial statutory requirements are quite stringent:

2. This Act applies to every hotel whether constructed before or after this Act comes into force.

3. No person shall

    (a) construct a hotel;

    (b) construct an addition to a hotel;

    (c) convert a building to a hotel; or

    (d) alter a hotel, until complete drawings and specifications thereof have been submitted to and approved by the Fire Marshal.

4. Every hotel ... shall have its structural assemblies ... constructed in the manner and of the materials prescribed ...

5. Every hotel shall have such exits, ... doorways, ... stairways designed, located, maintained, identified, lighted, and ... equipped with such hardware as the regulations prescribe.

6. Every hotel shall have in each building that

    (a) has a total floor area of more than 6,000 square feet;

    (b) is more than one storey in height; or

    (c) does not have direct egress to the outside from each ... suite, a fire alarm system ... prescribed by the regulations.

7. Every hotel four or more storeys in height and every addition four or more storeys in height ... shall have a standpipe and hose system ... prescribed by the regulations.

8. Every hotel shall install and maintain portable fire extinguishers of the type ... prescribed by the regulations.

14. Where an inspector finds that a condition exists in a hotel that makes the hotel specially liable to fire, the inspector may order the hotelkeeper to remedy the condition.

17. Every hotelkeeper who operates a hotel that does not conform with this Act and the regulations or who fails to comply with any order made by an inspector is guilty of an offence and on conviction is liable to a fine of not more than $1,000, and, in addition, the judge may order the hotel to be closed until it is made to conform with this Act and the regulations or with the order of the inspector.

Municipal bylaws require that all hotel rooms and restaurants be equipped with smoke alarms. The alarms should be checked regularly. Fire extinguishers should be readily available and should be inspected on a regular basis by a professional. The hoses and other pieces of equipment can be inspected by the maintenance staff. Fire pull stations should be periodically tested, and nothing should be placed in front of them. Time lost looking for a pull station may be the difference between life and death. The fire and smoke alarm systems should never be turned off even if there are frequent false alarms. (Despite what many people think, the most common perpetrators of false alarms are not children, but immature or impaired adults.)

In the event of fire, guests should not leave their rooms without first ascertaining that it is safe to do so. If the door feels too hot, the guest should place wet towels around the door to keep the smoke out. If the door feels cool enough, the guest should attempt to exit the hotel via the fire stairwell, never the elevator. If there is smoke in the halls, the guest should stay as low as possible below the smoke and avoid breathing it as much as possible. The greater danger in a fire is the smoke, not the flames.

Love v. New Fairview Corp. (1904), 10 B.C.R. 330 (C.A.)

L, a lodger living on the third floor of a hotel, was injured by a fire in the hotel. The action was based on the hotel's failure to supply adequate fire escapes as required by statute. L could have escaped without injury had he not delayed his escape to rescue a woman lodging on the same floor. The trial judge instructed the jury that, however praiseworthy L's act might have been, the law did not recognize heroism as a set-off to a plaintiff's own negligence or willingness to incur danger. The judge refused to put to the jury a question as to whether L had acted as a person of ordinary care and skill, but did put to the jury questions as to whether L delayed his exit to save the woman, and as to whether L could have left safely if he had not delayed his exit. On the basis of the answers to these questions, judgment was entered for the defendant hotel.

The above case might well have been decided differently today on the basis of negligence per se (i.e., the failure to abide by statutory requirements).

Emergency Exits

The fire exit lights must meet the local building code and should be inspected daily to ensure that they glow brightly and that no bulbs are burnt out. As noted earlier, fire exit information should be posted, along with the other important legal notices, on the back of each guest room door. Exit or back-of-the-house staircases are used primarily by staff but sometimes by guests as well. They should never be used for storage.

Emergency Lighting

Emergency lighting provides lighting only for a limited time. In one instance, Ontario Hydro was changing a transformer and made arrangements with the hotel to perform the job just after lunch. The job was scheduled to take only an hour or two, but was not completed until well past 10:00 p.m. Guests who were in the hotel sleeping during the day were warned of the situation. Many assumed that the power would be back on before nightfall; later, when they left their rooms, they did so in total darkness. The batteries and power sources for the emergency lighting should be checked regularly to ensure that they will be available during an emergency.

Intercoms and House Phones

Some hotels have intercoms and emergency telephones in elevators and hallways and at the front desk. They should be inspected regularly to ensure that they are operational.

Medical Assistance

An ambulance should always be called whenever a guest desires medical assistance. Wherever possible, medical attention should be left to the professionals. If a guest who appears to need medical treatment refuses treatment or refuses to allow an ambulance to be called, a written record of the refusal should be made and duly witnessed.

Staff Training and Inspections

All hotels and restaurants should ensure that their staffs are familiar with fire and other emergency procedures. In-house training programs are provided through fire departments and St. John Ambulance, among others. Those who work the evening and graveyard shifts may require special training, since there are often fewer staff members on duty during those shifts. All trainees should be advised of the room numbers of guests with disabilities, so that the numbers will be readily available to the fire department or other emergency services.

Each employee's job description should include various inspection responsibilities. It is recommended that 10 percent of guest rooms receive a thorough inspection by management on a daily basis, in addition to the daily inspections performed by the housekeeping staff. The front-desk staff should also perform inspections from time to time.

Daily Logs

All hotels and restaurants should keep a diary or computer log of events and emergency calls. Important messages that should be passed from shift to shift can also be included. The contents should be saved for several years.

Video Cameras

The front desk should have an all-purpose video camera on hand. If a guest complains about falling while showering, the staff should not engage in a discussion about potential liability. The alleged accident scene may be filmed in the presence of a witness. Valuable information may be gained that would otherwise be missed. However, a court may decide that videotaping someone's hotel room without his or her permission and knowledge is an invasion of privacy. Videotaping should occur during the regular housekeeping so that any infringement of the guest's right to privacy and exclusive use of the room is kept to a minimum.

Special Considerations

Children

The family market has long been a mainstay for the hospitality industry, and the demands made by families for amenities and safety are increasing. Many hotels now offer supervised play and craft centres. These centres should be operated by professional caregivers, and all toys and equipment should meet the requirements set by the Canadian Standards Association. The facility and its contents should be inspected on a regular basis.

> **Vannan v. Kamloops (City) (1991), 63 B.C.L.R. (2d) 307, [1992] 2 W.W.R. 759 (S.C.)**
>
> The infant plaintiff fell from a playground structure and fractured her skull. She recovered and sued the defendant municipality that owned the playground. The action was dismissed. The court ruled that the standard of care to be applied was one of reasonableness, not perfection. The defendant had a regular repair and inspection program that was found to be reasonable. Injuries that occur without a breach of a duty of care are not compensable unless the liability is strict.

There is another instance in which liability may arise with respect to children. Under provincial legislation, any person who has reasonable grounds for believing that a child is or may be in need of protection is required to forthwith report the belief (and the information upon which it is based) to a Children's Aid Society or other appropriate organization. A person who has such grounds and who fails to report may be liable for prosecution and civil damages.

Special Needs

If a guest advises a hotel of special needs, or if the special needs are plain to see, the hotel must respond appropriately and within reason. The physically challenged must be suitably accommodated. A person with a heart condition or a hip replacement should be booked into a room on a lower floor, so that he or she will have relatively few stairs to descend in the event of an emergency. A person who suffers from vertigo should be kept out of the penthouse. A claustrophobic should be given a bright and airy room. There are companies that will make all the travel and tourism arrangements on behalf of travellers with special needs. A travel agent can either assist directly or put the traveller in touch with such companies.

Pest Control

It is recommended that commercial hotels and restaurants make use of extermination services. The chemicals used in the extermination process are powerful and should be handled only by persons with the proper training. Professional exterminators understand the hazards associated with the chemicals they use (the danger to children and pets is a special concern), and have been trained in the proper handling and storage of these chemicals.

Rats are unwelcome guests. In most cases, keeping floor drains properly covered and shutting doors (especially those close to back alleys and garbage storage areas) is a sufficient means of control. Raccoons, skunks, and even bears are a common rural menace. Rural resorts are concerned about animals that have lost their fear of humans and are comfortable visiting the resort property in search of food. Children and family pets are often unaware of the danger that wild animals pose. All guests should be warned about wild animals. As a precaution against intrusions, all lower-level windows should be screened with heavy mesh. Garbage and picnic areas should always be kept clean and secure to reduce their attractiveness to animals.

Special Tours and Activities

Some special tours are offered directly by the hotel. If so, all liabilities rest with the hotel. In most instances, guests purchase the tickets from the hotel and the service is provided by another company. To avoid liability as a principal, the hotel must disclose to the guest that the hotel is only an agent. The status of agent will not protect the hotel from liability in every case if the principal delivers a negligent tour. The hotel has a duty not to engage or recommend a tour provider that it knows, or ought to know, has a poor record.

Exercise Trails

Some guests like to jog, cycle, or walk. Many hotels provide maps of trails and walking routes. The hotel should ensure that the routes are safe and advise guests of any changes in status.

Taxis and Shuttle Buses

Hotel staff are frequently asked by guests to recommend shows and other tourist attractions. Liability may arise if a guest is mugged returning from a show that was recommended by a staff member who knew, or ought to have known, that walking back from the theatre at night would pose a threat, and did not warn the guest to take a taxi.

Hailing a licensed taxi for a guest is a common courtesy that carries almost no risk. The greatest risk is associated with helping the guest into or out of the cab. If the assistance is negligent, the hotel may be liable.

Resorts and Recreational Amenities

Most hotels strive to offer good service in hopes of generating repeat business and favourable word-of-mouth advertising. If the variables of good service, location, name recognition, and advertising are comparable to those possessed by the competition, the only way a hotel can increase its market share is to offer additional amenities. Travellers today regard hotels as more than just a place to eat and sleep. Many hotels offer an array of amenities such as retail shops, swimming pools, saunas, and exercise rooms. For guests in urban hotels, particularly those who are occupied with business pursuits, amenities may be of secondary importance. By contrast, resorts—including traditional resort hotels, cruise lines, all-inclusive self-enclosed beach villages, and rustic ranches—owe their very existence to the natural, social, and sporting amenities they provide; the guests are there expressly to enjoy the resort's amenities.

The recreation sector of the hospitality industry includes the resorts themselves as well as the recreation facilities of urban hotels. Many of the issues of negligence prevention applicable to the recreation sector also apply to the accommodation sector in general and have been covered elsewhere in this book. Aspects of negligence prevention more closely identified with the recreation sector are discussed below. In general terms, the more extensive a resort's amenities are, the more important risk management becomes to the resort.

Natural Bodies of Water

Resorts located beside natural bodies of water may offer their guests swimming, diving, boating, and other activities. The resorts owe a duty of care to guests who use the waters as intended or in a reasonably foreseeable way. The swimming area should be safe for the type of activity that the guests are invited or likely to use it for. Warning signs should be posted wherever and whenever the water is not safe. Under general principles of occupier's liability and the common law, a duty may also be owed to nonguests and even to trespassers.

Swimming areas should be roped off so that boats, water skiers, and fishers cannot enter. The water beneath the surface down to the bottom must be inspected to ensure that dangers do not lurk below. Diving areas should be carefully inspected and monitored. Danger areas should be clearly marked. Otherwise, the resort may be liable for a failure to warn.

Recreational equipment loaned or rented to a guest must be used by the guest in an approved manner. The resort must consider whether some guests, particularly the young or inexperienced, may deliberately or inadvertently misuse the equipment. All equipment must be in proper condition and all safety features must be working. The guests should receive all required instruction in advance. In Hawaii, an accident occurred when a guest misused a surfboard owned by the hotel, which was found liable for improper instruction and supervision.

Other Water Attractions

Many resorts offer swimming pools and other attractions such as slides and whirling water rides. They are often preferred by guests for personal or safety reasons to natural water.

Atley v. Popkum Water Slides Ltd. (1992), 64 B.C.L.R. (2d) 1, 10 B.C.C.A. 193, 21 W.A.C. 193 (C.A.)

The defendant's water slide park included two wading pools separated by a raised walkway. At a point where the walkway dipped, forming a depression of about half an inch, a small amount of water flowed from one pool into the other. The walkway had a painted surface that was made slip resistant by the application of ground walnut shells. Nevertheless, the plaintiff slipped on the walkway and injured herself. Her action for damages was dismissed. The trial judge held that the defendant had used a recognized slip-resistant coating, and that persons using a water slide park had to expect slippery surfaces. The plaintiff's appeal was also dismissed. Based on all the evidence, the defendant had taken sufficient steps to ensure that the premises were reasonably safe. The Court of Appeal did not find that the trial judge's findings of fact were plainly wrong.

Targett v. Magic Mountain Water Park Ltd. (1991), 120 N.B.R. (2d) 95, 302 A.P.R. 95 (Q.B.)

T was injured when he slipped and fell entering the defendant's wave pool. He suffered a head injury, resulting in a personality change and a permanent loss of his senses of taste and smell. He was awarded general damages of $28,000. The defendant was liable because it had failed to ensure that the floor of the pool was not too slippery. The defendant had failed to paint the bottom of the pool with an abrasive coating.

Ski Areas

Ski runs should be ranked according to their degree of difficulty. The rankings should be explained and posted at all entrances to the hill and at the tops of the slopes, including crossover points. Slope boundaries should be apparent so that skiers unfamiliar with the hill do not ski over the edges. Qualified ski patrollers and other employees should be on the lookout for any existing or potential hazards, and for anyone who appears to be in need of assistance or heading down a slope that is beyond his or her skill level. Snow conditions and the depth of the base should be indicated at the entrances to the lifts. Skiers must be alerted if poor conditions exist or if good conditions take a turn for the worse. When rocks and straw bales become exposed, they should be marked with ropes and coloured flags or crossed poles. Moguls, ice, lift pillars, and other skiers are anticipated features of the slopes.

Ski rental equipment should be in proper condition. The staff who fit and adjust the bindings should be properly trained. Even an excellent skier can break an ankle if the binding release mechanism is set too tight and the skier encounters an unexpectedly soft mogul.

Many ski areas offer night skiing. The lighting is not particularly bright. Stadium lighting at a professional baseball park is much brighter than night skiing lighting. Unlighted runs should be cordoned off to reduce the chances of skiers accidentally crossing into them.

Lift equipment should be inspected regularly. There is little margin for error. Although more injuries occur in falls or collisions, injuries arising from defective lift equipment garner more media attention and often more liability. The lift operators must be well trained and responsible. They should also be trained to spot and cull from the line incompetent skiers, drunks, and troublemakers. Liability may befall the resort if an impaired skier boards a lift, shows off to the crowd during the lift's ascent, and falls to the ground as a result.

Gwynn v. Ochapawace Indian Band (1987), Vol. 6, No. 43, T.L.W. 644–016 (Sask. Q.B.)

The plaintiff was thrown from a T-bar when the cable was dislodged by an employee of the defendant who got off the ski lift part way up the hill. The operator of the ski hill was found liable for the injuries suffered by the plaintiff.

Marshall v. British Columbia (1988), 23 B.C.L.R. (2d) 320 (C.A.)

The skier was found two-thirds contributorily negligent for having skied too fast and for having failed to keep a proper lookout. The resort was found one-third contributorily negligent for having failed to mark the edge of a ravine with a warning fence or barrier.

Fink v. Greeniaus (1973), 2 O.R. (2d) 541 (H.C.)

A skier crossing a slope crashed into another skier descending the slope. The skier who had been crossing the slope was found contributorily negligent because she crossed the slope beneath a plateau that took her out of the field of vision of the skiers who were coming directly over the lip of the plateau. The skier who had been descending the slope was found contributorily negligent for skiing so fast in the vicinity of the ski run's blind spot that he was unable to avoid colliding with the crossing skier. Each skier was found 50 percent at fault. The resort was not liable. The reader is invited to consider on what basis the resort might have been found liable.

Ice Skating

Many Canadian rural resorts and some urban hotels offer outdoor ice skating as an attraction. Novice skaters and guests who are accustomed to the smooth ice surfaces featured in indoor rinks should be warned about the hazards posed by the irregularities of outdoor ice.

Hazardous Sports

Hazardous sports include mountain climbing, mountain biking, heliskiing, spelunking, bungee jumping, hang gliding, parasailing, whitewater rafting, scuba diving, and water skiing. Operators owe reasonable care and warnings of any dangers that might exist with respect to equipment, terrain, weather, and so on. Terrains that are safe for some sports may be dangerous for others. Clearly marked signs should be posted in appropriate places.

Horseback Riding

Horseback rides are a wonderful way to experience Canada's natural beauty. While the beauty is predictable, the horse is not. Horses, no matter how well trained, may react unexpectedly. Riders may not have the skill or time to take appropriate action. Guests must be warned of the dangers and shown how to deal with the situation. Trail leaders should check all equipment before each riding session. Saddles may become loose as the ride progresses. Trails should be inspected periodically for groundhog holes and other hazards.

Responsible leaders must ensure that activities are safe.

Burhoe v. Beach Grove Stables Ltd. (December 7, 1987) (B.C.S.C.), 7 A.C.W.S. (3d) 266

B fell off a horse she had rented from the defendant. The fall occurred when the horse began to gallop after being startled by the horn of a train. B suffered displaced cartilage in her nasal cavity, which required corrective surgery, as well as multiple contusions and abrasions on her face, arms, and legs. She was hospitalized for five days. There was no permanent damage. The rental contract contained a clause disclaiming all liability for injuries resulting from the rental. The disclaimer was clear and in a prominent place on the contract such that B should have read it. She voluntarily assumed the risk of injury when she signed the contract. The horse was not unruly or uncontrollable, and was properly equipped. It was reasonable for the train to sound its horn when approaching a public pathway. The defendant was not liable.

Saari v. Sunshine Riding Academy Ltd. (1967), 65 D.L.R. (2d) 92 (Man. Q.B.)

On October 31, 1965, Susan Saari, 17, and her friend Drena White, 17, went to the Sunshine Riding Academy to take part in a riding excursion with about 25 others, most in their early teens. Drena, an experienced rider, knew that Susan, who had ridden only twice before, wanted a quiet horse. Drena chose for Susan a seven-year-old horse, Select, who had been used for riding for the past four years. On the barn door was a sign (about a square foot in measurement) that read, "Riders Ride at Their Own Risk."

Nancy O'Connor, 15, was the lead guide. It was her duty to control the ride, including its pace. Linda Coyle, 14, was the middle guide and Drena was the end guide. It was their duty to keep the horses from bunching up and to provide assistance if anything went wrong. Nancy, Linda, and Drena were not permanent employees of the Academy, nor were they paid to serve as guides. None of the participants in the riding excursion that day had received any horsemanship instructions from the three teens.

The group proceeded in single file until they reached a field. There, everybody started trotting and cantering and getting out of line. The lead horse began galloping, and the other horses followed suit. As they galloped and bunched together,

Chapter 5 / The Accommodation Sector

Susan, who had lost control, screamed for someone to stop the horses. Then she fell off her horse and was fatally injured by one of the other horses. Her heartbroken mother sued the Academy.

The Academy argued that it was not an absolute insurer of the safety of the riders given that riding has an inherent element of risk, and that its only duty was to take reasonable precautions to prevent injuries.

The court found that the trail guides lacked the skills to control the horses properly and to save Susan from injury when the horses bunched together. It had been their duty to keep the horses safely spread out. Drena, the end guide, failed to remain behind to watch for trouble. At the time of the accident, Susan and several other riders were behind the guides. Given the number and youth of the riders, it was essential that the ride be controlled so that the horses could be slowed or stopped before an injury occurred. The Academy had failed in its duty to take the reasonable precaution of providing competent trail guides who could handle emergencies. Given Susan's inexperience, the Academy was also negligent in allowing her to canter without proper instruction. There was no evidence that the disclaimer had been brought to Susan's attention. Even if it had been, the court doubted that the language used in the disclaimer was wide enough to cover negligence on the part of the employees of the Academy. Susan's family was awarded general damages of $3500 and special damages of $916 for a total of $4416, in 1967 dollars, as compensation for their grief and expenses.

An award in such a case today would likely be much higher.

Rustic Accommodations

Noddin v. Laskey, [1956] S.C.R. 577, 3 D.L.R. (2d) 577, reversing in part [1955] 5 D.L.R. 442 (N.B.C.A.)

The plaintiff rented from the defendant a cabin that was heated by propane gas. The plaintiff applied a match to the gas heater. There was an explosion, and the plaintiff was severely injured. The defendant was found liable. The explosion had resulted from a failure to install a pilot light for which the defendant was responsible, and from an unexplained escape of gas for which neither party could be shown to be responsible. In these circumstances, the liability for the damage rested solely upon the defendant. While an owner is not required by law to install the most modern equipment, the defendant in this case was deemed to have known (1) that his guests would attempt to ignite the gas heater, and (2) that pilot lights are highly effective safety features. The defendant had a duty to make the accommodation reasonably safe for the guests. It was determined that the gas had escaped through the pipe leading to the burner, and that the explosion therefore would not have occurred had there been a pilot light.

The following case involved a private cottage, not a resort, but the principle is the same.

Mackniack v. Brown (1967), 62 W.W.R. 633 (Sask. Q.B.)

The plaintiff, a guest of the defendant's at the time of the incident, sued to recover damages for injuries the plaintiff sustained after falling into a manhole at the defendant's cottage. The manhole cover had recently been removed, probably by another guest. The action was dismissed. The defendant had no reason to anticipate any danger to the plaintiff arising from the correct use of the manhole. Moreover, the defendant was unaware that the manhole had become a hidden danger. For the duty of awareness to apply, more time would have had to have elapsed from the point at which the cover was removed. The occupier was not liable for damages inflicted on one of his licensees by the actions of another because the damages were not reasonably foreseeable.

Alderson v. North Pender Holding Inc., [1987] B.C.J. No. 1628 (Q.L.)

A lodge was found not liable for damages sustained by a guest who fell down steps described as "hewn." The court held that the steps were normal in a rustic setting but noted that the result may have been different had the steps been in an urban setting.

Emergency Telephones

Some resorts occupy many hectares of land. Guest activities may be spread all over the property. Although not a legal requirement, emergency phones in remote areas demonstrate a concern for the welfare of the guests.

Disclaimers and Waivers

The more hazardous the activity, the greater the potential liability. Many hotels and resorts use waivers and disclaimers to reduce liability. The waiver or disclaimer must be properly presented to the guest, and not be hidden among other written instructions, buried on the back of forms, or understated by staff. Staff should ensure that the guest has read the waiver or disclaimer and answered any questions. A waiver should be understandable to the guest signing it. Canada is officially bilingual. In British Columbia, the waivers may also need to be translated into Japanese and Chinese because of the size of those markets.

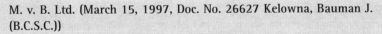

M. v. B. Ltd. (March 15, 1997, Doc. No. 26627 Kelowna, Bauman J. (B.C.S.C.))

M and his family had held season passes at B's ski resort for four years. M received the 1994 season renewal application in August. He did not review the application, but simply sent to the resort a cheque for the amount due. The application contained the following term: "All persons must sign a 'Release of Liability' prior to the obtaining of a pass. Parents and Guardians must sign on behalf of children under 19 years of age."

On opening day, M went to the resort's Pass Distribution Centre to retrieve the family pass. The passes were being distributed alphabetically, with each letter or group of letters assigned to a table for pickup. The "M" table was run by a woman who handed each person who approached the table a piece of paper to be signed. After signing the paper, a person would receive a pass and his or her paper would be deposited in a container that was overflowing by the time M arrived. When it was M's turn at the head of the line, he stated and spelled his name for the woman and gave her his photograph. She handed him a piece of paper and asked him to sign it. When he asked her why, she responded, "You have to sign this paper to get your pass." M signed the paper without reading it, and handed it back. Next to the signature line was the following statement in capital letters: "I HAVE READ AND UNDERSTAND THIS AGREEMENT AND I AM AWARE THAT BY SIGNING THIS AGREEMENT I AM WAIVING CERTAIN LEGAL RIGHTS WHICH I OR MY HEIRS, NEXT OF KIN, EXECUTORS, ADMINISTRATORS AND ASSIGNS MAY HAVE AGAINST THE RELEASEES."

The document had two sections headed "Assumption of Risks" and "Release of Liability, Waiver of Claims and Indemnity Agreement." Capital letters were used for the headings and set in bold type. The woman who received the release form from M returned it to him, saying, "You have to print your name and address here." She pointed to the lines under the "Release of Liability" heading, which read: "BY SIGNING THIS DOCUMENT YOU WILL WAIVE CERTAIN LEGAL RIGHTS, INCLUDING THE RIGHT TO SUE. PLEASE READ CAREFULLY!" M printed his name and address without reading the release. He handed it back to the woman and was given his ski pass.

In March 1995, M was injured when he collided with a snowmobile driven by an employee of B. M sued B and the employee. B and the employee moved for a dismissal of the action on the basis that the terms of the release precluded M from claiming damages from them. M maintained that he had not appreciated the nature of the release. He had mistaken it for an administration record and had assumed that its purpose was simply to ensure that the correct person received the pass. M did not recall signing a similar document in each of the previous four years. He admitted that had he been alerted to the fact that the document was a waiver, his right to claim damages would have been compromised.

The court had to decide whether M was bound by the release. The *Occupiers' Liability Act* provides that while an occupier can avoid his duty of care by express agreement, express stipulation, or notice, the occupier must take reasonable steps to bring the exclusion to the attention of the other party. The court found that the resort had taken reasonable steps to bring the release to M's attention. The application form carried notice of the release form. The Pass Distribution Centre would not release the pass until M signed the release. The use of bold type indicated that the release was an important legal document. The court held that M had been careless in signing the release. He had been given ample opportunity to read the release, but had chosen not to.

Generally in law, if a party has signed a written agreement, it does not matter whether or not he has read it. There was no fraud or misrepresentation in this case, and so it was immaterial whether or not M had read the document. The court concluded (1) that the release was binding and enforceable, (2) that the employee had acted within the scope of her employment, and (3) that M's accident fell within the scope of the release.

Another judge on another day may have found that not enough had been done to impress upon M the significance of the release. As with many court cases, the law was clear, but how the facts would be interpreted in light of the law was not clear.

Greeven v. Blackcomb Skiing Enterprises Ltd., 22 C.C.L.T. (2d) 265 (B.C.S.C.)

G, a first-time skier, had been surprised by a dangerous drop-off on a ski hill, fallen, and seriously injured herself. She sued the resort. The resort brought an application for summary judgment dismissing her action on the ground that the contract precluded any liability. The ticket given her that day bore on its face a request to read the back. The back contained conditions disclaiming liability on any basis. Evidence was given that red and yellow cards were posted in the ski areas announcing that exclusion of liability on the part of the resort was a condition of using the facilities. G acknowledged receiving the ticket, but stated that she had not read the back and had not seen the notices. The application for summary judgment was dismissed. The burden of proof lay on the ski resort to demonstrate that reasonable measures had been taken to draw the sweeping exclusions of liability to the attention of patrons. G had made out a *prima facie* ("on the face of it") case that there were triable issues. It was open to the trial judge to consider whether the resort had discharged the burden of showing that it had taken adequate measures to bring the exclusion clauses to the plaintiff's attention. The defendant's evidence on the application for summary judgment, including the location of the posted notices, was too vague to be relied upon.

Summary

Negligence prevention requires commonsense and constant vigilance. Where appropriate, legal advice can also be of invaluable assistance. An establishment should have written, standard operating procedures that are well thought out, regularly reviewed and updated, and applied faithfully in the day-to-day operations of the business. The premises and equipment should be kept in excellent working order at all times, and repairs should be made properly and without delay. Areas that are out of bounds should be clearly marked. All reasonable safety precautions should be taken and reviewed periodically. All staff should be well trained and monitored on a reasonably frequent basis. The more hazardous the activity, the greater the responsibility of the operator to ensure safety and adequate supervision and warnings.

Disclaimers and waivers are useful instruments with which to limit liability. However, they are not absolute guarantees. An operator will not be excused from gross negligence even if there is a disclaimer or waiver. To be effective, disclaimers must be clearly worded and brought fairly to the attention of the guest.

Discussion Questions

1. Outline some of the liability risks that may pertain to the following areas of a hotel:

   a) Doors, lobbies, and staircases

   b) Guest corridors

   c) Guest bedrooms, especially the bathrooms

   d) Dining rooms, bars, and banquet rooms

   e) Swimming pools, saunas, and hot tubs

2. For each of the above, what standard operating procedures (STOPS) could be adopted to reduce the risks?

3. Why should some repair and maintenance work be done by outside contractors?

4. Rank some of the standard operating procedures in order of importance.

5. Discuss how a telephone attendant should handle a call from a terrified female guest who says that she has been attacked and that the attacker might still be in the room.

6. Is a hotel an insurer of the guest's safety? Why or why not? Explain your answer in light of a nonstrict liability situation and a strict liability situation.

Chapter Six

The Restaurant Sector: Food

Learning Outcomes

1. Explain the negligence and regulatory issues particular to the food service industry.

2. Describe the standard of care imposed on the food
   service industry.

3. Describe the acts that govern the fitness of products
   in the food service industry.

4. Explain the *Food and Drugs Act, Sale of Goods Act,*
   and *Donation of Food Act.*

5. Explain truth in advertising and its impact on
   restaurant menus and offerings.

6. Describe liability for foreign objects found in food
   and drinks and for food poisoning.

7. List the seven major causes of food poisoning found
   in the food service industry.

8. Create standard operating procedures that would
   reduce the risk of food poisoning.

Introduction

This chapter deals with negligence prevention and regulatory issues of particular relevance to the food service industry. The restaurant sector includes any establishment that sells food and drink (whether licensed or unlicensed) to the public or members of a club, such as restaurants, bars, taverns, pubs, nightclubs, private clubs, lounges, takeout counters, refreshment booths, and hotel dining rooms. Although not specifically addressed, the principles also apply to food that is sold from display counters, such as potato chips and chocolate bars.

Food Standards

The Common Law

Just as an innkeeper may refuse accommodation to a transient if there are no vacancies in the inn, a restaurateur may refuse food and drink to a patron if there is insufficient food or drink in the premises to serve more than the patrons who have already ordered their meals. Although shortages are unlikely in urban or well-serviced rural settings, it can occur in remote lodges.

Food service operators have a duty of care to the public to avoid risks in the manufacture, preparation, and service of food. Under common law and pursuant to statute, there are implied conditions that any food offered for sale is of merchantable quality and fit for the purpose of digestion. Because the conditions are implied, it is not necessary for the parties—such as the customer and the waiter as representative of the owner—to turn their minds to them. Ordering a meal is not meant to be a thorough and detailed negotiation. The two implied conditions have been codified under sale of goods legislation. The food does not have to be tasty or nutritious, but it must be fit for human consumption. It must not contain foreign objects, poisons, or diseases. As was once famously observed, if one wishes to enjoy sausages and respect laws, one should not see either of them being made. Hot dogs often contain such cow and pig parts as connective tissue, lips, and lymph tubes; none of these off-putting ingredients is harmful to health; thus, they do not constitute a breach of the conditions.

Generally, when a patron suffers an injury or an illness as a result of eating or drinking at a restaurant, mere proof that the restaurant served the food or drink is enough to place the onus of disproof upon the restaurant. Food poisoning is a classic instance of the application of the negligence doctrine of *res ipsa loquitur*. Even if the precise manner in which the poisoning or contamination took place cannot be determined, the courts tend to find that the contamination could not have occurred but for the negligence of the manufacturer or server. The real question is often not whether the plaintiff will succeed, but against whom. The plaintiff can sue for breach of contract. The more common approach, however, is to pursue the action in negligence. As in any civil action, the burden of proof is on a balance of probabilities. The plaintiff does not have to prove beyond a reasonable doubt that the defendant caused the injury, only that it is more probable than not that the defendant did so.

> **Heimler v. Calvert Caterers Ltd. (1974), 4 O.R. (2d) 667 (H.C.J.), affirmed (1975), 8 O.R. (2d) 1 (C.A.)**
>
> The plaintiff contracted typhoid fever a week after eating food that he had consumed as a guest attending a wedding reception catered by the defendant. The source of the disease was a typhus-carrying employee of the defendant. The

disease was transmitted to the food when the carrier failed to wash her hands after using the bathroom. In finding for the plaintiff, the trial judge made the following statements:

> Is the defendant guilty of negligence? Generally, the law of negligence requires a restaurant operator to exercise a care proportionate to the serious consequences which may result from a lack of care. He is necessarily bound to ensure that the food prepared and served by him is fit for human consumption and may be eaten without causing sickness or endangering life by reason of its condition. The standard of care is to use the same degree of care in the preparation of food as would be exercised by a reasonably prudent person skilled in the art of preparing food. It has also been said that the standard of care would be the same as a person would use in preparing his own food ... A reasonably prudent restaurateur or caterer ought to anticipate the presence of foreign and potentially dangerous substances in his food ... The patron of a restaurant has the right to expect that all reasonable health precautionary measures are carried out and that the food served to him will be of high quality, well prepared, and free from any contaminating germs.

The Court of Appeal dismissed the appeal, stating that "the standard of care demanded from those engaged in the food-handling business is an extremely high standard."

McNeil v. Airport Hotel (Halifax) Ltd. (1980), 76 A.P.R. 490 (T.D.), 41 N.S.R. (2d) 490 (S.C.)

The plaintiff was one of several guests who suffered salmonella poisoning after eating Cornish game hens at the defendant hotel. He suffered through a miserable week and then was hospitalized for another three weeks. The cause was either poor hygiene on the part of the employees or a failure to cook the hens properly. The court ruled that the cause of the poisoning was the negligence of the hotel's employee in breach of the hotel's duty of care owed to the diner and assessed general damages for pain and suffering of $3,000.

In the *Heimler* case, despite the employee's testimony that she had washed her hands, the typhus bacillus had been transmitted to the food. In the *McNeil* case, despite the fact that no salmonella had been found in the leftover food, the salmonella germ had been transmitted to the plaintiff. The court found that it was improbable that the plaintiff had contracted salmonella anywhere else. In both cases, the food server had no satisfactory alternative explanation. Liability was imposed on the basis of *res ipsa loquitur*.

Keeping a kitchen sanitary is a never-ending battle. The bacteria cannot be eliminated, only kept at bay. A cutting board, for example, is host to literally trillions of bacteria. Of particular concern in any kitchen are the fats, oils, and grease. These substances can scald, causing severe injuries at temperatures well below their flaming points. Once afire, they can be more dangerous than other burning items because they burn with a white-hot intensity and can flow and spread the fire very quickly. Grease burning on a range or grill creates considerable smoke, which can trigger smoke alarms and heat sensors and provoke unwise chefs to disconnect them (clean cooking surfaces and proper ventilation are the better answers).

Operators and staff have a duty of care to staff and each other to avoid unreasonable risks in the operation of a kitchen. Keeping a kitchen safe is like trying to tidy a war zone. Many kitchen implements and pieces of equipment are dangerous including ranges, ovens, grills, deep fat fryers, garburators, meat slicers, blenders, knives, skewers, and breakable items. Many ingredients such as fats and oils are flammable or scalding. Quarters are usually cramped, and the cooks, busboys, and servers are usually rushed and preoccupied. Tidiness, courtesy, and good workplace policies help to minimize accidents.

Standard of Liability

The common law imposes a very high standard of care on the food service industry. Food manufacturers are held to a strict standard of care and are liable for injuries even though all reasonable precautions were taken. The rationale is that they are best situated to control the process and to blend the cost of insurance into the price of the product. Restaurateurs are held to a standard less than but close to strict liability. If they manufacture their own products, they also incur **strict liability**. Even if the problem originated with the manufacturer and the restaurateur could not have learned of it, the restaurateur will almost invariably also be found liable. In this situation, the restaurateur can make a third-party claim against the manufacturer.

The person who contracts to purchase the food from the restaurant has **privity of contract** with the restaurant and can sue directly in contract. Where there is no privity, such as when the purchaser of the food gives it to another person off the premises who eats it, the noncontractual consumer of the food can sue the restaurant using the tort law bypass (see Chapter 3) under the neighbour principle enunciated by Lord Atkin in *Donoghue v. Stevenson*, *[1932] A.C. 562 (H.L.)* (see Chapter 4). In another English case decided six years later, *Lockett v. A. & M. Charles, Ltd. et al.*, *[1938] 4 All E.R. 170 (K.B.)*, the court found privity of contract by implication arising out of the conduct of the parties. In Lockett, a husband and wife had lunch at the Hotel de Paris. The husband ordered and paid for both meals. The court held that there was "a contract implied by the conduct of the parties between the plaintiff, Mrs. Lockett, and the defendants when she ordered and was supplied with the [meal]." Although the order was placed through her husband, Mrs. Lockett had selected her own order. The defendants signalled their knowledge and acceptance of this by delivering the meal to her place setting.

Sometimes hotels and restaurants enter into contracts whereby the restaurant supplies in-room meals to guests, especially after the hotel's dining room has closed for the night. In such a case, it is likely that only the restaurant would be liable for any negligence. On the other hand, if a restaurant company licenses the hotel to produce and sell its products, the hotel would bear the liability unless the restaurant company supplied defective ingredients. If the hotel and restaurant are unconnected but are simply near each other, then the negligence of one does not affect the other, even if they are the only two businesses for miles around. Whether they will share in a joint negligence finding depends on there being a contractual connection between the two or a duty of care to the patron—that is, a duty not to recommend the local restaurant when it is known by the hotel that the restaurant has received work orders pertaining to unsanitary conditions.

The *Food and Drugs Act*

Part I of the federal *Food and Drugs Act* prohibits the sale, labelling, packaging, processing, and advertising of food, drugs, and cosmetics in any manner that is false or misleading. No food may be advertised as a cure or treatment for any of the afflictions listed in the Act. The Act makes it a criminal offence to breach its requirements. Penalties include fines and imprisonment. Sections 4 and 31 of the Act state the following:

4. No person shall sell an article of food that

    (a) has in or on it any poisonous or harmful substance;

    (b) is unfit for human consumption;

(c) consists in whole or in part of any filthy, putrid, disgusting, rotten, decomposed or dis-
eased animal or vegetable substance;

(d) is adulterated; or

(e) was manufactured, prepared, preserved, packaged or stored under unsanitary conditions.

31. Every person who contravenes [Part I] or the regulations made under [Part I] is guilty of an
offence and is liable

(a) on summary conviction for a first offence to a fine not exceeding five hundred dollars or
to imprisonment for a term not exceeding three months or to both and, for a subsequent
offence, to a fine not exceeding one thousand dollars or to imprisonment for a term not
exceeding six months or to both and

(b) on conviction on indictment to a fine not exceeding five thousand dollars or to imprisonment for a term not exceeding three years or to both.

Prosecutions under the *Food and Drugs Act* are undertaken by the Crown. Victims of
actions that constitute a breach of the Act may also sue in tort or for breach of contract.

The *Sale of Goods Act*

The *Sale of Goods Act,* or similar provincial legislation, imposes on a vendor a statutory,
implied warranty that the goods sold are of merchantable quality and are reasonably fit
for the purpose, which, in the case of foods and beverages, is ingestion and digestion. The
legislation codifies much of the law generated in the common law with respect to the sale
of goods. The British Columbia case of *Gee v. White Spot Ltd. (1986), 7 B.C.L.R. (2d) 235,
32 D.L.R. (4th) 238* confirmed that foodstuffs and beverages are goods within the
meaning of the legislation. To attach liability to the seller, the following rules apply:

1. Except for a purchase of an item specified by its patent or trade name, the buyer
expressly or impliedly must make known to the seller the purpose for which the
goods are required so as to show that the buyer is relying on the seller's skill or
judgment.

2. The goods must be sold in the course of the seller's business.

3. The goods must not be reasonably fit for the purpose, or must not be of merchantable quality, or both.

4. With respect to merchantable quality, if the buyer examines the goods such that
the defect should have been discovered, then the implied warranty is lost.

Unless the food is fairly bubbling with virulence, it is almost impossible for a diner
to discover upon examination that the food is not of merchantable quality and is contaminated with toxins. The discovery usually occurs hours or days later.

B.F. v. T. (1985), 8 O.A.C. 69

The plaintiff was a sausage manufacturer. A customer became ill from salmonella
poisoning after eating one of the plaintiff's sausages. The plaintiff successfully
claimed against the defendant who originally supplied the meat to the plaintiff.
The court ruled that the meat did not meet the requirements of merchantability
and fitness under the *Sale of Goods Act* and that, if it was impossible for the
slaughterhouse to deliver meat without any salmonella in it, then there was a duty
upon the slaughterhouse to warn the manufacturer of the possible presence of the
contaminant.

> **Tiro v. Old Country Smoked Meats, [1988] B.C.J. No. 168 (Q.L.), affirmed [1989] B.C.J. No. 304 (Q.L.)**
>
> The plaintiff purchased some pork and lamb from two men at a picnic, and later suffered salmonella poisoning. The court held that the *Sale of Goods Act* did not apply because the defendants were not in the business of selling meat to the public. The fact that the plaintiff had selected the meat directly meant that the sale was not by way of description and consequently the plaintiff had not relied on the skill and judgment of the defendants.

Good Samaritan Legislation

In the past, many restaurants and hotel dining rooms threw out unused food rather than risk liability claims from anyone who might have eaten it. While serving as a member of the official Opposition in the Ontario Legislature, Dalton McGuinty, now the premier of Ontario, sponsored a private member's bill to end the waste. The *Donation of Food Act* provides in part:

1.(a) A person who donates food or who distributes donated food to another person is not liable for damages resulting from injuries or death caused by the consumption of the food unless,

   (a) the food was adulterated, rotten or otherwise unfit for human consumption; and

   (b) in donating or distributing the food, the person intended to injure or to cause the death of the recipient of the food or acted with reckless disregard for the safety of others.

1.(b) (respecting directors, agents, employees or volunteers of corporations to essentially the same effect as subsection 1(a))

2. This Act does not apply to a person who distributes donated food for profit.

Similar legislation exists in several other provinces including Nova Scotia, New Brunswick, Quebec, and Manitoba. Partly as a result of the legislation, many communities have instituted Second Harvest programs whereby unused but usable food is collected from restaurants and hotels by volunteers who redistribute it to the needy.

Ingredients

Menus and Advertising

Menus are effective marketing devices. The customer is captive and wants to buy. The waiter proffers the menu, which boasts of the wares. The boasting, however, must be truthful. Diners realize that they have a legal right to get what they pay for. A 16-ounce steak must be a 16-ounce steak in precooked weight. Although the shaving of precooked steaks may be difficult for the diner to prove, the practice may come to light if the cook quits or is fired. Some bar menus advertise drinks containing a set amount of alcohol. With mixed cocktails, it would be difficult to prove the concentrations in each drink, but it could be embarrassing for the bar if a customer were to ask for a straight cocktail, remove the ice, and measure it.

Under false advertising and unfair business or trade practices legislation, it is false, misleading, and unfair to use a term if the food does not meet the standards suggested by the term. In our health-conscious age, many vendors offer foods purporting to be "light," "low fat," "low sodium," "heart-smart," or "part of a balanced breakfast." Many

Many hotels will arrange for specialty items, such as this birthday cake.

of these terms are meaningless. A blob of runny gelatin is part of a balanced breakfast provided the rest of the breakfast is nutritious. "Low sodium" may simply mean that the product contains less sodium than the company's similar alternative product. The company would be liable under the legislation only if both its products contained about the same amount of sodium or if it sold real salt as "low sodium." Less ambiguous are terms that express an absolute, such as "cholesterol-free" or "no-fat" (products so described must not contain cholesterol or fat). Other examples pertaining to truth in advertising include the following:

- "Fresh Fruit" should be fresh, not frozen or canned.
- "Canada's Grade A Beef" should be top Canadian grade, not top Argentine grade.
- "Grand Marnier Cake" should contain Grand Marnier, not just Grand Marnier flavouring.
- "Canadian Maple Syrup" must be Canadian, not an American substitute.
- "Dover Sole" must be Dover sole, not another type of sole.

In response to baby boomer anxieties about health and longevity, some companies have gone so far as to advertise that their products do not contain substances that never were in the products in the first place. "Caffeine-free" ginger ale is an example.

Allergies

Many customers are allergic to certain foods and food additives. Common serious, even fatal, allergens include nuts and peanuts, peas, dairy products, shellfish, regular fish, and sulphites that are used to keep salads looking fresh. Great care must be taken to ensure that, for example, ground nuts are not included in cakes unless proper warnings are included in the menu description of the dessert. The public has come to expect that French fries will be cooked in vegetable oil. To avoid the tragedy of a potentially fatal reaction, a restaurant keen to market the old-fashioned taste of French fries cooked in peanut oil must advise the public by means of emphatic warnings about the difference in food preparation. Food servers do not avoid liability merely by delivering to the table meals that were prepared elsewhere. Food servers must be able to advise their customers as to what they are serving. When guarding against food allergies, it is best for everyone concerned to err on the side of caution. It is recommended that an exact list of all ingredients for all food served be available for the guests and the service staff. The list should also include any menu items purchased from outside purveyors and sold in-house.

Religious Dietary Laws

Some restaurants cater to persons who follow religious dietary laws. Items on the menu that do not meet the requirements should be clearly marked. If the menu is ambiguously drafted, an attempt to serve food that has not met the requirements may be a breach under false advertising and duty of care.

Substitutions

Sometimes a restaurant must make substitutions; this is expected and cannot be helped. The menu should contain a fair disclaimer to protect the restaurant from a charge of false advertising—for example, "We strive to serve the freshest fruits and vegetables possible, and if these are not available, there may be a substitution." Restaurateurs and their staff must ensure that any substitutions do not endanger patrons with allergies.

Objects in Food

Some objects found in meals are not meant to be there. Some objects, such as glass, can be hard to detect. Glasses should never be stored above food preparation areas. Bartenders should not use the customer's glass as an ice scoop because it may chip and cut the customer. The chip itself might find its way into another customer's cocktail. Unless the bar can demonstrate that the chip was caused by the independent, intervening act of the patron, the bar will be liable for breaching the warranty of fitness of purpose.

> **Shandloff v. City Dairy Ltd. et al., [1936] O.R. 579**
>
> The plaintiff bought from the defendant a bottle of milk containing shards of glass. The court found that the defendant was liable because the product was not fit for the purpose intended and was not of merchantable quality under the *Sale of Goods Act*.

There are two tests applied to objects found in food. The foreign or natural test examines whether the object is foreign or natural to the food item. A fish bone in fish stew or seafood chowder is natural. A chicken bone in boneless chicken is not. On the other hand, a court may find chicken bones to be natural to chicken potpie. If the product is natural, there is no breach of the warranty of merchantable quality. If the product is foreign, there is a breach.

The second test, the reasonable expectations test, looks at whether the object would have been anticipated by a reasonable consumer. The presence of reasonably unanticipated objects constitutes a breach of warranty. Under the reasonable expectations test, a plaintiff may succeed even if the object is natural to the product, as long as the plaintiff would not reasonably have expected to find the natural object in the food. In *Zabner v. Howard Johnson's, Inc., 201 So. (2d) 824 (Fla., 1967)*, the court found that a walnut shell in walnut ice cream was not reasonably anticipated. Although walnut shells are natural to the food at first, the court felt that the public would not expect to find them in the final product. Whether or not an ingredient is reasonably anticipated will depend on the facts. Proper labelling is crucial.

Food Poisoning

Every year, over 10 000 cases of food poisoning are reported in Canada alone. It is estimated that another 100 cases are unreported for each case reported. Whether they occurred in the home or in a commercial establishment, virtually all of these cases could have been avoided. Vichyssoise (cold potato soup), steak tartar (raw meat), and hamburger because of E. coli; pork because of trichinosis; and poultry because of salmonella are common danger foods. Listed below are the major causes of food poisoning in the food service industry.

1. Contaminated raw material

2. Cross-contamination from raw to cooked food

3. Improper thawing, cooling, or heat retention

4. Inadequate reheating or cooking

5. Too much time between preparation and ingestion

6. Unsanitary kitchens and equipment

7. Infected persons handling the food

Food poisoning often goes undetected. The symptoms can be confused with other illnesses such as colds and upset stomachs. A healthy person can handle mild food poisoning, but it can be deadly to the elderly and the young. High regulatory and negligence standards and improved reporting systems virtually guarantee that unsanitary practices will come to light. Unfavourable publicity can embarrass or even bankrupt a restaurant. The guilty are not always the greasy spoons. In a recent case involving a five-star hotel, a gravy boat was removed from the hotel's buffet after lunch and allowed to stand in the kitchen until dinnertime. In another case, chicken wings were permitted to thaw on a counter for the better part of a day.

Proper kitchen procedures, personal hygiene, and proper use of sick leave help to reduce the risk of food contamination. Community colleges and programs such as the British Columbia Food Safe Program offer excellent food-handling courses. The Guelph Food Technology Centre is Canada's largest food services trainer. In an effort to consolidate all inspection services related to the food industry, the federal government created the Canadian Food Inspection Agency (CFIA). The CFIA has implemented the Uniform Regulation and Code of Practice for the Food Retail and Food Services Sector. Food manufacturers, retailers, and restaurants are all subject to a high duty of care. Liability for breaching this duty is found in the common law, the federal *Food and Drugs Act*, and the provincial sale of goods legislation.

N. v. W.S.L. (April 11, 1988, Spencer J. (B.C.S.C.))

The plaintiff contracted botulism at the defendant's restaurant and spent more than two weeks in hospital. The treatment was a very strong drug that caused much discomfort. The plaintiff never fully recovered. The court awarded $14,000 in general damages.

J. v. W.S.L. (June 21, 1988, Doc. No. C862739, Lander J. (B.C.S.C.))

The plaintiff suffered a mild case of botulism after ingesting a roast beef sandwich at the defendant's restaurant. It took the plaintiff three months to recover. The court awarded $8,500 in general damages.

The plaintiffs in the above cases were lucky. The antitoxin for botulism does not always work, resulting in a painful death. The defendants were also lucky: since their cases were decided, damage awards for food poisoning have risen substantially.

Smoking

Background Haze

In 1997, the major tobacco companies admitted that they have known for decades that cigarette smoke is a very serious and addictive health hazard. They are still trying hard to increase sales. Although tobacco advertising is limited by law, they have become adept at circumventing the laws, for example, by sponsoring cultural or sports events and placing their products on movie sets. Little can be done to increase market share among adult smokers whose value to the tobacco companies will increasingly become one of diminishing returns. Thus, the tobacco companies are looking to the young to sustain their profit margins in the future, despite the very high personal and public health and financial costs of smoking.

Although some would argue that smokers have a right to engage in what is still a legal activity, the fact remains that secondhand smoke is an infringement of the right of nonsmokers to breathe smoke-free air. More and more jurisdictions have acknowledged this fact by passing regulations that restrict smoking in public places. When it comes to smoking and its dangers, the accommodation and food service industries are finding themselves increasingly vulnerable to actions—or the threat of action—by members of the public and their own staff. The public may seek recourse through municipal bylaws and other regulations. Staff may seek recourse through occupational health and safety legislation. Both groups may seek recourse through civil action. Our society's ever-decreasing tolerance for secondhand smoke will be to the financial benefit of establishments that become known for their carcinogen-free air.

Municipal Bylaws

Many municipalities have passed clean-air bylaws that apply to all public buildings, leaving few indoor public places where one can legally smoke. Typical is the bylaw passed in London, Ontario, that allowed smoking in 50 percent of public seating areas in 1997 but called for that percentage to decrease to zero by the year 2002. The enforcement of the bylaw is generally left to the property manager. This demonstrates the genius of political compromise. On the one hand, passing the bylaw placates the anti-smokers. On the other hand, failing to enforce it placates the smokers. Passing the enforcement buck to the beleaguered operators cushions the municipalities from too much criticism while they wait for public sentiment to catch up to the bylaw. In recent years, however, municipalities have begun more diligent enforcement.

R. v. D. (Oct. 5, 1995, Lamkin, Prov. Div. J. (Ont. Prov. Div.))

A patron insisted on smoking a cigar in the nonsmoking area of a restaurant. He was asked to refrain or to move to the smoking area. He refused. Eventually, the operator called the police and the patron was arrested. The court ruled that the patron's refusal to leave was an offence under the *Trespass to Property Act*, and that his refusal to leave and use of profanity constituted undesirable conduct sufficient to entitle the operator to request him to leave the premises.

Restaurant & Food Association of British Columbia and the Yukon et al. v. The City of Vancouver (October 30, 1996, Doc. No. A961963 Vancouver, Cohen J. (B.C.S.C.))

Vancouver passed a bylaw that prohibited smoking in most indoor public places. The bylaw drew a distinction between restaurants where minors might be present and restaurants where minors were not permitted. Prior to passing the bylaw, the city held three days of hearings. Over 100 delegations were heard. The municipal medical health officer recommended that smoking be banned in all indoor public places. The restaurant industry favoured designated areas. The final bylaw was a compromise between the interests of the medical health officer and the lobbyists. The Restaurant & Food Association of British Columbia and the Yukon, and the F Restaurant, challenged the bylaw contending that it was discriminatory and *ultra vires* the city's charter. The charter gives the city council authorization to make health laws "for the care, promotion and protection of the health of the inhabitants of the city." The Association did not question the city's power to enact health laws but argued that the city had exceeded its powers under the charter and that the bylaw was invalid because it did not treat all establishments equally. The bylaw purported to distinguish between establishments that served children and those that did not. The city did not establish that children were any more susceptible than adults to the hazards of tobacco smoke. The Association pointed out that the bylaw did not apply to other areas where children gathered, such as bingo halls. There was also no indication that city council had been provided with any evidence pertaining to the effect of tobacco smoke on children. The Association argued that the main purpose of the bylaw was not to protect children, but to protect the public in general and hospitality workers in particular from "environmental tobacco smoke." The Association also suggested that the bylaw promoted the monied interests of the owners of a certain licence class of establishment. The court ruled that:

1. Bylaws are invalid if they draw distinctions between classes of persons where such distinctions are not authorized, expressly or impliedly, by the municipality's charter.

2. Bylaws cannot be challenged on the basis of unreasonableness or of being poor public policy.

3. Courts may intervene only if the bylaw is *ultra vires* the municipality.

The court found that Section 203 of the city charter expressly empowered the council to classify and discriminate. The issue was narrowed to whether the council had discriminated in accordance with its express powers. The court held that if the bylaw had a legitimate health-related purpose, then the city had the authority to draw the distinctions that it did. The court was satisfied that the medical health officer in his report had dealt with the impact of tobacco smoke on young people. The court also found that it was within the city's authority to effect a compromise when enacting a bylaw.

Civil Action

There is a cause of action for negligence if it can be proven (1) that the establishment is an occupier, (2) that the establishment has breached a duty, and (3) that the breach of duty is the cause of an injury. One difficulty with cases involving health-related injuries

Outdoor cafés, like this one, circumvent anti-smoking bylaws.

is the length of time it often takes for the injuries to become evident. Occupiers' liability legislation makes it the duty of occupiers to take such care as may be required by the circumstances to ensure the safety of all persons entering or present upon the premises. If a restaurant or bar fails to introduce fresh air into a smoke-filled area, then it may be that a duty has been breached. Air that is polluted with secondhand smoke is a medical hazard. There have been instances in which employees who were able to prove that their health problems were caused by their work environment have collected punitive damages from their employers. The day may not be far off when a nonsmoking waiter with lung cancer will successfully sue his or her employer in negligence on the basis that the smoke-filled working environment caused the disease.

Asthma sufferers constitute a significant portion of the Canadian population. In light of the thin skull rule in negligence law, susceptibility on the part of the plaintiff to the damaging effects of smoke-filled rooms will not necessarily excuse the hospitality industry from liability. This is another situation in which superior knowledge may impose upon the operators a duty beyond that of other citizens. If the evidence establishes hazardous air quality, the employee may well have a case against the operator even if the bylaw requirements were met.

Recommendations

1. Monitor food ingredients constantly, keeping in mind that many people suffer from potentially fatal allergies. Ensure that all menus, including those written on chalkboards, alert consumers to the presence of allergens. Ensure that any changes to the ingredients are brought to the attention of regular customers who might otherwise simply order their "usual" without realizing that it is now prepared with a different and potentially harmful ingredient such as peanut oil.

2. Establish and implement procedures relating to allergies, kitchen hygiene, and food-preparation techniques, and ensure that they err on the side of caution.

3. Institute safe procedures for kitchens and their deadly arrays of tools and equipment.

4. Deal only with reputable food manufacturers and suppliers.

5. Ensure that all menus are truthful and informative.

6. Respect the dietary requirements of religious patrons.

7. Consider joining a Second Harvest program for its own sake and for the good will.

8. If a lawsuit for food poisoning is filed, ensure that the claim is well founded and that the illness was not caused by some other source.

9. Ensure that smoking areas are well ventilated (preferably with ceiling vacuums) in order to protect other patrons and staff from the harmful effects of second-hand smoke.

10. Comply with all food service licence requirements and all anti-smoking bylaws.

11. Create standard operating procedures for kitchen emergencies, and train the staff.

Summary

Negligence prevention in the food services sector requires constant vigilance, common-sense, and, where appropriate, sound legal advice. The standard of liability pertaining to foodstuffs has been rising steadily over the past several decades. In many cases, the standard of liability is strict. Restaurateurs must take care to ensure that their food-storage areas, food-preparation areas, and dining rooms meet or exceed all applicable health regulations. Restaurateurs must also abide by all applicable municipal bylaws and other legislation regulating smoking, advertising, fitness of the food for consumption, and other related matters. Special care should be taken with people who suffer from food allergies or who have other special needs.

Discussion Questions

1. Visit two restaurants and learn what steps each has taken to warn patrons of allergens and to reduce the risks of an allergic reaction.

2. How is smoking in public places regulated in your jurisdiction?

3. What protection do staff have from the harmful effects of secondhand cigarette smoke?

4. What are the major causes of food-borne illnesses?

5. What are the most common sources of (a) salmonella, (b) trichinosis, and (c) E. coli? What steps can a restaurant take to avoid these types of food poisoning?

6. Describe a test that is used to determine whether an object ought not to be in food.

7

Chapter Seven

The Beverage Service Sector: Alcohol

Learning Outcomes

1. Describe the tort liability associated with the sale and service of alcohol.

2. Describe the regulatory liability associated with the sale and service of alcohol.

3. Describe the criminal liability associated with the sale and service of alcohol.

4. Describe the common law liability for injured third parties.

5. Assess the duty for the protection of person and property for a property serving alcohol.

6. Design strategies for handling disruptive or inappropriate behaviour by guests.

7. Create the standard operating procedures for the sale and service of alcohol.

Introduction

This chapter deals mainly with tort liability associated with the sale and service of alcohol. Liquor licences are dealt with in greater detail in Chapter 12. As there is considerable overlap between the various sectors of the hospitality industry, many of the principles discussed elsewhere in the book apply to servers of alcohol, and many principles discussed in this chapter apply elsewhere. For example, the duty to the public and employees is owed, and liability for permitted activities attaches, regardless of whether alcohol is involved. The difference lies mainly in the relative frequency with which alcohol is involved in instances of breach of duty or other liability.

The legal response to alcohol has changed over the years. During Prohibition in the United States, the bootlegging trade became entrenched and led directly to the rise of organized crime. Illegal distilleries, breweries, and speakeasies (illegal bars) flourished. Canadian laws concerning the manufacture, sale, and public consumption of alcohol were not as restrictive as American laws. The Seagram empire was built by Samuel Bronfman who legally sold alcohol, just inside the Canadian border, to Americans who then smuggled it into the United States during Prohibition. Today, the production and sale of alcohol are controlled by government.

Drinking today is a legal activity for persons of legal drinking age, which varies from jurisdiction to jurisdiction. A minor cannot escape culpability for drinking in a province that has a higher drinking age than his or her home province; ignorance of the law is no excuse. It has been well documented that alcohol is deleterious to the minds and bodies of people who abuse it. An estimated 20 percent of the population has a psychological or physical predisposition to addiction to substances ranging from caffeine, to nicotine, to alcohol, to hard drugs.

The consequences of overconsumption of alcohol are serious. The loss of natural inhibitions can lead to a loss of caution or anti-social behaviour, while the impairment of coordination can lead to accidents. According to the Traffic Injury Research Foundation of Canada, about 1 percent of hard-core drinking drivers cause 47 percent of traffic injuries and fatalities. On Friday and Saturday nights, it is estimated that about one in 10 drivers has consumed some alcohol. Drunk driving is the largest criminal cause of death and injury in Canada. More North Americans have died as a result of accidents caused by drunk drivers than in the First World War, Second World War, Korean War, and Vietnam War combined.

In order to minimize the damage caused by the overconsumption of alcohol, governments have enacted various laws including criminal code provisions, licence requirements, and a minimum legal age for anyone wishing to imbibe, purchase, or sell alcohol. Anyone wishing to sell alcohol must obtain a government licence and abide by the terms of the licence. Failure to do so leads to criminal and/or civil liability. Governments have also sponsored education and enforcement programs such as R.I.D.E. in which drivers are selected at random for Breathalyzer testing and the Last Drink project in which drivers are asked where they had their last drink. This can help identify licensed establishments that are lax in preventing impaired patrons from staggering to their vehicular weapons.

Alcohol, which costs about 26 cents for every dollar of revenue it produces, makes a significant contribution to the bottom line of a licensed establishment. Such after-dinner drinks as Spanish or Irish coffee, cocktails, and liqueurs are highly profitable. Not surprisingly, staff may be encouraged to promote their sale. However, since 1980, the attitude of the public toward drinking and driving has undergone a substantial change. Organizations such as Mothers Against Drunk Driving (MADD) have attracted the attention of the media and put pressure on lawmakers to effect change. It is no longer socially acceptable to drink and drive.

The law has evolved an ever-increasing duty of care not only upon those who take on the risks of alcohol impairment but also upon those who benefit from the provision of the alcohol. The underlying principle is that anyone who stands to gain from the provision of alcohol should contribute to the losses suffered by others resulting from that provision. The fact that they are liable for the damages caused by alcohol impairment has forced vendors of alcohol not only to increase their insurance coverage but also to monitor the consumption of alcohol by their customers. (The sit-

Alcohol should be consumed responsibly or not at all.

uation is different for the provincially owned liquor outlets, by far the largest retailers of alcohol in the country. Because their customers are prevented by law from opening the bottles on the premises, the provincial retail outlets are spared alcohol-related liability.) The liability of private providers of alcohol is not predicated on the commercial exchange of money for alcohol, but on tort law principles of negligence. Also accountable are private hosts who allow their private guests to leave the residence in a drunken state.

The alcohol consumer is not only a potential co-defendant with the alcohol server but is also a potential plaintiff against the alcohol server. The principles of voluntary assumption of risk and contributory negligence on the part of the alcohol consumer are of little assistance to alcohol servers because they have a responsibility to supply the consumer with the inhibitions that their offerings of alcohol have helped to suppress. The freedom to serve alcohol imposes responsibility on servers. Servers cannot simply stand by while a customer or guest becomes intoxicated. The law imposes on servers a duty to take positive steps to guard against the damages that their impaired customers or guests may cause to themselves and to others.

Liability for Alcohol Misuse

Types of Liability

Liability for the improper service or overconsumption of alcohol may arise in at least four ways:

1. Under the *Criminal Code of Canada*, an alcohol consumer can be charged with a criminal offence for driving with a blood alcohol level above the statutory maximum.

2. Under the *Liquor Licence Act* of the jurisdiction, a licensed alcohol provider can be charged with the offence of providing liquor to anyone who appears to be intoxicated or to a person who is or appears to be underage.

3. A licensed alcohol provider may be liable for negligence pursuant to statute, such as Ontario's *Liquor Licence Act*, which states: "*[I]f a person or agent or employee of a person sells liquor to or for a person whose condition is such that the consumption of liquor would apparently intoxicate the person or increase the person's intoxication so that he or she would be in danger of causing injury to himself or herself or injury or damage to another person or the property of another person ..., the [injured]*

person [or the estate of a deceased person] is entitled to recover an amount as compensation for the injury or damage from the person who or whose employee or agent sold the liquor."

4. An alcohol provider, licensed or private, may be liable under common law for breach of contract or for negligence for breach of duty of care or as an occupier.

Liability may be imposed on the server, and on the employer of the server through vicarious liability. The employer will not be liable for the actions of an employee who acts outside the scope of his or her authority. An employer may escape liability if it can be demonstrated that:

1. the employer gave clear and express instructions not to serve alcohol to a customer;

2. the server continued to serve alcohol out of friendship or infatuation; and

3. the server did not charge the customer for the drinks.

Notwithstanding these circumstances, a court could still find the employer liable for inadequate supervision or on some other basis.

Criminal Liability

A consumer of alcohol who drives or controls a motor vehicle or boat may be criminally liable for illegal consumption. When alcohol is consumed, it is dissolved into the fluids of the body. Alcohol in the bloodstream is measured in milligrams of alcohol per 100 millilitres of blood and is written as "percent milligrams." Pursuant to the *Criminal Code of Canada*, the maximum legal alcohol limit for drivers in Canada is .08 percent Blood Alcohol Level, or .08 percent BAL. Driving with a BAL above the limit is a crime that can result in loss of driving privileges, a fine, a jail term, or all three penalties. A driver's ability to drive may also be impaired at levels below .08 percent BAL.

Regulatory Liability

Liquor Licence Act Provisions

The following regulations pertain to the sale of alcohol and are examples of similar provisions found in the liquor licensing Acts of all jurisdictions:

Liquor Control and Licensing Act (British Columbia)
Drunkenness

45.(1) A person shall not sell or give liquor to an intoxicated person or a person apparently under the influence of liquor.

(2) A licensee or his employee shall not permit an intoxicated person to remain in his licensed establishment.

Request to leave licensed establishment

47.(1) A licensee or his employee may

(a) request a person to leave; or

(b) forbid a person to enter

if he believes the presence of that person is undesirable or the person is intoxicated.

Gaming and Liquor Act (Alberta)
Conduct on licensed premises

95.(2) No licensee or employee or agent of a licensee or permittee and no employee or agent of a licensee or permittee shall ...

(b) sell or provide liquor to a person apparently under the influence of alcohol or a drug,

(c) permit a person apparently under the influence of alcohol or a drug to consume liquor on the licensed premises or the premises described in the permit.

(3) No licensee shall ...

(c) allow a disorderly or intoxicated person to be in or about the premises.

Liquor Licence Act (Ontario)

Sale to person under influence

43. No person shall sell or supply liquor or permit liquor to be sold or supplied to any person in or apparently in an intoxicated condition.

Intoxication in a public place

45.(4) No person shall be in an intoxicated condition in a public place or in any part of a residence that is used in common by persons occupying more than one dwelling.

All the liquor licence Acts provide for penalties for the breach of the Act. Common law remedies are not precluded, but may be pursued concurrently with statutory remedies.

Apparently Intoxicated Persons

Throughout Canada, it is against the law to serve alcohol to any person such that the service will cause the person to become intoxicated or increase the person's intoxication. The Acts give the licensed establishments the right to refuse entry to persons already intoxicated and may even impose an obligation to do so. Liquor licensees also have the right, and perhaps the obligation, to evict from the premises persons who have become or who are intoxicated.

However, if the circumstances are such that the eviction would endanger the person or others, the licensee must take reasonable steps to ensure safe passage (e.g., calling a taxi). Alcohol vendors and servers are expected by virtue of superior knowledge to realize when a patron is apparently intoxicated. An obvious drunk is obvious to all. Liquor licensees are expected to detect more subtle signs of intoxication such as loss of coordination and changes in behaviour and speech patterns. Most jurisdictions offer government-approved training courses in alcohol management and service. If trained staff prevent one bad accident, the cost of the training will have paid for itself many, perhaps thousands of, times over.

Little Plume v. Weir, Marco Polo Pub Ltd., et al. (1998, 220 A.R. 332)
Alberta Court of Queen's Bench Judicial District of Calgary

The plaintiff pedestrian was rendered an incomplete quadriplegic as a result of a motor vehicle accident. The plaintiff sued the driver of the vehicle, the owner of the vehicle, the pub which the plaintiff had visited shortly before the accident and its owner and staff.

The plaintiff, an alcoholic, walked into a pub and sat down. He appeared to some of the pub staff to be intoxicated. He was not served. He was asked to leave and was offered a cab. He refused the offer and left on his own within a few minutes of entry. While attempting to cross the street, he was struck by a van and was rendered an incomplete quadriplegic. The Court held that the pub complied with its statutory duty to evict intoxicated persons and its common law duty to act reasonably when doing so. The pub's actions were reasonable and appropriate to the foreseeable risk.

Hague v. Billings (1989), 48 C.C.L.T. 192, reversed in part 13 O.R. (3d) 298 (C.A.)

A tavern had served alcohol to an already intoxicated patron. The patron drove and caused an accident, killing the plaintiff's mother and injuring the plaintiff. The tavern was found liable in negligence under common law and pursuant to section 53 of the *Liquor Licence Act.* The action was dismissed against another tavern that had served only one drink to the patron and whose owner had tried to dissuade the patron from driving.

Skinner v. Baker Estate (1991), 34 M.V.R. (2d) 157, [1992] I.L.R. 1–2809 (Ont. Gen. Div.)

The court held that the staff of the licensed establishment that had served two beers to the patron could not reasonably have discerned that he was already intoxicated. Several witnesses testified that the patron did not look intoxicated even though his blood alcohol level later tested at .24 percent, or three times the legal limit. The court found, on the strength of the independent testimony as to the patron's apparent sobriety, that the defendants had discharged their duty. The claim was dismissed.

Stewart v. Pettie (1993), 13 Alta. L. R. (3d) 142, [1995] 1 S.C.R. 131, 121 D.L.R. (4th) 222

The plaintiff, her husband, brother, and sister-in-law were patrons of the Mayfield Inn in Edmonton. Her brother consumed 10 to 14 ounces of alcohol during a five-hour period. Despite this, he showed no signs of impairment and assured her that he was capable of driving. As they were driving home on icy roads, he lost control of the car and struck a wall. The accident left the plaintiff a quadriplegic with damages in the $4-million range. His blood alcohol level was twice the legal limit one hour after the accident. The plaintiff's action against the inn was dismissed at trial on the basis that the brother's family members had been satisfied as to his sobriety and ability to drive such that it would be unfair to expect the staff of the inn to reach any other conclusion themselves. Ms. Stewart's appeal was allowed. The defendant inn then appealed to the Supreme Court of Canada. The appeal was allowed, restoring the findings of the trial judge.

The mere consumption of alcohol on the occupier's premises does not by itself impose liability on the occupier. The circumstances must be such that a duty has arisen and been breached. It is well-established law that a bar owes a duty of care to patrons and is required to prevent an intoxicated patron from driving if it is apparent that he or she intends to drive. The duty is also owed to third parties who might be using the highways. However, the duty to use positive action does not arise unless the risk is foreseeable. In the *Stewart* case, it was reasonable for the inn to have assumed that one of the patrons who accompanied the brother and who had not drunk any alcohol would be driving instead of the brother. In other words, it was reasonable for the inn to have assumed that sober persons would not let a drunken companion drive. In this case, the risk had not been reasonably foreseeable. Despite this case, commercial servers of alcohol owe a duty of high vigilance and are expected to be alert to signs of impairment that ordinary people might miss.

Underage Persons

Laws prohibit the sale of alcohol to anyone under the legal drinking age. For example, paragraph 61(1)(c) of Ontario's *Liquor Licence Act* makes it an offence to sell liquor to anyone who is underage or apparently underage. If the customer appears to be underage, the server must ask for valid identification. Further, if the liquor vendor has reason to believe that an adult is acquiring the alcohol for a minor, the vendor has a duty not to sell the alcohol to the adult.

> **Thomas v. Duquesne Light Co., 545 A. (2d) 289 (Penn., 1988)**
>
> An adult and a minor drove to a beer store to buy beer. The adult placed the order from his car. Upon reaching the car, the salesclerk saw the minor hand the adult money to pay for the order. After drinking the beer, the minor climbed an electrical transmission tower, touched a high-voltage wire, and fell 66 metres to the ground. The trial judge dismissed the case on the basis that the beer had been sold to the adult. The Court of Appeal ordered a new trial to determine whether the beer store, through its employee salesclerk, should have known that the beer was being purchased for the minor. The parties settled before a new trial could be held.

Common Law Liability

Originally, the common law did not avail innocent, injured third parties because they did not have privity of contract with the alcohol servers and the servers did not owe a duty to people they did not know. Cases such as *Donoghue v. Stevenson* (see Chapter 4) expanded the classes of persons to whom a duty of care is owed, and legislation further widened the liability net. Legislation and the tort law bypass (see Chapter 3) circumvented the privity problem.

Although accidents and injuries can occur in an almost limitless variety of ways, the customer who is served to or past the point of intoxication and who drives home represents the greatest liability risk. Time is often an enemy: there is generally not enough time between imbibing and departure from the premises for the blood alcohol level of an inebriated person to fall below the legal limit. Although drinking and driving constitutes the greatest risk, liability flows from any injuries caused or partly caused by the actions of intoxicated patrons or guests. Nondriving examples include riding an inner tube down a ski hill, jumping off a roof into a backyard swimming pool, or walking home and falling.

Under negligence principles, injured parties receive compensation intended to replace, as nearly as money can, the value of the loss. Special damages, such as the cost of prostheses and home nursing care, remain relatively easy to quantify. General damages for pain and suffering, on the other hand, are notoriously subjective. Since the 1960s, general damage awards in Canada have steadily increased. In an effort to curb ruinous awards, the Supreme Court of Canada, in three decisions known as the Trilogy, capped them at $100,000 in 1978 dollars. The awards have increased since then with inflation. Earlier awards were usually small enough to be covered by the normal public liability insurance of the tortfeasor. Later awards often exceed the coverage; therefore, to garner sufficient compensation, plaintiffs seek to sue an expanding body of defendants, including the providers of the alcohol and anyone else associated with the event. The leading Canadian case imposing a common law duty of care upon servers of alcohol is the *Menow* case discussed in Chapter 4.

Picka v. Porter and the Royal Canadian Legion (1980), 2 A.C.W.S. (2d) 428 (Ont. C.A.)

Porter consumed about 10 bottles of beer served to him on the premises of the Legion. The only staff person on duty was the bartender who never left his post behind the bar. Further, the Legion permitted patrons to buy rounds of beer. Porter left the Legion and drove through an intersection at an excessive speed. Several people were either killed or injured. The Legion was found liable because the manner of serving liquor was such that the staff had little or no opportunity to observe and monitor on a reasonable basis the level of intoxication of the patrons. The court awarded the plaintiff $400,000.

The *Picka* case demonstrates that, depending on the layout of the licensed floor area, it may not be sufficient to have a bartender permanently stationed behind the bar; it may be necessary to have roving, observant servers.

Schmidt v. Sharpe and the Arlington House Hotel (1983), 27 C.C.L.T. 1 (Ont. H.C.)

Schmidt was rendered a quadriplegic by Sharpe who had driven away from the Arlington House Hotel in an intoxicated state. His blood alcohol level had been .15 percent, or about double the legal limit. The court found that trained staff should have been able to detect that Sharpe was intoxicated and accordingly prevented his departure by car. The court awarded Schmidt $1,750,000.

Francescucci v. Gilker (February 12, 1996), Doc. CA C10259, C8229 (Ont. C.A.)

The victim of an accident sued a drunk driver and the restaurant that had served him. The restaurant employees had carried the clearly intoxicated driver to his car, unlocked the door for him, placed him behind the wheel, and tossed him the keys. The driver drove off and had an accident shortly thereafter. The restaurant was found to be 78 percent liable. The restaurant appealed the apportionment of liability, but the appeal was dismissed. The restaurant's employees owed a duty of care to the driver, as well as to others using the highway, to do everything reasonable within their power to prevent him from driving. Instead, they displayed a wanton disregard for the safety of the driver and others on the highway. Their acts were sufficiently shocking to differentiate the case from others involving hotels and bars in which lesser apportionments of liability had been made.

Commercial alcohol providers are not the only people being sued. Individuals, groups, and organizations that serve alcohol can expect to be named as defendants if there is an alcohol-related accident.

Baumeister v. Drake et al. (1986), 5 B.C.L.R. (2d) 382, 38 C.C.L.T. 1 (S.C.)

Baumeister and Drake had crashed a graduation party hosted by the Carefoots, the parents of one of their classmates. The Carefoots had invited about 25 guests, but about 175 people crashed the party, creating a chaotic scene. Baumeister and Drake had already been drinking and brought more alcohol to drink at the party. Although there was a wine punch at the party, Baumeister and Drake had not drunk much (if any) of it. After leaving the party, Baumeister fell off a truck and suffered severe brain damage. Drake had been driving the truck. The British Columbia Supreme Court held that, in these circumstances, the Carefoots could not have prevented the numerous guests from consuming their own alcohol or have distinguished who among the many guests was impaired. Thus, the Carefoots were not liable for the injuries. Significantly, despite absolving the Carefoots of liability, the Court held that their liability should be governed by the same standard applicable to commercial alcohol servers.

The reader may consider what small changes in the facts of the *Baumeister* case could have produced liability on the part of the hosts.

Occupiers' Liability

Statutory Provisions

As discussed in Chapter 4, all jurisdictions have **occupiers' liability** legislation that imposes upon an occupier responsibility for protecting the person and property of guests from injury or loss while on the occupier's property. Ontario's *Occupiers' Liability Act* states in part:

Section 1 (Interpretation)

1.(a) "occupier" includes,

    (1) a person who is in physical possession of premises, or

    (2) a person who has responsibility for and control over the condition of premises or the activities carried on there, or control over persons allowed to enter the premises;

  (b) "premises" means lands and structures, or either of them, and includes,

    (1) water ...

    (2) trailers and portable structures designed or used for residence, business, or shelter ...

Section 3 (Occupier's duty)

3.(a) An occupier of premises owes a duty to take such care as in all the circumstances of the case is reasonable to see that persons entering on the premises, and the property brought on the premises by those persons, are reasonably safe while on the premises.

  (b) The duty of care provided for in subsection (a) applies whether the danger is caused by the condition of the premises or by an activity carried on the premises.

The Act makes all occupiers responsible to provide safe premises and safe activities to anyone who enters upon property that they control.

Even light drinkers are less mentally and physically able than sober people. The risks inherent in the activities and premises of a hospitality business are greater for drinkers than nondrinkers. Occupiers may be liable if they fail to take into account the different skills of their drinking and nondrinking patrons. Some occupiers simply do not want to take on the additional risks that arise when alcohol is part of the mix. Many colleges have disallowed many of the initiation rights that once ushered in a postsecondary education, while many community-owned hockey rinks no longer tolerate the post-game beer in the dressing room.

Niblock v. Pacific National Exhibitions and the City of Vancouver (1981), 30 B.C.L.R. 20 (S.C.)

While intoxicated, the plaintiff fell over a low railing on the grounds of the Pacific National Exhibition. He had been drinking in one of the licensed premises on the grounds. The defendant argued that there had never been an accident involving the railing in the past, and that the fall was attributable to the intoxicated condition of the plaintiff. In rejecting this argument, the court stated that the *Occupiers' Liability Act* requires that occupiers ensure that the premises are reasonably safe for all people who might foreseeably enter upon them. The court held that in view of the fact that there were three licensed premises on a site that could be described as having a carnival-like atmosphere, the defendant should have anticipated that some of the people on the grounds would become caught up in the atmosphere and become intoxicated. However, the plaintiff was found to be 25 percent contributorily negligent.

The Conduct of Entrants

Patrons (or entrants) who are injured on the premises of a commercial establishment are not automatically guaranteed damages. Their conduct is also examined under such tort law principles as foreseeability, contributory negligence, and voluntary assumption of risk.

McGeough v. Don Enterprises Ltd., [1984] 1 W.W.R. 256, 28 Sask. R. 126 (Q.B.)

M was the victim of an unprovoked stabbing while a customer at the defendant's lounge. The attacker had been ejected from the establishment earlier in the day for bothering a female server. There had been no other indications that the attacker posed a threat to anyone. The court ruled that the attack was unforeseen. Because liability arises only when a risk is foreseeable, the lounge was not liable for the damages.

Stanton v. Twack et al. (1982), 14 A.C.W.S. (2d) 447 (B.C.S.C.)

Within hearing distance of the defendant's staff, the plaintiff was insulted and threatened by a female patron. Although the parties had been drinking, the defendant's staff ignored the situation. The female patron then picked up a glass and threw it into the face of the plaintiff. The court found that the verbal threats were a sufficient warning to the staff that the patron might become violent. By ignoring the verbal threats, the staff breached their duty to protect the plaintiff. The tavern was held liable for the damages.

Belligerent Customers

An establishment owes to its guests a duty to protect them from staff and other persons who represent a foreseeable risk. If the patron is well known for causing disturbances such that the establishment should have foreseen that trouble would ensue, the establishment may be liable for not evicting or controlling the patron. Even if the belligerent patron is not well known to the establishment, liability may still be found if the patron's dangerous behaviour became apparent to the staff prior to the infliction of the injury.

An establishment in a high-crime district has a higher duty than an establishment in a low-crime district to provide protection for its patrons. The standard of care imposed is one of reasonableness in light of all the applicable circumstances. Security measures include adequate staffing, bouncers, security guards, surveillance cameras, good lighting, handy police numbers and telephones, signs indicating that only small amounts of money are kept on the premises, and rehearsed procedures.

An establishment may use force to remove the person who is the source of the risk, but only sufficient or reasonable force. If employees use too much or unreasonable force, the establishment may be liable for damages. For this reason, bars with bouncers pay higher insurance premiums than those without. For many establishments, bouncers are a necessity. For others, a safer course is to contact the police. When there is not sufficient time to call the police, the staff must ensure that the actions taken are reasonable in the circumstances.

Permitted Activities

As the following case illustrates, liability may arise from an activity that the occupier does not offer but in essence permits.

Jacobson v. Kinsmen Club of Nanaimo (1976), 71 D.L.R. (3d) 227 (B.C.S.C.)

At a beer garden run by the Kinsmen Club, two patrons climbed onto the ceiling beams of the structure. A short time later, another patron joined them, but then fell, striking Jacobson, who sued. The court ruled that, had the accident occurred when the first two patrons climbed onto the ceiling beams, the Club would not have been liable because the first climb was not foreseeable. However, the first climb constituted sufficient notice of a risk to which the occupier should have responded. In failing to take steps to prevent the third patron from climbing onto the beams, the Club assumed the risk of allowing the activity. It therefore breached its duty to the plaintiff and was liable for his injuries.

In the *Jacobson* case, the occupiers became liable for an activity that they did not set out to offer by permitting it to continue after becoming aware of it.

Duty Owed to Employees

Many businesses host company parties. If alcohol is to be served, the business should consider providing overnight accommodation or transportation for its employees and their spouses and guests. Alternatively, a designated driver policy should be instituted and followed.

Jacobsen v. Nike Canada Ltd. (1996), 133 D.L.R. (4th) 377, [1996] 6 W.W.R. 488 (B.C.S.C.)

Jacobsen was employed by Nike as a warehouseman. Part of his job included using his car to transport goods to a trade show. During a workday, he and his co-workers and supervisors drank a substantial amount of beer freely supplied by Nike. After work, he and another worker went to two clubs and drank more beer.

After leaving the second club, he drove off the road and was rendered a quadri-plegic. Nike argued that its duty to Jacobsen was that of a tavern to a patron. The court found that Nike's duty exceeded a tavern's duty by virtue of its failure to provide a safe working environment. In requiring Jacobsen to bring his car to work that day and then supplying him with beer, Nike, in effect, made drinking and driving part of the working conditions that day. In the words of the court, "It is hard to imagine a more obvious risk than introducing drinking and driving into the workplace." The court awarded $2,719,213.48 and apportioned 75 percent liability ($2,039,409.82) to Nike and 25 percent to Jacobsen for contributory negligence.

Defences Against Liability

As in general negligence matters, the plaintiff's own conduct may be used to reduce or eliminate the liability of the defendant. Intoxicated patrons are frequently found to be contributorily negligent for their injuries. However, the defence of voluntary assumption of risk will almost never avail servers of alcohol. The rationale is that the intoxicated person is incapable of forming the informed intent to voluntarily assume a risk. Further, the defence is not available in cases where the injuries are derived from a breach of a statutory duty.

Crocker v. Sundance Northwest Resorts Ltd., [1988] 1 S.C.R. 1186

C had been drinking before arriving at a ski resort but also bought several drinks once there. He entered an inner tube race on one of the ski hills. The resort man-ager tried to prevent C from entering the race, but C belligerently insisted. The manager relented. During the race, C crashed and was rendered a quadriplegic. The resort argued that C had voluntarily assumed the risk when he entered the race. Although he did not remember doing so, C had signed a waiver before entering the race. The Supreme Court of Canada found that, even if he had remembered signing the waiver, he would not have appreciated its nature and import at the time of signing it or at the time the race began. The Court found C 25 percent liable and the resort 75 percent liable on the basis that, in backing down in the face of C's belligerence, the manager had not acted reasonably.

Recommendations

1. Review the alcohol revenue policies of the licensee. If the focus is on pumping up profits through the oversale of alcohol, the licensee is on a collision course with the courts. Management must make the responsible service of alcohol a top priority. Clear written policies should be posted and enforced. Even if the responsible service of alcohol reduces revenues (and that does not necessarily follow), it also reduces liability costs.

2. Train staff in the responsible service of alcohol and the handling of belligerent or departing patrons. Excellent training programs exist across Canada; however, training alone does not eliminate the risk. Training programs can engender a false sense of security if the policies and skills are not consistently implemented.

3. Train staff to recognize the signs of intoxication. Have effective, enforceable procedures for slowing or terminating the consumption of alcohol by a patron.

4. Instruct staff not to serve anyone apparently under the legal drinking age until valid proof of age has been proffered. Patrons who cannot prove they are of legal drinking age should be refused entry or evicted. Instruct staff to attempt (tactfully) not to serve alcohol to an apparently pregnant woman.

5. Encourage staff to offer alternatives to alcohol such as non- or low-alcohol beverages. Maximize the ability of customers to monitor their alcohol intake by recording the alcohol content of all drinks on the wine and spirits list.

6. Prevent staff and patrons from bringing alcohol onto the premises. Be on the lookout for packages and parcels that they may use for this purpose.

7. Recognize the dangers of such practices as shooter bars and drinking games.

8. Examine the condition of the premises and the activities that are allowed to take place. Ensure that all the conditions and activities are safe for the use of all customers, especially those who may have consumed alcohol.

9. Assess every potential customer. Control the gates. Troublemakers and persons already intoxicated should be refused entry at the door. They do not even represent a chance for revenue because they are already intoxicated and cannot be legally served.

10. Develop intervention procedures (including calling the police) to deal with patrons who become belligerent or uncontrollable and will not amend their behaviour.

11. Develop a plan for intoxicated patrons who want to drive home. Ascertain whether a sober person will be driving. If not, attempt to dissuade them from leaving or take their car keys. Participate in designated driver programs. Offer cab service even if it means absorbing the cost. Call the police if all else fails. It is not recommended that patrons be driven home by a staff member.

12. Encourage staff to take the Responsible Service of Alcohol Program now offered online by The Canadian Restaurant Association. All employees in the alcohol service industry should take this program.

Summary

Like negligence prevention in the accommodation and food service sectors, negligence prevention in the alcohol sector requires constant vigilance, commonsense, and, where appropriate, sound legal advice. As in the food sector, the standard of liability in the alcohol sector has been rising steadily for several decades. In many instances, the liability is strict. Operators who fail to abide by the liquor licence regulations and the *Criminal Code* may face heavy penalties. The loss of a liquor licence can bankrupt an establishment. It is vital for servers of alcohol not to serve a patron to or past the point of intoxication, and not to serve underage persons. Liability applies not only to business operators but also to private hosts.

The law has created the following three major duties owed to the public by commercial and private servers of alcohol: (1) not to serve alcohol to a person who is underage or apparently underage without first receiving proof of legal age; (2) not to serve alcohol to a person if doing so will render the person intoxicated or more intoxicated; and (3) to take all reasonable steps to prevent an intoxicated person from injuring himself or others or his property or the property of others. The duties are onerous. Alcohol servers should err on the side of caution, even at the risk of lost business or hurt feelings. Prevention is the best course. Even if the injuries are not prevented, the court may reduce the contributory negligence award against servers who have taken all reasonable alcohol-liability prevention measures.

Occupiers owe a duty to invitees, licensees, and even trespassers to take reasonable precautions against injury. Although the conduct of the entrants may play a role in the apportionment of liability, occupiers should take full responsibility for their own services.

Discussion Questions

1. Identify various characteristics of high-risk alcohol consumers.

2. Identify any factors other than alcohol that may lead to impairment.

3. Suggest ways in which the job of a responsible server of alcohol can be made easier.

4. Describe a scenario in which a licensee is held liable for an accident caused by an intoxicated patron.

5. Identify some alcohol sales and service training programs in your jurisdiction.

6. List some physical conditions and activities in a bar that may contribute to injuries, and describe what actions you would take to address them.

7. Draft policies that address entry to a bar, service to customers, eviction, and steps to be taken if an inebriated patron wishes to leave the bar.

8. Is it the main purpose of the court to punish the criminal in a drunk driving accident or to supply the victim with the means to live?

PART THREE

Innkeepers and Guests

8

Chapter Eight
The Innkeeper–Guest Relationship

Learning Outcomes

1. Analyze the innkeeper–guest relationship.

2. Distinguish the innkeeper–guest relationship from other relationships.

3. Describe registration, false registration, reservation contracts, and overbooking.

Introduction

At the core of hospitality law is the relationship between an **innkeeper** and the **guest**. The relationship is beneficial to both parties even though they rarely think about its myriad legal aspects. Those aspects hover over the parties largely unseen while the innkeeper thinks about service and payment, and the guest thinks about comfort and convenience.

The Foundation of the Relationship

History

Travellers have been accommodated since ancient times. Owners of property fortuitously located on a busy route at a convenient distance from other stopping places found they could make a living providing food and lodging even if all they had was a spare room in the barn. To understand the nature of the modern innkeeper–guest relationship, it is necessary to examine its origins in medieval England, as many of the principles developed then still apply today.

England in the Middle Ages was busy with commercial and social traffic, even though roads were poor and railways had not been invented. Heavy commercial travel was mainly by river and canal. Roads were either highways maintained mostly by the king or byways maintained, though less well, by local interests. Travellers by road typically walked or used pack horses; coaches were the preserve of the wealthy. The roads were infested with reivers and thieves, either highwaymen on horses or footpads on foot. Travelling nobility could find shelter in the homes of other noble families. The poor often bunked in churches. Most business travellers lacked the status to stay with the nobility and were not wretched enough to receive the charity of the church.

In response, inns began to dot the countryside and towns. A sign depicting crossed evergreen boughs indicated to passersby that food, drink, and safe accommodation were available inside. The early inns were simple establishments, often just one great room where all the cooking, entertainment, and even the sleeping took place. The innkeeper and his family typically lived in adjoining rooms. Gradually, as inns became more established and profitable, the number of persons per room decreased.

Sixteenth-century London boasted inns that could accommodate over 100 travellers. The demand was so high that innkeepers were accused of overcharging. The outrage reached the ears of King Edward III, who passed a statute in 1350 to constrain the amount that innkeepers could charge. This is the first recorded statute in the history of the Anglo-American accommodation industry. As innkeeping flourished, it became the innkeeper's legal responsibility to supply travellers with suitable accommodation and nourishment, subject only to ability to pay and availability of space, and to protect them and their property. Eventually, the innkeeper became subject to absolute liability for the protection of travellers and their property (see Chapter 11).

In North America, hotels were often the first sign of a European settlement and in many ways the centre of the community. Until other structures were built, they were used as seats of local government, courthouses, and places of worship, weddings, and funerals. Some hotel owners issued their own currency. Early American hoteliers often required that guests bathe before a room was let to them. This was done to cut down on the spread of lice and other bugs. To this day, an American hotel can refuse accommodation to someone who is unclean.

Since the Second World War, the industry has boomed as a result of a huge increase in tourism and business travel brought on by such factors as economic prosperity, increased leisure time, improved travel safety, and political stability. Accompanying the rise of the automobile was the emergence of motor hotels (motels). Entrepreneurs, recognizing a desire for quality control and familiarity, created chains of hotels and motels of which the Holiday Inn and the Hilton are among the best known. Hotels have always tended to cluster at transportation connection sites, such as train stations, docks, and highway interchanges. Of course, some are deliberately built off the beaten track to cater to those wishing to escape the hustle and bustle.

Definition

The Saxon word "inn" was introduced to Great Britain when the Angles, Saxons, and Jutes invaded the sceptred isle about 1500 years ago. "Hotel" is derived from the old French word "hostel" and the Latin word "hospes," meaning both lodger and master of the house. "Hostel," meaning youth hostel, and "hospice," meaning place of refuge for the ill, are also derived from "hospes." "Hotelier" was the Norman French word for "innkeeper." Historically, many words of French origin have denoted superiority over their Anglo-Saxon counterparts. Today, the word "inn" has regained some elegance, but "innkeeper" still sounds inferior to "hotelier."

The term **"inn"** covers such accommodations as inns, hotels, motels, tourist courts, cabins, trailer parks, lodges, bed and breakfasts, and resorts. The term "innkeeper" covers such accommodation providers as innkeepers, hoteliers, moteliers, and lodge owners. **Landlords** and operators of senior citizen homes and boarding and rooming houses are not included.

Landlord and senior citizen-home operators provide permanent residences. A boarding house provides rooms and meals but no housekeeping. A rooming house provides rooms but no meals and no housekeeping. Boarding and rooming houses cater to people who are intending to stay longer than hotel guests but not as long as apartment and senior citizen home dwellers. There is some overlap as people move and remain at different times. Also excluded are time-sharing arrangements because they involve ownership and periodic rights of occupancy by the owner, not temporary rental arrangements by nonowners.

Innkeepers and members of the public enter into legal relationships in a variety of ways and for a number of reasons. Some people may wish to book lodgings, eat in the hotel dining room, attend a business meeting, or meet friends staying at the hotel. Some may wish to shop at a store in the lobby, use the fitness facilities, or simply pass through on their way to an attached mall or office building. Some may be engaged by the innkeeper as employees, independent contractors, suppliers, entertainers, lawyers, and consultants. Each of these legal relationships gives rise to numerous rights, obligations, and remedies under contractual and negligence principles as the case may be. However, unless there is a component of temporary accommodation, the other legal relationships do not create an innkeeper–guest relationship.

Knight v. G.T.P. Development Co., [1926] S.C.R. 674

The plaintiff's husband attended a banquet at the defendant hotel. He was not staying at the hotel. While searching for a washroom, he wandered along a service hall until he reached a service elevator. He pried open the doors and fell to his death. The court held that no innkeeper–guest relationship had formed and that the husband, because he was not a guest, had no right to be in the service hall or the service elevator.

Although there are cases that have muddied the waters, the preponderance of the case law establishes that the innkeeper–guest relationship arises only between innkeepers and members of the public who have contracted for temporary accommodation in a room that is offered for that purpose, and that other relationships arise when the contracts are for other

Courtesy is central to the duty to entertain.

purposes. The innkeeper–guest relationship gives rise to a variety of rights and obligations that are unique to the parties to the relationship and to which nonparties are not entitled or subject.

One of the first recorded common law cases involving an inn was *Re Calye, 77 Eng. Rep. 520, 521 (K.B. 1584)*. The case attempted to define the responsibilities of an innkeeper, making innkeepers liable for the safety of guests and their property, but drawing a line at nonguests. The court held that "[c]ommon inns are instituted for passengers and wayfaring men ... and therefore if a neighbour who is no traveller, as a friend, at the request of the innholder lodges there and his goods be stolen, etc., he shall not have action." Thus, a traveller would have more recourse against the innkeeper than would the innkeeper's best friend if the friend had been merely invited to spend the night as a nontraveller. More recently, in the case of *Juengle v. City of Glendale, 164 S.W. 2d 610 (Mo., 1942)*, the court gave a considerably more diffuse definition of the innkeeper–guest relationship:

> A hotel is ... a house which is held out to the public as a place where all transient persons who come will be received and entertained as guests for compensation; or a house where travellers are furnished as a regular matter of business, with food and lodging while on their journey; or a house where travellers are furnished with everything which they have occasion for while upon their way; or a place where transient guests are admitted to lodge, as well as one where they are fed and lodged; or a place where every well-behaved stranger or traveller, who is willing to pay a reasonable rate for accommodation, is entitled to receive food, drink, and lodging; or a place kept for the entertainment of travellers and casual or transient guests; or a place where the proprietor makes it his business to furnish food or lodging, or both, to travellers.

Today, the provision of food is no longer a requirement. Thus, the definition can be expressed in the following (simplified) terms: When a business supplies accommodation and entertainment to a traveller for a fee, it is an inn; and when a person is well behaved and willing to pay for the accommodation and entertainment, he or she must be received as a guest if there is room. That is the basis of the innkeeper–guest relationship. An innkeeper is someone who is in the business of supplying accommodation to the public for a fee. Whether the accommodation for hire is an inn, hotel, motel, motor inn, bed and breakfast, club, tent, or igloo, as long as accommodation is being sold to a transient, the seller is an innkeeper with all the responsibilities of an innkeeper. The labels used do not matter. In one case, the judge said, "If in the eyes of the public, you are judged to be an inn, then you are an inn."

Fees are not an essential element. A person who receives accommodation at an inn without paying is still a guest. If she has won the accommodation in a contest or is receiving a complimentary room for promotional reasons, she is considered a guest, and the innkeeper has the same responsibility toward her as to a fee-paying guest. However, there must be a mutual intention to form the innkeeper–guest relationship. If a vagrant sneaks into a hotel room undetected, no innkeeper–guest relationship arises. On the other hand, a person who checks himself into a room, because the clerk is nowhere to be found when the hotel doors are open to the public, may be entitled to the rights and privileges of the innkeeper–guest relationship, even though the innkeeper does not learn of his presence until morning. In the right circumstances, the innkeeper would be estopped from denying the formation of relationship.

Transient Status

At one time, only transients used inns, and only **transients** could be guests in the legal sense. Today, inns are used not only by transients but also by local people. Attitudes toward drinking and driving have changed, and people now routinely seek local accommodation after weddings, graduations, and other festive events. A family may stay at an inn during home renovations or to enjoy a holiday close to home. The duty owed to them is no less than to persons who have travelled some distance. Hotels may refuse accommodation to people suspected of being prostitutes or undesirables or who are known for not paying their bills.

The Landlord–Tenant Relationship

Not all people staying in hotels enjoy the status of guests. They are not seeking temporary accommodation, but long-term shelter. A permanent resident in a hotel is not a guest, but a **tenant**, and the hotelier is a landlord. One famous tenant was photographer Yousuf Karsh, who resided in the Château Laurier in Ottawa for 16 years. In some situations, a person arrives at the hotel as a guest and later enters into a long-term agreement with the innkeeper. The guest's status may change to that of a tenant. The courts examine a variety of factors to determine which relationship exists, such as any change in rates, the length of the stay, the terms used by the parties to describe themselves in any written contract, the extent of control or supervision over the room, the provisions of incidental services and cooking facilities, and the ownership of the furnishings. Maid service may have been reduced from the standard daily service to twice a week. The guest may have personalized the room by adding pictures of his family and a stereo system. He may have changed the address on his driver's licence to that of the hotel, or he may have registered to vote in the riding in which the hotel is located. In the absence of a written lease, generally no single factor moves the occupant from the status of guest to tenant. The whole situation must be reviewed.

Ramsay v. Hesselman (1983), 148 D.L.R. (3d) 764, 42 O.R. (2d) 255 (Div. Ct.)

The defendant staying at the inn was held to be a tenant and not a guest when it was shown that she had no other residence from which it could be said she was travelling.

It is much easier for an innkeeper to evict a guest than a tenant. If the person is a tenant, then the rights of a guest and the responsibilities of an innkeeper no longer apply, and the provisions of the applicable landlord and tenant legislation do. Coincident with the loss of privileges as a guest, the person gains the benefits of being a tenant, a change in status that is reflected in the different responsibilities that are imposed on the landlord.

Foster v. Lewkowicz et al. (1993), 14 O.R. (3d) 339

The Windsor House rented rooms on a daily, weekly, or monthly basis. Foster resided there from August 1992 to January 1993. His room included a kitchen and bedclothes but no cleaning services. Pursuant to the Guest Registration agreement he signed, he was billed on a daily basis, could vacate without formal notice, agreed to the house rules, and agreed that his status was that of a guest in a hotel under the *Innkeepers Act*. In January 1993, he was evicted without notice. He brought an application seeking an order that he was a tenant and thus entitled to protection under the *Landlord and Tenant Act*. In finding that Foster was a tenant, the Court held that the status was to be determined without regard to what the parties called themselves but rather by using a predominant purpose test, which takes into account the following, among other, factors:

1. Is the occupation somewhat permanent? Has the occupant brought to the room personal items typically found in a home and not a hotel such as pictures?

2. Is cooking permitted in the unit?

3. Are typical hotel services such as room service available?

4. Does the occupant have control over the unit, or can the owner enter at will?

5. Who is responsible for cleaning the unit?

The evidence in the *Foster* case did not establish that the premises were accommodation provided to the travelling public. As a result, the premises were found to be rental accommodation to which the *Landlord and Tenant Act* applied.

Fraser v. McGibbon (1907), 10 O.W.R. 54 (Co. Ct.)

The plaintiff arrived at the hotel intending to register and stay the night. Without telling anyone at the hotel, he hung up his coat in the hotel and had dinner. His coat was stolen, and he never did register. The court held that the plaintiff became a guest from the moment he entered the hotel with the intention of being a guest.

The intention of the parties is important. In the *Fraser* case, it might have been argued that because the plaintiff had not drawn the attention of the staff to the fact of his intention, there was no mutuality of intention. Owing to the public nature of inns, there exists a presumption that the innkeeper intends to receive those who intend to be guests. The presumption is rebuttable but, absent rebuttal, it will apply to find an innkeeper–guest relationship if sufficient criteria are present.

The Public Nature of Inns

An innkeeper is imbued with a duty of accommodation to the public. An innkeeper has a duty to receive all well-behaved, paying transients seeking accommodation for whom there is room. This obligation even extends to minors, who cannot be bound by contracts. When dealing with minors, the innkeeper may be limited to collecting payment for necessities. A traveller who reaches an inn after it has closed is entitled to wake the innkeeper and demand accommodation. A shopkeeper who has retired for the night is not under any duty to answer the door for business reasons. Innkeepers are imbued with this duty because timely lodging is a human necessity. Innkeeping is truly a round-the-clock occupation.

The Duty to Receive

If there is room available in the inn, an innkeeper has a duty to receive a traveller who is presentable and willing to pay. An innkeeper is not discharged from the duty to receive simply because there is room at another inn, even if the other inn is next door. Rooms are not considered available if they (1) are unoccupied but have been legitimately reserved for a guest who has yet to arrive or (2) are out of service for repairs or renovations.

Accommodation is an essential requirement for the existence of an innkeeper–guest relationship. People visiting the hotel for purposes other than accommodation are not considered guests of the hotel. If their purpose is to shop in a lobby store, attend a banquet, dine in the restaurant, or have a cocktail in the lounge but not also to seek accommodation, then they are not guests of the hotel. The courts have ruled that a person who comes to a hotel and simply inquires as to whether accommodation is available has not acquired the status of guest until deciding to take up accommodation. In one case, a person who was not a guest placed money with the hotel for safekeeping. After the hotel lost the money, the person was unable to recover in court because the innkeeper–guest relationship, with its higher duty of care under common law, had not existed.

Hotels owe a higher duty of care to their accommodation guests than to casual diners. Once the relationship is formed, the rights and duties of the parties to the relationship are fixed and remain so for as long as the relationship exists.

Rex v. Ivens, 173 Eng. Rep. 94 [1835]

A few minutes before midnight on a Sunday, the plaintiff, Williams, a law clerk from Newport, arrived at the Bell Inn in Chepstow. The inn was closed; the defendant and his wife had long since retired for the night. Williams knocked on the door. Mrs. Ivens went to the window and asked his name. He replied, "What is that to you?" Mrs. Ivens said, "At such a late hour, I want to know your name and where you come from." He replied, "If you must know my name, it is Williams and I come from Newport; and now you are as wise as you were before, and be damned to you." Mrs. Ivens shut the window and did not open the inn to him. The judge in the case made the following summation:

> The facts in this case do not appear to be much in dispute; and though I do not recollect to have ever heard of such an indictment having been tried before, the law applicable to this case is this: that an indictment lies against an innkeeper, who refuses to receive a guest, he having at the time room in his house; and either the price of the guest's entertainment being tendered to him, or such circumstances occurring as will dispense with that tender. The law is founded in good sense. The innkeeper is not to select his guests. He has no right to say to one, you shall come into my inn, and to another you shall not, as everyone coming and conducting himself in a proper manner has a right to be received; and for this purpose innkeepers are a sort of public servant, they having in return a kind of privilege of entertaining travellers, and supplying them with what they want. It is said in the present case that Mr. Williams . . . conducted

himself improperly, and therefore ought not to have been admitted into the house of the defendant. If a person came to an inn drunk, or behaved in an indecent or improper manner, I am of the opinion that the innkeeper is not bound to receive him. You will consider whether Mr. Williams did so behave here. It is said that he came to the inn at a late hour of the night, when probably the family were gone to bed. Have we not all knocked at inn doors at late hours of the night, and after the family have retired to rest, not for the purpose of annoyance, but to get the people up? In this case it further appears that the wife of the defendant has a conversation with the prosecutor, in which she insists on knowing his name and abode. I think that an innkeeper has no right to insist on knowing those particulars, and certainly you and I would think an innkeeper very impertinent, who asked either the one or the other of any of us. However, the prosecutor gives his name and residence; and supposing that he did add the words "and be damned to you," is that sufficient reason for keeping a man out of an inn who has travelled till midnight? I think that the prosecutor was not guilty of such misconduct as would entitle the defendant to shut him out of his house. It has been strongly objected against the prosecutor ... that he had been travelling on a Sunday. To make that argument of any avail, it must be contended that travelling on a Sunday is illegal. It is not so, although it is what ought to be avoided whenever it can be. ... With respect to the non-tender of the money by the prosecutor, it is now a custom so universal with innkeepers to trust that a person will pay before he leaves an inn, that it cannot be necessary for a guest to tender money before he goes into an inn, indeed, in the present case, no objection was made that Mr. Williams did not make a tender; and they did not even insinuate that they had any suspicion that he could not pay for whatever entertainment might be furnished to him. I think, therefore, that cannot be set up as a defence. It however remains for me next to consider the case with respect to the hour of the night at which Mr. Williams applied for admission; and the opinion which I have formed is, that the lateness of the hour is no excuse to the defendant for refusing to receive the prosecutor into his inn. Why are inns established? For the reception of travellers, who are often very far distant from their own homes. Now, at what time is it most essential that travellers should not be denied admission into the inns? I should say when they are benighted, and when, from any casualty, or from the badness of the roads, they arrive at an inn at a very late hour. Indeed, in former times, when the roads were much worse, and were much infested with robbers, a late hour of the night was the time, of all others, at which the traveller most required to be received into an inn. I think therefore, that if the traveller conducts himself properly, the innkeeper is bound to admit him, at whatever hour of the night he may arrive. The only other question in this case is, whether the defendant's inn was full. There is no distinct evidence on the part of the prosecutor that it was not. But I think the conduct of the parties shows that the inn was not full; because, if it had been, there could have been no use in the landlady asking the prosecutor his name, and saying, that if he would tell it, she would ring for one of the servants.

Innkeeper Ivens was found guilty of not meeting his duty to receive a transient who appeared at his inn apparently in need of accommodation and apparently able to pay. A critical point in the judge's summation is that the later the hour, the more essential it is that a traveller be able to find accommodation when rooms are available. Innkeepers are in effect on duty 24 hours a day. Since the *Ivens* case, the law has evolved to allow innkeepers to require the name and address of a guest.

The Duty to Entertain

Entertainment is a required service to guests, but not in the show business sense. It simply means that guests must receive hospitality and be treated in a respectful and courteous manner. Simple, polite greetings clearly indicate a willingness to entertain and be hospitable. Gruff or informal greetings may also indicate a willingness to entertain and be hospitable. Short of clear rudeness, most words or deeds amounting to entertainment on the part of the innkeeper will be sufficient to create the innkeeper–guest relationship.

The Duty to Serve Food

Under common law, innkeepers have a duty to supply and serve food. In some jurisdictions, this requirement no longer exists. Many hotels that do not have dining rooms continue to offer food from vending machines.

The Formal Beginning of the Relationship
Presumption

For people who have arrived at and are staying at an inn, there is a presumption in favour of the existence of an innkeeper–guest relationship. Once formed, the relationship is presumed to continue until a sufficient change has occurred to end it. The relationship begins once all six essential elements of a contract are in place. One of these elements is mutual intent by the parties to enter into the relationship. Mutual intent may be demonstrated either through the nonwritten conduct of the parties or through written registration upon arrival. Mutual acts of registration by both guest and clerk establish the relationship, but it can also happen more subtly. When a traveller hands her valise to the porter, her action demonstrates her intention to become a guest in the inn. The porter, by accepting the valise, demonstrates the intention of the inn to accept her as a guest. Any relevant demonstration of mutual intent by the parties starts the relationship. Thus, handing over the valise to the inn's limousine driver at the airport starts the relationship, even though they are some distance from the inn. The relationship is not forged if the limousine driver is not an agent or employee of the inn.

The innkeeper–guest relationship is predicated upon the inn having a room available. If the inn does not have a room available when the transient arrives unannounced, then the relationship does not form. However, if the traveller has previously made a reservation and arrives only to find that the inn has no room, then the relationship has formed, at least for the purposes of assessing the innkeeper's liability, because the innkeeper had contractually promised to have a room available for the guest at the appointed time and date.

Registration

The innkeeper–guest relationship commences with the demonstration of mutual intent to exchange accommodation for money or money's worth. Under common law, registration is not an element of the relationship; however, some jurisdictions such as Ontario and British Columbia have enacted statutes making registration a legal necessity. For example, Ontario's *Hotel Registration of Guests Act* states in part:

2. A register shall be kept in every hotel in which shall be entered the name and usual place of residence of every person admitted as a guest in the hotel and occupying a room therein alone or with another person.

3. The owner and the manager of a hotel who fails to keep the register required by section 2 or to see that the particulars required by section 2 are entered therein, or who knowingly and

willfully permits an untrue statement as to the name or place of residence of a guest to be entered in the register is guilty of an offence and on conviction is liable to a fine of not more than $100, and in default of payment may be imprisoned for a term of not more than three months.

Ontario's *Tourism Act* imposes more stringent requirements on tourist establishments in Ontario by requiring operators to maintain registers containing the name and address of each person in the party, the unit occupied by the party, the dates of arrival and departure, and, if applicable, the make of the car, licence plate number, and province or state of origin. The applicable legislation in the other provinces and territories requires only that a register of guests be kept. Failure to do so does not result in penalties, although some Acts provide that the innkeeper shall not benefit from the other provisions in the Act unless the register is kept. For example, section 14 of Saskatchewan's *Hotel Keepers Act* states:

> Every hotel keeper shall keep in the hotel a register or record in which shall be entered the name and usual place of residence of every person admitted as a guest in the hotel and occupying a room therein alone or with any other person, together with the number of the room so occupied; and a hotel keeper shall be entitled to the benefit of the Act in respect only of goods or property brought to this hotel while such register or record is so kept.

Although the registration is often the first clear demonstration of mutual intent, there are instances in which people who have not registered have the status of guests. Tours and group travellers represent a significant segment of the population staying in hotels. Typically, only the tour directors are required by the hotel to register. It would be time-consuming to have every tour member register. In some instances, hotels do require it, but the inconvenience may drive the tour business to other hotels that are better prepared to handle large groups.

Large conventions often pre-register the delegates for convenience. As with tour members, all conventioneers recorded in this manner have the status of guests in the hotel. Although the pre-registrations may have taken place months in advance and kilometres away, a legal relationship begins once the parties demonstrate their mutual intention to contract, entitling the innocent party to sue for breach. It is not an innkeeper–guest relationship, however; as that can begin only when the guest arrives to take up the accommodation.

Regular customers are not always forced to go through the ritual of pre-registration. For these guests, checking in can simply involve signing in at a convenient time during their stay.

False Registration

Some guests register under false names or give false addresses and other information. While false registration may be a contravention of the applicable registration laws (thus giving rise to remedies), it does not invalidate the innkeeper–guest relationship. A guest who falsely registers has the same rights and obligations as a properly registered guest, but could be charged under the Act with false registration. Most of the innkeepers Acts deal with false registration. For example, section 8 of Nova Scotia's *Hotel Regulations Act* reads:

> Every person who applies for admission as a guest in any hotel and who registers under or represents himself as bearing some other name than his own, or who, in registering or procuring admission to a hotel, makes a false statement as to his ordinary place of residence shall be liable to a penalty of not more than two hundred dollars and in default of payment to imprisonment for a period not exceeding one hundred days.

Subsection 12(1) of the Yukon Territory's *Hotel Act* states, "No operator shall enter or knowingly allow to be entered any false information in the register." Further, pursuant to subsection 23(1) of the *Criminal Code of Canada*, a guest who fraudulently obtains food, beverage, or accommodation is guilty of an offence punishable by summary conviction.

Although false registration does not invalidate the innkeeper–guest relationship, the front desk clerks should be well trained in handling the registration of guests they suspect of registering falsely. There have been numerous cases of unmarried couples falsely registering for a room for "immoral purposes." In one case, the male half of the couple was injured in an accident involving the hotel elevator. The couple sued the hotel as guests, claiming failure on the innkeeper's part to provide for their safety. The innkeeper contended that there was no innkeeper–guest relationship because there was no mutual intent: it would never have been his intention to have on the premises a couple who were planning to use the hotel for an immoral purpose. The court found that the innkeeper–guest relationship existed regardless of the purpose of the stay. The purpose of the stay contributed nothing to the cause of the injuries. (The difference between this case and the *Knight* case described earlier in the chapter was that no innkeeper–guest relationship was held to have formed in the latter case; further, the elevator featured in the *Knight* case was a service elevator, not a public elevator.) The only circumstance that may relieve an innkeeper of liability is an illegal, as opposed to an immoral, act by the injured party. Even if the injured party had been committing an illegal act, the hotel may still have found itself liable if the elevator doors had malfunctioned due to negligence.

Termination of the Relationship

The innkeeper–guest relationship terminates when (1) due notice to vacate is given by the innkeeper to the guest; (2) the contracted time has elapsed; (3) payment is due and the guest will not pay; or (4) the guest has paid her bill. The innkeeper–guest relationship does not end immediately upon delivery of the notice or payment of the bill, but continues for a reasonable time until the guest has left. The guest is given leeway to return to her room, pick up her belongings, and exit the hotel. She is still a guest while loading her car in the hotel parking lot. The length of the time during which the relationship continues after payment varies depending on the circumstances. The guest who pays her bill early in the morning on the day she is checking out maintains her status as a guest until she exits. For those people who pay for their full period of accommodation in advance when they check in, such payment of the bill would obviously not terminate the innkeeper–guest relationship.

Summary

Innkeepers and members of the public enter into legal relationships in a variety of ways for a number of reasons. These relationships give rise to numerous rights, obligations, and remedies; however, unless there is a component of temporary accommodation, the other relationships do not create an innkeeper–guest relationship. If a room is available, an innkeeper has a duty to receive a traveller who is presentable and willing to pay. Under common law, registration is not required to begin the relationship. Some jurisdictions have enacted statutes making registration a legal necessity. While false registration may contravene registration laws (giving rise to remedies), it does not invalidate the innkeeper–guest relationship. Reservation contracts must have all six elements of a contract. Hotels should have fair cancellation, no-show, overbooking, and termination policies. A hotel should take all reasonable steps to assist a guest who has been badly served by the overbooking policy. Appendix 3 (Hotel Forms and Sample Contracts) contains a sample Guest Registration Form and a sample Registration Contract Reply Form.

1. Under what circumstances might a person entering a hotel not be a guest there?

2. Is there a difference in legal status between a person staying in a bed and breakfast and a person staying in a major downtown hotel? If so, what is the difference?

3. What is the meaning of "entertainment" in the context of the hospitality industry?

4. "Innkeeping is a round-the-clock business." What is meant by this statement?

5. A local person who checks into a hotel is not a transient under common law. When may a hotel refuse accommodation to someone who is not a transient?

6. What are some of the differences in status between a guest and a tenant in a hotel?

7. What is meant by "mutual intent" between guest and innkeeper?

8. Ronaldo made a reservation at the Stood Up Inn but failed to appear on the appointed day. As a result, the inn did not have to provide him with a room. Does the inn have a valid claim against Ronaldo for the price of the room? Why or why not?

9. Is registration required to establish an innkeeper–guest relationship? If not, why not?

10. Does the innkeeper–guest relationship end at the payment of the bill?

Chapter Nine

Innkeepers

Learning Outcomes

1. Analyze case law to identify the rights and obligations of innkeepers.

2. Design standard operating procedures for running an inn.

Introduction

The innkeeper–guest relationship is a legal relationship that bestows upon the two parties an assortment of rights, duties, and obligations. Innkeepers must honour their duties and respect the rights of the guests, just as guests must honour their obligations and respect the rights of innkeepers. In this chapter, we shall examine the rights of innkeepers. The duties of innkeepers are also discussed in conjunction with the rights of guests in Chapter 10. For example, the duty of innkeepers to post statutory notices is discussed as a right of the guest to the posting of such a notice. Many of the rights and duties that apply to innkeepers also apply to restaurateurs and bar owners, whose duties and rights were discussed in Chapters 6 and 7.

The Rights of Innkeepers

The Right to Refuse Accommodation When the Inn Is Full

An innkeeper has the right to refuse accommodation when there are no rooms available. The innkeeper retains this right even if some rooms are unoccupied, provided the unoccupied rooms have been legitimately reserved for guests who have yet to arrive or are out of service on account of repairs or renovations. In most circumstances, innkeepers cannot refuse accommodation if rooms are in fact available. If it is proven that rooms were available at the time the accommodation was refused, the innkeeper may be subject under human rights legislation to penalties for discrimination. Accurate and complete records of daily occupancy will assist an innkeeper's defence against such allegations.

Hotels often overbook to avoid losing revenue on empty rooms because experience shows that a percentage of people with reservations will not appear. If fewer cancellations occur than expected and a guest with a reservation must be refused, the hotel is in breach of contract with the refused guest. The hotel should take all reasonable steps to secure for the guest alternative and comparable accommodation. The guest has a duty to mitigate damages; therefore, provided the alternative accommodation is comparable, the guest must take it. If there are no damages, there is no cause of action. The hotel should treat the guest with the utmost courtesy and respect, and pay for the incidental costs of relocating (e.g., taxi fares).

The Right to Refuse Someone Without Luggage

The common law right to refuse someone without luggage is now largely an outdated concept. The rule evolved to discourage those who were not true travellers but who only sought the confines of a hotel room for the purpose of engaging in "immoral acts." In the past, hotels spent a great deal of time on the surveillance of guest luggage. Porters and the housekeeping staff would report any luggage of a suspicious nature. Guests were known to lug suitcases filled with bricks and magazines in order to meet the luggage requirement. Today, laundry is often so light that a full week's clothing can be carried in an overnight bag.

Although the attention paid to luggage is, sensibly, not what it was, the right to refuse on this ground technically still exists, and could be resorted to as an excuse to refuse accommodation to a person the innkeeper has good grounds to suspect of planning to misuse the room. However, the guest may thus acquire grounds, fair or not, for a cause of action.

The Right to Refuse Service Where Warranted

A hotel may deny accommodation to a person who has a history of failing to pay for services, refusing to abide by reasonable house rules, disturbing the peace, or using the establishment for illegal or immoral purposes. Accommodation may also be denied to persons known to be carrying a serious contagious disease or a firearm or other inherently dangerous substances such as explosives. Guests are the lifeblood of the hospitality industry, but some of them are consummate troublemakers. Some people with injuries have been known to check into hotels just so they can blame the hotel for the injury. Others claim to have lost phantom wallets, rings, and broaches. It is impossible to distinguish the honest from the dishonest based on appearances. In one case, a member of the clergy faked medical emergencies in order to avoid having to pay for his rooms. He would simply leave town from the hospital. He was not caught until he was recognized by an ambulance attendant.

To deny a guest on the grounds of anticipated dishonesty is a course fraught with potential liability. Except in obvious cases, the hotel must admit the guest. Often, the anticipations will prove groundless. Should they be borne out, however, it must be recognized that occasional losses due to dishonesty are simply part of the cost of doing business. The goal must be to minimize the losses. The decision to refuse accommodation to someone should not be taken lightly. Mere personal antipathy is insufficient grounds for refusing accommodation. The grounds for refusal should be compelling enough that a reasonable judge would in all probability find in the innkeeper's favour.

Operators may not discriminate on the basis of disability.

The Right to Refuse Pets

Unless the pet is a seeing-eye dog, an innkeeper has the right to refuse a guest who insists on bringing a pet, especially if the pet appears to be a threat or an annoyance to others. Most pet owners are very considerate, but others leave their pets alone in the room while they dine, tour, or attend meetings. A scared, nervous, or bored pet may disturb other guests and may cause damage to the room. Because it is impossible to anticipate with certainty which pets will cause problems and which will not, many hotels have a blanket policy not to accept pets.

R. v. Rymer, [1877] 2 Q.B.D. 136, 46 L.J.M.C. 108

The guest had been in the habit of bringing one or more dogs with him to the inn. The innkeeper had allowed the guest the privilege in the past, but the dogs had annoyed the other guests. Finally, the innkeeper forbade the guest from bringing the dogs again. On the next visit, the guest arrived with a large dog on a leash. The innkeeper refused to check him in, and the guest sued the innkeeper for the refusal. In finding for the defendant, the judge stated:

> I do not lay down positively that under no circumstances could a guest have a right to bring a dog into an inn. There may possibly be circumstances in which, if a person came to an inn with a dog, and the innkeeper refused to put up the dog in any stable or outhouse, and there were nothing that could make the dog a cause of alarm or annoyance to others, the guest might be justified in bringing the dog into the inn. But it is not necessary to decide any such question. In this case, looking at the previous facts, the number of dogs previously brought, and their kind and behaviour, the nature of the right [to "follow his inclinations" in bringing his dogs] claimed by the prosecutor in his letter, and the size and class of the dog, I think the defendant would have had ample ground for his refusal.

P. v. H., [1988] 3 W.W.R. 119 (Man. Q.B.)

A restaurateur refused a customer who was accompanied by his seeing-eye dog. The court found that the dog was an extension of the blind person, and that by refusing the dog, the blind person was also refused. The court held that this was discrimination on the basis of disability.

Many people involve their pets in all aspects of their lives, including family trips and holidays. Except in the case of seeing-eye dogs where there is no discretion, an innkeeper is free to decide whether or not to accept a pet. An innkeeper who agrees to accept a pet may request that the guest sign an undertaking to assume full responsibility for any expenses or liabilities incurred as a result of the pet being on the premises, including personal injuries and lost revenues if the room that the pet was in has to be cleaned or repaired after the visit.

The Right to Set the Rates

The innkeeper's right to set rates is subject to legislation designed to prevent price fixing. In a notorious case, the major hotels in a Canadian city learned confidential information as to what the federal government was willing to pay to accommodate civil servants visiting that city on government business. Aggrieved by what they thought was an unrealistically low rate, the hotels banded together to set rates above the government rate. The government was forced to meet the new prices or forgo accommodation at the major hotels. The hotels that participated in the rate hike were found guilty of price fixing and fined. In some jurisdictions, although there is no interference by the government with respect to the original rate that an innkeeper can set for the rooms, once the rate is set, it must be posted (by statute conspicuously in every room such as on the inside of the door). The rate can be set and reset (and reposted) almost at will, and seasonal fluctuations are permitted.

The Right to Privity of Contract

An innkeeper has the right to deal with the person that the innkeeper originally received as a guest. The guest cannot transfer or assign to another person the right to be a guest without the innkeeper's consent. Any assignee without consent is a trespasser. **Privity** in this context is not meant to exclude the guest's spouse or children who are travelling with him or her. Privity helps to shield the innkeeper from contractual claims from persons who are not parties to the contract. Privity applies to contractual relationships. As a result of the tort law bypass (discussed in Chapter 3) and the neighbour principle enunciated in *Donoghue v. Stevenson* (see Chapter 4), privity is not available to immunize an innkeeper from tort claims.

The Right to Select the Room

An innkeeper has the right to select the room that the guest will occupy. The innkeeper may not discriminate in the selection. For example, an innkeeper cannot move or confine visible minorities to separate areas or rooms that are substandard. In *Garnet Angeconeb v. 517152 Ontario Ltd. and Ruby Cullen (1993), 19 C.H.R.R. D/452 (Ont. Bd. Inq.)* discussed in Chapter 2, it was found that an innkeeper had discriminated by setting aside substandard rooms for his Native customers. The courts are more receptive to a seemingly discriminatory policy if the policy is a legitimate attempt to meet the needs of the guests. A hotel that sets aside an all-female floor in a high-crime area would likely survive a charge that such a policy was sanctionable discrimination.

The Right to Change the Room

An innkeeper may relocate a guest to another room provided there are reasonable grounds for the move. For example, if the guest is the only person on a floor, the innkeeper may wish to relocate the guest to a floor with other guests in order to streamline housekeeping and security measures. An innkeeper may need the entire floor for an incoming group of conventioneers or schoolmates, or for extensive renovations or other work. Most guests will agree to be moved if told the reasons for doing so. Failing to explain or to seek permission is poor public relations. If a guest is adamant about not moving, the hotel should consider not exercising its right if accommodating the guest would not unduly inconvenience the hotel.

Doyle v. Walker, [1867] 26 Upper Canada Queen's Bench Rep. 502

The plaintiff travelled to Toronto to visit his company's head office. He and his family became guests in the defendant hotel, occupying two rooms. By September 18, he owed the hotel $83.25, a substantial sum at the time. He could not or would not pay, and was asked to leave the hotel. He asked to remain in one of the two rooms so that his wife, who was ill, would not have to be moved. On September 21, he asked for his bill and received it at approximately 2:00 p.m. that day. The bill was delivered to him at his company's office by a clerk of the hotel. The bill was paid that same evening. However, on the morning of September 21, the hotel had entered the first of the plaintiff's rooms and had moved his belongings into the second room so that the next guest could move into the first room. The plaintiff sued the hotel for trespassing. At the trial, the jury awarded the plaintiff $100 on the basis that the hotel's actions amounted to an eviction that was unfair given the payment of the bill on the same day. The Court of Appeal overturned the trial decision and held that a hotel has the right to move a guest and his or her belongings to another room provided the actions are reasonable. In this particular case, the plaintiff was not being evicted, but simply moved into another room.

The Right to Enter the Room for Proper Purposes

Once a room has been assigned to a guest, the innkeeper has the right to enter the room only when invited by the guest or for the legitimate purposes of housekeeping, repairs, effecting valid terminations at the end of the stay, effecting valid evictions, and responding to emergencies. For example, if a fire has broken out overnight in an adjacent room, the innkeeper may enter to alert the guests to the danger and assist in their evacuation. If the children of guests are throwing items out the window of the room, the innkeeper may enter the room to prevent the activity on the basis that it constitutes a danger to people below.

The Right to Payment for Services

Under contract law, innkeepers have a right to be paid for the accommodation and other services they render to guests, such as movies and room service meals. This right can be based on a formal contract or upon *quantum meruit* principles (discussed in Chapter 3), although in the case of the latter disputes as to the quantum merited are more likely to arise.

Innkeepers may demand payment at the time of registration. A refusal to pay at registration is a valid ground to refuse admission. Many innkeepers collect payment some time later in the stay, most commonly at the end of the stay. To protect themselves, many hotels obtain an imprint of the guest's credit card in advance. Payment is not received until the end, but the means by which to receive it is secured at the beginning. Payment may be made by cash, cheque, or credit or debit card. Hotels may not refuse payment in cash unless it is done in fiddling change. Hotels may refuse payment by cheque unless it is certified or a bank draft. A hotel that might otherwise have accepted a personal cheque may refuse a cheque that has been endorsed. Endorsement occurs in the following manner:

1. Tom writes a cheque in favour of Dick.

2. Dick signs, or endorses, the cheque.

3. Dick gives the cheque to Harry, who wishes to use it to pay for his stay at the hotel by further endorsing the cheque to the hotel.

Once a cheque has been endorsed, it is almost as liquid as cash, and some security is lost. Although Tom remains liable to pay the face amount of the cheque, each time the cheque is endorsed by someone else, there is less certainty that the money is in Tom's bank account.

Hotels may refuse payment by credit or debit card if, upon attempting to verify the card, it is learned that the card has expired or the credit limit has been exceeded.

A hotel may also accept payment in kind or in services. Payment in kind refers to accepting physical property in exchange for accommodation. An example would be a guest who pays for her room by giving the hotel an oil painting. Depending on the artist, the hotel may come out ahead. Similarly, a guest may pay by performing such services as dishwashing, landscaping, or marketing. Any such payments are a taxable benefit to the hotel, which must include the value of them in annual taxable revenues.

Guests are often granted credit for their stays until they check out. There are practical limits to the amount of credit a hotel can extend. Well-run hotels monitor the guest accounts; when a limit has been reached, payment is requested. The limit may be a limit personal to the guest or set by house policy and applicable to all.

As discussed later in this chapter, if the guest is unable or unwilling to pay, the innkeeper has the right to end the innkeeper–guest relationship and evict the guest from the hotel. It stands to reason that if the obligations to serve and to be paid for serving are not regarded as complementary by the guest, the innkeeper need not continue the relationship.

Hotel and dining room services are like any other goods and services—they can be stolen. If it can be proven that the guest or diner had an intention not to pay for the services (*mens rea*) and did not pay for them (*actus reus*), criminal charges for theft or fraud may be laid against the guest under the *Criminal Code*. Other crimes for which a guest could be charged include forgery, which occurs when someone signs someone else's name to a registration or payment, and uttering, which occurs when a person knowingly with intent to defraud writes a cheque on a bank account with insufficient funds. Unless there is restitution, the criminal charges will not result in recovery of the payment, but the enforcement of the law in this manner may discourage similarly inclined guests.

The Right to Collect Payment

Lawsuits and Collection Agencies

Along with the right to be paid for the accommodation and services they render to guests and patrons, innkeepers have all the rights of any business to collect payment. Hotels may hire lawyers and collection agencies to pursue outstanding bills. The hotel should ensure that the collection agencies act appropriately and do not overstep the boundaries of proper collection procedures; otherwise, the hotel's reputation may suffer. Hotels do not have to monitor the activities of lawyers because lawyers are bound by professional codes of conduct.

Liens on Guest Property

In addition to legal remedies available to most businesses, innkeepers have a right to a **lien** on the goods of a nonpaying guest. Liened or abandoned property may be sold provided the rules governing such sales are followed. Pursuant to the case of *Bank of Montreal v. 414031 Ontario Ltd. (1983), 45 C.B.R. (N.S.) 77*, an innkeeper's lien has priority over persons who have registered an interest in the goods under personal property security legislation. Every province and territory of Canada extends to innkeepers a right to a lien on the goods of guests who have not paid the bill. Alberta, which does not use the term "lien," grants an innkeeper the right to "detain" the personal effects of guests who fail to pay for accommodation. The lien can be used to cover all expenses, and is not limited to the amount of the lodging bill. The articles that can be seized under the lien are the luggage, trunks, valises, and personal effects of the guest. Some provincial statutes still provide for innkeepers' liens on horses and carriages. Innkeepers have the right to break open locked luggage under common law.

The lienholders are responsible for the goods liened or detained. Each jurisdiction has its own requirements for liened goods. After holding the goods for a period varying from one to three months, the innkeeper must advertise the sale (usually by auction) in a local newspaper in the hotel's town at least a week before it occurs. The advertisement includes the following:

1. The name of the guest

2. The amount of indebtedness

3. A description of the property to be sold

4. The date, time, and place of the sale

5. The name of the auctioneer

Manitoba requires that a hotel apprise an indebted guest of an intended sale by way of registered mail to the person's last known address.

The proceeds of sale are to be applied to the amount due the hotel for the most recent stay and the costs of the sale. The proceeds cannot be applied against money owing for a previous stay sufficiently separated in time from the current stay; however, a current stay is not ended merely by temporary absences from the premises by the guest. What constitutes a sufficient interruption is a question of fact. The innkeeper does not have to sell all the goods, only enough to cover the indebtedness and the costs of the sale. The surplus should be paid to the guest or to whomever is entitled to them, such as a judgment creditor.

There are times when liens are useful in collecting overdue charges. The lien threat may produce the payment. However, liens are usually of little value. Although occasionally the liened luggage contains furs, jewellery, and laptop computers, most often it yields low-value clothing and personal effects. The hotel is often better advised to pursue nonpaying guests in the civil courts or, in extreme cases, to seek to have them charged with fraud.

If two people are sharing a hotel room and one of them leaves without paying, the remaining guest may be subject to a lien against his or her luggage if the total bill is not paid.

Hotels are sometimes used as places of temporary refuge for battered women and their children. Rather than add to their misery by liening their luggage, the hotel should put them in contact with social agencies that can assist them.

Generally, the lien rights apply only to the property of the guests. The property of nonguests cannot be claimed under the innkeeper's lien. A casual diner in the hotel dining room lacks the status of a guest and is therefore not subject to the lien. However, casual diners who fail to pay for the meal may be pursued in civil court or charged with fraud. The patron in a restaurant is in the same position. Restaurateurs do not have a right to a lien when payment is not received, but may sue the diner for breach of contract or claim fraud. Sometimes the property of nonguests is in the possession of a guest. Provided the innkeeper has no actual notice that the property does not belong to the guest, the lien will attach to the goods. In other words, in the absence of knowledge to the contrary, the innkeeper may assume that any property in the possession of the guest belongs to the guest.

The Right to Establish House Rules

An innkeeper may establish and enforce reasonable **house rules**. For example, a resort may ask that no glasses of any type be brought to the pool area, and that all drinks be contained in sturdy plastic cups. The reasonable purpose of such a rule is to protect barefoot guests from stepping on broken glass. House rules protect the inn and protect guests from themselves and from other guests. Restrictions on bare feet in lobbies, horseplay, and wet bathing suits outside the pool area are just some examples of appropriate house rules. The onus is on the house to make reasonable attempts to communicate the rules in an appropriate manner to the guests. Posting them in the guest rooms and in the applicable public areas is recommended.

The Right to Evict Guests

Tort Liability

Sometimes an innkeeper has the right to end the innkeeper–guest relationship and may do so by evicting the guest from the hotel. Eviction must be done properly and for proper cause, or the innkeeper may be liable under the law of tort.

McLean v. University Club, 97 N.E. (2d) 174 (Mass., 1951)

McLean was a member of the University Club, which offered its members overnight privileges. From time to time, McLean availed himself of the accommodation and used the opportunity to drink fairly heavily. On one such occasion, he mentioned to the staff that he was feeling ill. They discounted his claim, assuming that he was simply feeling the effects of the alcohol, and did nothing to assist him. On the day McLean was scheduled to leave, the Club evicted him one hour prior to checkout time. For the next couple of days, he lived in his car, which was parked in the Club's parking lot, and was attended to by sympathetic staff members of the Club who brought him food and coffee. McLean sued the Club for breach of duty of care. The court agreed that the manner of the eviction had not been humane and decent, and that it constituted a breach of the duty of care owed by the Club to its member guests. McLean would probably also have been successful had he chosen to sue for wrongful eviction.

For an innkeeper to be found liable for improper eviction, it is not necessary that the guest be harmed physically while being removed from the property. The eviction takes place at the moment the guest is informed that the innkeeper wishes him to leave. The conduct of the hotel from that moment on must withstand close scrutiny by the court.

The request to leave should be made privately. At the discretion of the innkeeper, the guest may be informed of the reason for the eviction. An evicted guest who fails to leave should be politely asked to do so again. If the guest persists in staying, the police should be called. Discretion and courtesy should be employed at all times. The guest should be left with as much dignity as possible. Hurt feelings and emotional distress only worsen an already tense situation and increase the likelihood of a claim for damages by the evicted guest.

Innkeepers and their employees may use force, but only enough to effect the eviction. Even if the eviction was justified, the use of excessive force during the eviction may result in a damages claim. Most innkeepers have never had to resort to force either by themselves or by employees under their direction. Once apprised of the reasons for the eviction, most guests will leave quietly. If called, the police are generally cooperative, and will remove the guest, sparing the innkeeper potential liability for excessive force. An innkeeper who calls the police to effect an eviction may be liable to the guest for the embarrassment if it is later shown that there was no just cause for the eviction. On occasion, an innkeeper cannot wait for the police to arrive. A guest who is presenting a danger to anyone, including himself, may be removed immediately (again, with no more than the amount of force reasonably required).

A major drawback of using force is that it will be judged afterward in the cold light of a courtroom. Contrary to what one might expect, gauging the amount of force to use is less difficult when it comes to dealing with belligerent males than when others, such as inebriated or distraught guests, are the subject of the force. The courts allow some leeway in determining the appropriate amount of force. The force does not have to be measured too finely, but it must not exceed a reasonable amount in the circumstances.

Eviction at the End of the Stay

When guests check in, they are typically given their rooms for specified periods. At the conclusion of the period, the innkeeper has a right to expect the guest to check out. The business of innkeeping would be impossible if an innkeeper could not keep a reliable record of the availability of rooms. Bookings are made in advance, and innkeepers have obligations to individuals and groups who are expecting to check in on the appointed day and time. Despite what many innkeepers and guests believe, guests who choose to stay beyond the contracted time can be asked to leave, and then evicted (forcibly if necessary) if they refuse.

Evicting paying customers who think highly enough of the establishment to want to remain for a longer stay than planned is not a happy business decision. During the check-in, innkeepers should remind guests of the length of their intended stay. If the period subsequent to the guest's stay is heavily booked, the guest should be advised at the beginning of the contracted stay that the likelihood of an extension is remote.

Many hotels require that a departure date be noted in writing at the time of registration. Some extremely busy hotels go as far as to insist that the guest fill in the date on the registration card or initial any printout with the date on it, thereby acknowledging the agreed-upon checkout date. This practice reduces the chances of misunderstandings when the date arrives. Planning allows innkeepers to meet their obligations and allows guests who have not extended their reservations to make alternative plans.

During heavily booked periods, it is a good idea to inform guests early in the day that this is the day of their expected departure. The midnight shift can remind guests via their message boxes. Many hotels slip the invoice under the guest's door on the night preceding the day of departure. These are nonconfrontational ways of informing guests that the hotel has not experienced any cancellations, and that their rooms will still be required for the day's incoming guests. Checkout warnings provide a valuable service to guests who may then make timely arrangements for suitable alternative accommodation if they are not ready to leave town.

Nonpayment

Before the end of the reserved stay, the hotel may request payment for the services rendered so far. If the guest refuses to pay and does not offer an adequate explanation for the refusal, the hotel may evict the guest for nonpayment.

Before evicting a guest for nonpayment, the hotel must first ensure that the guest did not receive additional credit privileges from a hotel employee who had apparent authority to grant them. For instance, the guest may have made a binding arrangement with a staff member to pay his account on the day he receives his monthly paycheque. Evicting a guest who has made a proper and binding alternative arrangement is, of course, unwarranted. To avoid this kind of nonpayment situation, only certain employees should be given the authority to grant credit or enter into other arrangements, and all such arrangements should be recorded on the registration card or guest information sheet.

Persons of Ill-Repute

A hotel has the right to evict persons of **ill-repute**, such as prostitutes, gamblers, and drug dealers. Eviction is always distasteful, and should be handled with care. The chances of legal action are increased if the grounds were false or the eviction was performed improperly. It is rarely obvious that a room is being used for prostitution or gambling and the like. In most instances, the occupants will go to considerable lengths to avoid drawing attention to themselves. Most often, the evidence is discovered inadvertently. In addition, many activities are ambiguous in the sense that they may be either legitimate or illegitimate. An activity that appears to be illegal gambling may be nothing more than a friendly game of Monopoly. In the event that illegal gambling is taking place, the innkeeper has the right to evict the gamblers.

Some of these situations can be avoided if guests were screened carefully at the time of check-in. As in other situations, the decision to refuse accommodation or to evict should be made only after careful consideration.

Disorderly Conduct

Guests who insist on behaving in a disorderly fashion—for example, by parading around in no or almost no clothes—may be evicted. An innkeeper must use discretion in determining what constitutes disorderly conduct. The use of undergarments such as boxer shorts as all-purpose outer clothing is becoming more common. A thong may be underwear or a bathing suit.

Provided it is not done deliberately to shock or to attract commercial activity, it is no longer considered disorderly in Ontario for a female to bare her breasts in public. It goes without saying that breast-feeding is not disorderly conduct. Spanking a child is not normally considered disorderly unless the punishment is so severe as to constitute criminal assault.

Loud, boorish behaviour caused by inebriation may be either merely rude or disorderly depending on the degree. Clear and persistent belligerence is usually considered disorderly, and may constitute disturbing the peace, discussed below. Disorderly conduct is examined in light of community standards, which are constantly shifting. Without legitimate complaints from other members of the community close in time to the behaviour complained of, many types of eyebrow-raising behaviour are not disorderly to the degree required to justify eviction.

Disturbing the Peace

Guests are entitled to use hotel rooms as they would use rooms in their homes, provided the uses are reasonable. For example, guests are entitled to entertain friends in their hotel rooms. However, guests and their invited friends do not have the right to disturb the peace and enjoyment of the other guests. At a reasonable hour, the hotel can ask guests to reduce noise levels and request their unregistered acquaintances to leave the hotel.

A hotel may set special rates for its party rooms because these rooms typically require much more attention and cleaning than rooms used for sleeping and luggage storage. As a result of paying additional charges, some party room patrons believe that they have purchased a licence to disturb. Others are more considerate and will immediately reduce the noise levels upon request. A person who uses a room purely as a party room and not for accommodation is not in an innkeeper–guest relationship, and consequently does not enjoy all the rights of a guest. If the disturbance is a threat or a sufficient annoyance to other guests, the innkeeper has a duty to protect the other guests as well as outsiders, and may evict the disturber.

For people wishing to use the hotel as both a venue for a social event (perhaps a wedding or a graduation party) and a place of accommodation, it is good practice to book the accommodation and the event together, keeping the revellers together on the same floor or floors and away from the other guests.

Carrying a Contagious Disease

Innkeepers may refuse or evict guests suffering from contagious diseases such as cholera, influenza, and tuberculosis. Common colds do not qualify because they are not usually serious. The innkeeper should refuse or evict only if the disease presents a real or imminent danger of transmission. AIDS does not fall into this category and therefore does not constitute grounds for refusal or eviction. If the alleged disease is in fact a disability rather than a contagion, then the innkeeper who refused accommodation or evicted on the latter basis might be held to have discriminated on the basis of disability. Given that few staff are medical experts, care must be exercised lest someone be misidentified as a carrier of a contagious disease.

Breaking House Rules

Hospitality business owners have the right to establish and enforce reasonable rules of conduct for persons enjoying their hospitality. The rules may ban a wide range of activities, from using drinking glasses in pool areas to drinking alcohol in the rooms. Guests who breach reasonable and advertised house rules should be warned of the consequences of further breaches. If they persist, they may ultimately be evicted. Evictions are the capital punishment of the hospitality industry, and for that and other reasons should be used only as a last resort.

The Right to Evict Nonguests

The fact that hotels are both public and private places causes many problems for innkeepers. At virtually any time, anyone can walk through the front door of a hotel and wander around the lobby. People with no intention of reserving a room may come to dine, shop, await others, or simply to make inquiries. It is not uncommon for a hotel lobby to be a rendezvous for people who are not staying in the hotel. Most of this activity is of little concern to the hotel, and may even be considered an opportunity to market the hotel.

Hotels also attract persons who wish to use the lobbies as they would use benches in a park. They may be hitchhiking across the country or tired from shopping and wish to rest in the comfort of a clean and climate-controlled space. If the conduct and appearance of the loiterers are not up to the standards of the hotel's guests, many of those guests may be discomforted by the loiterers' presence in the hotel. An innkeeper has the right to ask loiterers and other nonguests to leave and, if they refuse, to remove them. The innkeeper should first ask the nature of their business in the hotel to establish that they are indeed loiterers. A person who looks and acts like a loiterer may in fact have legitimate business in the hotel.

Some nonguests may be in the lobby to solicit business. The solicitation may be for prostitution or for legitimate reasons such as to promote a local tourist attraction or restaurant. Even if the solicitor is a guest of the hotel, if he or she is attempting to solicit the hotel's patrons, the innkeeper has a right to ask that individual to leave the premises.

Some people try to exploit the semi-public nature of hotels. An innkeeper who finds an unwanted person in the hotel may have difficulty charging him with trespassing if he tells the police that he was simply looking for a washroom. Such a person can be asked to leave, given notice that he is not welcome, and advised that in future he will be charged with trespassing.

If a person on the premises has no intention of becoming an invitee or a guest, the hotel may ask the person to leave. A person who fails to leave when properly asked becomes a trespasser, thereby entitling the innkeeper to use reasonable force. Any eviction should be handled with care. As with the eviction of guests, no excessive force should be used.

The Right to Make a Citizen's Arrest

In the case of exceptional, qualifying conduct, an innkeeper may make a citizen's arrest of a guest or nonguest. Section 494 of the *Criminal Code of Canada* states:

(1) Any one may arrest without warrant

    (a) a person whom he finds committing an indictable offence; or

    (b) a person who, on reasonable grounds, he believes

        (i) has committed a criminal offence, and

        (ii) is escaping from and freshly pursued by persons who have lawful authority to arrest that person.

(2) Any one who is

    (a) the owner or a person in lawful possession of property, or

    (b) a person authorized by the owner or by a person in lawful possession of property, may arrest without warrant a person whom he finds committing a criminal offence on or in relation to that property.

For the citizen innkeeper, the tricky part is knowing whether an indictable offence is being or has been committed by the person, or knowing whether an indictable, summary, or hybrid offence is being committed by the person in relation to property the citizen innkeeper owns or has possession of. A mistake can lead straight to tort liability for false imprisonment.

Summary

The rights of innkeepers and the rights of guests are intertwined. Innkeepers have the rights incidental to ownership and control of the business and premises subject to, for example, the rights of guests to privacy in their rooms. In certain circumstances, innkeepers may bar nonguests from the premises, may refuse accommodation to a potential guest or, having granted accommodation, may evict the guest. Innkeepers may set house rules, and are entitled to be paid for their services. Innkeepers must exercise their rights legally and reasonably or face liability for improper conduct.

Discussion Questions

1. Can a hotel deny accommodation to someone who has no baggage? If so, under what circumstances?

2. Can an innkeeper discuss with another innkeeper the rates that he or she would like to charge next season? Why or why not?

3. Under what circumstances can an innkeeper refuse accommodation to a person with a pet? When does the innkeeper not have the right to refuse?

4. Is putting a lien on the luggage of a nonpaying guest a good idea? Why or why not?

5. What is the purpose of house rules?

6. Under what circumstances can a guest in good standing as to payment be evicted?

7. What steps should a hotel take when evicting someone?

8. Who can an innkeeper refuse to accommodate?

10

Chapter Ten

Guests

Learning Outcomes

1. Analyze case law to identify the rights and obligations of guests.

2. Describe the rights of guests for mail and other forms of messages and deliveries.

Introduction

As noted in Chapter 8, the innkeeper–guest relationship is a legal relationship that bestows an assortment of rights and obligations upon the innkeeper and the guest. An innkeeper must respect the rights of the guest, just as the guest must respect the rights of the innkeeper. In this chapter, we shall examine the rights of guests. The duties of guests are also discussed in conjunction with the rights of innkeepers in Chapter 9, e.g., the duty of guests to pay for the accommodation and services was discussed as a right of the innkeeper to receive payment.

The Rights of Guests

The Right to Be Received

Except in limited circumstances, transients have a right to be **received** by the innkeeper. The obligation to receive even extends to minors, who cannot generally be bound by their contracts unless necessities are involved. The innkeeper may be limited to collecting from the minor for the cost of the room and regular meals, but not for the in-room movies and the depletion of the minibar. A traveller who reaches an inn after it has closed is entitled to wake the innkeeper and demand accommodation. Unlike the innkeeper, a shopkeeper who has retired for the night is not under any duty to answer his or her door for business reasons. Innkeepers are imbued with this duty because timely lodging is a human necessity. An innkeeper may refuse accommodation when there are sufficient grounds to believe that the transient is:

1. more than minimally impaired;
2. carrying a dangerously contagious disease;
3. well known for causing damage or disturbances;
4. well known for failing to pay; or
5. likely to engage in illegal or immoral acts on the premises.

An innkeeper may also refuse a paying transient seeking accommodation when there is no room at the inn. *White's Case, [1558] 2 Dyer 158b* expressed the following principle:

> If the inn is full and the innkeeper properly refuses a traveller, and if the traveller receives the permission of a guest to share the guest's room without the assent of the innkeeper, then the traveller is not a guest.

In *Carriss v. Buxton, [1958] S.C.R. 44*, it was found that a person who has been improperly refused accommodation has been treated tortiously by the innkeeper and may sue the innkeeper either in tort or in contract.

The Right to Be Entertained

Upon being received, the guest is entitled to be entertained. As noted in Chapter 8, "entertainment" here simply means that guests are entitled to receive hospitality and be treated in a respectful and courteous manner for the duration of the innkeeper–guest relationship.

Under tort law, the intentional infliction of emotional harm by an innkeeper may give rise to damages. Derogatory comments, outright insults, or psychological pressures can distress some guests. Many insensitive comments do not invite court remedies because the courts are often reluctant to reward plaintiffs who are unreasonably sensitive. On the other hand, the courts may invoke the thin skull rule to find in favour of an emotionally fragile plaintiff if the hotel staff behaved in a sufficiently insensitive manner. As noted elsewhere, legal principles can often be found to support whatever decision the judge wishes to render. A judge may find that the distress was not reasonably foreseeable in the circumstances and dismiss the claim or may invoke the thin skull rule and allow the claim. Although some give and take in communication and discourse is normal (especially between parties of roughly equal stature), innkeepers serve an exceptionally broad spectrum of personality types, from the rhinoceros-skinned to the emotionally fragile. Innkeepers have an obligation to be sensitive toward the public that well exceeds the obligation of the public to be sensitive toward innkeepers.

Guests are entitled to full disclosure of all charges.

An innkeeper should ensure that guests endure no willful or careless treatment that could cause humiliation or distress. Staff should be trained in this regard, and management should be alert to any failures by staff to exercise reasonable courtesies. Liability may also arise if the staff become aware that one guest is abusing another and fail to take appropriate action. On the other hand, problems can arise when staff are too quick to judge a situation. Guests should be given the benefit of the doubt. Staff should be cautious in responding until sufficient evidence is in. The case of *Dewolf v. Ford, 86 N.E. 527 (N.Y., 1908)* involved the discovery by hotel security staff of a man in the room of a female guest. Unbeknownst to the security staff, the man had a valid reason to be in the room. The hotel was found liable for the distress that resulted when the security staff insulted the female guest by insinuating that she was a prostitute. (The staff may have escaped civil liability had they insulted the man, who was not a guest, instead of the woman.) In another case, *Emmke v. Desilva, 293 Fed. 17 (1923)*, a husband and wife were accused by hotel staff of not being married. They recovered damages for their humiliation. Both of these cases demonstrate the need for discrete, noncommittal behaviour on the part of staff. In the following case, the plaintiffs lost.

Hurd v. Hotel Astor Co., 169 N.Y.S. 359 (1918)

A man was found by the hotel staff in a room that was registered to his wife and another woman. The husband had not received permission and his presence in the room contravened a hotel rule. In the hallway, the hotel discussed the matter with him in a nonoffensive manner. Although the wife was accused of soliciting for the purpose of prostitution, there was no damage award because there had not been an intrusion into the guest room, and the two women guests had knowingly broken a valid house rule.

In the bygone era of the above cases, hotels often had floors designated for male or female guests only. For many years, such designations were no longer made. Today, however, some hotels are designating certain floors for special uses such as nonsmoking or females only. For reasons of security, some women travelling on their own prefer a floor of rooms designated for females only. Others who may benefit from designated floors include school tours, sports teams, and trade or club associations.

The obligation of an innkeeper to treat guests in a respectful and courteous manner does not apply to the same degree to nonguests or to casual patrons of the hotel restaurant, bar, banquet room, or any other area of the inn. The duty owed by a hotel to a casual patron of its dining room is comparable to the duty owed by a restaurant.

Wallace v. Shoreham, 49 A. (2d) 81 (D.C., 1946)

A patron of a hotel restaurant who was not a guest of the hotel was insulted because of a mistake in the amount of change due on the bill. The patron sued for insult, claiming the rights of a guest. The action failed because the patron was found not to be a guest of the hotel, only a patron of the hotel's restaurant. The result would probably have been different had the patron been found to be a guest. The result might also have been different had the case been heard in today's pro-victim litigation climate.

Jenkins v. Kentucky Hotel Co., 87 S.W. (2d) 951 (Ky.,1935)

Jenkins waited in the hotel lobby for her brother, who was attending a banquet. A hotel detective asked her to leave. She managed to stay out of his sight and continued to wait. Upon rediscovery, the detective insisted that she leave. Fearing for her safety, she left. She sued the hotel, alleging that the detective had addressed her in a rude and objectionable fashion. The court found that she was at most a mere licensee and had been asked to leave properly the first time. The second request showed bad manners but, in the circumstances of this case, it was not actionable, at least by a nonguest.

While nonguests are not owed the same degree of courtesy as guests, accommodation-sector personnel should treat everyone on the premises with proper respect and avoid defaming anyone. Prostitutes who frequent hotels and hotel bars are often indistinguishable from legitimate guests and passersby. Innkeepers should be loath to accuse anyone on the premises of being a prostitute. An innkeeper who knows with all human certainty that a person is a prostitute, and who wishes to evict the person from the premises, should simply inform the person that the reason for the eviction is that there have been too many visitors to the room. In these and other circumstances, tact and diplomacy are essential tools of hoteliers.

The Right to Have Luggage Admitted

An innkeeper must admit not only the guest but also his or her luggage. However, the right of the guest in this regard is not unlimited. There are reasonable restrictions on what is considered luggage and baggage.

Waters v. Beau Site Co., 114 Misc. 65, 68, 186 N.Y.S. 731, 732 (N.Y. City Ct. 1920)

In this case, it was held that "[l]uggage and baggage are essentially the bags, trunks, etc., that a passenger takes with him for his personal use and convenience

> with reference to his necessities or to the ultimate purpose of his journey, and in this connection it has been held that, within limits, the same include such jewelry as may be adapted to the tastes, habits and social standing and be necessary for the convenience, use and enjoyment of the traveler either while in transit or temporarily staying at a particular place."

In other words, items of convenience and personal use are receivable without controversy. Items that are not automatically receivable could include items that are not needed for convenience or personal use. Thus, a hotel could refuse to receive as luggage construction tools, life-size stuffed elephants, and a myriad of other things.

An innkeeper is not required to accept a traveller's baggage if the traveller has no intention of being accommodated at the inn. Under common law, an exception is made for a traveller's horse. As a result of this anomaly, travellers can park their horses at the Banff Springs Hotel and then stay at the Chateau Lake Louise.

The Right to Full Disclosure of All Charges

Guests are entitled to be advised in advance of the room rate and that they may be billed for extra services such as use of the room telephone and minibar. Guests are entitled to be billed only for the services that they have contracted for. Hidden charges are not allowed. This does not mean that each guest must endorse in advance all amounts being charged for all services. Rather, it means that the charges should come as no surprise and that hotels should not concoct amounts to add to the bill. In the 1960s, the Waldorf Astoria Hotel in New York City attempted to add a 2 percent surcharge to each bill. The hotel expected to raise from the surcharge as much as $126,000 annually. If a guest questioned the charge, it was removed without debate. An action akin to a class action suit was successfully brought against the hotel on behalf of all guests who were overcharged during the period identified in the action.

The Right to Information Required by Statute

All provinces have legislation requiring that a notice of certain statutory provisions relating to liability limitations and property protection be posted in every hotel bedroom. Some provinces require that the notice be posted in other rooms as well. For example, section 5 of British Columbia's *Hotel Keepers Act* states:

> 5.(1) Every innkeeper must keep conspicuously posted in the office and public rooms and in every bedroom in the inn a copy of section 3 [limitation of liability], printed in plain type.
>
> (2) An innkeeper is entitled to the benefit of section 3 for the goods or property brought to the inn only while the copies are posted.

Innkeepers should consider posting the notices in any location that might serve as the site of the commencement of the innkeeper–guest relationship, such as the cab of the hotel's private limousine. Some provinces require that the room rates be posted in the rooms themselves. For example, section 5 of Ontario's *Hotel Registration of Guests Act* states:

> 5.(1) In every room used for sleeping accommodation in a hotel there shall be kept posted in a conspicuous place a notice specifying the rates charged for the room.
>
> (2) Every owner and every manager of a hotel who fails to keep posted the notice required by subsection (1) is guilty of an offence and on conviction is liable to a fine of not more than $550.

The Right to Privacy and the Exclusive Use of the Room

Once assigned a room, the guest has a right to privacy and the exclusive use of the room. The hotel may enter the room only:

1. with the permission of the guest;

2. in the case of an emergency;

3. to perform legitimate housekeeping duties;

4. to perform reasonable maintenance work;

5. to move the guest from one room to another; and

6. to re-enter the room and terminate the innkeeper–guest relationship if payment is past due and the guest is unable or refuses to pay.

In all other circumstances, the hotel must treat the guest's room like a private residence. The hotel must also protect the guest from intrusion on the part of unauthorized staff and outsiders. This includes refusing to allow a guest's nonregistered spouse access to the room, even if the spouse can prove the marital relationship. It may be that the spouse is the last person that the guest wishes to have access to the room. The hotel would be liable for any reasonably foreseeable damages arising from the failure to safeguard the guest's privacy. Let us revisit a case that was first introduced in Chapter 9.

Doyle v. Walker, [1867] 26 Upper Canada Queen's Bench Rep. 502

The plaintiff had rented two rooms from the defendant hotel. The plaintiff fell behind in his payments and was unable to pay upon request. The hotel asked him to leave whereupon he requested that he be allowed to remain in one of the two rooms so that his wife, who was ill, would not have to be moved. The hotel entered the first of the plaintiff's rooms and moved his belongings into the second room so that the next guest could move into the first room; in the evening of the same day, the plaintiff paid his bill. The plaintiff sued the hotel for trespassing. The court held that the hotel has the right to move a guest and his belongings to another room provided the actions are reasonable.

In the *Doyle* case, even if the hotel had liened the plaintiff's belongings or delivered them to the office where he was working and not simply moved them into another room, the hotel would not have been liable for trespass because it could not have known that the late payment would be made. The hotel had acted reasonably given the facts known at the time.

In another case, hotel staff inadvertently turned over a key to the next guest before the first guest had vacated the room. Valuable items belonging to the first guest went missing. The hotel was found liable on the basis that there had been an infringement of the first guest's right to exclusive use of the room.

Unauthorized entries of rooms should be discouraged. If a person who is not the registered guest asks for a key to the guest's room, the key should not be given out even if the person making the request claims to be, or is in fact, the guest's spouse, child, parent, or employer. If someone claims to have permission to enter the room on behalf of the guest, hotel staff should contact the guest for confirmation. An infringement of the guest's right to privacy and exclusive use of the room can be embarrassing for the guest and costly for the hotel.

Hotels do not have the right to open a guest's door for the police unless the police have a proper warrant. Staff are entitled to assume the validity of the warrant. The hotel would not be liable if the warrant turned out to be invalid, rendering the search illegal. Beyond asking the officers to identify themselves and to confirm that they have a warrant, the innkeeper owes no further duty in this circumstance. The recourse of an innocent, aggrieved guest would be an action not against the hotel but against the police officers and their governmental employer.

In some instances, the police may insist upon the door being opened even though they lack a warrant or the warrant is defective. The guest's right to privacy and the exclusive use of the room is such that the innkeeper does not have the right to open the door. If the police indicate that they will use force if the innkeeper does not open the door, the innkeeper should not interfere but should instead ask for an address to which the repair bill can be sent. Recent Supreme Court decisions have curtailed police entries in situations where there is no warrant or where the warrant is defective. The police have learned to be careful in obtaining warrants, which has lessened any dilemmas faced by innkeepers.

It is also an infringement of the guest's right to privacy and exclusive use of the room if a member of the housekeeping or other staff leaves the door open such that the police or anyone else can observe the room, its contents, and any activities taking place therein. Guests are entitled to the presumption that they are behaving legally and appropriately in their rooms. Quite strong evidence is needed to rebut the presumption.

The police and suspicious spouses are not the only people who may wish to gain access to a room. Parents, children, employers, frustrated creditors, disgruntled lovers, close and well-intentioned friends and relations, and even the innkeepers themselves may seek to gain entry to a guest's room. Except in the circumstances outlined above, no one—not even the innkeeper—may enter the room without the permission of the guest. When additional information about a guest is required by the front desk, even if the information is innocuous and legitimately required, hotel staff cannot enter the room without the guest's permission. The staff must attempt to obtain the information at the door or over the telephone.

Lee v. Jacobson; Weber v. Jacobson (1992), 87 D.L.R. (4th)

The plaintiffs were successive tenants of a log cabin owned by a company controlled by the defendant. Lana Weber was the first occupant followed by Ina Lee. One night when Ina Lee was reading in bed, she heard an unusual noise coming from behind her head. Initially, she thought it was a bear grunting or a person quietly clearing his throat. She discovered that a hole had been cut in the wall above her bed, giving a person standing outside a clear view of the room and the bed. The hole was behind a two-way mirror that appeared to be a conventional mirror. Attached to the exterior wall of the bedroom was a small shed. The hole was inside the shed, concealed by a dustpan hanging on a nail. Fibrous insulation was used to plug the hole. The court found the defendant made the peep-hole. The court awarded Lana Weber $2,000 and Ina Lee $5,000 for damages. Punitive damages of $25,000 were also awarded to the plaintiffs to be divided between them.

The Right to Proper Handling of Mail, Messages, and Packages

The innkeeper has an obligation to deliver mail, faxes, telegrams, and parcels to the guest as soon as reasonably possible (there may be a greater urgency with faxes and telegrams). The contents of faxes and telegrams should be kept in the utmost confidence. Most modern hotels offer message services that are connected to room telephones and that inform a guest that a message is waiting at the reception desk or on the telephone voice mail. If these or similar features are absent, then a hotel must make an effort to bring the fact of the message to the attention of the guest or to deliver the message by hand as soon as reasonably possible. If a delay in delivery is the fault of the hotel, the hotel may be held responsible for any financial losses arising from the delay. Hotels should follow any reasonable instructions that the guest may give them concerning guest mail, messages, and packages.

Berlow v. Sheraton Dallas Corp., 629 S.W. (2d) 818 (Tex., 1982)

A jewelry designer sent a package by courier to her parents who were staying at the Sheraton Hotel for four days. The package did not arrive during the stay. The plaintiff's parents instructed the hotel to refuse delivery if it arrived after their departure, so that the courier company would return it to their daughter. The hotel agreed. The package later arrived at the hotel, where it was accepted and kept at the front desk for a month. Following standard procedure after the month, the hotel marked the package "Return to Sender" and put it in the mail. The package was lost. The court found that the hotel had been negligent in its acceptance and handling of the package, and in failing to attempt to contact the guests. The courier company had delivered the package properly (if a little late) to a person who accepted it and was therefore not negligent. The plaintiff testified that the package had contained jewelry worth over $10,000 (U.S.). The court accepted her evidence and awarded her the full claim.

The Right to Telephone Service

Although the telephone is not a recent invention and is often a critical safety feature, it is not a legal requirement that every guest room have a telephone. Most hotels supply a telephone in every room, but there are some locations where it is acceptable that a phone not be in a guest room. For example, some resorts, lodges, and bed and breakfasts—particularly those whose clientele are seeking a rustic holiday—do not supply a phone in every room. All but a very few of such establishments nevertheless offer access to a telephone, which is usually located in the lobby or front office. Under the tort concepts of reasonable expectation and duty of care, it is likely that guests have a right to the use of a telephone unless the innkeeper forewarns the guest prior to registration that no access to a telephone will be provided.

Hotels routinely charge their guests for local and long-distance calls. To many guests, the charges seem excessive. In one recent case, a young man from Belleville, Ontario, used a pay phone outside his hotel in Florida in order to avoid the high cost of using the phone in his room. While he was using the public telephone, he was surrounded by several youths in a robbery attempt and shot dead. Although modern telephone systems require little servicing by the hotels, hotels in Canada may charge whatever they wish for the use of the phone. Hotels and especially those located in high-crime areas should seriously consider the potential dangers of using a telephone off the premises. Among guests it is the young, the elderly, and the impecunious who are most likely to cut down on their expenses by using an off-site telephone. These are the same people who tend to be most vulnerable to criminal acts.

The Right to Security of Property

Under common law, innkeepers have a duty to protect the property of guests for the duration of the innkeeper–guest relationship. Statutes have placed limitations on the liability for lost or damaged guest property provided the provisions of the applicable statute are followed. It is left to the discretion of the innkeeper and the guest to contract out of the limitation if they wish.

Under common law, title to lost property devolves upon the finder, and title to abandoned property devolves upon the first claimant. However, title to mislaid property remains with the guest and cannot be turned over to someone else without the permission of the guest, even if he or she has vacated the room. If a guest has mislaid or left behind property, the innkeeper may open or examine it to discover its owner. Such actions do not constitute an invasion of the former guest's privacy, but are necessary to serve that guest and to protect the hotel from potential liability under its duties as a bailee of the property. Bailment and other security of property issues are discussed in detail in Chapter 11.

The Right to Security of Person

Under common law, innkeepers have a duty to protect the guests themselves for the duration of the innkeeper–guest relationship. The guest's right to protection extends to protection from outsiders, other guests, staff, and the guest himself when, for example, his judgment is impaired by substance abuse or depression. Although innkeepers are not insurers, adequate measures must be taken to secure the premises against intruders, respond to intrusions or misconduct on the part of other guests, and assist guests who are suicidal or who have overdosed on drugs. The backgrounds of staff should be investigated. Staff should be supervised and be subject to clear codes of conduct. Failure to exercise due care may result in the hotel being liable for any reasonably foreseeable personal injuries arising out of the failure. Such injuries include physical and emotional damages, and lost income for time missed.

Innkeepers should watch for con artists on or near the premises. Pickpockets sometimes distract their targets by touching a lit cigarette to their hands. In another scam, swimmers cry for help while their accomplices steal the property left unguarded by the rescuer. In the case of the sadistic pickpockets, there is injury to both the person and the property.

McKenna v. Greco (1981), 33 O.R. (2d) 595 (C.A.)

The plaintiff was assaulted. The court held that knowledge on the part of the hotel of previous violent incidents by the assailant was relevant to whether or not the hotel should have anticipated trouble and taken steps to prevent it.

Faltus v. Bazel (1990), 73 Alta L. R. (2d) 75 (Q.B.)

T and the plaintiff engaged in a fight that began and ended quickly. The fight was spontaneous and the innkeeper had no reason to expect trouble from T. The court held that, in the circumstances, the innkeeper had no opportunity or obligation to risk injury to himself by intervening. The innkeeper was not negligent in not calling the police because the fight was short-lived.

The Right to Assistance in the Event of Illness, Injury, or Death

In Canada, most medical care is covered by provincial health programs. If a guest claims to be ill or injured, the solution, where reasonable, is to call an ambulance. Any guests who are truly ill or injured will be taken care of by trained paramedics. If the situation is an emergency, an ambulance should still be called, but the staff may have to render immediate assistance.

Pursuant to statute, everyone has a duty to inform a coroner or a police officer of a death. Failure to do so is a provincial offence. For example, Ontario's *Coroners Act* states:

10. Every person who has reason to believe that a deceased person died,

   (a) as a result of

      (i) violence,

      (ii) misadventure,

      (iii) negligence,

      (iv) misconduct, or

      (v) malpractice;

   (b) by unfair means;

   (c) ... pregnancy ...;

   (d) suddenly and unexpectedly;

   (e) from disease or sickness ...;

   (f) from any cause other than disease; or

   (g) under such circumstances as may require investigation,

   shall immediately notify a coroner or a police officer of the facts and circumstances relating to the death. ...

55. Any person who contravenes section 10 ... is guilty of an offence and on conviction is liable to a fine of not more than $1,000 or to imprisonment for a term of not more than six months, or to both.

The Right to Freedom from False Detention or Arrest

Hotels have the right to report suspicious behaviour to the police. If room attendants observe firearms or illegal drugs in a guest's room where there is a reasonable apprehension of criminal activity, the hotel may report their observations to the police with impunity.

Hotel and restaurant staff may not interfere with a police arrest of a guest. Further, staff must not do anything, such as providing incorrect information, that could lead to a **false arrest** of a guest. For example, a police officer may arrest a guest for disturbing the peace because the desk clerk has embellished some facts about the behaviour of the guest. If the unembellished facts are such that the person would not have been arrested, the hotel may be liable for wrongful imprisonment or malicious prosecution.

If a hotel detains someone without cause (i.e., the staff have no reasonable grounds to believe that the person has committed a crime), then the hotel may be found to have falsely arrested that person. The person may then sue the hotel in tort for wrongful imprisonment. Proper grounds for detention include damaging hotel property or the property of other guests and making threats toward staff, other guests, or other persons on the premises.

Bahner v. Marwest Hotel Company Ltd., and Muir (1970), 75 W.W.R. 729 (B.C.C.A.)

While entertaining two friends at the defendant's restaurant, B ordered a bottle of wine with dinner. At 11:30 p.m., the waiter asked him if he would like a second bottle, even though the first bottle was only half empty. B agreed, and the second bottle was opened and brought to his table. At 11:50 p.m., the waiter correctly advised him that, under current provincial law, the second bottle would have to be finished by midnight. B replied that he and his companions could not drink a bottle of wine that quickly without getting drunk, and that he would take the bottle home with him. The manager informed B, again correctly, that his proposed course of action was illegal. B subsequently refused to pay for the wine. The manager summoned a security guard who said to B, "You cannot leave." B reasonably expected to be restrained by force if he tried to leave and the law does not require that he attempt to run away. The manager also called the police. Constable Muir placed B under arrest without a warrant and took him to the police station. Muir was advised by a justice of the peace that B could not be charged with obtaining goods under false pretences. Muir then went to the cell and told him that he was being charged with being intoxicated in a public place, a charge that was totally unsubstantiated and even contradicted by the evidence.

The trial judge found that, while B may have been wrong and may have been under a civil liability to pay for the wine that he could neither consume nor take with him, he had made no false pretence and had used no force; he had simply refused to pay a sum that he, honestly and in good faith, believed that he did not owe. The hotel manager, who could not have believed that a criminal offence had occurred, had called the police simply as a means of collecting the amount owing. The trial judge found that there were two false imprisonments. The hotel was liable for the actions of the security guard, but not for the arrest by Muir because all the manager did was apprise Muir of the incident, leaving it to him to decide whether to arrest B. However, in the assessment of damages, the trial judge noted that the miseries inflicted on B by Muir would never have happened had the manager not called the police. Muir was also liable for false imprisonment.

The Court of Appeal upheld the trial judge's finding that the defendants had acted outrageously, and quoted with approval the words of the trial judge:

> The arrogance and stupidity of ... the hotel authorities cannot be overstated ... (T)he fact that he was publicly humiliated by detention by the security officer in the hotel in the presence of the staff and a dozen guests, and by subsequent interrogation and arrest by a uniformed policeman was known to a considerable number of people, who have in all probability and very naturally told other persons about it. It is hard to calculate how far news of this kind may spread and what harm it may have done. Few persons who witnessed his arrest are likely to be aware of his subsequent acquittal. The ripples from the boulder thrown into the water by the defendants may spread far. The degradation consequent upon the experience suffered by the plaintiff is sore and not easily forgotten. Muir's assertion ... that he arrested the accused to prevent a breach of the peace and because he was intoxicated in a public place is a mendacious afterthought devised at a later time to try to defend an indefensible position ... a sorry course of conduct and one which it saddens me to discover in a member of our usually fair-minded and well-conducted police force.

The Court of Appeal upheld the awards of $3,500 against the hotel and $2,500 against Constable Muir; each award included costs and $1,000 in punitive damages.

Summary

The rights of guests and innkeepers are intertwined. In most circumstances, guests are entitled to be received and be entertained. They are entitled to disclosure of the charges and other information required by statute such as liability limits. Except in emergencies or in the event of their own improper conduct, guests are entitled to privacy in their rooms and to security for themselves and their property. Guests are subject to reasonable house rules, and are required to pay for the services received. Guests must exercise their rights legally and reasonably or face liability for improper conduct.

Discussion Questions

1. Describe how an innkeeper can avoid liability for hurting a guest's feelings.

2. Under what circumstances might a hotel consider having floors designated for females?

3. Are all persons who frequent a hotel owed the same degree of care? Why or why not?

4. How should a front desk clerk respond if a guest complains of a medical problem?

5. Under what circumstances is a hotel entitled to enter a guest's room?

11

Chapter Eleven
Protection of Guests and Their Property

Learning Outcomes

1. Assess an innkeeper's common law liability for a guest's property.

2. Describe the importance of insurance for an innkeeper.

3. Assess the liability of a bailee for the property of a bailor.

Introduction

As discussed in Chapter 8, travelling in medieval England was a risky proposition. Inns became a refuge for travellers seeking to protect themselves and their property from attack by reivers and thieves. These early travellers often found that they and their goods were equally vulnerable inside the inn. It was fairly easy for thieves to separate travellers from their belongings as they slept in the communal great room. Unscrupulous innkeepers employed decoy travellers to carry out the looting. Since the victims were from outside the district, the decoys could be used repeatedly.

The common law judges, frequent travellers themselves, were quick to respond to the problem. Their solution was to impose upon the innkeepers absolute liability for the safety of guests and their property. In this way, the innkeepers could not gain by looting, but stood to lose whatever they had looted in addition to whatever independent thieves had taken. The only economical course for innkeepers was to make their establishments very safe. This was, and is, even for honest and diligent hoteliers, a formidable task. Intruders and untrustworthy employees are a constant threat. Some guests are a double threat in that they may rob other guests or else claim to have been robbed. Some professional guest/thieves, sophisticated and studiously well dressed, are experts in obtaining copies of keys and eliciting confidential information from staff.

Over time, the courts have evolved different standards of care for different classes of contractual relationships. The nature of the responsibility depends on the legal relationship between the innkeeper and the other party. The innkeeper's greatest responsibility is owed to guests. If the relationship is between an innkeeper and a nonguest, the duty of care is generally the same as that between any two members of the public, and therefore lower than the duty owed to guests. Security of the person and property of guests is one of the major undertakings of innkeepers. The property of guests includes items kept or left in the room, in the hotel safe, or inside the guest's parked car (and, of course, the car itself). The protection of nonguest property, generally by bailment, is discussed later in this chapter.

Common Law Liability for Guest Property

The Absolute Liability Rule

Under common law, innkeepers are absolutely liable as full insurers for the safety of the property of their guests. Under **absolute liability**, it does not matter whether the innkeeper has exercised all due care and is not negligent. If the innkeeper–guest relationship has been established and the guest suffers a loss, the innkeeper, negligent or not, becomes liable for the entire loss under common law. Liability is imposed as soon as both the innkeeper–guest relationship and the fact of the loss are established.

From its inception, the absolute liability rule contributed greatly to the protection of guests and their property. When a guest checks in or hands her bags to the hotel's porter or to the hotel's limousine driver at the airport, the parties have demonstrated their mutual intent to enter into the innkeeper–guest relationship. Under the absolute liability rule, throughout the duration of the relationship, the innkeeper is responsible for the guest's property and must pay for any losses or damages to it. The English case of *Williams v. Linnit, [1951] 1 K.B. 565* confirmed that an innkeeper could not, under common law, contract out of strict liability. Further, innkeepers could not avoid strict liability by warning their guests to keep their belongings under lock and key because there were possible miscreants staying at the inn.

To be liable under the absolute liability rule, the owner of the hotel must be acting as an innkeeper and the occupant of the room must be acting as a guest. If the relationship is one of restaurateur and patron, the absolute liability rule does not apply. Unlike innkeepers, restaurateurs are not insurers under common law. If the relationship between the owner and the occupant is essentially that of landlord and tenant, the owner is subject only to the standard of care owed by a landlord, not by an innkeeper. Under common law, a landlord is not liable absolutely, but liable only if negligence is established.

Ford v. Seligman, [1954] O.R. 957, [1955] 1 D.L.R. 796 (C.A.)

Ford, a long-term lodger at the defendant hotel, had his room forcibly entered twice and his property stolen. The relationship was found not to be that of innkeeper and guest, but of landlord and lodger. Therefore, there was no absolute liability and the hotel could be liable to Ford only if negligence could be proven. Because no such negligence was proven, the defendant was not liable for the loss.

Lynar v. Mossop (1875), 36 U.C.Q.B. 230 (Ont. C.A.)

Lynar arrived at the hotel with a portmanteau and several other articles of luggage. While booking the room, he stated that he wanted to use the room only to change his clothes before visiting a friend. His luggage was taken to his room. When Lynar returned the next morning for his portmanteau, it could not be found. In the ensuing action for damages, it was held that the loss had occurred when Lynar was not acting as a guest. Thus, the defendant was not liable as an innkeeper and the absolute liability rule did not apply. This case might not have been decided the same way today.

Exceptions to the Absolute Liability Rule

There are three exceptions to the common law absolute liability rule. The hotel will not be absolutely liable where the loss or damage to the goods is attributable to the guest's own negligence, an act of a public enemy, or an act of God.

The Guest's Own Negligence

If the damages are attributable to the guest's own negligence, the hotel cannot be held absolutely liable for the loss. For instance, if a group of guests occupying rooms on the same floor all leave their room doors open to facilitate a social gathering, and some property goes missing, the loss would be attributed to the guests' decision to leave their doors open. The hotel would not be liable for the damages or losses. Applying basic negligent principles, liability may be apportioned between the hotel and the guest if both parties are negligent.

Barrie v. Wright (1905), 1 W.L.R. 412, 15 Man. R. 197 (C.A.)

Barrie, a guest at the defendant's hotel, was given his room before the luggage he had left with a cartage company was delivered. When it arrived, it was left standing in the lobby. Although both the defendant and the plaintiff were aware of its presence there, neither party acted to remove it. The luggage disappeared. At trial, the defendant was held liable. The appeal was dismissed, but the appeal judges differed on the question of which party had actual custody of the goods left in the hall. However, they agreed that a guest's contributory negligence could exonerate a hotelkeeper from liability, and that the degree of care owed by a hotel can be based on such factors as the capacity of the hotel, the number of guests, and the size of the community in which the hotel is located.

There is no rule of law that guests who fail to lock their rooms are negligent. However, pursuant to *Armistead v. Wilde, [1851] 17 Q.B. 261*, guests can be found negligent if they make an ostentatious display of their money or valuables and then leave them in an ill-secured place in the presence of several people.

Acts of Public Enemies

A public enemy is a person or group that is recognized as an adversary of the government in times of war or terrorism. When a terrorist group detonates in a hotel a bomb that damages guests and their luggage, the innkeeper is not liable for the resulting losses and damages.

Acts of God

Under common law, innkeepers are not responsible for losses or damages resulting from an act of God. Acts of God include such events as hurricanes, floods, tempests, lightning strikes, avalanches, and earthquakes. If such an event causes a loss or damage to guest property, the innkeeper is not liable for the loss. Liability would be found, however, if the damage were the result of some form of negligence on the part of the innkeeper. For example, if water pours into a guest's room during a heavy rainfall and the innkeeper had failed to repair a leaky roof, then the hotel would be liable. Innkeepers must take all reasonable steps to minimize the consequences of adverse weather. For example, they must remove from the roof excessive buildups of snow. Attributing any subsequent disaster to an act of God is no defence.

Infra Hospitium

The innkeeper is responsible only for the property of the guest that the guest has brought onto the premises of the inn. This principle is called ***infra hospitium***, which means "within the inn." Pursuant to this principle, an innkeeper is not responsible for property that the guest leaves at the airport, in the taxi, or at another site in the city. Conversely, if the guest hands the luggage to a limousine driver (who is engaged by the hotel) at the airport, the luggage is *infra hospitium*. The limousine is regarded as a temporary mobile extension of the hotel. While the property of the guest is within the precincts or control of the inn (i.e., on the grounds or inside the inn or in the care of the inn's agent), the innkeeper has the opportunity and responsibility to protect the property. A guest who hangs up a coat in a hotel cloakroom provided for that purpose has placed the coat *infra hospitium*, even though the innkeeper is unaware of the presence of the coat. Stables are considered *infra hospitium*.

An innkeeper has the right to expect that the guests will bring into the inn all the property with which they are travelling. An automobile is an obvious exception. However, if the automobile is parked in a garage or on a lot owned or operated by the hotel, the parking lot or garage is *infra hospitium* and the innkeeper has a responsibility to protect the automobile and any contents that are reasonably associated with it, such as car batteries, folding sun visors, and snow scrapers. The innkeeper is not responsible for the loss of or damage to any contents of the automobile that are more reasonably associated with the guest than the automobile, such as suitcases and cameras. Such items must be brought into the inn itself before they are considered *infra hospitium*. The innkeeper is not responsible for automobiles that the guest parks in a garage or on a lot that is not owned or operated by or affiliated with the hotel.

George v. Williams, [1956] O.R. 871, 5 D.L.R. (2d) 21 (C.A.)

The plaintiff, George, had arrived by automobile as a guest at the defendant's hotel, and had parked his car in a parking lot marked at the entrance with a sign that read "Parking for Chateau Hotel Guests Free." Because it was raining, George left most of his belongings in the locked automobile. Despite the fact that the parking lot had an attendant, the belongings were stolen from the car. Although it was separated from the hotel by a lane, the parking lot was found to be *infra hospitium*. The issue was not the separation of the parking lot from the hotel, but rather the degree of care and control exercised by the hotel over the parking lot. Although the car was *infra hospitium*, it did not necessarily follow that the chattels in the car were also *infra hospitium*. While an innkeeper's liability for injury to the person and goods of a guest extends to the guest's automobile, the property of the guest that is more reasonably associated with the guest than with the automobile must still be carried into the hotel itself before the innkeeper will be liable for its loss. In this case, the hotel had every reason to expect that George would bring any property not associated with his automobile into the hotel, where the innkeeper would have a better opportunity of protecting the hotel against liability. Thus, the personal chattels in the car were *extra hospitium*. Notwithstanding its failure to post any legal notices in the parking lot, the hotel was found not liable for the loss.

Statutory Limitations

Purpose of the Limitation

The purpose of the common law absolute liability rule was to end the frequent losses incurred by guests at medieval British inns. The judges were keen to transfer the risk to the innkeepers. While there is no doubt that the rule greatly reduced the losses of guests, it left the innkeepers with a very heavy burden. The shoe was now on the other foot as unscrupulous guests began to bring unfounded and fraudulent claims for nonexistent losses. To correct the imbalance and distribute the risks more fairly, the British government enacted legislation to soften the sometimes harsh effects of the common law. All the provinces and territories have enacted similar legislation that limits an innkeeper's liability for loss or damage to the property of guests provided the conditions set forth in the legislation are met. Essentially, the conditions require that notices of the limitation be posted in specified locations, and that the loss not be the result of the willful act, default, or neglect of the innkeeper. As with any statutory restriction of a common law right, the courts generally require strict compliance with the statute on the part of the person wishing to rely on the restriction. If the statute is not complied with, the common law applies and the innkeeper's liability is that of an absolute insurer. Provided the innkeeper complies with the statutory requirements, the limitation statutes help to protect innkeepers from unwarranted claims by unscrupulous guests, as well as from ruinous claims by honest guests who travel, unbeknownst to the innkeeper, with large amounts of money or other valuables.

Limitation Provisions

As an example, sections 3, 4, and 5 of Newfoundland's *Innkeepers Act* set forth limitation and notice provisions as follows:

3. The liability of an innkeeper for the loss of or damage to the goods or property of a guest is limited to two hundred dollars except where the goods or property have been

    (a) stolen, lost or injured through the act, default or neglect of the innkeeper or his servant; or

    (b) deposited for safe custody with the innkeeper, except in case of such deposit the innkeeper may, if he thinks fit, require as a condition of his liability that the goods or property shall be deposited in a safe or other receptacle.

4. Where an innkeeper refuses to receive for safe custody any goods or property of a guest or if the guest, through any fault of the innkeeper, is unable to deposit such goods or property for safe custody, the innkeeper shall not be entitled to the benefit of this Act in respect thereof unless he establishes that his inn was not equipped with a proper safe or vault and that he so informed the guest at the time of refusing to receive the goods or property.

5. (1) Every innkeeper shall keep conspicuously posted in the reception area, public rooms and in every bedroom of the inn, a copy of section 3 and such copy shall be printed in plain type.

    (2) An innkeeper shall be entitled to the provisions of this Act only while the copy of section 3 is posted.

The Acts in the other jurisdictions differ in some important respects. Innkeepers who fail to follow the exact requirements of the Acts in their respective jurisdictions will likely lose the protections and benefits to which they are entitled under those Acts.

> ### Laing v. Allied Innkeepers Ltd., [1970] 1 O.R. 502 (Div. Ct.)
>
> Laing, a registered guest at the defendant's motel, had money taken from his wallet, which he had left on the top of the dresser before falling asleep in his room on the second floor. Laing had locked the door to the hall, but the thief had entered through a door opening onto the balcony, which Laing had left open for ventilation. As required by the *Innkeepers Act*, notice of the limitation of liability had been posted in the guest's room. There was evidence that the notice had not been posted in the office, public rooms, and in every bedroom as also required by the Act. The court found that the defendant had not complied with the posting requirements of the statute, could not rely on the statutory exemption, and was therefore liable as an absolute insurer under common law for the loss. The plaintiff was found not to be contributorily negligent. The defendant was aware of the benefits of the statutory limitation in reducing the amount of money paid out for guest's loss. However, the defendant failed to recognize the importance of following exactly the posting requirements set forth in the Act.

The dollar value assigned as the limited liability for an innkeeper varies from jurisdiction to jurisdiction. The $200 limit in Newfoundland is the highest in Canada. Some provinces limit the loss to $40. Manitoba innkeepers have no liability at all unless they caused the loss themselves or else received an express deposit of the property for safe custody. Section 8 of Manitoba's *Hotel Keepers Act* states:

8. (1) No hotel keeper is liable to make good to any guest of the hotel any loss or injury to goods or property brought to his hotel except

(a) where the goods or property are stolen, lost or injured, through the fault or neglect of the hotel keeper or any servant in his employ; or

(b) subject to subsection (2), where the goods or property are deposited expressly for safe custody with the hotel keeper.

(2) Where a deposit is made, as mentioned in clause (b) of subsection (1), the hotel keeper may, if he thinks fit, require, as a condition of his liability, that the goods or property be deposited in a box or receptacle fastened and sealed by the person depositing it.

Few members of the public are aware of the limitations under the legislation. Those who are aware tend to be people who have already suffered losses. At the time the various statutes were written, the amounts that were established to cover the losses of the travelling public may have been fair. Today, most people travel with basic clothing and personal effects that exceed in value even the $200 established under the Newfoundland legislation. The $40 limit of some provinces barely covers the cost of a good umbrella.

Subsection 3(a) of the Newfoundland statute prevents innkeepers from limiting their liabilities for loss or damage to guest property if the innkeepers or their staff are the cause of the loss or damage. A similar provision exists in all other jurisdictions in Canada. Innkeepers remain absolutely liable for the negligence and dishonesty of themselves and their staff. In the case of a staff member who neglected to close and lock the door of a guest's room after vacuuming, thereby enabling a thief to abscond with the guest's property, the statute would be unavailable to limit the hotel's liability for the loss. Under the innkeeper–guest relationship or under the laws of tort, the guest could sue the innkeeper in contract for recovery.

Under subsection 3(b) of the Newfoundland Act, a guest can ask the hotel to store such valuables as jewellery or large sums of money when they are not in use. If the innkeeper does so, the statutory limitation will not apply and the innkeeper will become once again absolutely liable for the full value as an insurer under the common law. By implication, subsection 3(b) allows innkeepers to require that guests keep items of special value in the hotel's vault or safe. If the innkeeper does so require and the guest fails to make use of the vault, then the innkeeper will not be responsible for more than the amount of the statutory limitation, absent negligence or dishonesty on the part of the innkeeper or the staff.

What is of special value to some people is of ordinary value to others. If a sable hat is the guest's normal apparel, the innkeeper will be liable for its loss as part of everyday property. In order for absolute liability to attach to the innkeeper for extraordinary valuables, a guest who has been clearly informed of the requirement of storage must store the valuables in the hotel's vault. The guest who wears a Timex watch for everyday use and a Rolex for special occasions must deposit the Rolex in the hotel's vault when it is not being worn.

Disclosure of Value

If a hotel believes that the amount of money or valuables that the guest wishes to store is excessive, it may insist that the guest use an outside storage facility such as those offered by banks. Whether or not an inn can refuse storage depends on the province. For example, section 4 of the Newfoundland Act provides that if, through any fault of the innkeeper, the guest is unable to deposit his property with the innkeeper for safe custody, the innkeeper is not entitled to the limitation benefit of the Act unless the innkeeper establishes that the inn is not equipped with a proper safe or vault and so informed the guest at the time of refusing to receive the goods or property. Thus, a timely warning that there is no vault absolves a Newfoundland inn from absolute liability, but a Newfoundland inn that has a vault cannot take advantage of the provision. Unlike Newfoundland,

Ontario does not give the innkeeper the option of advising the guest that the inn has no vault. Sections 4 and 5 of Ontario's *Innkeepers Act* state in part:

4. (1) No innkeeper is liable to make good to any guest any loss of or injury to goods brought to the inn ... to a greater amount than the sum of $40 except, ...

   (b) where the goods have been deposited expressly for safe custody with the innkeeper.

   (2) In case of such deposit, it is lawful for the innkeeper ... to require, as a condition of liability, that the goods shall be deposited in a box or other receptacle, fastened and sealed by the person depositing the goods.

5. If an innkeeper refuses to receive for safe custody, as mentioned in clause 4(1)(b), any goods of a guest or if the guest, through any default of the innkeeper, is unable to deposit such goods, the innkeeper is not entitled to the benefit of this Act in respect thereof.

Thus, in Ontario, if the hotel refuses to store the goods because it has no vault, it is still absolutely liable on the basis of the refusal. When there is a vault, the statutory limitation does not apply for property stored in the vault, and the innkeeper could be liable for enormous sums of money in the event of loss or damage to the contents of the vault. For many people, items of jewellery are normal accoutrements. They can also be worth a considerable amount of money. An Ontario inn cannot insist that an expensive diamond ring be stored off site, nor can it refuse to store it in its vault. The inn is caught between a rock and a hard place. If the guest keeps the ring in the room, the limitation avails the innkeeper; if the guest stores the ring in the vault, the limitation does not avail the innkeeper. Thus, a secure vault and adequate insurance are essential. Fortunately for innkeepers, as demonstrated in the following case, the imposition of liability for property placed in the vault is tempered by the concept of "express deposit."

Whitehouse v. Pickett, [1908] A.C. 357 (H.L.)

In this case, the House of Lords held that in order for an "express deposit" to take place, something must be said or done to convey the guest's intention to deliver the property and the innkeeper's intention to receive it such that the innkeeper agrees to make himself liable for the property. Property is deposited for safe-keeping with the innkeeper only if the guest informs the innkeeper in a reasonable way that the deposit is for safe custody. Leaving a bag with the hotel without declaring the value of the contents does not constitute an express deposit.

If a guest has made an express deposit, and if the guest removes a valuable item from the vault, the innkeeper once again enjoys the protection of the Act until the guest returns the item to the vault by way of an express deposit. Once the guest checks out, the innkeeper is no longer responsible. It should be pointed out that the process of checking out is not complete until the guest is off the premises. Safe delivery of the guest and the guest's property to the exterior of the hotel's property is necessary to terminate the innkeeper–guest relationship.

Some innkeepers use disclaimers in an attempt to cater to the desire of guests to store valuable property while simultaneously limiting the liability of the hotel. Many hotels offer deposit envelopes that are designed to hold a guest's property. Printed on the envelopes are disclaimers informing guests that the hotel has limited its liability to pay for property loss or damage, usually to the same statutory limit applicable to property outside the vault. Such disclaimers are a derogation of the innkeeper's absolute liability and are invalid upon the authority of *Williams v. Linnit* discussed earlier in this chapter.

Any limitation of the innkeeper's liability lies in determining whether or not the deposit was express. For example, deposit envelopes often contain a statement that an employee who agrees to make the hotel liable for more than the statutory maximum, and who does so without actual knowledge of the contents of the deposit envelope, is acting outside of the scope of his or her authority and cannot make the hotel liable. Such a statement is proper because, in the absence of actual knowledge of the value, the deposit is not express. If the employee has actual knowledge of the value of the deposit, the deposit is express and the amount of the innkeeper's liability is increased to the known value. Employees should follow clear procedures when dealing with guests who wish to deposit with the hotel property whose value exceeds the statutory maximum. They should also be circumspect when receiving a guest's property for safe custody. If an estimation of the value of the deposit is not offered by the guest, the employee should not elicit one because doing so will increase the liability of the hotel.

Suppose a guest claims that he lost a satchel containing $10,000 that he had deposited in the hotel vault. If it turns out that the guest had not advised the hotel of the value of the contents of his satchel, and that the hotel had taken all reasonable precautions against theft, then it would be unfair to saddle the hotel with the entire risk of the loss. To gain additional security, the guest should have advised the hotel of the true value of the contents, thereby giving the hotel the opportunity either to seek from him a higher payment (to cover the higher risk) or to refuse to accept the contents. The law allows a hotel to enjoy a fair opportunity to refuse to accept a risk that exceeds the statutory maximum.

Sufficient insurance is a must. To defray the cost, some hotels charge guests a service fee on valuable deposits. Other hotels have installed safes in the guest rooms. These safes, many of which are little more than fire boxes, are intended to prevent the contents from being consumed in a fire. In a major fire, however, the heat often chars the contents beyond recognition. Fire boxes are not generally very secure; they are light and can be removed with relative ease. Proper vaults are anchored and can be removed only with special tools or explosives. Despite their drawbacks, storage boxes in the rooms do serve two functions. First, they

Hotels should have well-thought-out delivery policies.

provide some additional security, at least against amateur or opportunistic thieves. Second, they reduce the number of guests who choose to store their goods by means of an express deposit with the hotel. By storing their goods in their rooms, guests limit themselves to the statutory recovery and save the hotel from the greater liability of the express deposits.

Posting Requirements

Section 5 of Newfoundland's Act requires that section 3 of the Act be posted in a number of conspicuous locations in the hotel. The posting requirements vary from jurisdiction to jurisdiction; innkeepers should know the requirements of their own jurisdiction. If an innkeeper fails to meet the posting requirements, the limitations in the Act will not avail the innkeeper. As noted in Chapter 10, innkeepers should exceed the posting requirements by posting the Act wherever the innkeeper–guest relationship might begin. If the hotel offers its own limousine service, the Act should be posted in the cab of the limousine. The Act can also be posted in the lobby, in the parking lot or parking garage, and on the back of reservation confirmations.

It is important to ensure that, as soon as a person becomes a guest, she is informed of the limitation of the innkeeper's liability for property loss or damage. Compliance with the Act greatly reduces the amount of money paid out in damages. The posting locations should be inspected regularly to ensure that the notices are still in place and legible. The Act requires not just that the notice is posted, but that it is posted conspicuously. The benefit of the Act may be lost if the notice is posted in an obscure location, buried among other notices, or if the print size is too small or the font too ornate.

The Acts also require that the statutorily required notice provisions be posted in their entirety. Abridged versions of the pertinent sections of the Act will not afford the innkeeper the protection of the Act. If the notice states that the hotel is responsible for guest property to a limited amount but fails to specify the amount, the limitation will not avail the hotel. Unless they were apprised of the limited amount, few guests would realize that a first-class hotel is required to pay only between $40 and $200 for a loss of belongings worth several thousand dollars.

Sherrill v. King Edward Hotel Co. (1929), 63 O.L.R. 528, [1929] 2 D.L.R. 612 (H.C.)

Sherrill was a guest at the King Edward Hotel. During the stay, his property was stolen from his room by another guest. The notice informing guests of the availability of a vault for valuables and of the limitation of liability was not conspicuously posted in his room as required by law, although he did have actual notice that there was a vault available. In finding the defendant hotel liable for the loss, the court stated that to benefit from the statutory limitation an innkeeper must post the statutory notice in a conspicuous place in each bedroom so that every guest may read every word of it. Actual notice by the guest of the availability of a vault does not confer upon an innkeeper the benefits of the Act when the guest does not have notice of the statutory provisions limiting liability.

The aging of the baby-boom generation raises the question of whether notices in the future will need to be even more conspicuous—particularly with respect to print size—than they are now. Many hotels cater directly to seniors and have demonstrated sensitivity toward their needs by improving lighting in dining rooms and printing large-type menus. Related to this issue is the extent to which people with disabilities should be accommodated. Should notices be posted in Braille for the benefit of guests who are blind? Should they be posted at an appropriate level for guests who use wheelchairs? Some hotels have printed menus in Braille and taken other steps to attract the business of these valued guests. In the absence of cases directly on point, general principles of negligence and contract law must cover these situations.

Seller's Samples

Innkeepers are generally responsible for personal-use items. Items such as the samples of travelling sellers are not considered part of a guest's personal property, and therefore the innkeeper is not responsible for them. However, if the hotel receives actual notice that the guest has brought samples and is apprised of their value, then the hotel will be responsible for them. The liability will be no greater than the amount specified by the statutory limitation, unless the hotel is negligent in handling the property.

Equitable Estoppel

If an innkeeper gives notice to a guest that the hotel's liability is greater than the limitation amount, the courts will estop (prevent) the innkeeper from relying on the statutory limitation. Under vicarious liability, if a hotel employee informs a guest that the hotel will be responsible for the full value of valuables left in the hotel safe, the hotel will be responsible for the full amount of the loss. Further, if a hotel employee gives the guest reason to ignore the posted notices or discourages the guest from placing valuables in the safe, estoppel will apply. Assume that a guest asks the desk clerk to place her valuables in the hotel vault, whereupon the desk clerk assures her that her property will be just as safe in her room. If the guest accepts the clerk's assertion and does not place her property in the vault, the hotel will be estopped from relying on the statutory limitation in the event of a loss. Estoppel can be contrasted with disclaimers on deposit envelopes, which limit the employee's authority to bind the hotel. Sorting out the responsibilities and liabilities can be a challenge for the courts.

Animals

Many jurisdictions provide that the horses or other live animals and any gear appertaining thereto, or a carriage, of a guest are not subject to a statutory limitation. The innkeeper remains absolutely liable under common law.

Vehicles

Liability for vehicles may be the subject of a statutory limitation. For example, subsection 10(1) of Saskatchewan's *Hotel Keepers Act* addresses the issue in this manner:

> No hotel keeper shall be liable for loss or injury to a vehicle of a guest or its contents except where the loss or injury occurs when the vehicle is stored or parked in a garage of the hotel or in a car park within the precincts of the hotel or maintained elsewhere by the hotel keeper and where a fee is charged by the hotel keeper for the storage or parking or where the hotel keeper or his servant expressly accepts the vehicle for handling or safe keeping.

Fire Damage

If a guest's property is lost or damaged by fire, the innkeeper's financial responsibility is limited to the statutory amount applicable to other losses, unless the innkeeper was responsible for the fire or otherwise liable in negligence.

Ponson v. Premier Hotel Ltd. (1957), 21 W.W.R. 664 (B.C.S.C.)

Ponson had for some years occupied a room at the defendant's hotel, paying a monthly rental. Fire destroyed the hotel and his property. He sued the hotel on the basis of innkeeper's absolute liability for guest property. The court held that the plaintiff was a permanent lodger to whom the defendant owed only the more limited obligation to take reasonable care for the safety of the property of lodgers brought onto the premises. The hotel was not found to have been negligent in the performance of its duties. Even if an innkeeper–guest relationship had existed, the posting of a notice under the statute of limitations would have protected the innkeeper from greater liability.

Liened Property

When an innkeeper claims a **lien** against the property of a guest for nonpayment of an account, the innkeeper must hold it for a prescribed length of time (three months in Ontario) and post a notice of sale before it can be sold. The innkeeper is responsible for the guest's property until it is sold. If the property is lost or damaged in the meantime, the innkeeper must reimburse the guest for the loss, although the statutory limitations would apply.

Frank v. Berryman, [1894] 3 B.C.R. 506 (C.A.)

F had stayed at the defendant's hotel for one month. When F was unable to pay, the hotel liened his trunk. The hotel's baggage room was full and, with the help of F himself, the hotel staff placed the trunk in the hotel's reading room. When F returned, he found that the lock on the trunk had been cut and some of his property was missing. The court held that in retaining the trunk under the innkeeper's lien, the defendant had failed to take reasonable care of the goods. F had not left the trunk voluntarily and had done nothing to expose the trunk to additional risk by helping to move it into the reading room; thus, there was no contributory negligence or voluntary assumption of risk.

The Guest's Conduct

The various innkeeper Acts limit an innkeeper's liability for property loss or damage. The limitation is lost if the provisions of the statute are not strictly followed. The limitation is also lost if the innkeeper is negligent in the handling of the property. On the other hand, negligence such as unreasonably foolhardy behaviour by the guest may negate or reduce the liability of the innkeeper. Guests may not leave their doors wide open for long periods of time, exposing the room and its contents to passersby. Further, the guest may be precluded from full recovery for lost or damaged valuables if the value was not revealed to the innkeeper as required at the time of deposit in the vault. The relative responsibilities for the negligence must be determined on the basis of the facts of each case.

No duty is cast upon a guest to request a key. A hotelier wishing to escape common law liability as an insurer of goods *infra hospitium* must furnish each guest with a key and the means of securing the room against third parties. The concept of third parties is not limited to outsiders. It also applies to staff members and other guests.

> **Vicars v. Arnold (1914), 7 W.W.R. 676, 7 Sask. L.R. 298, 20 D.L.R. 838 (C.A.)**
>
> At the defendant's hotel, Vicars was given a room for which he was told there was no key. While he was having a meal elsewhere on the premises, his overcoat was taken from his room. The court held the defendant liable as an innkeeper. There was no contributory negligence on the part of the plaintiff, who did all he reasonably could in asking the porter for a key.

Property Left Behind by Guests

A surprising amount of property is left behind by guests. Deciding what to do with it can be a headache. The last known occupant may not have been the person who left the item. Some former guests may be hard to locate or may not want their personal items returned. Property left behind by guests falls into one of three categories: lost, mislaid, or abandoned. It is not uncommon for hotel staff to acquire from the hotel's lost and found such items as raincoats, umbrellas, and gloves. However, the status of each piece of property must first be ascertained to determine the innkeeper's responsibility with respect to it.

Lost Property

Lost property is property that has been involuntarily separated from its owner, which is to say the owner of the property has lost it and is unaware of its location. The wallet found lodged between two sofa cushions has likely been lost, not mislaid or abandoned. In dealing with lost property, the hotel must take reasonable steps to contact the guest, perhaps by writing to the guest at the address on the registration card. If the hotel is unable to locate the owner, under common law, title to the property falls to the person who found it. Thus, the property would go to the room attendant who located it, not to the attendant's supervisor who stored it.

Some hotels do not allow their staff to keep property that once belonged to a guest, even if it was probably left as a gratuity for the staff member. Guests have been known to leave behind bottles of beer or half-empty bottles of liquor. Hotels are concerned about ambiguous circumstances that might leave them or their staff open to claims of misconduct. Hotels also fear for the safety of their staff, especially when it comes to open bottles of liquor. A mentally disturbed guest may have adulterated the liquor by mixing it with a dangerous substance. It is good policy to require that all items left in a guest room be delivered to management without delay. This practice not only minimizes the dangers, but it also discourages employees from developing a sense of entitlement toward lost guest property. The return of lost property to the guest is excellent public relations.

Mislaid Property

Mislaid property is property that the owner has knowingly placed in a special location but then forgot. Unlike the wallet embedded in the sofa, a wad of bills placed in a dresser drawer has probably been mislaid, not lost. Legal title to mislaid property stays with the original owner. Mislaid property should be stored for the owner to claim at a later date. In the case of money, the hotel should maintain a special bank account for this purpose. There is no time limit on the owner's claim; title remains with the owner until he or she claims the money. After the expiration of a reasonable period of time, the hotel may wish to make use of the money, but the hotel will still be liable to the owner. To avoid excessive claims, the hotel should be scrupulous in its record keeping.

Abandoned Property

Abandoned property is property to which the owner has given up all his or her rights and interests. It is property that a reasonable person would conclude that the owner does not want. Title to abandoned property passes to whomever claims it. Old shoes left in the garbage pail are considered abandoned; should someone claim them, title goes to the claimant.

Questions of Fact

It is a question of fact as to whether property has been lost, mislaid, or abandoned. All the circumstances must be considered, and an innkeeper is well advised to err on the side of the guest by assuming that the property was only mislaid. After a reasonable attempt has been made to find the owner, lost property may be returned to the room attendant who found it or used in accordance with the hotel's lost property policy. During and after a reasonable attempt to find the owner, mislaid property should be stored or accounted for because the title remains with the original owner. Abandoned property may be thrown out or given to the first claimant without first searching for the owner.

Access to the Guest's Room

As we have seen, guests are entitled to their privacy and to the exclusive use of the room throughout their stay. No one else, including hotel management, may enter the guest's room except in certain circumstances. Guests must have not only unfettered access to their own rooms but also the means to secure the room and any property they are storing in the room.

At one time, hotels had large ornate keys whose presence was conspicuous in a pocket. As the cost of producing these keys rose, they were replaced by the smaller, more economical metal keys of today. While the older keys often had the hotel's logo embossed on the head, modern keys simply carry a postal identification so that a guest who inadvertently checks out without turning in the key can later drop the key in a postal box for redelivery. In the event that a guest loses a key, a duplicate can be used until the lock is re-keyed.

Most room thefts are not the result of the theft of single-room keys. Single-room thefts are a risky proposition. The thief would have to visit only that room, the room would have to be rented yet unoccupied at the time of the visit, and the guest would have to have left in the room property that was sufficiently valuable and marketable. Breaking and entering hotels is usually worth the risk only if the thief has a master key and can roam the halls waiting for guests to leave their rooms. Unfortunately, some employees are willing to sell master keys to thieves.

More secure than the traditional metal keys are plastic keys that resemble credit cards and are coded for one room and one visit. These keys are not coded until the guest arrives. Once the guest has checked out, the door lock is recoded so that the old key can no longer be used to gain access to the room. Although coded key systems are more expensive than the metal key systems, the added security is generally worth the extra cost.

Most hotels feature three locks on guest room doors: (1) the main lock opened by the room key, (2) a night lock opened from the outside only with a grandmaster key (not just a master key), and (3) a mechanical lock, either a chain or moveable bar. Smart guests lock their rooms with both the night lock and mechanical lock once they are inside. When the mechanical lock is fastened, the door can be opened only a few centimetres. Although mechanical locks are not particularly effective as barriers, the sounds of a thief trying to break through one may alert the room's occupant to the fact that an intruder is attempting to gain access. Of course, for such an event to occur, both the main lock and the night lock would have to be breached.

Proper maintenance and prompt repairs of defective doors and locks are essential. Until its door and lock are up to standard, a room should not be booked; the potential liabilities for assaults and thefts are too great. It is also essential that all hotel staff are well trained in both room key procedure and ferreting out thieves and con artists. The challenge of the latter requirement lies in the fact that con artists make their living by fooling even those people who are on guard against them.

One technique that confidence tricksters use is to have a spotter sit in the lobby near the front desk and record the names of guests as they check in. An accomplice of the same sex as the guest later approaches the desk and, using the registration information gained by the spotter, requests a key for the room. This ruse has a better chance of succeeding if the desk staff have changed shifts in the interim. Instead of assuming that the person standing at the counter is a registered guest, hotel clerks should ask for more than just the person's name and room number when giving out a key. Hotel switchboard operators are trained not to reveal room numbers or guest information; front desk clerks should be equally, if not more, careful.

Most room thefts occur when a thief enters an open room. Guests may leave such items of value as cameras and purses in view from the hall. They may leave the room door open while they go to an ice machine. Housekeeping staff may leave guest room doors ajar when returning to their carts for supplies. In all these instances, the lapse in security invites trouble.

Hotels should monitor persons who wander around the guest room floors. All persons on a guest floor should have a legitimate reason for being there. They should be moving purposefully to a destination rather than loitering. In most circumstances, all nonregistered persons should be refused access to guest floors after 11:00 p.m. Outside personnel such as taxi drivers and pizza deliverers should be met in the lobby.

A police information officer once commented that most property that goes missing in hotels can be attributed to theft by staff or to the guests' own negligence. It is unlikely that theft by staff is primarily to blame. People who steal tend to do it only if they believe that they can get away with it. If the room attendant is the only hotel employee on a particular floor with access to a particular room, he or she is unlikely to feel confident enough to remove something of value from the room. It is unfortunate that the lowest-paid people on staff are often the first to be suspected. Probably more common than thefts by staff are attempts by guests who have lost their property to blame it on staff. Members of staff who have developed a well-earned reputation for honesty and integrity deserve the support of their co-workers and managers.

That said, staff thefts do occur, and policies and procedures are necessary to minimize them. Many hotels and restaurants have house rules that prohibit staff from bringing large purses or bags with them to their workstations, and that prohibit them from carrying too much of their own personal property on the job. Small purses and bags, and a minimum amount of their own personal property, make it more difficult for staff to disguise and remove a guest's property. In the case of restaurants, large bags can give a dishonest waiter or cook the means with which to remove property or bring in their own liquor for private resale.

Proper procedures properly followed by alert management and staff greatly reduce the number of thefts and other dishonest acts. Many guests have only vague recollections of a pleasant hotel experience, but they tend to recount unpleasant experiences endlessly to family, friends, and acquaintances, inflicting incalculable damage on the hotel's reputation.

Insurance

Hospitality businesses should maintain adequate fire, theft, business interruption, and public liability insurance. From the point of view of the guest, it does not matter whether the claim is paid by the hotel or its insurance company. Sometimes guests naively submit their claims to their own insurance company. Unless the guest's insurance company recovers the payout from the hotel or its insurance company, the guest's claim may result in a premium increase for the guest, even though the guest was not responsible for the loss. Both hospitality businesses and guests should find out how the insurance claim is being handled by the insurers and whose company is paying the claim. There is a tendency to wash one's hands of the matter once the insurers have stepped in. As with any business issue, matters that are not monitored closely have a tendency to return to haunt the participants.

Property of Nonguests

If a person is not a guest, then there is no innkeeper–guest relationship. The innkeeper owes no duty to protect the property of nonguests beyond basic negligence principles or, if applicable, rules of bailment (discussed below). Section 5 of Alberta's *Innkeepers Act* states:

> 5. No innkeeper is liable to make good to any person who is not registered as an occupant of a room or rooms in his inn any loss of or injury to property brought into his inn, except
>
> (a) when the property has been lost, stolen or injured, through the default or neglect of the innkeeper or his employee, or
>
> (b) when the property has been deposited expressly for safe custody with the innkeeper and a cheque has been issued for the property.

When dealing with the property of nonguests, innkeepers generally have the responsibility of a bailee. The coats, boots, umbrellas, hats, automobiles, and other belongings of nonguests that are left in the care of the innkeeper are examples of bailments.

Legal cases have not been consistent in determining who is and who is not a guest. Some cases have found a person who was intending not to stay the night but only to have a meal in the hotel dining room to be a guest within the context of the innkeeper–guest relationship. Other cases have drawn a distinction between a guest who intends to stay the night and a patron who intends to make use of some of the hotel's services but who does not intend to stay the night. The distinction is important because if the innkeeper–guest relationship does apply, the innkeeper may be protected by the statutory limitation of liability. If the plaintiff is not a guest, the claim may be for the full amount of the loss under a bailment, which is the delivery of personal property by one person to another for safekeeping.

Fraser v. McGibbon (1907), 10 O.W.R. 54 (Co. Ct.)

The plaintiff arrived at the hotel in the morning, intending to register as a guest later in the day. He hung his coat in the cloakroom without notifying the hotel, and had lunch in the hotel before leaving to attend a local fair. When he returned, the coat was missing. He brought an action to recover his loss. Although the plaintiff had never registered as a guest and did not spend the night in the hotel, the court found him to be a guest and held the hotel liable. Had the hotel been simply a bailee for the sole benefit of the bailor, it would not have been liable. Judge Gorham offered the following definition of a guest:

> A guest is one who resorts to and is received at an inn for the purpose of obtaining the accommodation which it purports to afford. He may be a wayfarer, traveller, or passenger who stops at or patronizes an inn as such. ... He comes for a more or less temporary stay ... and may go when he pleases. ... His stay and entertainment may be of the most transient kind. One who goes causally to an inn and eats or drinks or sleeps there, is a guest, although not a traveller.

The judge in the following case took issue with Judge Gorham's definition.

Philp v. Hunts Limited, [1947] O.W.N. 529

P entered the beverage room of the Savarin Hotel to have a beer. He hung his coat on a stand provided for the purpose. Forty-five minutes later, his coat was gone. Citing the *Fraser* case, Judge MacDonnel stated, "I do not think that the last sentence quoted [from Judge Gorham's decision] can be said to be fully justified by the authorities." Based on the facts of the present case, P was held not to be a guest. As such, he was able to recover the full value of the coat rather than the limit under the *Innkeepers Act*.

In determining what constitutes a guest, the line must be drawn somewhere; otherwise, anyone entering the premises to pick up a brochure or to buy a trinket in the gift shop would qualify as a guest. A distinction should be maintained between guests and nonguests. Many of the cases confuse the innkeeper–guest relationship as it applies to the property of guests with the law of bailment, which applies when the relationship is not that of innkeeper and guest. Under the law of bailment, a restaurant is responsible for the property of its patrons given to the restaurant for safekeeping or placed in locations identified by the restaurant as repositories of patron's property, such as cloakrooms. A patron of a hotel dining room who is not staying in the hotel should be in the same legal position as the patron of a restaurant.

Bailment

Definition

A bailment is the transfer of possession of personal property from the owner or possessor of the property to another person with the understanding that the property will be returned to the owner or first possessor at a later time. The person transferring the property is the bailor. The person receiving the property is the bailee. The only change is actual physical possession; title to the property does not change. When a person who is not a guest leaves her coat with a hotel cloakroom attendant, a bailment has taken place. The owner of the coat has transferred to the cloakroom attendant only possession of the coat, not title to the coat. The cloakroom attendant has only temporary possession of the coat. Title to the coat remains with the owner, although the coat is no longer in her immediate possession. The understanding is that when the owner wants her coat back, she will regain possession of it without difficulty, subject only to any reasonable or posted charges for the services of the bailment.

The duty owed by an innkeeper to a guest is higher under common law (but may be lower by statute) than the duty owed by a bailee to a bailor. Which relationship is applicable is a question of fact. As the following case illustrates, if the innkeeper–guest relationship has ended, the innkeeper's liability can be as low as that arising under a gratuitous bailment whereby the bailee (the innkeeper in this case) is liable for only gross negligence.

Lynar v. Mossop (1875), 36 U.C.Q.B. 230 (Ont. C.A.)

The guest checked out of the hotel but, unbeknownst to the innkeeper, left luggage behind. The court held that because the innkeeper–guest relationship had ended, the innkeeper's responsibility had fallen to that arising under a gratuitous bailment.

Elements of a Bailment

1. Bailment applies only to items of personal property such as cars, clothes, luggage, and computers. It does not apply to real property or to intangible personal property such as shares in a company, although it does apply to the share certificates themselves.

2. The **bailor** must transfer physical possession of the personal property to the **bailee**.

3. The bailee must acknowledge the receipt of the property.

4. The transfer and receipt must occur under an express or implied agreement that the bailee will return the property to the bailor upon the request of the bailor.

The transfer of possession must involve a transfer of control over the property. A nonguest who delivers his car and its keys to a hotel parking lot attendant has entered into a bailment. He has transferred possession of his personal property by giving the attendant control over it by way of the keys, and the hotel has acknowledged receipt by taking the keys and the car. Possession of the property must be returned to the bailor, upon his request. In the meantime, the hotel is liable for the property in its control under bailment. If the bailor simply parks his car in the hotel parking lot and keeps the keys, he has not given up control of the car, and a bailment probably does not exist. Some hotels operate indoor parking garages with automatic ticket-dispensing gates. To exit, the driver must present the ticket and pay the charge to the garage attendant. The driver is expected to retain the keys, but effective control over the vehicle has passed to the operator of the garage. In such a case, there most likely is a bailment. Bailment is a question of fact.

If a bailment exists, then the bailee must return the property to the bailor upon request. If there is no bailment, then the hotel never had control, never became a bailee, and has nothing to return to the bailor. If there is no bailment and the car goes missing, the bailor cannot recover from the hotel. If there is a bailment, failure to return the property can expose the bailee to a claim for damages, depending on the type of bailment and whether the bailee breached the duty of care owed to the bailor.

A bailee has the right to request a receipt for payment for a lost item to ensure that an overpayment or windfall to the bailor does not take place.

Types of Bailment

There are three types of bailment: bailment for the sole benefit of the bailor, bailment for the sole benefit of the bailee, and bailment for hire. Each type has a different duty of care.

Bailment for the Sole Benefit of the Bailor

When a bailee receives no fee or benefit for performing the bailment, the bailment is for the sole benefit of the bailor. This is also known as gratuitous bailment. The bailee in this situation is required to exercise only a slight degree of care, and is liable only for gross negligence. Suppose a former guest (specifically, a guest who has just checked out and is no longer a guest) asks the front desk clerk to store, for no fee, some luggage behind the counter while the ex-guest/bailor visits one last museum. The bailment would be for the sole benefit of the bailor. If the luggage were stolen or damaged, the bailor would not recover from the hotel or the clerk unless the clerk had been grossly negligent. Leaving the luggage within easy reach of passersby and not watching it at all would constitute gross negligence.

Bailment for the Sole Benefit of the Bailee

A bailment for the sole benefit of the bailee occurs when the bailor delivers possession of the property to the bailee, who may then use the property. The bailor is not receiving any benefit at all, not even temporary storage. On the other hand, the bailee has not only possession of the goods but also the right to use them. In a bailment for the sole benefit of the bailee, a high degree of care is owed by the bailee. If a hotel borrows some cots from another hotel that receives nothing in return, a bailment for the sole benefit of the bailee has taken place. The bailee will be liable to the bailor for virtually any damage to the cots.

Bailment for Hire

A bailment for the mutual benefit of both parties is called a bailment for hire. In this case, the bailee must exercise ordinary care. An example of a bailment for hire is a restaurant's cloakroom for which a fee is charged. The bailee receives the benefit of the storage of the coat, and the restaurant receives the benefit of the fee. The coat is expected to be not only returned, but returned in substantially the same condition in which it was delivered. It is reasonable to expect that a coat packed into a crowded cloakroom will sustain the odd wrinkle. On the other hand, if the bailee allows the coat to fall on the slushy floor, the coat will not be returned in proper condition. The bailee will be held liable for damages.

To avoid liability for bailment, a business must not take control of a person's property. For example, a restaurant may prefer that the patrons place their coats in an unattended cloakroom. The restaurant never acknowledges receipt of the coat, and therefore no bailment is created. If a patron takes her coat to her chair and a solicitous waiter takes the coat and hangs it in the cloakroom, then a bailment is created. When there is no bailment, restaurant patrons can better secure their coats and other belongings by keeping them at the table.

Liability in Bailment Cases

To substantiate a claim for damages for bailment, the bailor must establish the following:

1. The property was delivered to the bailee.
2. The bailee accepted the property.
3. The property was not returned, or not returned in substantially the same condition as when delivered.
4. The bailee breached the duty owed to the bailor.

These four circumstances would establish a *prima facie* case entitling the bailor to judgment. To avoid liability for the damages sustained by the bailor, the bailee would have to prove that the presumption of negligence on his part is false, or that there was another intervening cause of the damages, or that the requisite duty of care was not breached.

Property Concealed Inside Bailed Property

A bailee is not responsible for property about which he has no knowledge. A wallet in the pocket of a bailed coat is not the subject of a bailment unless the bailee is aware of the wallet's presence in the pocket. If a parking lot attendant is unaware that there is a computer in the trunk of the car that has been delivered to the hotel for bailment, then the hotel is not responsible for any loss of or damage to the computer, but only for any loss of or damage to the car. However, if the attendant were to open the trunk and see the computer, then the hotel's responsibility as a bailee would extend not only to the car but also to the computer. Most automobiles today are manufactured with valet keys that prevent parking lot attendants from gaining access to the trunk. An attendant who receives only the valet key cannot become a bailee of the contents of the trunk unless the owner reveals or describes the contents to him.

Limitations and Bailment

Limitation provisions in the various innkeepers Acts apply to the innkeeper–guest relationship, not to the bailment relationship. Innkeepers who take control of guests' property under a bailment may not rely on the limitation provisions in innkeepers Acts to reduce the losses. The casual patron in a hotel dining room is in the same legal position as the customer of a restaurant. Because there is no innkeeper–guest relationship, the Act will not restrict the damages that a customer may seek for breach of bailment. A guest whose coat is stolen from the cloakroom and who subsequently sues for recovery under bailment will most likely recover the full cost of the coat. A guest who sues under the innkeeper–guest relationship will, absent negligence by the innkeeper, likely recover only the limitation amount. Often, the wrong claim is brought or the wrong defence is invoked.

Restaurant and Bar Cloakrooms

Restaurateurs and bar owners who operate cloakrooms for a fee should be aware of the risks. If a coat is not returned (or not returned in proper condition) to the bailor, then the bailee will be liable for the loss. A guest who is forced to leave a restaurant or bar without her coat in the middle of winter may have increased damages if she becomes ill as a result of not having her coat. In such circumstances, and if the guest did not use personal transportation to travel to the restaurant or bar, the restaurateur should offer her complimentary taxi service.

Cloakrooms Run by Concessionaires

Concessionaires who pay a fee to hotels to run hotel cloakrooms are not in an innkeeper–guest relationship with the hotel's guests. They are contractors independent of the hotel, and are bailees of the property of the hotel's guests. Concessionaires cannot use the innkeeper–guest relationship and the limitation provisions in the innkeepers Acts to limit their liability for bailments. Hotels should ensure that all concessionaires operating on their premises have adequate insurance. The posted limitation provisions might mislead a guest into assuming that the concessionaire is liable for as little as $40.

Security of the Person

As discussed in Chapter 10, the hospitality industry has a duty to take all reasonable steps to prevent crimes against the person. The duty is owed to guests and to employees. As a horrifying example of what can go wrong, in May 1992 three employees of a McDonald's in Cape Breton were brutally murdered and a fourth employee left permanently disabled during a robbery. The killers, who had thought that the restaurant's safe held between $80,000 and $200,000, left the bloody scene with $2,000.

While hotels are more prone than restaurants to be the scene of sexual assaults because of the privacy of the rooms, restaurants tend to experience more robberies than hotels. Part of the reason for this is that restaurants generally have more cash on hand (credit card use is the norm at hotels). In addition, restaurant cash registers are often close to the door, thereby allowing for quick getaways. Gas stations and convenience stores were once the targets of choice, but they have changed their money-collection and storage procedures, and now advertise the fact that they do not keep large amounts of money on the premises.

The hospitality industry owes its guests and employees a high level of protection. The premises should be examined for problems relating to access. New employees should be investigated. Security and surveillance activity should be instituted or expanded. Important phone numbers (police, fire department, hospital) should be posted by telephones. Substantial sums of money should be routinely removed from the premises, perhaps by bonded couriers. Employees should be discouraged from heroics during a robbery. To help identify robbers, there should be height strips on the door jams and strategically placed closed-circuit cameras.

Summary

Property losses are a constant concern. Innkeepers and restaurateurs must know their responsibilities. Knowledgeable operators can benefit from statutory limitations, and can take other steps to reduce not only liability for property losses but also the expenses associated with wrangling in the court system and the damages resulting from loss of goodwill. Additional protection can be obtained through liability insurance. Assaults and other crimes against the person are rarer occurrences but must also be the subject of constant vigilance on the part of hospitality operators. The damage caused by crimes against the person is incalculable.

Appendix 3 contains a sample Deposit Box Agreement.

Discussion Questions

1. What are the posting requirements for the jurisdiction in which you live?

2. What kind of liability did the common law judges impose on the early innkeepers?

3. What are three exceptions to the liability rule imposed by the judges cited in question 2?

4. Who has legal title to property deemed lost, abandoned, or found? When can title change?

5. What problem is addressed by the statutory limitations of loss and damage recovery provided for in the various innkeepers Acts?

6. What is the statutory limit payable to a guest for lost luggage in your jurisdiction?

7. What must an innkeeper do to benefit from the statutory limitation in your jurisdiction?

8. How is the statutory limitation affected by negligence on the part of the innkeeper?

9. Discuss how the liability changes depending upon the innkeeper's knowledge or lack of knowledge of the value of goods stored in the hotel's vault.

10. What would your ruling be in the following case? A person wins a large amount of money in a card game in one of the rooms. After the game he approaches the desk and asks about the availability of a room. The clerk responds that a room is available. The person places an envelope in the safe and says he will return to check in. Latter that day he returns for his money. The money is missing. He never checked in.

PART
FOUR

Management in the Hospitality Industry

Chapter Twelve

Regulatory Requirements

Learning Outcomes

1. Describe the purpose of zoning bylaws, building codes, fire codes, *Food and Drugs Act*, *Meat Inspection Act*, *Canada Agricultural Products Act*, *Hazardous Products Act*, *Hotel Fire Safety Act*, *Tourism Act*, and *Copyright Act*.

2. Define licence, licensor, licensee.

3. Describe the authority and responsibilities of a licensing board.

4. Explain the requirement for public approval in the granting of certain licences.

5. List some licence requirements for an accommodation and a food service business.

6. Describe how a liquor licence may be lost or revoked.

7. Explain federal legislation designed to protect consumers.

8. Explain provincial legislation designed to protect consumers.

9. Describe the tax responsibilities of residents in Canada.

10. List the tax-collection duties of a business in Canada.

Introduction

In Chapters 6 and 7, we discussed some of the regulatory requirements pertaining to food and alcohol service. Requirements particular to the travel industry will be described in Chapter 15. In this chapter, we focus on general regulatory requirements affecting the hospitality industry.

General Regulation

The regulation of trade and commerce is a federal responsibility under section 91 of the *Constitution Act (1867)*. The regulation of civil (meaning property) rights is a provincial responsibility under section 92 of the *Constitution Act (1867)*. There is an effort to keep overlap to a minimum. The federal government concerns itself more with regulating federal enterprises and matters of national, interprovincial, and international interest. Most business regulation emanates from the province either directly or through authority delegated to boards and municipalities. Both the federal and provincial governments extensively regulate employment and employees (see Chapter 14). Breach of governmental regulations constitutes negligence per se and leaves the occupier open to claims that are difficult or impossible to defend.

Federal regulation of business may be indirect, as provided in the *Criminal Code*, or direct, as provided in the *Food and Drugs Act* and the *Competition Act*. Provincial regulation of business may also be indirect, as provided in negligence legislation, or direct, as provided in sale of goods, liquor licence, and business practices legislation. Many of the regulatory functions of the provinces and territories are carried out by municipal enforcement officers.

Building Codes

Provincial **building codes** set minimum standards of construction and renovation, including materials, doors and windows, and electrical, heating, and plumbing systems. Enforcement is delegated to the building departments of municipalities. Before a new construction or renovation can occur, the owner must pay a fee to the municipality and obtain from the building department approval for the construction plans and a building permit. The permit must be prominently displayed on the site. The work must be undertaken in accordance with the approved plans. The municipality will inspect the progress of the work at appropriate stages and, if warranted, issue interim inspection reports. Once the work has passed a final inspection, the municipality will issue an occupancy permit or certificate of completion.

Thereafter, the municipality may re-enter the premises to assess continuing compliance. The inspectors may issue work orders or deficiency notices requiring the owner to make repairs or alterations to bring the property up to the standard of the code. Persistent failures to meet the code may result in fines and condemnation orders. A condemned building usually causes land to lose market value. When the real value is in the land, the buildings, even ones in good condition, can lower the value because of the expense of removing them.

Fire Codes

Provincial **fire codes** regulate minimum standards of construction and operation of premises, including construction and decorating materials, number and placement of smoke alarms and fire extinguishers, ventilation systems, and exits. Fire marshals and municipal inspectors have the right to enter and inspect the premises for compliance and to issue work orders for deficiencies or other failures to comply. In extreme cases, a business may be ordered shut until the code has been complied with. It is an offence under the codes to allow the premises to be built contrary to the code or to allow the premises to deteriorate to a level below the required standards. For example, exits must not be blocked or locked on the inside. In addition to general fire codes, most provinces have a fire safety statute specifically for the accommodation industry. For example, Ontario's *Hotel Fire Safety Act* states in part:

2. This Act applies to every hotel whether constructed before or after this Act comes into force.

3. No person shall,

   (a) construct a hotel;

   (b) construct an addition to a hotel;

   (c) convert a building to a hotel; or

   (d) alter a hotel,

   until complete drawings and specifications thereof have been submitted to and approved by the Fire Marshal.

4. Every hotel ... shall have its structural assemblies ... constructed in the manner and of the materials prescribed. ...

5. Every hotel shall have such exits ... doorways ... stairways, designed, located, maintained, identified, lighted, and ... equipped with such hardware as the regulations prescribe.

6. Every hotel shall have in each building that,

   (a) has a total floor area of more than 6,000 square feet;

   (b) is more than one storey in height; or

   (c) does not have direct egress to the outside from each ... suite, a fire alarm system ... prescribed by the regulations.

7. Every hotel four or more storeys in height and every addition four or more storeys in height ... shall have a standpipe and hose system ... prescribed by the regulations.

8. Every hotel shall install and maintain portable fire extinguishers of the type ... prescribed by the regulations.

14. Where an inspector finds that a condition exists in a hotel that makes the hotel specially liable to fire, the inspector may order the hotelkeeper to remedy the condition.

17. Every hotelkeeper who operates a hotel that does not conform with this Act and the regulations or who fails to comply with any order made by an inspector is guilty of an offence and on conviction is liable to a fine of not more than $1,000, and, in addition, the judge may order the hotel to be closed until it is made to conform with this Act and the regulations or with the order of the inspector.

Municipal bylaws require smoke alarms in all hotel rooms and restaurants. The alarms should be checked regularly and approved fire extinguishers should be readily available.

Health and Food Regulations

Both the federal and provincial governments regulate food safety, which prohibits the sale of food that is unfit for human consumption. Sections 4 and 31 of the federal *Food and Drugs Act*, which are reproduced on pages 151 and 152 in Chapter 6, spell out the prohibitions and penalties. Other federal statutes applicable to the food sector include the *Meat Inspection Act* and the *Canada Agricultural Products Act*; contained in the latter statute are the egg regulations, the dairy products regulations, and the livestock and poultry grading regulations. At the provincial level, sale of goods legislation prohibits the sale of goods that are unfit for the purpose or that are of unmerchantable quality. (For more on the sale of goods, see Chapter 4.)

Each province maintains minimum health standards applicable to all qualifying commercial enterprises and public undertakings. Enforcement is delegated to the health departments of municipalities. They may initiate inspections or respond to complaints from the public. Within the hospitality industry, the health standards are of particular relevance to the commercial and institutional food service sector. They govern such matters as:

- the manufacture, processing, preparation, storage, handling, display, distribution, transportation, and sale of foods to the public, including detailed rules for problematic foods such as eggs and meat;

- the construction of food services establishments including the food-storage facilities, lighting, ventilation, and the number and type of washrooms; and

- the operation of the establishment including permitted equipment, hygiene of employees, hygiene of the premises and utensils, and handling of the food.

The Canadian Restaurant and Foodservices Association in Toronto, Ontario, provides on request a useful compendium of the applicable health regulations across Canada.

The most common health-related complaints in the food sector are unsanitary washrooms, the presence of vermin and other pests on the premises, and improper storage of food. All of these conditions can lead to disease and even death. Persistent or serious breaches of the health regulations can result in prosecutions and potentially ruinous publicity. Most often, the health department prefers that the food operators simply abide by the regulations. The inspectors will close or condemn only those food operators who leave them little choice. Even a citation for a minor matter can seriously damage a food operator's reputation. Operators who wish to remain in business over the long term should ensure that they are meeting or exceeding the regulatory minimums at all times.

Environmental Protection

Human beings generate a colossal amount of waste. Businesses that cater to basic human needs, such as food and shelter, also create waste on enormous scales. Only recently have governments taken a deep interest in protecting the environment. As late as the 19th century, Great Britain, the most technologically advanced nation at the time, had no formal regulations governing waste disposal. Today, the protection of the environment and adequate waste disposal are regarded as vital to the health of the population. Through the *Hazardous Products Act*, the federal government regulates the handling of hazardous and toxic products and their interprovincial and international transportation. Through environmental protection legislation, the provinces regulate the storage and disposal of waste. The legislation divides businesses into categories and imposes increasingly stringent standards upon larger waste generators.

The hospitality industry is a large waste generator, but some individual businesses may qualify for membership in a category where the standards are less stringent. The rules are less onerous for businesses located in small communities or rural settings; however, businesses located within national or provincial parks or heritage sites may be subject to more exacting requirements. Like building and fire codes, the legislation empowers inspectors to enter the premises to determine compliance and to issue work orders for violations. The regulations are technical, varied, and subject to change. The Canadian Restaurant and Foodservices Association will provide on request copies of its publication *Going Green without Seeing Red: An Environmental Guide for the Foodservice Industry.*

Tourism

Ontario's *Tourism Act* requires that all operators of Ontario tourist establishments maintain registers containing the name and address of each guest, the unit occupied by the guest, the dates of arrival and departure, and, if applicable, the make of the car, licence plate number, and province or state of origin. Operators are also required to file their room rates (though they may be easily changed) and post the rates in all the rooms. The Act prohibits misleading advertising. Unless breakfast, lunch, and dinner are offered, the word "restaurant" cannot be used. Unless at least 90 percent of the rooms have colour televisions or air conditioning, the advertising cannot refer to those amenities. In jurisdictions with enforceable day-of-rest legislation, hotels and restaurants usually receive a tourism exemption.

Intellectual Property

Pursuant to the federal *Copyright Act*, many books and other printed materials, music, art, movies, and broadcasts enjoy copyright protection. For example, a restaurant called Goaltenders could not use a reproduction of the Ken Danby painting *At the Crease* on its menu covers without first receiving the permission of the artist. Most telecasts and movie productions contain a notice stating that their rebroadcast, retransmission, or any other use without the express written authorization of the owner is prohibited. Presenting Pay-Per-View events in bars without paying the promoter is pirating, a criminal offence.

Under the *Copyright Act*, any broadcaster, entertainment club, or other business that plays recorded music or dance or background music must pay royalties. In Canada, the Society of Composers, Authors and Music Publishers (SOCAN) monitors the use of the music and collects the royalties for redistribution to the artists. In the case of radio, SOCAN computers are tuned to every station and, through recognition technology, note every song played and tally the royalties for each artist. If a radio station plays a song that the computers do not recognize, such as an in-studio, live version, the station's program director will receive a telephone call from SOCAN asking that only the recognizable version be broadcast.

Copyright does not last forever. If it has expired or if it never applied to a particular intellectual property, the property is said to be in the public domain and may be used freely by anyone. Trademarks are protected intellectual property, as are patents and industrial designs.

Municipal Bylaws and Zoning

Municipalities are territories created by provincial statute. They are governed by elected councillors and govern and regulate certain matters of local jurisdiction. The councils enact an official plan that governs the overriding planning principles for the municipality. In accordance with the official plan, municipalities enact **zoning** and other **bylaws** to regulate such matters as:

- Creation, density, use, and size of private lots, and adjustments to existing lots
- Types of residential uses
  - single-family, attached, multilevel, trailer parks, campgrounds
- Types of commercial uses
  - agricultural, offices, small retail, large retail, warehousing, manufacturing, institutional, religious, adult entertainment

- Business activities

  — hours of operation, smoking rules, density, and layout

  — number of patrons per square foot

  — exterior character and advertising

- Residential and commercial building construction standards and upkeep

  — type, size, height, quality of construction, and fitness for occupancy

  — exterior presentation such as colour, clotheslines, satellite dishes, garages, sheds, and tree planting

- Noise and nuisance levels, ice and weed removal

- Animal control, including cleanup

- Dumpsites, garbage and recycling collection

- Public roads, rights of way, and parklands

- Traffic patterns, including road closures

- Road servicing, drains, snow removal, water mains and sewers

Municipalities also run social assistance programs, set licensing conditions and inspection requirements, levy licence fees and taxes on land and businesses, and collect education taxes from landowners on behalf of local school boards. In addition, they enforce numerous provincial regulatory matters through authority directly delegated to them by statute, such as building and fire codes. They may also acquire regulatory authority by taking advantage of opportunities available in provincial legislation. For example, based on their authority to enforce matters of public health derived from the provincial health standards statute, municipalities may enact and enforce bylaws restricting smoking on public premises.

Municipalities may regulate but not prohibit legal activity. For example, a municipality cannot place a blanket prohibition on strip clubs within its boundaries, but it may limit their numbers, designate their locations, set working conditions, levy hefty licence fees, and impose other conditions provided they are not unreasonable. Municipalities cannot pass bylaws that are in substance criminal law enactments because such enactments are *ultra vires* municipal jurisdiction; they may, of course, prohibit activity that is illegal under federal or provincial law.

Re Adult Entertainment Bar Association and Metropolitan Toronto (Municipality) (1997); Thomas-Johns, Goldberg et al., interveners, 35 O.R. (3d) 161

In an effort to control "lap dancing," the Municipality of Metropolitan Toronto enacted a bylaw that purported to address "public concerns for the health and safety of the public and the women employed in these businesses." The bylaw states in part:

36. No owner or operator shall, in respect of any adult entertainment parlour owned or operated by him, knowingly permit any attendant, while providing services as an attendant, to touch, or be touched by, or have any physical contact with, any other person in any manner whatsoever involving any part of that person's body.

37. No attendant shall, while providing services as an attendant, touch or have any physical contact with any other person in any manner whatsoever involving any part of that person's body.

The Ontario Adult Entertainment Association brought an application for judicial review to the Divisional Court, arguing that the bylaw was in substance a criminal law and thus *ultra vires* the municipality. The court dismissed the application. The Association appealed. In dismissing the appeal, the Ontario Court of Appeal made these findings:

- The bylaw is a valid exercise of provincial legislative authority delegated to the municipality, and not an invalid attempt to legislate in matters beyond its law-making competence.
- The bylaw is not an attempt to raise the level of the permitted standard for indecent or immoral acts proscribed by the Criminal Code of Canada.
- The bylaw is regulatory in nature and could not be said to legislate on matters of morality even though its ancillary effect is to touch on matters of morality.
- The bylaw is not so overly broad as to prohibit rather than regulate. The bylaw does not restrict the general operation of an adult-entertainment business and does not restrict the core activities such as the sale of food and alcohol, sporting activities, nude or erotic stage performances, and table dancing.
- The bylaw regulates only the conduct of "attendants" performing "services." It restricts touching during the performance of the "services," but it does not restrict benign touching or table dancing.
- Assuming that lap dancing could be said to be an expression within the meaning of section 2(b) of the *Canadian Charter of Rights and Freedoms*, the bylaw is a justifiable limit on that freedom of expression under section 1 of the Charter.

Bylaws that contravene the official plan of the municipality are invalid. Properties that contravene the bylaws may be subject to compliance orders. If the contraventions are minor, a committee of adjustment may allow a minor variance. For example, if the bylaw requires that the front of the building be set not less than 4.5 metres (15 feet) back from the road and the building is 4.25 metres (14.5 feet) back, the committee may grant a minor variance allowing the contravention. Major derivations from the bylaw would require a zoning amendment.

Unlike the federal and provincial governments, which may act autonomously without soliciting public representations, municipalities must give notice to the public whenever they wish to enact, repeal, or amend a zoning bylaw, and must hear submissions in public from those affected. A municipality may not retroactively change the use of property. Despite any change in the bylaw, the use by the owners of their land is grandparented and the land is said to enjoy a "valid, nonconforming use." However, if the owners ever change their use, they can do so only in accordance with the amended bylaw.

A great deal of planning goes into the layout of a town or city. The residential and commercial users demand an ever-increasing variety of services and facilities. Small businesses and heavy industries consume huge amounts of water, hydro, and fuel, and require access to sophisticated transportation systems to ensure timely distribution of their products to the world markets. High-tech companies need modern facilities, a highly educated workforce, and a lifestyle that appeals to their employees.

Parents in a family neighbourhood do not want their children crossing busy streets, breathing polluted air, or viewing commercial activities that might be considered unsuitable for children. Residential areas must be separate from business districts and must feature good schools, recreation facilities, parks, playgrounds, shopping centres, and health facilities.

The creation of separate zones and the supply of utilities and other amenities are some of the tasks that city planners face. If they do their job well, they may attract more residents to their municipality, thereby increasing the tax base and generating the additional revenues that will pay for even better services. Bylaws, ordinances, and civil engineering are some of the tools that municipal planners use to perform their complicated job.

L.E.C. v. N.Y. (February 7, 1996, Rosenberg J. (Ont. Gen. Div.))

In the fall of 1994, the plaintiff was considering opening a restaurant, club, and entertainment facility in a building that bordered on a residential neighbourhood. The building had previously housed a furniture store and a warehouse. The plaintiff provided the zoning examiner in the building department with a marketing plan and a bylaw study that addressed the feasibility of the business and the intended use of the property. The project was to include a restaurant, club, travel agency, and entertainment facility for the use of 2500 people. The bylaw study suggested that the plan was permissible under existing municipal requirements. The zoning examiner confirmed to the plaintiff that the proposal met the zoning requirements and was permitted under the bylaw. With that assurance, the plaintiff entered into a ten-and-a-half-year lease and hired consultants and design experts to commence the planning of the project. The city asked for a site plan, which was submitted in February 1995. The city responded with a list of conditions for plan approval and a building permit. The conditions did not include a parking study. The conditions that were requested were met. The plaintiff submitted his application for a building permit in March 1995 and paid the $7,600 permit fee. The zoning examiner conducted a formal review that confirmed that the use, setback, loading, and parking requirements were in compliance with the zoning bylaws. The transportation department reviewed and approved the plan in the spring of the same year.

Upon learning of the plan, local ratepayers voiced their objections to the plaintiff and a city councillor. The councillor wrote to the Liquor Licence Board objecting to the granting of a licence so close to a residential area. The councillor wrote that the project was unsuitable and called it an "after-hours club" that would feature "adult entertainment." The councillor also referred to the high incidence of crime associated with such clubs. In an effort to appease the councillor, the plaintiff wrote him a letter in which he clarified the intended use of the property and explained the plan. In April 1995, the councillor met with the city solicitor and chief building official to discuss the building permit, the liquor-licence application, the right to street parking, and the case law on building permit appeals. In June, the councillor, who by this time had become chair of the planning committee, met with the commissioner of planning regarding the proposed project. After this meeting, the commissioner contacted the transportation department to review the parking issue. As a result of the review request, the commissioner wrote to the plaintiff requesting that a qualified traffic consultant prepare a study on the availability of parking for the proposed use of the site. The plaintiff complied with the request, and the study was submitted to the transportation department in August.

In the same month, the building department informed the plaintiff that the parking did not comply with the zoning requirements, but that all the other requirements had been met. Shortly thereafter, the transportation department informed the plaintiff that the study that he had completed was insufficient. The plaintiff, who had already invested close to $2 million, applied to the court to direct the city to issue a building permit. On the day that the hearing was to be held, the city requested and received an adjournment. Prior to the new hearing date, the council enacted an interim bylaw that prohibited the establishment of the club at the proposed location.

Alleging that the city was acting in bad faith, the plaintiff moved for an order quashing the bylaw and requiring the city to issue the building permit. The court concluded that the city's real concern was not parking but whether the club was suitable for a residential neighbourhood. The court recognized the concern but felt that it was not appropriate to use the parking problem as grounds for stopping the project. The city argued that the extraordinary circumstances, although not necessarily a condition of a building permit, required a site-plan approval. The court found that extraordinary circumstances did exist, but that the city had acted in bad faith in enacting the interim bylaw. A municipality should act in good faith in an impartial, open, and fair way. The court quashed the bylaw, ordered that the building permit be issued, and awarded costs to the plaintiff.

1 Ont. Inc. v. City of Toronto (Sept. 27, 1995, Doc. No. 5697/95, Kitely J. (Ont. Gen. Div.))

The City of Toronto tried to stop the establishment of a restaurant that planned to offer entertainment and dancing. The site was zoned for a restaurant but not for an entertainment business. The court was asked to decide whether the proposed establishment was an entertainment facility or a restaurant with dancing and entertainment as an accessory use. If the latter, it would be permitted by the zoning bylaw. If the former, it would be prohibited. The court ruled in favour of the applicant in finding that the entertainment and dancing was ancillary to the dining. The court stated that "[t]he difference between an entertainment facility and a restaurant appears to be one of emphasis. In an entertainment facility, the primary function is entertainment and the secondary is dining. In a restaurant, the primary function is dining and the secondary is entertainment."

City of Saint John v. 5. N.B. Ltd. (June 27, 1996, Doc. No. S/M/44/96 Jud. Dist. Saint John, Turnbull J. (N.B.Q.B.))

The City of Saint John applied to the court to stop a numbered company from running a club that featured exotic dancing. Exotic dancing was not allowed under a bylaw. The court found that the exotic dancing was in operation before the zoning bylaw was passed, and that no terms or conditions had been placed on the land by the planning commission. Where a use exists prior to the enactment of a zoning bylaw, the owner enjoys a valid nonconforming use that entitles the owner to continue the use. This policy is consistent with a general prohibition against laws that retroactively deprive someone of a previously enjoyed right. The court ruled that when one examines how a building is used, the general use should be considered. In this case, the general use was the club, not the exotic dancing. The judge ruled that even if he were wrong, he would not order the company to cease and desist because the company had operated openly. If the city had wanted more information, it should have requested it on the application form. The lack of such a request should not be held against the company. Further, the business enjoyed a valid nonconforming use. The city's application was denied.

Prior to incurring any great expenditures in acquiring and planning the location of a hotel or restaurant, it is essential to ensure that the location is zoned properly for the intended business and that there are no restrictions against the proposed plans. This is particularly important for hospitality businesses that intend to serve alcohol and provide entertainment, and that require street parking. If there are zoning restrictions, the battle is not necessarily lost. Provided it would be in accordance with the official plan, the municipality may be willing to amend the zoning bylaw to accommodate the new business. Normally, the municipality will be forthcoming about the procedure and the nature of any foreseen public opposition.

Licences and Permits

A licence is an authorization granting the licensee a right to do something that may not be done legally without the licence. A driver's licence, issued by a province, gives an individual the right to drive a motor vehicle. Without it, the individual does not have the legal right to drive. To obtain a driver's licence, the applicant must pass a written exam and a driving test. Many jurisdictions require that the licensee demonstrate competence at various levels before obtaining the final and full licence. To operate a hotel, restaurant, tavern, and many other businesses in Canada, one or more licences are required. As with driver trainees, the applicant must meet the initial requirements of the licence. Once the licence is granted, the applicant will be subject to its restrictions and must meet its continuing requirements.

A licence is not granted as of right. It is issued only to those who meet the licensing requirements and who undertake to operate the business according to the conditions of the licence and the regulations of the Board or Commission or Tribunal (BCT). The BCT may refuse to grant a licence to (or revoke the licence of) anyone whom the BCT believes will not operate (or is no longer operating) the business in accordance with the terms of the licence.

Not all governmental approvals are issued in the form of a licence. In order to construct or renovate a hotel, the owner must first obtain a municipal building permit by filing with the municipality the construction or renovation plans and by paying the prescribed fees. While the work is being done, the municipality conducts inspections to ensure that the work is in compliance with the plans and the provincial building code. Once the work is satisfactorily completed, the municipality issues a completion certificate. In the case of a new construction or a substantial renovation during which the hotel was not occupied, the municipality will issue an occupancy permit, which means that the hotel is fit for human habitation.

The approval of the Fire Marshal is also required to construct, convert, or alter a hotel or restaurant or addition. Section 3 of Ontario's *Hotel Fire Safety Act* states:

No person shall

(a) construct a hotel;

(b) construct an addition to a hotel;

(c) convert a building to a hotel; or

(d) alter a hotel

until complete drawings and specifications thereof have been submitted to and approved by the Fire Marshal.

A hotel or restaurant must obtain a certificate of compliance, issued by the health department, before it can operate its kitchens, dining facilities, and bars. Before the hotel or restaurant can offer liquor for sale on its premises, it must obtain a licence from the applicable liquor licence board.

Should an inspection by the municipal building department, the fire marshal's office, the health and safety branch, or the liquor licence board discover substandard workmanship or materials, missing required equipment, or other defects under the terms of the licence, each of these bodies may issue a work order requiring the establishment to correct the defect. Failure to do so may result in fines, revocation of licences, or court injunctions. In the case of liquor licences, the police are empowered to report to the board any violations of the licence.

The fundamental purpose of licensing legislation is to protect the public interest and public safety through the regulation of business operations. In each of Canada's jurisdictions, there are numerous building, fire, health, elevator, innkeeper, and liquor licence codes, and other statutory and regulatory requirements. It is the responsibility of every hospitality business owner or manager to meet all the applicable regulatory and licensing requirements.

Licence-Granting Bodies and Permit-Granting Bodies

Federal and provincial governments may grant administrative law bodies such as boards, commissions, and tribunals (collectively referred to hereafter as "boards") the authority to issue and regulate licences and permits. Provinces may also delegate authority to municipalities. The jurisdiction and mandate of each licence- and permit-granting body is set forth in the enabling legislation of the body and is sometimes augmented by common law. Boards are created by statute or by regulation. The government appoints the board members, who are generally chosen from a pool of individuals with expertise in the subject area. The power of the boards is shown in the following excerpt taken from section 50 of Nova Scotia's *Liquor Control Act*. Pursuant to subsection 4(1), the board may:

(a) grant a licence or any renewal thereof, upon such conditions as it may prescribe;

(b) refuse to grant a licence;

(c) order the suspension of a licensee;

(d) restore any licence suspended on such conditions as the Board may prescribe;

(e) after notice and opportunity for hearing, cancel or refuse to renew any licence;

(f) impose conditions from time to time, upon the continuance or renewal of a licence;

(g) fully or partially license an establishment; or

(h) at its discretion request the attendance of a licensee for the purpose of a discipline hearing when an infraction of these Regulations has occurred.

Granting Requirements

A licence or permit (hereinafter "licence") is issued pursuant to the enabling legislation, the regulations made thereunder, and the discretion of the granting body. A licence is issued only if certain minimum standards, deemed necessary in the public interest, are met. Normally, a licence will be issued if the applicant meets all the requirements of the licence.

Shooter Sports Inc. v. Nova Scotia (Liquor Licence Board) (May 24, 1996, Doc. No. S.H. No. 127717 Halifax, Gruchy J. (N.S. S.C.))

W wanted to open a billiards club. He was convinced that the project would be viable only if the club had a liquor licence. He met with the CEO of the Liquor Licence Board to discuss the proposal. The CEO advised W to meet with the manager of the board, and advised W in writing that a public hearing would be necessary before such a licence could be granted. Prior to meeting the manager, W made a conditional offer to lease the premises. W's meeting with the manager left him with the understanding that, provided he met certain requirements, a Special Occasions Liquor Permit could be issued monthly for one year; in addition, a Special Premises Licence for the billiard club could be applied for at the end of the year without a public hearing being required.

W then proceeded with the work, intending to meet all the requirements within the year. He committed $180,000 to the project. In a follow-up discussion with the manager of the board before the end of the year, W revealed the person whose name would appear on the licence. About a month later, the manager informed W that a hearing would be required prior to the issuing of a Special Occasions Permit. W tried to contact the CEO but was obliged to discuss the matter with an assistant. The board continued to insist that a hearing be held. W believed that a public hearing would put his investment at risk.

W brought a court application for an order that the licence be issued without a public hearing. He argued that the manager had assured him that the permit would be issued if he fulfilled the requirements, and he proved that he had met almost all of them. The manager agreed with W's version of their prior conversations and also stated that a public hearing was a highly unusual prerequisite to the granting of a Special Occasions Permit; in his memory, no such hearing had ever been required.

The court concluded that the manager had given W assurances that the licence would be granted without a hearing if certain requirements were met. Although W had been warned of the possibility of a hearing by the CEO, this concern was removed by the assurances of the manager. The court determined that the licence had already been approved and that it would be unfair to require a public hearing. The court found that the only reason the board had attempted to hold a hearing was to placate various persons opposed to the licence. The court ordered that W be granted the licence without a public hearing conditional upon compliance with a few outstanding work requirements.

Public Notice of Application

When an application for a licence is submitted, the board will normally advertise the application in a local newspaper, along with the time and place of the hearing, in order to give the public a chance to make representations concerning the application. The board considers the representations of the public when determining whether to grant the licence.

In July 1997, several applications to open strip clubs were the subject of public hearings in Kanata, Ontario. As a result of representations by the public, the locations where the clubs could be housed were greatly reduced. The board had to balance the interests of the public with the interests of the applicants. The restrictions made the clubs who did obtain licences more lucrative by significantly reducing the possibility of competition.

Grounds for Refusal

Some boards are concerned only with whether the applicant has met the technical requirements of the licence and are not concerned with the character of the applicant. Even known criminals can get a building permit for a clubhouse provided they meet the technical requirements and pay the fee. If a municipality refuses to issue a permit to an applicant who has met the technical requirements, the municipal board can order the issuance.

Other boards such as liquor control boards are very concerned about the character, history, and expertise of the applicant. Such boards have the discretion to refuse the licence even if the technical requirements have been met if they believe that the applicant lacks the honesty, responsibility, expertise, or training necessary to operate the business safely and properly. If a board having discretionary jurisdiction is concerned that a licence might be misused, it may refuse to grant the licence. For instance, if an applicant has a criminal record for selling drugs to minors, a licensing board may refuse to issue a liquor licence based on its concern that the applicant would sell alcohol to minors. Even an applicant who does not have a criminal record but who has known links to criminals may be refused a licence.

Mohammed v. British Columbia (Liquor Control and Licensing Branch) (1994), 51 B.C.A.C. 62, 84 W.A.C. 62 (C.A.)

M was the principal owner of two hotels, Hotel R and Hotel V. The British Columbia Liquor Control and Licensing Branch (the "board") had suspended the licence of each hotel for two months. In doing so, it invoked section 16(1) of the *Liquor Licence Act*, which states that "[a] licence shall not be issued, renewed or transferred to a person who ... in the general manager's opinion is not a fit and proper person."

The board ordered M to divest himself of his interest in the two hotels as a condition of reinstating the licence. M felt that the penalty was unduly harsh, and so appealed to the Court of Appeal. At the appeal, the board presented evidence that its inspectors had found 123 bottles of whisky in Hotel V's liquor lockup. Four more bottles were found hooked up to the liquor-dispensing equipment in the bar, and nearly a full bottle was found behind the bar at Hotel R. The whisky had been stolen from a shipment of liquor destined for Japan. The whisky was packaged for the Japanese market and did not carry any of the distribution stickers required by the board. The liquor was not legally available for sale within the province. M had not been charged with any crime because it could not be proven beyond a reasonable doubt that he had known about the whisky in Hotel V's liquor lockup. It also could not be proven beyond a reasonable doubt that he had known the whisky was not lawfully available for sale in the province. It was proven that he had handled some of the liquor himself, that he should have known it was packaged differently, and that it did not have the required government labels.

The Court of Appeal ruled that, upon finding M to be unfit, the board had no choice but to order him to divest himself of his interest in the hotels. The court found no jurisdictional error, failure of natural justice, or error of law on the face of the record. Thus, the court could not interfere with the decision of the board. The court also recognized that it owed a degree of deference to those involved in the day-to-day administration of the *Liquor Licence Act*. The appeal was dismissed.

The Public Interest

As we have seen, a licence may be refused if it is in the public interest to do so. A licence may also be revoked for the same reason. A licensee should cultivate good relations with its neighbours. The following case stands for the proposition that the "public interest" should be interpreted broadly.

Major Mack Hotel v. Ontario Liquor Licence Board (1994), 76 O.A.C. 326 (Div. Ct.), affirmed April 30, 1999, Doc. CA C21043 (Ont. C.A.)

The plaintiff operated a hotel, strip club, and bar under a licence issued by the Liquor Control Board of Ontario (now the Alcohol and Gaming Commission of Ontario). In early 1992, the board issued a Notice of Proposal to Suspend Licence for 21 days, alleging that the plaintiff–licensee had failed to comply with the *Liquor Licence Act* (LLA), the licensee or an employee or agent had knowingly permitted a person under the age of 19 to consume liquor on the licensed premises, the licensee or an employee or agent had allowed a person who appeared to be under the age of 19 to consume liquor on the premises, and the licensee had failed to inspect the identification of a person apparently under 19 years of age. Later that year, the board issued a Supplementary Notice of Proposal to Suspend Licence, alleging that a 17-year-old person had been allowed to consume alcohol on the premises, and that the licensee had allowed drunkenness and riotous, quarrelsome, violent, and disorderly conduct to occur on the premises.

In June 1992, the police laid over 55 charges against the hotel owners, alleging conspiracy to keep a common bawdy house, prostitution, obstruction of police, possession of proceeds of crime, and endangering life. The charges led the board to believe that the business was not operating with integrity and honesty in accordance with the LLA. In September 1992, the board filed a Notice of Proposal to Revoke Licence. In October 1992, the board filed a second Notice of Proposal to Revoke Licence because the residents had complained that, despite their previous objections, the activities in and around the hotel, including the loud, drunken, and disorderly conduct of the patrons, were continuing to disrupt the quiet enjoyment of their homes.

Following a hearing, the board imposed a 45- to 60-day suspension for the disciplinary matters and a 60-day suspension pending determination in the criminal court of the bawdy house and related charges. Ultimately, guilty pleas were entered on various of the criminal charges and, in 1994, the board ordered the revocation of the licence as being the only way to safeguard the public interest.

The plaintiff appealed the revocation to the Divisional Court. The court ruled that the board had not denied the plaintiff natural justice, that the board was entitled to consider the overall conduct of the business, that the board had been correct in linking the neighbourhood problems to the licensee, that the revocation of the licence was reasonable, and that the LLA was not vague and was therefore enforceable.

The plaintiff appealed to the Court of Appeal, which dismissed the appeal in April 1999. The court held that the "public interest" should attach to the behaviour of the licensee and its patrons both inside and outside the licensed establishment "including noise, disturbance, profanity, parking infractions, driving infractions, fighting, violent behavior, urination, defecating, vomiting and passing out on public streets and on private property and littering same, such litter including needles and condoms." The court went on to state that the meaning of "public interest" "is not so uncertain or imprecise a concept as to be beyond legal debate." Thus, a seven-year-long legal battle ended in the board's favour.

Inspections

After a licence has been issued, the board's designated inspectors may conduct periodic inspections of the property at reasonable times to ensure that the provisions of the statute and regulations and the terms and conditions of the licence or permit are being complied with. "Reasonable time" means any time that the licensed establishment is open or that persons other than staff are on the premises. No person shall obstruct the inspector or withhold, destroy, conceal, or refuse to furnish any information or thing relevant to the inspection.

Some licensees contravene the terms and conditions of the licence or permit, or fail to comply with the provisions of a liquor licence Act. Some chronic offenders operate with little regard for the law, and inspectors often find numerous licence infringements. Other offenders may simply be cutting corners, looking for a marketing advantage over their competitors. Non-compliance for economic or other purposes is not fair to operators who are in compliance or to members of the public, who are relying on the enforcement of minimum standards.

When a board moves against a licensee, it will often first build an impressive list of infractions based on inspections and complaints. While a licensee will normally be given a chance to correct honest mistakes, serious and persistent mistakes may not be regarded with the same tolerance. The Major Mack Hotel had been guilty of technical infractions in the past, but for these the board had simply issued suspension orders. By contrast, the criminal guilty pleas and the legitimate complaints of the neighbours could not be ignored and led to the revocation of the licence.

Decisions and Appeals

An application for a licence or for a project may require the approval of many boards and municipal departments. The approval of each board and municipal level is independent of any other approval. An applicant or owner who has obtained approvals for the application or the project from all but one of the boards or departments may be denied the licence.

Decisions to grant a licence are usually made without a hearing and are based on the application material filed by the applicant. If an objection to the application is filed, a hearing is often held so that all parties may be heard. When a board makes a decision to refuse to issue or renew, or to suspend or revoke, a licence, it will inform the applicant or licensee in writing of its decision. The suspension may take place immediately. If a hearing is required, an extension of an existing licence until the hearing is concluded will often be granted. The board will inform the applicant or licensee of the time and place of the hearing.

Generally, any internal appeal process must first be exhausted before accessing the traditional courts. Thereafter, appeals of federal board rulings are made to the Federal Court of Canada. Appeals of provincial board rulings are generally made to a superior court of a province (the Divisional Court in the case of Ontario). Appeals from municipal government rulings are made to the Ontario Municipal Board or its equivalent in other provinces. Appeals from a Municipal Board are made to a Superior or Divisional Court. Further appeals are made to the provincial Court of Appeal. An appeal of a board ruling is called an application for judicial review. A judicial review considers only the process that brought about the decision of the board. It does not reconsider the decision. The court looks for jurisdictional error, failure of natural justice, or error of law on the face of the record.

Errors of Jurisdiction

The decisions of some boards are stipulated to be final by the legislation. In such an event, the appeal court will not overturn any decisions unless a jurisdictional error has been made or the board went beyond its statutory mandate. A board can err in its decisions as long as it acted within its mandate and there is some evidence supporting the decision. A board cannot act in areas beyond its jurisdiction. For example, a Liquor

Licence Board cannot rule on zoning issues. Typically, to succeed on an appeal, the applicant must establish that the process was incorrect rather than that the decision was incorrect.

Rudy's Enterprises Ltd. v. New Brunswick (Liquor Licensing Board) (1993), 139 N.B.R. (2d) 307 (Q.B.)

The board refused to grant a beverage room licence to the applicant on the grounds that the applicant would not be able to provide proper service to alcohol consumers in light of the number of other businesses requiring the applicant's full-time attention. The board also considered the condition of the building, its proximity to a residential neighbourhood, and the likely parking problems. In applying for judicial review of the decision, Rudy's argued that the board had considered matters outside its jurisdiction. The application was dismissed. The court held that the board had made its decision reasonably based on sound evidence, and that it had done so following a fair hearing and without error of jurisdiction or error on the face of the record.

Errors of Natural Justice

All boards owe a duty of fairness to the parties they regulate. Boards must not act in a capricious, unreasonable, or arbitrary manner when exercising their powers to deny a licence or discipline a licensee. Before a person's licence privileges are suspended or revoked, he or she must be advised of the nature of the complaint and be given an opportunity to be heard. These rights are fundamental to the fairness of the process. The licensee need not speak, but must be afforded a reasonable opportunity to do so.

Fog Cutter Inc. v. New Brunswick (Liquor Licensing Board) (1989), 99 N.B.R. (2d) 392 (Q.B.)

A three-day suspension of a licensee's licence was overturned when it was shown that the lawyer for the licensee had been refused an opportunity to speak before the suspension was handed down. When a licensee is denied an opportunity to be heard, the fairness of the hearing is called into question. In this case, it was not necessary to demonstrate that the board was biased against the licensee, only that there was a reasonable apprehension of bias.

Gal-Cab Investments Ltd. v. North West Territories (Liquor Licensing Board), [1986] N.W.T.R. 90 (S.C.), affirmed [1987] N.W.T.R. 100, 34 D.L.R. (4th) 363 (N.W.T.C.A.)

A liquor inspector who had given evidence against the licensee remained in the room with the board members while they deliberated the case. There was no proof that the liquor inspector participated in the deliberations, but his presence created a doubt as to whether or not he might have influenced the board's deliberations.

Errors on the Face of the Record

Errors on the face of the record are usually technical or clerical errors. For example, if a board issues a licence suspension against Smith's Restaurant when it meant to issue the suspension against Smyth's Roadhouse, and if for some reason the board will not correct the error, an application for judicial review may be necessary. In the absence of jurisdictional error, failure of natural justice, or error of law on the face of the record, the courts are unlikely to overturn board decisions. Therefore, a licensee or applicant should be well prepared for the hearing before the board at first instance, rather than hope for a reversal by the court of the board's decision.

Responsibilities of the Licensee

Applying for a Licence

The applicant must qualify for the licence by paying any application fees and meeting the criteria set forth in the enabling legislation and regulations. For some licences, the granting is discretionary in that the board need not issue the licence even if an applicant has met the criteria. Refusals must be on reasonable grounds and not arbitrary. For other licences, there is no discretion. If the applicant has met the criteria, the licence must be issued. The criteria should be carefully reviewed. Although most applications are fairly straightforward and can be filled out by the applicant, it is recommended that legal counsel be sought because there are pitfalls to be avoided and deadlines to be met. An application that does not meet the exact requirements can be a costly mistake in terms of time and lost revenue.

Renewing a Licence

Usually, the renewal of a licence for a licensee in good standing is a formality. The board will generally renew the licence upon the completion of the renewal form and payment of the fee. Some licensees fail to return the application form on time or fail to complete it properly. In that event, the renewal may become very complicated. If the licence has lapsed, the operator may have to apply for a new licence—a longer and more expensive process than a renewal.

Transferring a Licence

Because a licence is a privilege, not a right, it may not normally be assigned or transferred without the approval of the licence granter. The assignee or transferee must meet all the requirements of the licence. A person who is not entitled to a new licence cannot gain one by purchasing a business that already has a licence. Most boards have strict procedures for transferring a licence. There may be a transition period in which the original licensee is required to oversee the operation until all the paperwork and investigations are completed. A purchaser of a licensed establishment should make the due transfer of the licence a condition of the sale. If the existing licence cannot be transferred or a new one obtained, the new owner may have to convert the establishment (e.g., from a pub into a dairy bar).

Complying With the Licence

It is the responsibility of the licensee to comply with all the terms and conditions of the licence. The responsibility cannot be delegated or sidestepped, as is made evident by, as an example, section 21 of Ontario's *Hotel Fire Safety Act*, which states:

> Neither the granting of a permit by an authority having jurisdiction, nor the approval of drawings and specifications by the Fire Marshal, nor inspections made by an inspector or any other authority having jurisdiction during the construction or alteration of a hotel shall in any way relieve the hotel keeper of such hotel from full responsibility to carry out the work in accordance with the requirements of this Act and the regulations.

This Act relieves inspectors of any responsibility should they fail to inform a licensee of a requirement or regulation that the licensee is not meeting. If an inspector passes the property, and it is later found that a requirement was not met, the licensee will have to meet the requirement regardless of the cost. A licensee who fails to meet a statutory requirement may be found liable for **negligence per se.**

Operating Without a Licence

The consequences of operating without a licence or outside the bounds of the licence can be severe. For example, the operator of an after-hours bar may be charged with offences that carry penalties ranging from hefty fines to jail terms. Conviction for such offences makes it extremely difficult for an operator to obtain a licence in the future.

In the event that a liquor licence has expired and not yet been renewed, the operator must not serve alcohol to customers until the renewal has been received by the operator. The suspension for the violation will likely be longer than the wait for the renewal. Suspensions are costly and damaging to the reputation of the establishment.

A business that lacks a licence may not pursue in court any revenues derived from sales requiring a licence. Thus, an unlicensed innkeeper could be prevented from collecting revenues generated by the minibars, and an unlicensed hotel or restaurant could be prevented from collecting the liquor-sale revenues generated at a convention or a large reception.

Business Licences

Few jurisdictions have a separate category for hotel licences. Generally, hotel operators need only obtain a regular business licence from the municipality.

Elevator Licences

All provinces have legislation governing the installation and operation of elevating devices such as escalators and elevators. Such devices cannot be used without a licence. The Acts provide stiff fines and imprisonment for contraventions such as operating an unsafe device.

Food Premises or Victualling House Licences

Given that the mishandling of food can have tragic consequences, most if not all municipalities require licences for food premises; some jurisdictions refer to food premises as victualling (pronounced "vittelling") houses. Licensing allows the municipality to inspect the premises and food-handling policies and, if appropriate, to issue work and other orders in the public interest. Needless to say, a food-service operator should comply strictly with or exceed the terms and conditions of the food-premises licence.

Liquor Licences

All provinces regulate the sale and service of alcohol through a liquor control board. The controls are detailed and strict. Anyone wishing to gain the economic benefits associated with the sale and service of alcohol must qualify for and obtain a licence from the board and comply fully with the regulations or risk losing the licence. Operators of licensed establishments must familiarize themselves with the regulations because ignorance does not excuse contravention. Operators should obtain a copy of the liquor control and licensing Act and regulations in their jurisdiction and take advantage of information material and training programs that may be offered by the board or approved agencies. Many if not all of the liquor licence boards in Canada publish for their licensees newsletters that are good sources of current and practical information about the attitudes of the boards. Hospitality trade associations, which can be found in every jurisdiction, are also excellent sources of information.

A purchaser of a licensed business should include as a condition of the agreement that the licence is in good standing, that the owner has done nothing that would cause an informed inspector to take action, and that the purchaser will be granted a licence by the board. As the new owner assumes responsibility for the inventory, it should also be a condition of the agreement that the liquor included in the inventory was validly purchased through the licence.

Categories of Liquor Licences

A liquor licence is required for a variety of activities. Some of the major categories are:

1. Manufacturer's licence—required by a manufacturer to produce alcoholic beverages for sale to the province's liquor control board.

2. Manufacturer's agent's licence—required by an agent to solicit or receive orders for the sale of alcohol.

3. Arena licence for the sale of alcohol in a tiered section of an arena or stadium.

4. Delivery licence.

5. Sales licence for the sale and service of alcohol on premises where meals are available.

6. Minibar licence for the sale of alcohol from a minibar in a room rented for overnight accommodation. Food must also be available. Minibars must be secure against access except by the renter of the room using a special key, not the room key.

7. Special-occasion licence for the consumption of alcohol at an event for which a government permit has been issued. The licence may allow the alcohol to be supplied at a fee or at no charge to the attendees. It is usually not required that food be available.

Applying for a Liquor Licence

Any person may apply for a liquor licence subject to various restrictions and conditions. A licence may be refused in the following circumstances:

1. The applicant cannot reasonably be expected to be financially responsible in the conduct of the applicant's business.

2. The applicant is not a Canadian citizen or a person lawfully admitted to Canada for permanent residence and ordinarily resident in Canada.

3. The applicant is a corporation and a majority of the members of the board of directors are not Canadian citizens or persons lawfully admitted to Canada for permanent residence and ordinarily resident in Canada.

4. The past or present conduct of the applicant affords reasonable grounds for belief that he will not carry on business with integrity and honesty and in accordance with the law.

5. The applicant makes a false statement or provides false information in an application.

6. The applicant is carrying on activities that are (or will be if the license is granted) contrary to law.

7. The premises, accommodation, equipment, and facilities in respect of which the licence is to be issued are, or will be, contrary to law.

8. The issuance of the licence is not in the public interest with respect to the needs and wishes of the residents in the municipality in which the premises are located.

The various liquor licence Acts provide that the board must give notice of the application to the residents of the municipality in which the premises are located. The notice may announce a public meeting or contain a request for written submissions as to whether the issuance of the licence is in the public interest, having regard to the needs and wishes of the residents. The boards are required to consider the representations of the residents.

Duties of the Licensee

The licensee must abide by the terms of the licence or risk losing the licence. The licence must be posted in a conspicuous place where it may be seen by the public and by the inspectors. Many of the duties of the **licensee**, such as the duty not to serve minors or persons who are intoxicated, are discussed in Chapter 7.

Renewals and Transfers

Provided that the licensee has abided by the terms of the licence and is continuing to meet the requirements of the board, a licence renewal is usually granted with little difficulty. Liquor licences cannot be transferred except in accordance with the applicable regulations. In most cases, the licence is not transferred and a purchaser of licensed premises must apply for and obtain a new licence. Any agreement to purchase a licensed establishment should be conditional upon the purchaser obtaining a licence.

Suspensions and Revocations

The boards retain the right to suspend or revoke a liquor licence for such violations as failing to remit sales taxes and selling illegal liquor. Liquor sales generate large tax revenues. If an establishment is caught failing to remit payment for federal, provincial, and corporate taxes, its liquor licence will be in great jeopardy. The sale of illegal liquor can involve smuggling cheap foreign liquor into Canada and selling it to the bars at prices more attractive than those set by the liquor control board. More frequently, the charges are for illegal liquor that owners, management, and staff bring into their establishments. Any liquor brought on site that is not purchased by the licensee in the prescribed manner is illegal liquor. A business liquor licensee who is short of inventory cannot replenish it from a personal supply. Further, the transfer of liquor from one bar to another is illegal. Any person who replaces a lost bottle by bringing illegal liquor on site could be charged with bootlegging. It is also illegal for staff or, in most municipalities, customers to bring personal liquor on site; doing so could result in the loss of the licence.

When a liquor licence is revoked in Ontario, the board may suspend applications for a new licence at the location for up to two years. A landlord should make sure that the tenant is reputable and in compliance with the liquor licence. If the tenant's liquor licence is suspended, the site's ability to generate liquor sale revenues could be lost for a lengthy time, possibly causing the landlord to lose rental income.

Hearings

If the board intends to deny, suspend, or revoke a licence, notice is given to the licensee of a hearing into the matter. While such hearings are before an administrative tribunal and are therefore less formal than court hearings, the licensee should prepare the case very carefully. It is difficult to successfully appeal the decisions of the board. A licensee's best chance at obtaining or preserving a licence is at the hearing before the board.

Examples of Disciplinary Dispositions

Liquor licence boards take their responsibilities very seriously and do not shirk from disciplining those who transgress against the requirements of the licence. The Alcohol and Gaming Commission of Ontario publishes a regular report containing, among other news, a list of recent dispositions. From it, readers can learn about current trends in discipline matters. Below is a sampling. The names of the guilty have been deleted to protect the unwise.

Infraction	Disposition
• Failing to collect and remit retail sales tax	Licence revoked
• Permitted narcotics and drunkenness on the premises, selling illegal liquor, failing to have an experienced food and beverage supervisor on premises	Licence revoked
• Permitting narcotics on premises, adulterating liquor, breaching the public interest	Licence revoked
• Serving minors, permitting drunkenness, serving illegal liquor, permitting removal of liquor from premises	30–day suspension
• Serving illegal liquor, breaching the public interest	30–day suspension
• Selling liquor to a person appearing to be intoxicated, permitting drunkenness, over–serving alcohol, serving minors, failing to inspect identification	21 days
• Serving minors, failing to provide light meals, permitting narcotics on premises	18 days
• Obstructing an inspector, serving minors, overcrowding	15 days
• Overcrowding, serving minors, failing to inspect identification	14 days
• Permitting the operation of a business not permitted under the Act under the Act or regulations	14 days
• Serving outside prescribed hours	14 days

Failing to be financially responsible, especially by breaching the conditions of the licence or the provisions of the statutes and regulations, accounts for a significant proportion of the infractions. Liquor licence revocations and suspensions are embarrassing, costly, and potentially ruinous. It is better to avoid them through comprehensive standard operating procedures and alert management practices.

Consumer Protection

Under common law, the general rule affecting consumers was *caveat emptor* ("let the buyer beware"). Until rules of fitness for the purpose and merchantable quality began to evolve, a consumer who did not negotiate terms of warranty was often left with little or no remedy. Consumer-protection legislation was regarded as an interference in the freedom of contract. In this environment, many innocent parties were disadvantaged because of an inequality of bargaining power, or because of special knowledge or unscrupulous behaviour on the part of the other party. In the post–Second World War period, governments have been increasingly willing to enact consumer protection legislation in response to the problem. The legislation typically gives the government broad powers to investigate and punish violators.

No statute can eliminate unfairness. Although the legal situation is much improved today, there will always be people looking to take advantage of gullible and unsophisticated individuals who are prime fodder for everything from telemarketing scams to get-rich-quick schemes. Some protection for consumers is provided by private agencies such as better business bureaus and credit bureaus, which keep files on businesses based on inquiries and complaints made by consumers. A consumer can use the information provided by these agencies to assess the creditworthiness and ethical track record of a given business.

The *Competition Act*

The *Competition Act* is the main federal law regulating advertising, competition practices, restraint of trade matters, mergers, and pyramid and other referred selling schemes. The Act gives the federal government broad powers of investigation, and makes it a criminal offence to engage in false or misleading advertising, price fixing, restriction of trade, and predatory practices. Penalties include fines of up to $10 million and imprisonment for up to five years.

False or Misleading Advertising
Advertising may be found to be false or misleading based on the general impression it makes, the literal meaning of the words used, the truth of any testimonials or claims, or the price or quality of the goods or services. Benign puffing is allowed; the prohibition extends essentially to misrepresentations of fact and statements that are calculated to mislead. In promotions that involve an element of chance, the odds of winning must be clearly revealed.

Price Fixing
Agreements to fix prices to the detriment of the public are prohibited. In the accommodation industry, it is illegal for hotels of virtually identical quality to conspire to charge the same room rates such that the public interest is harmed. However, similar hotels may charge highly similar rates if doing so is the result of a bona fide attempt to compete in the marketplace and not a conspiracy to harm the public. Also illegal is bid rigging, a practice whereby a group of bidders decide among themselves whose turn it is to submit the lowest bid on a given project. See the discussion in Chapter 9 regarding the right of an innkeeper to set room rates.

Unfair Competition Practices
Unfair competition practices include selling a product for the higher of two displayed or ticketed prices (double ticketing), selling a product for more than the advertised price, and baiting customers with low prices and then switching them to higher-priced products by claiming, for example, that the supply of sale items has run out. Bait-and-switch techniques are illegal only if an unreasonably small number of sale items are offered at the sale price. If the number of sale items is reasonable, the retailer will not be liable. Predatory pricing is an illegal activity in which one business with economic clout sells its products at deep, long-lasting discounts in order to harm a competitor. Reasonable loss-leader sales are allowed provided the intention is not to prey unfairly on competitors.

Mergers and Acquisitions
Business mergers and acquisitions that unduly limit trade or restrict competition are prohibited under the *Competition Act*. Mergers and acquisitions are not necessarily bad. They may be essential for parties that would not otherwise survive in an environment of larger or more-established competitors. Mergers that do not unduly limit trade or restrict competition are legal. In assessing a proposed merger, the competition tribunal considers both the potential to harm the public and the potential to benefit the public. In some

cases, there is identifiable potential harm, but the benefits outweigh the harm. If the public interest is unlikely to be materially harmed by the merger, or if the benefits outweigh the harm, the merger will not be opposed by the tribunal except in exceptional circumstances. There are three types of mergers:

1. *Vertical merger*. In this form of merger, a supplier of a good or service merges with a retailer of the same good or service. In such cases, the supplier could favour its own retail arm to the detriment of other retailers who need supplies from the same source. For example, a cheese supplier enjoying a near-monopoly of supply in a community could buy several pizza outlets within a local business radius. It would be unfair if the supplier charged non-owned outlets more for its products than it did its owned outlets.

2. *Horizontal merger*. Here, a business merges with a direct business competitor. For example, one hotel chain could merge with another. The effect may be to drastically reduce or eliminate competition in a given area. Given the vast number of accommodation businesses and tourist destinations, it is unlikely at least in the foreseeable future that the accommodation business will become so concentrated as to attract the attention of the competition tribunal.

3. *Conglomerate merger*. A conglomerate merger occurs when a business merges with another business that has not been a direct competitor. For example, a holding company that owns a steel mill could buy a travel wholesaler. Conglomerate mergers are essentially attempts to diversify corporate activity and revenue streams. As such, they are less likely to harm the public than are vertical or horizontal mergers.

Other Federal Laws

Other federal laws that protect the public in general and the consumer in particular include:

- The *Hazardous Products Act*, which regulates the importation, manufacture, handling, and sale of hazardous products. Most such products are merely controlled; others are banned. Some inherently dangerous materials or products are covered in separate legislation, including the *Pest Control Products Act*, the *Explosives Act*, the *Motor Vehicle Safety Act*, and the *Food and Drugs Act*. The *Food and Drugs Act*, discussed in Chapter 6, regulates the advertising and sale of food, drugs, and cosmetics; it also bans many substances and makes trafficking in or possessing certain of them an offence.

- The *Consumer Packaging and Labelling Act*, the *Textile Labelling Act*, and the *Weights and Measures Act*, which regulate the manner in which products are labelled and measured, and require that manufacturers and vendors disclose such information to the consumer.

- The *Bills of Exchange Act*, which regulates the use of bills of exchange such as cheques, promissory notes, and other negotiable instruments and money products.

Provincial Legislation

All provinces have consumer-protection and business-practices legislation that prohibits unfair or deceptive practices such as performing and charging for unnecessary repairs, suggesting that a product or service is on sale when it is in fact being offered at the regular price, and overstating the difference between a sale price and a regular price. See, for example, British Columbia's *Trade Practice Act*, Alberta's *Unfair Trade Practices Act*, Ontario's *Business Practices Act*, and the *Direct Sellers Acts* of Newfoundland and Labrador, and Nova Scotia.

Some of the legislation endeavours to protect the public from enticing but problematic sales schemes and tactics. Pyramid and other referred-selling schemes are tightly controlled or prohibited in several provinces, including British Columbia and Ontario. To provide some protection against the high-pressure tactics of door-to-door salespeople, many provinces allow for a cooling-off period during which the purchaser may repudiate the contract without penalty. Each province has enacted legislation that requires lenders to disclose the true cost of the borrowing; in addition, each province controls the methods by which debts may be collected.

All provinces have unconscionable transactions relief legislation that permits the courts to set aside money-lending transactions that are unconscionable. A very high rate of interest charged for a loan does not necessarily make the loan unconscionable. The level of risk must be examined before such a determination can be made. Prince Edward Island, Ontario, and British Columbia have extended relief for unconscionable transactions to goods and services. In cases in which the price for the good or service is grossly excessive, or in which the complaining party was unduly influenced or suffered from an unfair disadvantage such as mental incapacity or illiteracy, the Acts in those provinces may provide relief in the form of rescission or damages, and even exemplary damages.

Liability

It is the responsibility of business owners and managers to know the requirements specified by all applicable federal and provincial legislation. The general rule is that ignorance of the law is no excuse. However, there are tempering provisions. For example, under the *Competition Act*, the advertiser or business may escape liability if it demonstrates that the mistake was honest and that reasonable steps were taken initially to avoid, and later to correct, the mistake. Advertisers or businesses will also escape liability if they first obtain from the Bureau of Competition Policy an advance ruling authorizing the advertisement or business practice.

In addition to (or even in the absence of) a claim or prosecution brought pursuant to a statute, those engaged in the practices impugned by the legislation may find themselves liable for damages to injured parties under common law principles such as breach of contract and negligence. Statutory remedies do not preclude common law remedies unless the statute expressly so states, e.g., workers' compensation and no-fault automobile legislation.

E-Commerce Considerations

Federal statutes such as the *Competition Act* and the *Personal Information Protection and Electronic Documents Act* (see Chapter 13) and provincial statutes such as Ontario's *Electronic Commerce Act* (see Chapter 3) have either been amended or enacted partly to protect consumers in the e-commerce world. Many other legislative provisions, such as the *Criminal Code* provisions against fraud and other consumer-protection provisions, apply to e-commerce as much as to any other form of commerce. Increasingly, governments are engaging in activities, including international cooperation, to halt or hinder e-commerce abuse.

Taxation Matters

Tax legislation is extensive and filled with innumerable qualifiers and exceptions that are themselves qualified and excepted. What follows is a brief overview of the tax provisions that are applicable to a typical hospitality business. For guidance on tax planning and

Sound professional advice pays dividends.

preparing tax returns, professional advice from a lawyer or accountant who specialize in this field is essential.

Residents of Canada are required by law to pay income tax on their taxable income earned inside and outside Canada. Persons who are not residents of Canada but who earn income in Canada are required to pay tax on their Canadian earnings but not on their earnings earned outside Canada. Taxation is based on residency, not citizenship. Most governments have tax treaties with other governments to ensure that taxpayers do not pay tax twice on the same income (double taxation) and do not avoid paying taxes to the appropriate authority.

Although tax law is complex, at the core of the *Income Tax Act* is a fairly straightforward process. Taxpayers calculate their taxable income (leaving out nontaxable income such as gifts and lottery winnings), subtract the allowable deductions, and pay tax at the applicable rate on whatever is left. That is all there is to it. The complexity lies in determining which receipts are taxable and which deductions are applicable and to what extent.

In addition to paying income tax, businesses are required to collect the goods and services tax (GST) on their sales and services, calculate the net GST owing, and remit it. There are penalty and interest charges for failing to comply. Most businesses are also required to collect and remit the provincial sales tax (PST).

Income Taxes on the Business

Sections 91 and 92 of the *Constitution Act (1867)* grant the federal and provincial governments the authority to levy income taxes. Provincial income tax is collected by the federal government and remitted to the provinces. Residents of Quebec are required to prepare a separate provincial income tax return. Some provinces require the preparation of a separate corporate income tax return; others require only a capital tax return; Ontario requires both.

An individual in business (sole proprietor or partner) must file an income tax return by April 30 for the previous year. Because no employer makes source deductions or remittances for them, self-employed people must pay tax in quarterly instalments calculated on the basis of either one-quarter of the previous year's tax liability or the estimated income tax liability for the current year. Any shortfall, including interest charges for underpayments, must be paid by the end of the next April.

A corporation must file a return within six months of its fiscal year-end. Corporations must pay monthly tax instalments based on either one-twelfth of the previous year's tax liability or the estimated income tax liability for the current year. Any shortfalls and interest charges must be paid by the end of the third month following the corporation's fiscal year-end in the case of a Canadian-controlled private corporation (CCPC) and by the end of the second month in the case of all other corporations.

Statutory Remittances for Employees

Employers are required to withhold at source and remit to the Receiver General of Canada three statutory remittances on behalf of their employees:

1. Federal and provincial income taxes,

2. Employment insurance premiums, and

3. Canada (or Quebec) Pension Plan contributions.

All salaries, wages, or other remunerations paid or made to the employee, and all tips and gratuities earned by the employee, must be included in his or her taxable income in order to calculate the amount of the remittances. Only the employee contributes to the income tax statutory remittance, but both the employer and the employee contribute to the employment insurance (EI) and pension plan remittances. (Quebec operates its own pension plan.) Strictly speaking, employment insurance premiums and Canada (or Quebec) pension plan contributions are not taxes but an insurance premium in the case of the former and an investment in the case of the latter.

Employers are required to deduct the income tax, EI, and pension plan amounts at source (i.e., from the employee's paycheque) and remit them to the government, together with the employer's portion of the EI and pension plan contributions, by the 15th day of the month following the month in which the remuneration was paid. An employer must file a detailed report specifying employee earnings and deductions by the end of February in the following year. To assist in the process, employees must provide their employer with their social insurance number within three days of being hired. The employer must in turn provide employees with information slips (e.g., T-4 slips) that outline the remuneration and source deductions and assist employees in filing their tax returns.

The employer's EI premium is typically 1.4 times the EI premium of the employee. The federal government also contributes to the EI plan out of general revenues. To receive benefits, an unemployed person must have been employed for a minimum period, which may vary depending on the unemployment rate in the locale and the work history of the claimant. Claimants can receive up to 55 percent (to a maximum of $413 per week) of their average insured earnings over the 26 weeks immediately preceding their unemployment.

Employer Health Tax

Health care is primarily a provincial responsibility. Some provinces tax employees directly by means of a source deduction. Ontario levies an employer health tax (EHT) that is based on the total amount of remuneration paid by an employer to its employees in a calendar year. Calculated on the basis of the size of the annual payroll, the rate ranges from .98 percent for small employers to 1.82 percent for large employers. Employers whose gross annual payroll or remuneration is less than $400,000 are exempt from EHT. Employees are not subject to the tax; thus, EHT is not a source deduction. In Ontario, eligible employers are required to file an annual EHT return and remit the balance payable by March 15 in the following year. Depending on the size of their payroll, employers remit annually, quarterly, or monthly. The larger the payroll, the more frequent the instalments. As with income and sales taxes, the employer is required by law to maintain accurate books and records for audit purposes.

Workers' Compensation

Like employment insurance contributions, workers' compensation contributions are an insurance premium. Workers' compensation plans were introduced to help workers with work-related injuries or diseases to bypass the lengthy, costly, and uncertain outcomes of civil litigation against employers, as well as to save employers from potentially ruinous claims. Except where the injury is caused by the worker's own willful and serious misconduct, the plan is a no-fault insurance scheme that pays benefits according to rates set forth in the enabling legislation. The benefits vary depending on the type, duration, and severity of the injury or illness. Independent contractors are not included in the definition of worker.

Workers' compensation contributions are not source deductions because they are made only by employers pursuant to a formula that varies depending on the type of business and the size of the employer's payroll. Many employers, including smaller travel agencies, are exempt. Employers that are not exempt, such as hotels and restaurants, face penalties if they fail to register or remit the contributions. Accommodation businesses and food and alcohol service businesses typically pay at different rates. In the case of a hotel that operates a dining room, the rate will be that of the primary activity—likely the running of the hotel—unless the payrolls of the two operations are kept separate.

Goods and Services Tax

Pursuant to the *Excise Tax Act*, the GST is a multi-stage, value-added tax levied on each supply of goods and services except exempt and zero-rated supplies. Exempt supplies include such things as used residential real property, health-care services, educational services, financial services, legal aid, and road, ferry, and bridge tolls. Zero-rated supplies include such items as prescription drugs, medical devices, basic groceries, and travel services.

The GST is collected by the supplier. The current GST rate is 7 percent. The GST in a tax-included price may be calculated by multiplying the price by 7 and dividing the total by 107. The GST is calculated on the price of the supply net of provincial sales taxes. In other words, there is no tax on tax. In some circumstances, nonresidents of Canada may apply for a rebate of GST including GST paid on short-term accommodation and convention costs.

With the exception of persons qualifying for a small-supplier exemption who have gross annual revenues of less than $30,000 (not applicable to taxi drivers and non-resident performance entertainers, though they must still register), all persons engaged in commercial activity must register with Canada Customs and Revenue Agency (CCRA), and collect and remit the GST. Registrants are entitled to a refund, or input tax credit, for the tax they pay on their purchases; i.e., the amount of GST remitted is the excess of the amount of GST collected on supplies over the amount of GST paid for supplies. Where the GST paid exceeds the amount collected, the registrant is entitled to a rebate. Suppliers of exempt supplies are not entitled to claim input tax credits on purchases related to the exempt supplies. For example, fees received for educational services are not subject to GST; however, GST paid on furniture and books in relation to the educational services is not claimable. No GST is payable on zero-rated supplies, but registrants may claim input tax credits on their related purchases.

Registrants whose gross revenues from taxable and zero-rated supplies in the previous year are below $500,000, and whose GST payable is less than $1500, may file their GST return annually and may remit the GST owing annually. Registrants with gross revenues below $500,000 and GST payable of $1500 or more may file their GST return annually and must pay quarterly instalments based on the previous year's GST liability or the estimated GST liability for the current year. The instalment form and remittance are due within one month following the end of the quarter. Registrants with revenues between $500,000 and $6 million must file their GST returns and make their remittances quarterly. Registrants with revenues greater than $6 million must file their GST returns and make their remittances monthly. For the purpose of calculating revenues, registered businesses are defined as including associated businesses. Any refunds of GST are payable by the government at its leisure, usually within six weeks.

In the hospitality industry, all goods and service supplies are subject to GST except rentals for less than $20 per day, tips unless they are a mandatory gratuity shown on the bill, basic groceries, and some foods not intended for immediate consumption, such as baked goods sold in packages of six or more. Thus, while a package of five doughnuts would be taxable, a package of six would not, unless the

Sales taxes are mostly unavoidable—we might as well grin and bear them.

doughnuts were consumed on the vendor's premises. Most foods and beverages are taxable, including wine, beer, other alcoholic beverages, carbonated drinks, fruit drinks containing less than 25 percent natural fruit juice, most snack foods, and prepared foods and beverages intended for immediate consumption, such as hot meals, salads, sandwiches, and food platters.

Provincial Sales Tax

All persons engaged in qualifying retail activity are required to register with the province and to collect and remit provincial retail sales taxes (PST) on the sale of taxable goods and services. Alberta does not levy a provincial retail sales tax. In the four Atlantic provinces and Quebec, the PST has been blended with the GST to produce a single value-added tax called the harmonized sales tax (HST). In British Columbia, Saskatchewan, Manitoba, and Ontario, PST is separate from GST and is a single-stage (i.e., applied at one level) tax imposed on the final retail consumption of taxable goods and services. In some circumstances, nonresidents of a province may apply for a rebate of PST for goods purchased in the taxing province and delivered to the purchaser's home or office in another province.

PST is calculated on the sale price net of GST (except in Quebec). The vendor is required to charge, collect, and remit the PST, and to keep records of the transactions and exemptions. There are innumerable exceptions and qualifications in the list of taxable goods and services. The retail sales tax legislation in force in the province must be consulted to ensure that the tax is being collected only on taxable items and at the correct rate. Typically, PST returns and remittances for the previous month must be filed with the provincial revenue office before the end of the next month. Small vendors may be allowed to file and remit on a less frequent basis. Although the ultimate liability for the collection of the PST rests with the vendor, the Minister of Finance may assess either the purchaser or the vendor for any deficiency. This right is regularly exercised. Consider a hotel that purchases linens for use in the hotel. If the linen vendor neglects to charge the sales tax, the hotel may be liable to pay the PST, as well as interest and penalties. A purchaser cannot take advantage of a vendor's failure to charge PST.

Municipal Taxes

Pursuant to authority delegated from the province, municipalities may levy business (but not income) taxes on businesses to whom they have issued licences. The municipalities may also levy property taxes. Municipal taxes are typically paid annually or biannually.

Miscellaneous Taxes

Hospitality businesses are generally subject to the same taxes imposed on other businesses. Provincial governments in particular sometimes assess special taxes to defray costs of public facilities or events. A room tax may be added to defray the costs of building a convention centre or financing an exhibition, carnival, trade fair, or major sports event such as the Olympic or Commonwealth games. An airport tax may be added to the cost of each airplane ticket to help pay for airport renovations or security initiatives.

Interest and Penalties

Interest is charged by the federal government on outstanding tax balances at a prescribed rate plus 4 percent (the government pays interest on overdue refunds at the prescribed rate plus 2 percent). Currently, the prescribed rate is set quarterly and is the average rate on 90-day treasury bills sold by the government during the first month of the preceding quarter. The interest compounds daily. As a result, the effective annual interest rate can be very high. Penalties are in addition to interest charges, and are themselves subject to interest charges if left unpaid. Provinces and municipalities also levy interest and penalty charges.

Assessments

The CCRA may assess tax returns, and the information used in the preparation of the returns, for the preceding three years. The most controversial tax assessments occur when the government makes an error in an assessment in the taxpayer's favour, adjusts the error, assesses the taxpayer for the additional tax, and applies the interest retroactively. Such action is legal, and is one of the reasons why the onus is on the taxpayer to ensure that the correct amounts are remitted. The statute requires taxpayers to retain their tax records for at least seven years; however, it is frequently a very good idea to retain the records indefinitely, particularly in commercial matters. It is commonsense, good business practice, cheaper in the long run, and a legal requirement that accurate and detailed books and records be maintained. In all matters of taxation and record keeping, professional advice should be sought.

Directors' Liability

Many people welcome their election to a corporate board of directors. However, directors may be personally liable for the torts or other wrongdoing of their companies. Liability for employees' wages is discussed in Chapter 14. Directors should also be aware of their personal liabilities for the remittance of taxes. Pursuant to federal income tax and GST legislation, where a corporation does not remit all the tax as required, the directors sitting at the time the remittance was to have been made are jointly and severally liable to pay the missing tax and any applicable interest and penalties. Joint and several liability means that each director may be held fully liable for the whole debt even in the absence of financial contributions from the other directors. However, under the tax legislation, a director is not liable if he or she has exercised the care, diligence, and skill that a reasonably prudent person would have exercised in comparable circumstances to prevent the failure to remit the full amount of the tax. The case law provides that making general inquiries about the status of remittances is insufficient. The directors must regularly require assurance and possibly proof that the remittances are duly and fully being made. They cannot be careless, reckless, negligent, or willfully blind.

Most often at risk are remittances of employee source deductions for income tax, employment insurance, and pension plans. When a business is strapped for cash, the owners may covet the remittance amounts as interest-free loans. Businesses are well advised to remember that the penalties levied on late payments are not tax deductible. The cost of deferring remittances can escalate rapidly.

Avoidance and Evasion

Tax avoidance is a legal activity, one that keeps hordes of tax experts and financial planners busy into the night. Tax law is as intellectually stimulating as a never-ending game of chess. A good accountant is a must. Accountants can save a business far more than the cost of the accounting. Accurate bookkeeping is also a must. Books that are in disarray are a time-consuming headache to correct, and rob the owners and managers of the financial information they need to run the business soundly.

Tax evasion is a crime that the government takes rather seriously. Al Capone went to Alcatraz (derived from the Spanish word for pelicans) not for murder, but for tax evasion. Sometimes the line between avoidance and evasion is grey. The best way to stay on the right side of the line is to seek professional advice and to err on the side of caution.

Recommendations

1. Ascertain all licensing requirements for the business, including renewal dates. Abide by all the terms and conditions of the licence.

2. Be familiar with the various inspections required to ensure compliance with the applicable Acts or codes. Many administrative boards publish newsletters. Read them to keep abreast of changes and current issues.

3. Check the legal status of any licence that is to be acquired by purchase or transfer. Note that licence transfers are not automatic and can take a long time to complete.

4. Comply with all municipal bylaws.

5. Be fully prepared for any appearance before a board or tribunal.

6. Be fully prepared for any public hearings on a licence application. Market studies should include neighbourhood-impact information.

7. Check all zoning requirements before investing. Zoning changes are costly and time-consuming, and may be difficult to obtain.

8. Before and after licensing or zoning approvals are acquired, exercise good public relations as a way of fostering goodwill within the community.

9. Select the business name wisely and protect it through registration or trademark filing.

10. Hire an excellent lawyer, accountant, and bookkeeper.

11. Avoid as many taxes as you can; evade none.

Summary

Businesses are subject to an enormous variety of laws and regulations, such as building codes, fire codes, health and food regulations, environmental-protection matters, record keeping, and so on. In addition, municipal zoning and other bylaws regulate land use, including the type of business that may be conducted upon the land, the hours during which the business may be open to the public, and numerous other matters.

A licence is an authorization issued by a competent body that grants qualified applicants the right to do something that may not be done legally without the licence. After the licence has been issued, it may be revoked or suspended if the conditions of the licence are not being met. Licences should only be refused, revoked, or suspended upon reasonable and proper grounds. An applicant or licensee who believes that the refusal, revocation, or suspension is unfair may appeal to the appropriate administrative tribunal for relief. The licensor generally has the right to inspect the premises and business of the licensee. The licensor may issue work orders and compliance notices, which are remedies less drastic than revocation.

Liquor licences are heavily regulated and carefully monitored. It is essential for a liquor licensee to comply with the requirements of the licence. Loss of a liquor licence for a restaurant can be catastrophic to the business.

Under common law, the general rule in consumer transactions was "let the buyer beware." Although case law and especially consumer-protection legislation have softened the rule, a consumer is better advised to investigate and exercise due caution before entering into a consumer transaction. The *Competition Act* is the main federal law regulating advertising, competition practices, restraint of trade matters, mergers, and pyramid and other referred-selling schemes. Several other federal and provincial statutes also regulate consumer transactions in the public interest. In general, the legislation shifts much of the responsibility for ensuring fairness in consumer transactions from the consumer to the supplier. The statutory protections are in addition to any common law protections.

All individuals and businesses in Canada are subject to various tax laws. The services of a lawyer, accountant, and bookkeeper are very beneficial. Businesses must calculate and make statutory remittances, such as Canada Pension Plan contributions, employment insurance premiums, income tax, and, where applicable, health tax and workers' compensation premiums, for their employees. Businesses must also remit goods and services tax and, where applicable, provincial sales tax, and municipal business and property taxes.

1. List and describe the types of licences that are required for a hotel or a restaurant in your jurisdiction.

2. Visit three establishments that hold a liquor licence and report on the type of licence each has. Describe three offences under the liquor licence Act in your jurisdiction.

3. What is meant by the adulteration of liquor, and how can it occur quite innocently?

4. Are underage persons allowed to sell and serve liquor in your jurisdiction?

5. Are underage entertainers allowed to work in licensed premises in your jurisdiction?

6. Is a hotel allowed to rent one of its licensed rooms to another hotel operator?

7. Contact a law firm and learn the nature and cost of the services it provides.

8. Contact an accounting firm and learn the nature and cost of the services it provides.

13

Chapter Thirteen

Ownership and Management

Learning Outcomes

1. List the various forms of ownership for a business.

2. Assess the legal advantages of each of the types of ownership.

3. Discuss the most important factors that should be included in an offer to purchase.

4. List and discuss the most pertinent factors that should be included in a lease.

5. Explain what is meant by the term "trademark."

6. Explain the legal protection offered by a trademark.

7. Analyze insurance requirements and recommend the protection required.

Introduction

Anyone going into business should ensure that the structure is sound and that any **statutory** or regulatory requirements are met—they are there for a reason. If the structure is sound, success can more easily be draped on it.

Ownership of a Hospitality Business

Types of Business Structures

Any business, including a hospitality business, may be structured in one of three ways: sole proprietorship, partnership, or corporation. Sole proprietorships, partnerships, and provincially incorporated corporations are governed by provincial law. Federally incorporated corporations are governed by federal law.

Sole Proprietorship

A business owned by one individual is a sole proprietorship. There are over 200 000 sole proprietorships in Canada, which makes them the most common form of business organization in the country. All the assets and liabilities of the business belong to the individual, not the business. The income must be reported on the individual's income tax return. Losses incurred in the business may be used to offset income from other sources. The individual's personal assets, such as a house and a bank account, are at risk should the business fail or any successful lawsuits against the business exceed the insurance coverage.

Sole proprietorships are relatively easy and inexpensive to commence and to dissolve. The name of the owner, the name of the business (if different from the owner's name), and the place of business must be filed with the provincial government. The filings must be kept current and renewed periodically.

Partnership

A partnership is created whenever two or more persons carry on business together with a view to profit (actually turning a profit is not necessary). Most partnerships are created by an express agreement between the partners, but some may be created by the conduct of the parties. Thus, a person may become the partner of another person even though the two parties have not expressly discussed the matter. In the absence of an express agreement to the contrary, the law supposes that the parties are equal partners entitled to an equal say in the operation of the partnership and to an equal division of the profits and losses. As with sole proprietorships, the income, assets, and tax and other liabilities are personal to the partners and must be dealt with as such, and each partner's personal assets are at risk.

Disputes among partners are not uncommon. Partnership agreements minimize disputes, or at least provide an expeditious method of resolving them, by setting forth such terms of the partnership as division of income, authority to bind, and rights upon incompatibility, dissolution, or death. A party may remain liable even after leaving the partnership unless certain provisions are made and statutory requirements met.

Partners owe each other a duty of **good faith**, which is to say they must act only in the best interests of the partnership. Partners may bind the other partners to contracts and obligations. The partner need not have actual authority to do so provided he has apparent authority, i.e., he appears to a reasonable third party to have authority whether he does or not. If a partner binds the partnership to an arrangement with an innocent third party that is unfavourable to the partnership, the innocent third party will be able to hold all the partners to the arrangement. The innocent partners may be able to claim over against such a partner.

Partnerships are relatively easy to commence and dissolve. The name of the partner-ship, the names of the partners, and the place of business must be filed with the government. The filings must be kept current and renewed periodically.

A special kind of partnership, called a limited partnership, allows the limited partners to limit their liability to the amount of their financial contribution provided certain con-ditions are met. In Ontario, the *Limited Partnerships Act* requires that there be at least one general partner whose liability is unlimited, and that the limited partners declare the amount of their respective contributions. The limited partners are subordinate to the general partner for most purposes, including the ongoing operation of the business. If a limited partner begins to operate the business, he may become a general partner by default and lose the benefit of limited liability.

Corporation

The word "company" is derived from the Latin *cum panis*, meaning "with bread." Roman businessmen would gather for a meal and form business ventures. It was a common fea-ture of these arrangements that no member could lose more than the amount he had invested in the venture. His liability was limited to the amount of his investment and his other assets were sheltered from claims—hence the inclusion of the word "limited" in many corporate names.

Companies proved to be an effective means of creating and operating business ven-tures. Eventually, governments enacted legislation governing their creation and formal operations. The legislation refers to "corporation" as opposed to "company" because the latter word has too broad an application. The formal filing and other requirements are more detailed than those for sole proprietorships and partnerships. The registered head office and place of business of the corporation, together with the names of the directors and the officers, must be filed with the government and kept current. It is not necessary to file the names of the shareholders. A corporation must maintain its bylaws, resolutions, and detailed records at its head office where they may be reviewed by the shareholders, directors, and government inspectors during reasonable hours. These records, together with the minutes of the meetings of the shareholders and the meet-ings of the directors, are stored in the minute book.

As creatures of statute, corporations can act only in accordance with the statutory framework and the corporate bylaws and resolutions derived from it. In law, a corpora-tion is a separate "person" from its owners and managers, which means that it can sue and be sued, enter into contracts, and otherwise act in its own name. Corporations may be "offering," which means their shares are traded on a public stock exchange, or "nonoffering," which means their shares are not publicly traded but held and traded privately. Most corporations are Canadian-controlled private corporations (CCPCs). There are well over 100 000 active corporations in Canada. Many are incorporated at the provincial level. A business should incorporate federally if it expects to do business in more than one province or internationally.

Corporate structure has four tiers. At the top are the **shareholders**, who are the owners of the company. Generally, their liability is limited to the amount of their investment; however, in some circumstances, the courts may "pierce the corporate veil" and assess additional liability upon them. The share (or stock) certificate is their evidence of own-ership. They must meet at least once a year, either in person or by proxy. They are entitled to share in the profits by receiving dividends, to recover their investment if the corpora-tion is wound up and the creditors have been paid, and to participate in the management and direction of the corporation by voting for and directing the directors.

Occupying the second tier is the **board of directors**, which is elected by the share-holders and which must direct the broad policy affairs of the corporation in the best interests of the corporation. Boards must also meet at least once a year. Below the board of directors in the third tier are the three statutory officers—namely, the president, the secretary, and the treasurer, who are appointed by the board to run the company on a daily basis. Some large companies delegate some of the nonstatutory functions of the president to a chair of the board and a chief executive officer. Vice-presidents are optional. The fourth tier comprises the employees who are hired by the officers to fill the remaining roles in the business. Many corporations have a fifth tier that consists of creditors. Under the laws of creditors' rights, creditors may in certain circumstances have a direct say in the affairs of the company.

In a one-person corporation, the owner wears all the hats, serving as shareholder, director, officer, and employee. If this person lends his or her own money to the corporation, he or she becomes its creditor and may stand in line with other creditors if the corporation fails. The ability to be both a shareholder and an employee is important because dividends (i.e., the payments made by a corporation to a shareholder and which represent a return on the investment) are treated differently from salaries under the *Income Tax Act*.

One major respect in which corporations differ from sole proprietorships and partnerships is that the income, losses, assets, and liabilities of a corporation belong to the corporation, not the individual. The corporation files its own tax return. Tax planning within the context of a corporation can save investors large amounts of money. The limitation of liability and the ability to hold money in the corporation until it is needed are two great advantages of incorporation. Another advantage is that its legal position as a separate person from its owners means that its existence does not come to an end if the owners die or sell their shares.

Hospitality business owners, even those who expect that their business will lose money such that the losses can be netted against income from other sources, are generally better advised to incorporate their businesses in order to take advantage of limited liability and to effect a more professional public presentation.

Chains and Franchises

Many hospitality businesses are stand-alone, one-location enterprises. Others are chains, meaning that one owner operates several locations. Still others are **franchises** in which control is shared by the franchiser and the franchisee. A franchise is a business arrangement in which one party, the franchisee, obtains the benefits of the market development and goodwill of another party, the franchiser, in exchange for a fee. Typically, the franchisee owns the business location but must pay royalties and other fees to the franchiser and follow the business practices of the franchiser. Depending on the agreement, the fees may be a percentage of the gross revenues of the franchisee's business, or a flat fee independent of revenue, or some combination thereof. In many instances, the franchisee must also purchase the goods of the franchiser for resale. Some franchisees are little more than redistribution centres for the products of the franchiser. Others are relatively autonomous businesses that make use of little more than the well-known name and advertising programs of the franchiser.

Franchising allows franchisers to expand their market penetration without risking too much of their own capital. Franchisees are able to buy into a business that has a track record. Thus, the benefits are mutual. The parties enter into a franchise agreement that details the responsibilities of each party. The agreements are drafted by the franchisers in their favour, so it is essential that the franchisees have legal advice during the negotiations. The agreement sets the standards of business operation and determines how the royalties and other charges will be calculated and remitted. The agreement may specify that regular inspections will be held and that failure to pass them may result in penalties including loss of the franchise. The agreement may limit the franchisee to one location or may grant the franchisee exclusive rights to a territory with one or more outlets permitted. Some agreements allow the franchisee to grant subfranchises provided the consent of the franchiser is first obtained.

Brand name recognition is
one of the major advantages
of franchise operations.

C H O I C E   H O T E L S   C A N A D A ®

Some agreements are loosely drafted (usually because the franchiser does not want to be too beholden to the franchisee), but the majority are very detailed because the franchiser has built a reputation for quality that it is anxious to preserve. Less strict franchise arrangements occur when otherwise stand-alone businesses enter into royalty or licensing arrangements with national marketers and booking agencies. Best Western International does not own, operate, or manage any hotels or motels. It is primarily a referral agency to which members pay a fee for the marketing and booking services. However, to maintain its reputation and commercial viability, Best Western requires members to at least meet minimum standards.

There is no limit to the clauses and conditions that can be included in the franchise agreement and the disputes that can arise. Common bones of contention include the following:

- Extent, frequency, and quality of any training
- Extent, frequency, and quality of any advertising
- Details of the standard operating procedures
- Calculation of the franchise fee and royalty payments and the timing of the payments
- Extra charges such as management and advertising fees
- Exclusivity of the territory and right of first refusal for additional franchises
- Requirement to buy tied supplies from the franchisers
- Right to a fair price when buying tied supplies
- Right to buy supplies from outside suppliers
- Right to grant subfranchises
- Right to review the financial records and conduct operational inspections
- Rights upon breach of franchise agreement
- Conditions of termination of the agreement
- Notice, renewal, and option rights

P.P.H. v. N.F. (June 29, 1995, Doc. No. 166/91, Fleury J. (Ont. Gen. Div.))

The plaintiff sold frozen food franchises. The defendants were led to believe by the plaintiff's material that a store they intended to open would generate pretax income of $51,000. In August 1988, the defendants paid $15,000 of the $25,000 franchise fee. They were then informed that they would be required to raise financing of about $140,000, and that this amount did not include payment of the first and last months' rent and other closing expenses. The final amount due was substantially greater than the amount forecast by the franchiser. The store remained in operation for about a year. The franchisees finally realized that the store would never generate the revenue expected, and they abandoned the franchise. The franchiser sued to recover damages.

The court found that the forecast pretax income was not realistic. Such amounts had never been attained by even the most established franchise in the group. The statements made by the franchiser during the invitation to treat had been reckless and misleading. The action was dismissed and the contract rescinded. Normally, when a contract is rescinded, there is a return of some money, but not so in this case. The court found that the franchisees had acted negligently when they abandoned the store without notifying the franchiser. By the time the franchiser finally learned of the abandonment, the inventory was beyond recovery, resulting in unnecessary losses to the franchiser.

As this case illustrates, even when morality is on your side, you must behave in a commercially reasonable manner.

Buying a Hospitality Business

The vendor of a hospitality business invites interested buyers to submit an offer. The buyer prepares the offer and submits it to the vendor. Once the offer is submitted, it is out of the control of the buyer. No one should bind themselves to an offer until it has been reviewed by a lawyer; otherwise, the offer may be deficient, and the buyer may be bound to a bad bargain. A properly drafted agreement of purchase and sale is in the interests of all parties. The agreement should take into account, among other things, the following:

- Satisfactory review of the agreement by the buyer's lawyer
- Satisfactory review of the books and records by the buyer's financial adviser
- Satisfactory review of the ownership structure of the business
- Satisfactory review of title to the land, buildings, equipment, and other assets
- Vendor's pre-closing obligations such as disclosure and maintaining the business
- Vendor's post-closing obligations such as training, noncompetition, and confidentiality
- Rights to use the trade names, telephone numbers, and other intellectual properties
- Rights to transfer or assign licences, leases, and supply and other contracts
- Need for consents from the franchiser or licensers
- Zoning and regulatory compliance
- Union issues, and continuity of employees and key management personnel
- Lists of inventories, suppliers, and other business contacts
- Land and equipment leases
- Real and personal property encumbrances
- Existing or pending lawsuits, liabilities, and contractual obligations
- Disclosures of any defects relating to property, licensing, and other matters
- Risk allocation and insurance pending the closing of the transaction
- Rights to terminate the agreement with or without financial penalties

Agreements of purchase and sale may be either share purchases or asset purchases. Vendors sometimes prefer share purchases because the purchaser of the shares assumes all the assets and liabilities of the business. Purchasers sometimes prefer asset purchases because they can eliminate assets they do not want, sidestep liabilities attached to the shareholding of the business, and reap tax advantages by increasing the adjusted cost base of the assets for depreciation purposes. Goodwill is an asset. Within the purchase price, vendors tend to want a high value placed on goodwill so that they can sell the tangible assets at a low gain or at a loss. Purchasers tend to want a low value assigned to the goodwill in order to keep the adjusted cost base of the tangible assets high for depreciation purposes.

The purchase price may be payable in full on closing or in instalments. A lump-sum payment on closing is cleaner, but payments over time can benefit both parties by deferring the sale revenues for the vendor and reducing the up-front financing needed by the purchaser. As collateral for any instalment plan, the vendor may wish to take back a security interest in the assets of the business. Because of the tax and other consequences arising out of the agreement, both parties should seek professional advice before committing to the agreement.

Once the agreement has been negotiated and executed, numerous documents must be prepared, such as inventories, financial statements, financing documents, letters to suppliers and customers, corporate or partnership resolutions authorizing the sale, and sworn declarations by the vendor as to capacity, ownership, disclosure, informational accuracy, and the state of the business, the assets, and the liabilities. Before the transaction is finalized, various searches against the vendor and the business must be done, including the following:

- Corporate or other status of the vendor
- Real property title searches for ownership and encumbrances
- Personal property title searches for ownership and encumbrances
- Security interests under the federal *Bank Act*
- Writs of execution for judgments obtained in court
- Bankruptcy proceedings
- Employment and union contracts
- Pension or health benefit plans
- Income tax, CPP and EI remittances
- Workers' compensation and employer's health tax remittances as applicable
- Utility company accounts
- Provincial retail sales tax account
- Municipal tax account
- Municipal building and zoning requirements
- Licensing and other regulatory requirements
- Work orders issued by the municipality, fire department, environmental authority, etc.

Noncompetition/Nonsolicitation Clauses

Noncompetition and nonsolicitation provisions are commonly found in agreements of purchase and sale of businesses. Typically, a purchaser of a business will protect the competitive position of the business by including in the purchase agreement clauses that restrict the seller from competing with the business for a certain time and within a certain territory. Otherwise, sellers could reopen across the street and solicit their customers. The victim of a breach of such clauses may enforce them in court by seeking either an injunction restraining the offending party from competing, or damages for the loss of income from the increased competition, or both. However, the courts will not enforce unreasonable clauses. In *Elsley v. J.G. Collins Insurance (1976), 13 O.R. (2d) 177 (C.A.)*, the Court of Appeal addressed the issue as follows:

> The general rule is that clauses restricting the scope of a man's future business activities, whether contained in agreements of employment or of sale of a business, must be reasonable both between the parties and with reference to the public interest. Otherwise such a clause is unenforceable as being in restraint of trade and contrary to public policy. ... The old doctrine that any restraint on trade was void as against public policy must be balanced against the principle that the honouring of contractual obligations, freely entered into by parties bargaining on equal footing, is also in the public interest ... and the question whether a particular noncompetition agreement is void and unenforceable is one of law to be determined on a consideration of the character and nature of the business, the relationship of the parties and the relevant circumstances existing at the time the agreement was entered into. ... In cases dealing with sales transaction, the courts have been reluctant to interfere with restrictive covenants ... entered into by businessmen having a presumed equality of bargaining power. On the other hand, such clauses in employment agreements are carefully scrutinized and are frequently held unenforceable on the ground that they extend beyond the interest which the employer is properly entitled to protect. ... The generally accepted test as to which employees may be restrained is set out ... as those employees who will acquire not merely knowledge of customers, but in addition, influence over them: "A restraint is not valid unless the nature of the employment is such that customers will either learn to rely upon the skill or judgment of the servant or will deal with him directly and personally to the virtual exclusion of the master, with the result that he will probably gain the custom if he sets up business on his own account. (Cheshire and Fifoot, *Law of Contract*, 8th ed. (1972))

In *Elsley v. J.G. Collins Insurance, [1978] 2 S.C.R. 916*, the Supreme Court of Canada affirmed the judgment of the Court of Appeal, stating:

> A covenant in restraint is enforceable only if it is reasonable between the parties and with reference to the public interest. As in many of the cases which come before the courts, competing demands must be weighed. There is an important public interest in discouraging restraints on trade, and maintaining free and open competition unencumbered by the fetters of restrictive covenants. On the other hand, the courts have been disinclined to restrict the right to contract, particularly when that right has been exercised by knowledgeable persons of equal bargaining power. In assessing the opposing interests, the word one finds repeated throughout the cases is the word "reasonable." The test of reasonableness can be applied, however, only in the peculiar circumstances of the particular case. ...
>
> The distinction made in the cases between a restrictive covenant contained in an agreement for the sale of business and one contained in a contract of employment is well-conceived and responsive to practical considerations. A person seeking to sell his business might find himself with an unsaleable commodity if denied the right to assure the purchaser that he, the vendor, would not later enter into competition. Difficulty lies in definition of the time during which, and the area within which, the noncompetitive covenant is to operate, but if these are reasonable, the courts will normally give effect to the covenant.
>
> A different situation ... obtains in the negotiation of a contract of employment where an imbalance of bargaining power may lead to oppression and a denial of the right of the employee to exploit, following termination of employment, in the public interest and in his own interest, knowledge and skills obtained during employment. Again, a distinction is made. Although blanket restrictions on freedom to compete are generally held unenforceable, the courts have recognized and afforded reasonable protection to trade secrets, confidential information, and trade connections of the employer.

A noncompetition clause that is too restrictive will be severed from the agreement, leaving the purchaser with no remedy at all. What is or is not reasonable depends on the circumstances. A noncompetition clause that precludes a seller from carrying on a similar business anywhere in Canada for 50 years would in almost all cases be struck out. However, a large restricted territory and a lengthy restricted time may be reasonable if the business involves selling exclusive products or services to a thinly scattered clientele (e.g., providing helicopter skiing in the Canadian Rockies).

Financing a Hospitality Business

Unless the purchaser can pay cash to purchase the business, financing through a lender is usually necessary. Sources of financing include the owners themselves, banks and other institutional lenders, family and friends, stock market investors, and federal and provincial government programs. The federal government finances qualifying ventures through the Business Development Bank of Canada (BDBC) and through loan guarantees under the *Small Business Loans Act* for purchases of land, premises, and equipment. The provinces have their own programs. Government loans are generally available for ventures deemed worthwhile but too risky for the banks, which are answerable to their shareholders for the quality of their loans.

The lender will require evidence of the buyer's financial wherewithal before it will commit money to the venture. Typically, a satisfactory down payment and a viable business plan are needed. The lender will take a security interest in everything it can, from land mortgages to chattel mortgages to pledges of earnings to the personal assets of the buyers.

Once the business has been purchased, it will need operating capital to meet routine expenses (salaries, supplies, property taxes, and so forth) and extraordinary expenses such as a new roof or the installation of a pool. The operating capital will come from the receipts from guests, but more often than not, a line of credit with the bank will also be necessary to smooth the frequent lack of synchronicity between income and expenditure. As the business prospers, the mortgages will be reduced and eventually retired. The business will then be owned outright by the owners, subject possibly to any security given for a continuing line of credit.

It is a serious error to undercapitalize a business acquisition. Without proper funding, the business faces an uphill struggle to survive. A purchaser is better advised to purchase a less expensive business with adequate capitalization than to overextend on a more costly venture. Once the original ownership or shareholding has been settled, there are three methods by which a business can raise additional financing.

1. Increasing the equity in the business. To raise equity financing, the business may sell more shares or partnership interests in the business to the existing or new shareholders or partners. Alternatively, one or more of the existing shareholders or partners may sell shares or partnership interests to existing or new investors. A new shareholders' or partnership agreement should be negotiated upon each equity infusion. The advantages of equity financing lie in not having to deal with outside lenders and in not having to pay a return on the investment for a period of time (in some cases indefinite). The disadvantages of equity financing are that the existing shareholders or limited partners may be placing more of their personal money at risk, and that the ownership may become more widely held, with an accompanying loss of control or independence.

2. Increasing the debt of the business. To raise debt financing, the business must obtain a loan from a lender. The advantage of debt financing is that once the debt has been retired, the owners are no longer beholden to a creditor and they

have not given up control over a percentage of the business. The disadvantages of debt financing include the following:

- Payments usually begin immediately, affecting the cash flow of the business.
- The interest rate will vary depending on the economic climate and the perceived risk of the business (pubs, bars, taverns, and restaurants are considered to be risky ventures; accommodation business and travel agencies somewhat less so).
- The loan may involve conditions that the owners may find intrusive.
- The loan may involve pledging business assets as collateral for repayment.
- The lender may require personal guarantees from the major owners, which for shareholders and limited partners greatly lessens the benefits of a limited liability.
- If the assets of the business and the personal guarantees of the owners are insufficient to secure the loan, the owners may be forced to obtain the personal guarantees of outsiders such as spouses and prosperous relatives.
- The lender will be less likely than the owners to ride out difficult periods and more likely to require repayment of the loan at an inopportune time.
- Various assets of the business may be lost if the lender is able to exercise any rights to retain or sell the collateral.

3. Selling assets of the business. Assets that may be sold include fixed assets, inventory, such rights as territorial rights, franchises, and subfranchises, such intellectual property rights as trademarks and copyrights, and even entire divisions, subsidiaries, and business opportunities. The business may also sell at a discount its accounts receivable to a company that then takes on the risk of collecting the receivables—the higher the risk of nonpayment, the higher the discount. This is called factoring. The advantage of a sale of assets is that the business need not dilute the ownership or deal with lenders. However, sales are generally more public than debt or equity financing. Unless the sale is for market or strategic purposes, the sale may be regarded by observers as a sign that the business is in financial difficulty, especially in the case of factoring.

Each method of financing discussed in this section has distinctive tax and other consequences. It is essential that a business have a full understanding of all the implications before entering into any financing arrangement. (See also Chapter 3 (The Law of Contracts).)

Property

Property is almost always a valuable asset and is subject to a huge number of laws, statutory and common. Property is divided into (1) **real property**, which is further divided into real estate (land) and fixtures (buildings attached to the land and items affixed to the buildings); and (2) personal property, which is further divided into **chattels** and intangibles (rights such as contractual entitlements, financial paper such as stocks and bonds, and intellectual property such as trademarks and goodwill).

The distinction between fixtures and chattels is best illustrated by examples. Ceiling lamps, wall-to-wall carpeting, curtain rods, built-in dishwashers, hood fans, and shelving brackets are all fixtures. Floor lamps, area rugs, curtains, rollaway dishwashers, stoves, and shelf boards sitting on brackets are examples of chattels. An aluminum shed sitting on the ground without a foundation is a chattel. A mobile home still on wheels is a chattel, whereas a mobile home bolted to concrete blocks set into the ground is a fixture. In essence, a fixture is anything that is affixed to the building or is an integral part of the building, including the building itself and other structures attached to the land. Everything else is a chattel. In Quebec, the distinction is between movables and immovables.

Failure to properly acquire or adequately protect one's interests in property can result in heavy losses. In advance of any purchase or leasing of land on which to operate a hospitality business, it is essential that the property issues be investigated. It may be that a prospective hospitality operator is interested in buying a vacant lot and building a motel on it. If the property is not or cannot be zoned for that use, or if there are restrictive covenants or easements that materially interfere with the proposed use of the property, the acquisition of the land may be an expensive mistake. Investigation of property issues is also necessary in advance of any purchase or leasing of equipment and other chattels.

Real Property

Ownership

Some hospitality businesses are located on land owned by the business. The outright owner of land has a freehold interest in the land and fixtures. The evidence of the ownership is a deed registered on the title at the local land registry office. In some jurisdictions, the deed is called a transfer. Freehold is the highest form of ownership, but carries with it the highest form of responsibility. The owner must pay all property taxes and maintain the property in good condition or suffer the loss of value as the property deteriorates. If the fair market value falls, the investment will decline through no fault of the owner. Values may fall to below the original purchase price. Like other forms of ownership, land ownership is inherently more risky than renting; thus, owners are justly entitled to the greater rewards that ownership can bring.

Adverse Possession

Title to land may also be acquired by an unregistered party who possesses the land adverse to the interest of the registered owner for at least 10 years (20 years in the case of easements). Title to land may be lost in exactly the same manner. In order for a claim of adverse possession to succeed, the adverse possession must exhibit the following characteristics:

1. *Open and notorious.* The possessor may not possess the land in secret but must do so openly so that the adverse possession will become known to the owner.

2. *Unchallenged.* The owner must be aware of the possession and allow it to continue without asserting rights of ownership (e.g., by giving a warning).

3. *Exclusive.* The possessor must be the only nonowner in possession; there cannot be competing claims of adverse possession.

4. *Continuous.* If before the required time period has elapsed the possessor interrupts the possession or the owner asserts ownership rights, the claim for adverse possession will fail.

When a fence is erected in the wrong location, one neighbour may eventually acquire title to the part of the neighbouring land lying inside the fence and the registered owner eventually loses title to it. Acquiring title by adverse possession in this manner can occur only with respect to land that is registered under the *Registry Act*. Land that is registered under land titles or similar legislation cannot be gained or lost by adverse possession.

Easements and Rights of Way

An **easement** is a right enjoyed by one landowner over the land of another landowner for a specific purpose. The dominant tenement is the land enjoying the benefit; the servient tenement is the land that is subject to the easement. In Quebec, an easement is called a servitude. Examples of easements include a right-of-way over the servient tenement to and from the dominant tenement, a right to effect repairs for dwellings that share common walls, a right to install and repair utility services, and the right to have an eavestrough hang over another's property. Easements may be given by registered grants or may be acquired by 20 years' adverse possession for land not registered under land titles or similar legislation.

Restrictive Covenants

Restrictive covenants run with the land, which is to say they are registered against the title and bind the owner to their terms. Provided they are not void for being against public policy, they are enforceable. A covenant not to sell the land to persons of a particular race is obviously void. Covenants restrict a wide variety of matters, from changing the drainage slope of land to planting fast-growing trees. If the covenant is unduly restrictive, a court may terminate it.

Zoning

Zoning bylaws are, in effect, municipally imposed restrictive covenants. The bylaw prevents the owner from using the land except in accordance with the bylaw. For example, the bylaw may prohibit construction of a structure of more than five storeys or confine the use of the land to residential. In the case of the former example, a hotel higher than five storeys could not be built; in the case of the latter example, a hotel could not be built or operated at all.

Mortgages

Real property can be given as security for a money loan. The documentary evidence of the debt is called a **mortgage** (old French for "dead bet," as in "I bet I'll pay you back, and if I do, the debt is dead"). It is registered against the title to the land so that anyone else who might be considering lending the landowner some money can verify how many other lenders already have a security interest in the land. It is pointless to lend money on a mortgage where the loan exceeds the realizable value of the land and the costs of collecting on the mortgage. The person borrowing the money is the **mortgagor** because he is giving his land as the security. The person lending the money is the **mortgagee** because she is receiving the land as security. A first mortgagee enjoys more security than a second mortgagee who enjoys more security than a third mortgagee, and so on. Because the risks rise for subsequent mortgages, so do the interest rates. When a mortgage is registered, it becomes an encumbrance to the title.

Except for interest-only mortgages, a mortgage payment is a blend of principal and interest. In contrast to rental payments, which are made in advance, mortgage payments are made in arrears such that a payment due on May 1 pays for the interest on the debt for April plus a contribution toward the principal. Each payment reduces the total debt. Thus, every successive payment features slightly less interest and slightly more principal. The period required to retire the principal in full at a constant interest rate is called the amortization (French for "toward the death") period and is typically 25 years, although it can be any finite period. Most lenders will not guarantee an interest rate for more than a few years. The guaranteed period is called the "term." Hence, a mortgage can have a 15-year amortization and a three-year term. At the end of the term, the mortgage must be repaid or renegotiated. Some mortgage interest rates float—that is, they fluctuate with another rate such as the lender's prime rate or the Bank of Canada prime rate plus a few percentage points. A fixed rate offers certainty; a floating rate offers the opportunity of a better rate and the risk of a worse one.

Upon sufficient default (failure to make the mortgage payments by a deadline), the mortgagee has various remedies, the most important of which are:

1. *Foreclosure,* or taking over the land in lieu of recovering the balance of the debt.

2. *Power of sale*, or selling the land at fair market value. The mortgagor is entitled to any amount remaining after payment of the principal, interest, and proper costs of the sale. The mortgagor may convert a foreclosure action into a power of sale.

3. *Action on the covenant.* If there is a shortfall after the sale, the mortgagee may sue for the difference on the mortgagor's personal covenant in the mortgage.

4. *Taking possession* of the property and seizing the rents and other property receipts. The mortgagee must behave in a commercially reasonable fashion and render an accounting for all monies received.

5. *Seizing and selling by public auction* ("distraining") the chattels of the mortgagor until the debt is repaid. "To distrain" is "to seize goods under distress." Such goods as tools of trade and necessities of life such as clothing are exempt.

Upon repayment, the mortgagor is entitled to a signed discharge from the mortgagee that is registered to clear the title. In some jurisdictions, the mortgage is called a charge.

Land Liens

Under mechanics' or construction **lien** legislation, a supplier or worker who has supplied goods or performed services on or in respect of land and fixtures may register a lien against the title if the owner or tenant fails to pay for the goods or services. If the lien is not preserved by proper registration (e.g., in Ontario, within 45 days of substantial (97 percent) completion of the work), the right to preserve is lost. A preserved lien must be perfected, in Ontario, within 90 days of substantial completion of the work, or the right to sue under the lien legislation will be lost. Failure to meet the deadlines limits the supplier or worker to ordinary civil court remedies. The right to a **land lien** is valuable because it is easier to seek lien remedies than civil court remedies. Another advantage is that the land is not going anywhere, whereas other assets that might be attachable by the claimant following a regular civil court action may be moved or sold.

Real Property Leases

A lease, whether for real or personal property, is a contract whereby the owner (lessor) of the property gives the renter (lessee) the right to use the property for a period of time in exchange for rent. Hospitality businesses that do not own their own land and premises must rent them from a landowner. The renter has a leasehold interest. The landowner has a freehold interest and is entitled to the return of the land at the end of the lease. The terms landlord or lessor and tenant or lessee are often used interchangeably. Commercial leases are almost invariably in writing. They may be registered on the title, but most contain a clause stating that they will not be registered. A periodic tenancy may run daily, weekly, monthly, or yearly. A tenancy at will occurs where there is no certain tenancy period, or where the tenant is overholding after the certain period has expired. Commercial lease terms are entirely negotiable by the parties. By contrast, many residential lease terms such as notice periods are set by statute and cannot be varied by contract. The remedies of a residential landlord for a breach of the lease are substantially curtailed by law. It is no picnic being a residential landlord.

A commercial lease is often lengthy because it must cover a wide range of terms and circumstances. The lease should be conditional on such matters as securing adequate financing, ensuring that satisfactory inspections have been performed, and obtaining any applicable governmental licences or approvals. Some of the terms of the lease include:

- The starting date of the lease
- The length (or term) of the lease
- The starting date of the rent
- The amount of the rent and any other charges, including cost-of-living provisions
- Location of the premises and guarantees of visibility, such as in a mall
- Permissible uses of the premises and exclusivity of the use
- Penalties for failing to pay or for abandonment, bankruptcy, failing to insure, and selling substantially all of the tenant's assets
- Responsibility for taxes, utilities, insurance, repairs, and maintenance
- Responsibility for conforming to building codes and other licensing requirements
- Rights in the event of fire or other damage
- Rights to sublet or assign the lease
- Rights of renewal, notice, and termination

An offer to lease is a short document that typically binds the tenant to the provisions, sight unseen, of the landlord's standard lease. Once the offer to lease is signed, it may not be possible to amend the terms of the standard lease. No tenant should sign an offer to lease or standard lease without first obtaining legal advice. A person who signs a commercial offer to lease or standard lease is almost always regarded by the courts as a businessperson who intended to be bound by the terms of the document. It is no picnic being a commercial tenant.

With respect to franchises, many franchisers insist that they be entered as the tenant in the lease. This gives them greater control and allows them to replace the franchisee without jeopardizing the lease. In such a case, the franchisee is the subtenant of the franchiser.

Tenants do not normally have the right to withhold rent in the event of a breach of the lease by the landlord. Instead, they must sue for damages. If the tenant can be adequately compensated by an award of damages, the lease will continue in effect; otherwise, the court may terminate the lease. Upon sufficient default of payment by the tenant under the lease, a landlord may obtain a court order for repossession of the premises, sue for back rent and costs, or distrain against the nonexempt goods of the tenant on the premises provided the landlord has demanded payment in writing and has distrained in the daylight and on weekdays without force. The landlord may distrain only if the tenant has not gone bankrupt. Upon an assignment or petition into bankruptcy, the landlord's claim is (1) limited to the arrears of rent during the three months preceding the assignment or petition, and (2) subordinate to the claims of the tenant's other creditors having a higher priority in law, such as secured creditors.

Termination of the lease may occur pursuant to the lease automatically at the end of the term or upon notice as set forth in the lease. It may also occur in response to a serious breach of the lease; or by frustration, a situation whereby the premises are destroyed through no fault of the party wishing to terminate; or the insolvency or bankruptcy of the tenant. In the case of bankruptcy, the trustee may step into the shoes of the tenant and continue to honour the lease; this is often done for hotels and restaurants because the trustee wishes to maintain the business presence and goodwill while searching for buyers.

At the end of the lease, the landlord may be entitled to the fixtures. If an innkeeper leases vacant land and constructs an inn on it, the building will belong to the landlord at the end of the lease. The inn is said to be an improvement to the land. If the lease specifies that the land must be returned in its pre-lease condition, the innkeeper may be liable for the cost of demolishing the inn and restoring the land. In this circumstance, the inn is said to be a waste to the land. Whether a change to land is an improvement or a waste often depends on the needs and perspectives of the parties and the provisions of their contract. A commercial tenant may retain any fixtures that can be removed without causing any material damage to the premises.

Personal Property

Chattels and Chattel Mortgages

Chattels are items of physical personal property that are not attached to or an integral part of the land or the buildings. At the end of a lease, they remain the property of the chattel owner. A chattel mortgage is a document in which chattels are given as security for a loan. Evidence of the security interest may be filed under provincial personal property security legislation. The filing requirements are highly technical. Even trivial defects may invalidate the filing. A subsequent security interest holder who did not learn of the prior interest due to a filing defect will prevail against the prior interest holder. If the chattel mortgagor has no other assets, the prior chattel mortgagee may have no recourse. Sometimes the chattels are not specific or fixed, such as dishwashers and turbines, but are items of inventory that are sold and replenished quickly, such as trinkets in a gift shop. In such a case, the chattel mortgage is a "floating charge" that floats above the inventory, allowing it to be sold and replenished, but swooping down and immobilizing the inventory still in stock upon default.

Intangibles

Intangibles are neither real property nor chattels but include such things as shares in a company, debt instruments, goodwill in a business, trademark ownership, rights to insurance proceeds, rights under a contract, and so on. "Chattel paper" is sometimes used as a term to describe debt instruments, bonds, shares, and other paper proofs of financial ownership.

Equipment Leases

Instead of buying a chattel and using it as security for a financing loan, a business may prefer simply to lease the equipment. At the end of the lease, the equipment reverts to the owner.

Conditional Sales Contracts

Instead of leasing a chattel (e.g., kitchen equipment) with a reversion to the lessor at the end of the lease, a business may prefer to acquire ownership of the equipment at the end of the payment period either as of right or upon payment of a final lump sum. Such an arrangement is called a conditional sales contract.

Chattel Liens

A person who repairs or stores chattel property is entitled to be paid and has a lien against the chattels until payment is made. Each jurisdiction has slightly different laws that provide and regulate this right. The right is not absolute, but depends partly on the circumstances of the work or storage and partly on the degree to which the chattel is a necessity for the owner.

Trademarks

Trademarks are intangible intellectual property. A trademark is a symbol, word, name, or device adopted to identify a company or its product. Businesses operate under a name and style. Recognition of the name and style and the willingness of patrons to recommend the business constitute the goodwill of the business. Goodwill is an asset on the balance sheet that may be more valuable than the fixed assets. The golden arch logo of McDonald's is one of the best-known trademarks in the food, or any, business. Holiday Inn uses a star-like symbol that evokes decent, affordable accommodation. The names Hilton and Ritz evoke luxury accommodation. Other hotels may not use slightly altered versions of these and other trademarks in order to take business away from their competitors. The importance of trademarks is not restricted to international chains. Businesses in local markets also depend on reputations that have become established over time. They may also enjoy trademark protection. Some brand names are so popular that they have become synonymous with the product itself. Kleenex, Xerox, Coke, and Ski-Doo are just a few examples. Competitors are prevented by law from using these and other famous brand names. For example, John Deere sells snowmobiles, not Ski-Doos, and Procter & Gamble sells tissues, not Kleenex.

Registration and Protection of Trademarks

Businesses should protect their goodwill and name, style, and logo by obtaining a trademark from Industry Canada upon meeting the requirements of the federal *Trade Marks Act*. The owner of the trademark is granted exclusive use of it throughout Canada, and may obtain injunctions enjoining others from using it or a mark confusingly similar to it. Trademarks must be registered and guarded in every country in which the company intends to do business. Some large companies have full-time trademark departments. The following case illustrates an improper attempt by one company to disguise itself as another company in the same field.

Holiday Inns, Inc. v. Holiday Inn, 364 F. Supp. 775 (S.C., 1973)

The Holiday Inn Corporation of Tennessee, one of the world's largest hotel chains, was the plaintiff. The defendant was a hotel called Holiday Inn that operated in Myrtle Beach, South Carolina. The plaintiff in the case made the following charges:

1. The defendant adopted and used a sign substantially similar to the registered "Great Sign" logo of the plaintiff.

2. The defendant used a mark ("Your Host on the Coast") similar to the registered mark of the plaintiff ("Your Host from Coast to Coast").

3. Items 1 and 2 were likely to cause confusion, mistake, and deception among customers of hotel services in the Myrtle Beach area of South Carolina.

4. Items 1 and 2 constituted a trademark infringement.

The court's findings were as follows:

1. The plaintiff was founded in 1952 and operates 1300 facilities in the United States; the state of South Carolina is home to 33 of these facilities. The operations are either owned outright or franchised.

2. The plaintiff's original concept was to establish a chain of hotels and restaurants of dependable quality across the U.S. Chain members were easily identifiable by such common features as free cribs, free accommodation for children under 12 staying in their parents' room, kennels, and a standard credit card affiliation.

3. All facilities in the chain use the "Great Sign." The sign is large and has a green background. The words "Holiday Inn" appear in large, distinctive script. A large star is located at the top of the sign, and smaller stars surround the name. A large orange arrow points the way to the inn.

4. One of the slogans used in advertisements is, "Your Host from Coast to Coast."

5. The aforementioned marks appear in countless advertisements and promotions, as well as in over 10 million chain directories. The marks are all registered.

6. The defendant was incorporated in 1960 and operates one hotel with 87 units.

7. The plaintiff first learned of the defendant in 1966 when a franchisee of the plaintiff received a letter from the defendant's lawyer objecting to the use of the franchisee's name in the Myrtle Beach area. The franchisee, operating as the Holiday Lodge, had received permission from the plaintiff to use the name. The words "Holiday Inns of America System" appeared in large script above its sign.

8. In 1968, the defendant hired a signwright to build a sign that would resemble, but not duplicate, the sign used by the plaintiff. The signs are so similar that the public could easily mistake the defendant for a franchisee of the plaintiff.

9. Over the years during which the parties have been in simultaneous operation, countless pieces of mail and reservations were delivered to the wrong party.

10. The defendant nurtured the confusion in order to profit from the plaintiff's name and the goodwill associated with it.

The test for trademark infringement is whether or not it is likely that an ordinary consumer who has previously been exposed to the old mark would be likely to confuse it with the new mark. The court concluded that there was compelling evidence that the defendant was guilty of trademark infringement. The court ordered that:

1. the defendant be restrained from using any sign, script, slogan, star design, colour combination, or other indicia tending to suggest a link with the plaintiff;

2. the defendant be given 90 days to provide proof of compliance; and

3. the defendant be allowed to continue to operate under the name "Holiday Inn" within the town of Myrtle Beach, South Carolina.

McDonald's Corp. v. C.H. Stores Ltd. (June 5, 1996, Doc. No. A-278-94 Ottawa, Marceau, Hugessen and Decary JJ. (Fed. C.A.))

The defendant sought to register the name "McBeans" as a trademark for a business that intended to sell tea and coffee makers, grinders, teas, and coffee beans. McDonald's Corporation opposed the registration of the name. The Trial Division ruled against McDonald's, which subsequently appealed. The Appeal Division agreed with the prior decision. The justices did not find that the defendant had any intent to enter the fast-food restaurant business. Further, the justices stated, "[We] do not think that [McDonald's] claim to monopoly can be extended to the use of these syllables when used as separate words either alone or in combinations with other words." The two businesses were not competing with each other and therefore the public would not conclude that there was a connection between them. McDonald's Corporation could not be given a monopoly on the syllables in its name. The similarity was allowed.

Most cases of trademark infringement are concluded before court action is required. General Motors Corporation, which owns all rights to versions of the name "Chevrolet," moved quickly to stop a roadhouse in Ottawa, Ontario, from using the name "Chevy's."

The roadhouse continued its business under a new name. Given the number of lawsuits stemming from drinking and driving, one can understand why General Motors would not want the public to associate its vehicles with a liquor-serving business. Wise corporations protect their goodwill.

The names, signatures, and likenesses of well-known persons may also be protected by trademark registration. Anyone wishing to use the name must obtain the permission of the owner of the name, who will usually require a fee or royalty for the use of the name. The owner of the name may not be the well-known person. A celebrity can sell the use of the name to another person. Upon the owner's death, ownership of the name is assumed by another person, either the estate or a purchaser of the right.

Statutory Protection of Trademarks

Under the federal *Trade Marks Act*, the following are prohibited:

- The use of false or misleading statements that discredit the business, wares, or services of a competitor
- The use of words or symbols that suggest royal or governmental approval
- The use of the signature or likeness of any person who is living or has died within the last 30 years unless the consent of the person, or the consent of the estate of the deceased person, has been obtained
- The use of a trademark confusingly similar to the registered trademark of a registrant
- Holding out a business in a manner likely to cause confusion with another business in the minds of reasonable members of the public (a tort called passing off)

Passing Off

A trademark, whether registered or not, may be enforced under the common law with a suit against an unauthorized user for the tort of passing off. To obtain injunctive relief and damages, the plaintiff must demonstrate five elements, namely, that there has been:

1. a misrepresentation, even if it is innocent,
2. made by the defendant trader in the course of trade,
3. to prospective customers of the defendant trader or to ultimate consumers of goods or services supplied by the defendant trader,
4. which has a reasonably foreseeable consequence of injuring the goodwill of the plaintiff trader, and
5. which actually injures the business or goodwill of the plaintiff trader or will probably do so.

In the case of a registered trademark, the first person to register will enjoy protection of the trademark against any other potential registrant. In the case of an unregistered trademark, to be successful at trial, the plaintiff must establish usage of the trademark prior to the usage of the trademark by the defendant.

Dino's Place Ltd. v. Corfu Restaurant Ltd., Geordino Restaurant Ltd. et al. (1991), 36 C.P.R. (3d) 146 (B.C.S.C.)

The plaintiff was a restaurant franchise company with outlets in Vancouver and Victoria operating under the name "Dino's Place." The defendant had operated one of the restaurants as a franchise, but when the franchise agreement came to an end, the defendant continued to operate under the name "Geordino Family Restaurant." In court, the plaintiff pointed out the following similarities between the two operations:

1. The name "Geordino" was similar to and in the same format as "Dino's Place."
2. The name "Geordino's" on one of the outdoor signs was even more similar.
3. Geordino's phone number was the same as the old restaurant's number.
4. The new restaurant went to some length to appear to be still associated with the old restaurant. Advertisements stated that the restaurant was formerly Dino's, and had been at the same location under the same management for ten years.
5. The logo, which featured two classic pillars with crowns on top, was similar to the pillars-and-fire symbol used by Dino's.

Geordino's owner testified that the name "Geordino" was derived from her husband's name, "George." The court found little connection between the names "Dino's Place" and "Geordino Family Restaurant," and noted that the use of pillars in logos is common among Mediterranean-style restaurants. However, the court found that the name and logo in combination with the same phone number and the description in the advertisements would lead reasonable people to think that the restaurant was another Dino's franchise, albeit with a somewhat different name. The owners of the Dino's franchise had not registered the name as a trademark, but they did operate a successful franchise under that name and had developed the type of reputation with which the owners of Geordino wanted to be associated without paying a franchise fee. Geordino did what it could to pass itself off as a Dino's restaurant, to the financial detriment of Dino's. The court found Geordino liable for the tort of passing off. The court held that the misrepresentation could cause financial loss to Dino's and ordered Geordino to change the telephone number immediately and to stop advertising any connection with Dino's.

Marketing and Public Relations

The public presentation of a commercial establishment will often dictate the type of consumer who chooses to go there. The property should be clean and safe. Patrons should feel welcome and comfortable. Unlike good maintenance, bad maintenance is almost always noticed. Owners and staff should at all times have good manners, use common courtesy, dress and speak well, and convey a positive attitude. Leadership by owners and management is essential; past success is no guarantee of future success.

A business may improve its bottom line either by decreasing costs or by increasing revenues. Decreasing costs is a matter of sound fiscal management. Increasing revenues is a matter of sound overall management and successful marketing, both direct and indirect. Direct marketing includes signs, brand-name recognition, business cards, brochures, newsletters, and advertising. For many accommodation businesses, marketing consists of being in the right location at the right time with a sign designed to alert passersby. For weary highway travellers, few sights are more welcome than a "Vacancy" sign. For other accommodation businesses, marketing consists of having a well-known name. People who stay at the Hilton or Holiday Inn for the first time may do so because they are familiar with the name. Such hotels have built loyal clienteles and could probably survive on repeats and referrals for years to come if they arrested all direct marketing initiatives. For many establishments, however, direct advertising is essential to survival. Even the Hilton chain would slowly and inexorably lose market share to its competitors if it abandoned direct marketing. Other forms of direct marketing include promotions such as enrolling repeat guests in reward clubs. Some hotels offer points programs, similar to air-mile programs, in which points may be accumulated and redeemed for upgrades, free nights, meals, or event tickets. Customers can be put off by an overly complex points program; hotels should make the programs as user-friendly as possible.

♦ The federal *Competition Act* prohibits misleading advertising and provides stiff penalties for transgressions, especially for factual misrepresentations. There is still wide latitude for trumpeting the features of the establishment, especially in the form of an expression of opinion.

Indirect marketing includes good service, attractive amenities, and word of mouth. The best marketing tool is good service. Bad service repels more customers than good service attracts. In fact, an essential component of good service is avoiding bad service. Guests who are happy with the service will be inclined to return. If these contented guests recommend the hotel to family and friends, the hotel will reap the added benefit of favourable word of mouth.

Hybrids of direct and indirect marketing include sponsoring charitable events and participating in community endeavours. Whether the business chooses to sponsor a Terry Fox run or help organize a Second Harvest food program, the payback in terms of goodwill will be immeasurable. More subtle benefits are derived from the teamwork and accomplishment that management and staff generate.

Insurance

The purpose of insurance is to protect the insured against an onerous loss by spreading the cost of a given risk among a group of similarly affected parties. Each member of the group pays a premium, which is a fraction of the total cost of the assessed risk. The premium is calculated to cover the operating expenses and profit margin of the insurer, and the costs of the small number of members in the group who do suffer the losses associated with the risk.

Insurance companies are the primary source of insurance. Another source is agricultural cooperatives in which farmers band together to take advantage of bulk buying and to protect each other against crop and other losses. A third source is industry-funded compensation programs such as the travel compensation fund. This program has lowered many of the risks associated with the travel industry and elevated the industry's public image.

All the provinces and territories have an insurance Act that sets forth the conditions of an insurance policy or contract. The Acts state that certain provisions must be printed in every policy and that no subsequent variations, omissions, or additions shall bind the insured. The Acts also state that the provisions cannot be waived in whole or in part unless the waiver clearly states the terms and is duly signed. In addition, the Acts set forth requirements for the renewal of insurance contracts and protect the insured from unjust stipulations and exclusions.

The hospitality and travel industries are subject to horrendous potential liabilities, some of which stem from:

1. the duties owed to guests, invitees, licensees, the public, and even trespassers;

2. the nature of such physical assets as boilers, swimming pools, and marble floors;

3. the nature of the services provided, such as food and alcohol service;

4. the large numbers of members of the public who use or visit the premises; and

5. the large and revolving number of employees.

Insurance must be part of the business's financial protection plan. Deductibles are an effective way to reduce the cost of insurance. Higher deductibles produce lower premiums, but also lower payouts. If a high deductible would hinder a business from recovering from a loss, then the deductible may have to be reduced. From time to time, the insured should review the amount of compensation required to adequately protect the business. Insured property is generally replaced at a depreciated value. In the case of a housekeeper's uniform that was purchased for $75 and subsequently damaged in a fire, the insurance payout will be very low compared to the cost of purchase. Replacement-cost policies help to defray the cost of depreciation, but they tend to feature higher premiums.

Types of Insurance

Listed below are the most common types of insurance coverage:

- Public liability insurance for injuries to the person and property of guests, patrons, employees, and other members of the public.

- Fire insurance. The protection normally covers the building and contents. Some losses, such as medical expenses or losses of property belonging to others, may not be covered. Expanded protection can be purchased to cover some of these items.

- Automobile insurance for a wide variety of vehicles from delivery trucks to snowblowers.

- Driver's insurance.

- Plate-glass insurance.

- Business-interruption insurance for loss of business and profit.

- Event insurance for liabilities (such as ticket refunds) arising out of the cancellation of an event or performance that was to take place on the premises.

- Theft (the simple taking of someone else's property), burglary (theft following break and entry), and robbery (theft with violence or weapons) insurance for nonemployees.

- Fidelity insurance (bonding) for theft or criminal behaviour by employees.

- Directors' and officers' liability insurance to protect against claims of bad management.

- Key-person life and disability insurance. The success of many companies depends on key employees. Their death or disability can greatly affect a company's financial health and even its chances of survival. The risks can be lessened by taking out a life insurance policy on the key person, naming the company as beneficiary. The money may be used to tide the company over until a new key person has been engaged, or it may be used to buy from the estate the shares owned by the deceased.

- Employee insurance. Many companies offer employees health insurance that goes beyond the provincial health plans by extending to such things as dentistry, extended health care, long-term disability, parental leave, and sick leave. Such insurance is often paid for by contributions made jointly by the employer and the employee.

- Statutory insurance. There are statutory insurances for which an employer must remit employer and employee contributions. These include employment insurance, worker's compensation, and health insurance, which are discussed in Chapter 14.

- Travel insurance for trip cancellations. Compensation funds may provide this insurance.
- Weather insurance for damage caused by natural phenomena such as storms.
- Environmental insurance for losses resulting from natural contamination (e.g., sulphur in the drinking water) or man-made pollution (e.g., leaks from buried service station gas tanks).
- Other insurable losses as may be applicable.

Reporting Claims

After an insured person has suffered an insured loss, he or she must follow certain steps as required by the terms of the policy or by statute. The following excerpt is from a fire insurance policy, but similar requirements exist for most insured losses.

1. Upon the occurrence of any loss of or damage to the insured property, the insured shall, if such loss or damage is covered by the contract,

   (a) forthwith give notice thereof in writing to the insurer,

   (b) deliver as soon as practicable to the insurer a proof of loss verified by a statutory declaration,

      (i) giving a complete inventory of the destroyed and damaged property and showing in detail quantities, costs, actual cash value and particulars of the amount of loss claimed;

      (ii) stating when and how the loss occurred, and if caused by fire or explosion due to ignition, how the fire or explosion originated, so far as the insured knows or believes;

      (iii) stating the loss did not occur though any willful act or neglect or the procurement, means or connivance of the insured;

      (iv) showing the amount of other insurances and the names of other insurers;

      (v) showing the interest of the insured and of all others in the property with particulars of all liens, encumbrances and other charges upon the property;

      (vi) showing any changes in title, use, occupation, location, possession or exposures of the property since the issue of the contract; and

      (vii) showing the place where the property insured was at the time of the loss;

   (c) if required, give a complete inventory of undamaged property showing in detail quantities, cost and actual cash value;

   (d) if required and if practicable, produce books of account, warehouse receipts and stock lists, and furnish invoices and other vouchers verified by statutory declaration, and furnish a copy of the written portion of any other contract.

Fraudulent Claims

Each of the provincial insurance Acts states that any fraud or willfully false statement in a statutory declaration in relation to any of the particulars of the loss shall vitiate (erase) the claim of the person making the declaration. Under the fraud provisions in the *Criminal Code of Canada*, an insured may face criminal prosecution for making false insurance claims. Provisions against fraud are also found in the policies themselves. If an insured deliberately overstates the value of the property lost or stolen, the policy may be voided. If an insured intentionally starts the fire, insurance will not cover the loss. If the fire is started with criminal intent, the insured may be charged with the crime of arson. If death results from the fire, the insured may be charged with murder or manslaughter.

Prevention of Claims

While insurance lessens the financial impact of a loss, it does not always restore the business to its former stature. The insurance may cover the financial loss, but the community may lose confidence in the company if it was not sufficiently prepared for the disaster. Insurance does not replace effective management and staff training, and an abiding concern for the safety of staff, guests, neighbours, and property. Standard operating procedures and safety measures should be in place and followed; however, even the best management and strongest commitment to accident prevention cannot guarantee that insurance will never be needed. Hospitality businesses should periodically review their insurance situation with an insurance professional to ensure that their protection is still adequate in light of such factors as renovations, equipment acquisitions, changes in the law of duty of care, and damage awards.

E-Commerce Considerations

Marketing on the Internet is becoming increasingly important and useful, but serious issues remain to be resolved. For example, the Internet compromises a person's privacy to some extent and exposes one's cyber-information to security breaches. Further, one is never really sure of the identity, location, and *bona fides* of the other cyber-party. The Canadian Association of Internet Providers and the Canadian Marketing Association have developed voluntary codes of conduct. Governments are helping to create enforceable standards of conduct by amending existing legislation such as the federal *Competition Act* and by enacting new legislation such as (1) the federal *Personal Information Protection and Electronic Documents Act*, which requires that consent be obtained for the collection, use, or disclosure of personal information; and (2) the *Electronic Commerce Act* of Ontario discussed in Chapter 3.

Businesses must take reasonable steps to protect themselves from vandals, viruses, and hackers—for example, by having secure business premises; using up-to-date anti-virus programs, anti-worm programs, and intrusion detection systems; installing firewalls where applicable, backing up data including laptop data on a regular basis; storing backed-up data in safe off-site locations; changing passwords frequently especially when disgruntled employees leave; and monitoring the use of computers and their whereabouts. Businesses should also consider insurance for damage to hardware, software, and electronic records information, and for economic losses such as information theft and inability to serve customers.

Websites should be easy to find and navigate, current, uncluttered, and informative without being wordy. For many consumers, they are the business's first public face. It should not be a scowl, a smirk, or a blank. Weblinks should be investigated before being offered.

Recommendations

1. Operate the hospitality business as a registered corporation. If there is more than one shareholder, have a shareholders' agreement. Provide for the continuity of the business.

2. Know the people you will be doing business with. Check their backgrounds. As with all business and legal dealings, trust but verify.

3. Seek legal advice before entering into any important legal relationship or signing any document relating to the acquisition, financing, or operation of a business or to the acquisition or leasing of land, premises, furnishings, or equipment.

4. Engage in effective direct and indirect marketing. Take part in community or charitable initiatives. Ensure that the public presentation of the business is as good as it can be.

5. Protect the intangible property and trademarks of the business.

6. Ensure that the business has adequate insurance. Consult an expert.

7. Learn to manage time as a highly perishable, irreplaceable resource.

8. Maintain a comprehensive and current operations manual containing:

   a) Copies of relevant legislation such as the *Canadian Charter of Rights and Freedoms, Employment Standards Act, Fire Safety Act, Food and Drugs Act, Human Rights Code, Innkeepers Act or Hotel Keepers Act,* and *Occupational Health and Safety Act.*

   b) A list of the names, addresses, and telephone numbers of such federal offices as the District Tax Office, Employment Insurance Office, GST Information Office, Health Protection Branch Office, and Product Safety Bureau (Health Canada).

   c) A list of the names, addresses, and telephone numbers of such provincial offices as the Corporations Branch, Employer Health Tax Office, Employment Standards Office, Health Insurance Office, Human Rights Commission, Liquor Licence Board Office, Liquor Service Training Program Office, Ministry of Labour Office, Occupational Health & Safety Division, Pay Equity Office, Retail Sales Tax Office, Tourism Office, Workers' Compensation Office.

   d) A list of the names, addresses, and telephone numbers of such local offices as the Building Code Office, Environmental Regulation Office, Fire Marshal's Office, Licensing Department, and Municipal Tax Department.

   e) A list of such private bodies as:

      • Canadian Restaurant and Foodservices Association, 316 Bloor Street West, Toronto, Ontario, M5S 1W5, 416-923-8416, 1-800-387-5649

      • Canadian Specialty Food Association, 409-1 Eva Road, Etobicoke, Ontario, M9C 4Z5, 416-626-6239

      • The provincial hotel association

   f) A list of other useful numbers such as:

      • Medical emergency assistance

      • Ambulance

      • Hospitals

      • Coroner's office

      • Fire department

      • Police department

      • Lawyer's office

      • Landlord's office

      • Repair services (e.g., elevator)

   g) Standard operating procedures designed to

      • establish the line of authority and legal responsibilities;

      • delineate work responsibilities and define terms;

      • provide clarity, certainty, and continuity;

- provide for continuous two-way communication with staff; and
- establish standards and procedures concerning
  - medical and other emergencies
  - vandalism, thefts, and robberies
  - acceptance and storage of guest property
  - health and safety of guests and staff
  - inspections and monitoring
  - cleaning, maintenance, and repairs
  - handling complaints by guests and the public
  - reporting to supervisors
  - traffic control and access by the aged and physically challenged
  - enforcement of house rules
  - general public and media relations
  - selling and sales promotions
  - purchases and acquisitions
  - inventory and storage of assets and acquisitions
  - storage of animals, bicycles, etc.
  - accident reporting forms
  - financial and accounting reporting forms
  - audio/library/documentation cataloguing
  - special-event programming
  - outdoor programs (e.g., hiking, bicycling, etc.)
  - special requests such as access to faxes
  - special needs as to medical conditions and environmental sensitivities
- establish employee-related policies concerning
  - qualifications, recruitment, and selection
  - duties, orientation, training, conduct and deportment
  - salary and wage rates
  - overtime, vacations, statutory holidays, and leaves of absence
  - pensions and health plans, expense accounts, and vehicle costs
  - complaint procedures regarding other staff and management
  - acceptance of gifts and gratuities from guests
  - budgetary guidance
  - performance appraisals and disciplinary procedures
  - dress, appearance, smoking, drugs, liquor, and political activities
  - the use of the telephone and facilities

h) Copies of precedent forms such as reservation forms and storage box forms.

i) Copies of major contracts for insurance, maintenance, supplies, and catering.

j) Checklists for such matters as:
- work schedules

- safety and maintenance inspections
- security measures, first-aid and emergency equipment
- motor vehicles
- pools, watercraft, and related facilities
- storage safety for chemicals and other dangerous substances
- electrical and lighting
- food and alcohol storage
- loading/unloading/receivables

Summary

A business may be owned by a sole proprietor, a partnership, or a corporation. The choice of structure depends mainly upon the number of people involved, the desire to limit liability, the desire to separate business life from private life, and other advantages and disadvantages concerning financing, marketing, and operations. Some businesses stand alone, others are parts of chains, and others are franchises. Franchise and other licensing agreements require that minimum operational standards be met. The franchisee trades loss of control for access to regional or national goodwill and management assistance.

It is unwise to enter into an agreement to purchase a business without legal advice. Noncompetition clauses are found in business purchase agreements and in employment contracts. Such clauses must be reasonable to be enforceable. Proper capitalization and financing of a business is important. Many business acquisitions are financed through bank loans. Ongoing operational expenses often require a bank line of credit. Capitalization and financing may be in the form of shares and partnership interests or in the form of bank debt. Equity financing dilutes the ownership and control of the business, while debt financing increases financial liability to outsiders.

Property is divided into real property (land, buildings, fixtures) and personal property, which is divided into chattels (tangible personal property) and intangibles (trademarks, goodwill, stocks, contractual entitlements). Ownership and security interests in land must be registered on title to protect the security. Ownership of chattels need not be registered; however, security interests in chattels should be registered under personal property security legislation. Property, whether real or personal, may be leased from the owner. Breach by one party entitles the other party to various remedies, such as forfeiture of the lease by the tenant.

Goodwill is an important asset and should be protected. The registered owner of a trademark may prevent others from using a mark that is confusingly similar to the registered mark. If the mark is not protected, the owner may lose the exclusive right to the mark.

Effective marketing and good public relations are important. Premises should be clean, safe, and well maintained. Owners and staff should be clean, courteous, and helpful. Marketing endeavours and opportunities are limited only by imagination, finances, and the law of diminishing returns. Excellent service, sound marketing, and creative advertising can significantly increase the popularity and profitability of a hospitality business.

Insurance is essential to protect the business from loss, damage, and public liability. It is a mistake to be overinsured, but it is worse to be underinsured. Insurance claims and premiums can be minimized through good management, standard operating procedures, sensible safety measures, and other preventative measures.

1. Discuss two advantages of incorporating a hospitality business.

2. Discuss why a landowner might regard an inn constructed on her lands as "waste" and want it demolished at the end of a long lease.

3. Select a restaurant or hotel operating in your province that is a member of a national chain and describe the uses and locations of its trademark.

4. Is a business that has not registered its name as a trademark without legal remedy if another person begins using a confusingly similar name? Why or why not?

5. Discuss the advantages and disadvantages of (a) buying a franchise, and (b) opening a stand-alone business.

Chapter Fourteen

Employees and Employment Standards

Learning Outcomes

1. Define master, servant, and independent contractor.

2. List what should be included in a job description.

3. List the legal protections that Canadians have against discrimination.

4. List the exceptions to the discrimination legislation.

5. Describe the legislated duties of an employer.

6. Describe the employee's rights and the employer's duties in the following areas: contractual dismissal, rightful dismissal, and wrongful dismissal.

7. Describe the constitutional powers granted to the Parliament of Canada and the legislatures of the provinces and territories for the passing of labour legislation.

Introduction

Good employees are essential to the health of a hospitality business. Without them, most businesses would fail.

The Nature of the Employer–Employee Relationship

Master and Servant

Modern employment law is derived from the concepts of master and servant in old English law. Masters engage servants to perform tasks that the master cannot or desires not to perform. The master determines the services to be performed, as well as when, where, how, and to which standard they are to be performed. The servant has some input into the process and decides whether to serve given the terms offered.

Independent Contractors

There are two classes of servants—employees and **independent contractors**—that are differentiated largely in terms of the amount of control the employer exercises over them. In making the distinction, the courts ask a multitude of questions, including the following:

- To what degree does the employer control the working conditions of the servant?
- Does the servant have the freedom to work for other employers?
- Who is entitled to the profit of the enterprise?
- Who bears the risks of the business?
- Who owns the equipment the servant will use?
- Does the servant have the authority to hire staff?

It is the true nature of the relationship, not how the parties label themselves, that governs. The distinction is important because independent contractors and employees have different rights with respect to their employment. An employer must calculate and make the statutory remittances for income tax, employment insurance, and CPP/QPP contributions for employees, but not for independent contractors. Independent contractors are not offered contracts of employment. They enter into contracts as between separate businesses. If the employer terminates the contract before it has been fully performed, the remedy of the independent contractor is not one of wrongful dismissal, but of breach of contract.

Live Entertainers

Live entertainers are independent contractors typically engaged through a booking agency for set periods of time. They may be self-employed or employees of someone else, but they are generally not employees of the establishment where they perform. However, the establishment is obliged to monitor the entertainment because it may be found vicariously liable for unlawful conduct (such as obscenity) on the part of the entertainer during the performance.

The Duties of Employers

Job Descriptions and Application Forms

An employer must first identify the need for services and describe them with sufficient clarity and detail to enable applicants to know what is expected of them. The job description should include the required duties and standards of performance, the remuneration offered (including salary, bonuses, perks, and benefits), the length of the term, the likelihood of changes to the description over time, and other provisions as necessary. Advertisements need not contain as much information as the job description.

Employers should avoid overselling the position. An employer who entices a new employee to join with promises that are not kept may be sued for misrepresentation. Applicants are also under legal constraints. They must not submit dishonest applications or otherwise mislead prospective employers by, for example, lying about their qualifications or providing false references. If they do, they may be fired for cause as well as sued for damages. The application form should state that the applicant is providing true and accurate information, is aware that the employer is relying on the truth and accuracy of the information, and is aware that a false statement may serve as grounds for dismissal and other action.

The Contract of Employment

Many employees are hired without a written employment contract. When there is a dispute, the courts tend to side with employees on the basis of their weaker bargaining position. The consequences may not be too onerous for a position paying minimum wage, but the legal costs of battling over the matter will almost certainly exceed the costs of drafting a template employment contract. A well-drafted employment contract should contain the following:

- The names of the parties
- The start date and, if applicable, the end date
- A meaningful job description, and a statement that it may change over time
- The salary and benefits to be paid and the method of determining changes
- The rules for any bonuses and perks, and how they may change over time
- The frequency and type of performance reviews
- A statement that the qualifications submitted by the applicant are true and that the employer is relying on their truth
- A statement that the employer did not induce the employee to breach another contract of employment
- Noncompetition/nonsolicitation provisions
- Confidentiality requirements
- The possible causes for termination
- The method and notice of termination

A contract of employment is like any other contract. There are also implied terms such as the duty of the employer to provide a safe working environment. All provinces have occupational health and safety legislation that applies regardless of the terms of the private employment contract. Other legislative requirements include the duty of the employer to make statutory remittances, and to provide a workplace environment that does not breach human rights codes. Of particular importance is the vicarious liability of the employer. Owners and employers are liable for the negligence, breaches of contract, and other workplace misbehaviour of their employees arising out of their status and activities as employees.

Human Rights Protection

Employers must ensure that their job advertisements, job descriptions, recruitment and interview procedures, hiring and promotion policies, workplace environments, and public relations practices are not in contravention, inadvertently or otherwise, of the Charter of Rights and Freedoms, if applicable, and provincial human rights legislation. Employers must not discriminate on any grounds prohibited under human rights legislation, including race, colour, creed, ethnic origin, place of origin, religion, sex, sexual orientation, marital status, family status, age, and disability (the latter of which includes drug or alcohol dependency). A breach may result in a complaint. Employers must implement appropriate policies and inform their employees of all relevant aspects of the legislation and policies. To maximize compliance, employers must monitor themselves and their employees. Publications on human rights in the workplace are available from umbrella hospitality organizations and government bookstores.

The legislation allows for affirmative action programs designed to assist certain groups in society who have historically suffered hardship or economic disadvantage, as well as for employee benefit plans that discriminate on the basis of age, sex, marital status, or physical disability. Employers may also discriminate for or against granting employment to the spouses, children, or parents of an employer or an employee. An employer may include in the ad or job description any reasonable requirements that are directly related to the job, such as a driver's licence for a job requiring a driver or a recognized certification for the position of lifeguard. An employer may discriminate if an objective, honest analysis shows that the discriminatory qualification is a bona fide ("good faith") occupational requirement, known by its acronym "BFOR." For example, a model with Asian features may be selected over other candidates to appear as a flight attendant in a Canadian-made advertisement for Cathay Pacific Airlines.

Serious thought should be given to the development of job application forms and interview questions. On both the application form and during the interview, questions must seek to determine only whether the applicant is qualified for the job. Questions relating to any of the prohibited grounds under the legislation are improper. Questions unrelated to the job requirements may lead to human rights complaints. It is less trouble to design an appropriate application form or interview policy than it is to defend oneself against a complaint.

An employer may not ask for an applicant's photograph before hiring the applicant; ask whether the applicant wishes to be referred to as Mr., Mrs., or Ms.; or ask whether the applicant has children, is pregnant, or is planning to have children. An employer may ask whether the applicant would be able to relocate or accept reasonable amounts of travel, shift work, or overtime. An employer who is concerned that a married applicant may not be able to work the long hours that the job requires should ask the applicant about his or her ability to work the hours, not about his or her marital status; a married applicant may well be fully able and prepared to work the hours required. An employer may ask the applicant if he or she is of legal working age and is legally able to work in Canada. With respect to criminal convictions, an employer should use such wording as, "Have you ever been convicted of an offence for which you have not received a pardon?" An employer may pursue this line of questioning if there are particular convictions relevant to future job performance, such as an assault conviction for a bouncer or a drunk-driving conviction for a taxi driver.

An employer is required to attempt to **accommodate** the protected needs of employees. For example, an employee may refuse to work on a day of religious significance such as Sunday for Christians and Saturday for Seventh Day Adventists and Jews. The refusal can be used neither to hire nor to fire the employee. Instead, the employer must accommodate employees, perhaps by having the Sunday worshippers work on Saturday and the Saturday worshippers work on Sundays. A job advertisement or description cannot make working on a worship day a requirement of the position. Within reasonable limits, an employer must accommodate an employee who suffers from a drug or alcohol dependency. The duty to accommodate does not apply if to do so would cause an undue hardship upon the employer as measured objectively and reasonably. For a discussion of human rights, see Chapter 2.

The Duties of Employees

Proper Performance

It is an implied term of every contract that the parties will perform their respective obligations with proper care and skill. For employees, this means that they may be liable to the employer under negligence law for a breach of the duty of care, and under contract law for a breach of the implied warranty to render proper performance. Proper performance also includes abiding by the requirements of human rights legislation. Employees themselves must be mindful of the law when interacting with their employers, other employees, and the public.

Good Faith and Loyalty

It is also an implied term of every contract that the parties will act in good faith toward one another. With some exceptions under other laws such as occupational health and safety legislation and the common law duty to warn of serious, imminent dangers, all employees must act in good faith toward and be loyal to their employers. The degree of the duty tends to fluctuate with the level of responsibility of the position. Management employees are impressed with a fiduciary duty to act in the best interests of the employer even at the expense of the interests of the employee. The question of whether an employee has a fiduciary duty is determined not merely by the employee's title, but by the level of decision making, knowledge of the employer's secrets and customers, and degree of responsibility. Although most fiduciaries are found in management, all employees who handle money or assets or who have access to confidential information have a fiduciary duty to their employers.

Confidentiality

Confidentiality provisions are commonly found in employment contracts. If they are missing, reasonable provisions may be implied. It is reasonable for an employer to wish to preserve the confidential nature of such aspects of the business as customer lists, marketing plans, expansion plans, product development plans, salary structure, financing arrangements, formulas, recipes, technology initiatives, manufacturing processes, and unique trade practices. A confidentiality clause is enforceable only where the information is unique to the employer and the employee knew, or ought to have known, that it was confidential. Generally, employees cannot be forced to keep confidential their personal skills and knowledge, the nature of their employer's organization, and trade practices that are standard in the industry. If the information is no longer confidential, as when expansion plans have been publicly announced, the employee may disclose it.

However, the employee may not disclose any details of the expansion plans that have not been announced. The duty to hold information in confidence usually continues for some time after the termination of the employment.

Noncompetition/Nonsolicitation

Noncompetition/nonsolicitation provisions are commonly found in contracts of employment, especially for key employees. Typically, employers wish to protect their competitive positions by including in the employment contract a noncompetition clause that restricts the employee from competing or planning to compete with the employer while employed, or from jumping to a competitor within a certain territory for a specified period following termination. The employer may seek to enforce the noncompetition clause, usually by applying to the court for an injunction and bringing a claim for damages. However, the courts may not enforce unreasonable clauses. A noncompetition clause that is too restrictive may be severed from the agreement, leaving the employer with no remedy at all. What is or is not reasonable depends on the circumstances. Nonmanagement employees are generally treated differently from management employees. It may be reasonable to require that the hotel manager not manage a directly competing hotel for a year, but it may be unreasonable to stop a chef from joining a competing hotel unless the chef is a well-known major attraction of the dining room.

In the case of *Elsley v. J.G. Collins Insurance (1976), 13 O.R. (2d) 177 (C.A.), affirmed [1978] 2 S.C.R. 916* (also discussed in Chapter 13), the Ontario Court of Appeal, affirmed by the Supreme Court of Canada, had this to say with respect to the reasonableness of noncompetition clauses between employers and employees:

> ... [S]uch clauses in employment agreements are carefully scrutinized and are frequently held unenforceable on the ground that they extend beyond the interest which the employer is properly entitled to protect ... The generally accepted test as to which employees may be restrained is set out ... as those employees who will acquire not merely knowledge of customers, but in addition, influence over them: "A restraint is not valid unless the nature of the employment is such that customers will either learn to rely upon the skill or judgment of the servant or will deal with him directly and personally to the virtual exclusion of the master, with the result that he will probably gain the custom if he sets up business on his own account." (Cheshire and Fifoot, *Law of Contract*, 8th ed. (1972))

Reasonable Notice

Employees who wish to quit are required to give their employers reasonable notice. Failure to do so may injure the employer, giving rise to a cause of action against the employee.

Termination of Employment

Contractual Dismissal

A contract of employment may terminate as planned, such as on the date specified in the contract or upon the occurrence of a triggering event that the parties recognize as terminating the contract. An example of the latter is a lifeguard who is hired for the summer. The most reasonable interpretation of the contract is that it terminates at the end of the Labour Day weekend. Other seasonal jobs fall into this category.

Rightful Dismissal (Termination for Cause)

Unless a contract (most often a collective agreement with a union) provides otherwise, an employer has the right to dismiss any employee at any time for any reason. The only questions are whether the dismissal was rightful or wrongful and, if wrongful, the nature of the remedy. A dismissal is rightful if the termination is for **just cause**, such as financial dishonesty, falsified qualifications, or gross and continuing incompetence. Under common law, if the dismissal is for cause, the employer is not liable for severance and other post-employment matters. As a practical matter or pursuant to legislation, employers often pay the employees as though they had been wrongfully dismissed.

Wrongful Dismissal

Unless the dismissal is contractual or rightful (i.e., for cause), then the dismissal is wrongful. The employee is entitled to notice (or cash in lieu of notice) and fair dealing in all other respects. Even if the dismissal is wrongful, the employer should assist the employee with supportive (though truthful) letters of reference, career counselling, access to outplacement assistance, and other reasonable assistance as the circumstances warrant. The remedies to which the wrongfully dismissed employee is entitled vary depending on such factors as

- job description;
- length of service;
- remuneration level attained;
- level of responsibility attained;
- employee's age;
- employee's job prospects; and
- manner of termination.

The amount of compensation tends to rise with the level attained in the management hierarchy. The rationale is that it is easier for a waiter or housekeeper to find alternative comparable employment than it is for a hotel manager or comptroller. No termination of employment or severance package should be offered or accepted without legal advice.

Robertson v. Red Robin Restaurants of Canada Ltd. (1998), B.C.J. No. 884 Vancouver Registry No. 96-29769

Robertson began work for the Victoria branch of the defendant restaurant in 1991. By 1995 he was assisting the manager. With the company's support, Robertson moved from Victoria to the Guildford branch. He was the assistant to the General Manager in Guildford, earning $30,000 a year. In May of 1996, a new Acting General Manager was appointed and Robertson was told that he needed further development before he would be given the store. He was under the impression that he was a valued employee. On July 15, 1996, he was called to a meeting in the public area of the restaurant, where he was told that he did not have the "right stuff," and that both parties should cut their losses, and he was terminated. Robertson stated that he was given no option by the defendant employer but to leave. He was given five weeks' severance for the five years that he was employed. The defendant stated that Robertson chose to terminate his employment and that payment in lieu of notice was reasonable and that Robertson had failed to mitigate his damages. Robertson sued for damages, including punitive damages, for breach of employment contract and termination.

Robertson was awarded judgment in the amount of $8,538.48, including additional damages due to the manner of dismissal. The defendant conceded that the plaintiff was dismissed without cause. The employer's actions constituted a wrongful dismissal without notice, without warning, and without documentation. The employer's conduct was insensitive, but not intentionally malicious. The claimant was terminated from the position of middle manager, and the reasonable notice period would have been 15 weeks. The claimant did all he reasonably could in mitigation. The court held that employers ought to be held to an obligation of good faith and fair dealing in the manner of dismissal. A breach of those principles would be compensated for by adding to the length of the notice period. The claim by the defendant that the claimant had left by his own choice was high-handed and offensive. The position of the employer was indefensible and combined with the public nature of the termination meeting resulted in a loss of self-esteem, public humiliation of the claimant, and a loss of confidence. An appropriate addition to the notice period in this case was two months.

Bennett-O'Brien v. Village Green Inns Ltd. (1998), B.C.J. No. 2049 Vancouver Registry No. C980001

In July 1993, O'Brien began working as the general manager of the defendant hotel. Poor financial performance caused the defendant to close the coffee shop, the lounge, and the dining room. The location that housed these services was leased out for a new bar and grill. The manager and O'Brien could not get along. The hotel terminated O'Brien's employment without notice in November 1997. She sued. The hotel claimed that reasonable notice was four and one-half to five months. The court awarded her damages for 12 months citing, in part, her level of responsibility and the fact that she had been terminated without cause.

Statutory Obligations

Canada Labour Standards

The *Constitution Act (1867)* grants authority to pass labour legislation to the Parliament of Canada as well as to the provinces and territories. Section 91 authorizes Parliament to legislate "[l]aws for the Peace, Order and good Government of Canada." This clause greatly expands the jurisdiction of the federal government. Subsection 91(2) empowers Parliament to regulate trade and commerce. As a result of these two provisions, the federal government is free to legislate labour standards virtually unchecked. Federal authority governs industries and undertakings that are interprovincial, national, or international in scope, including banking, transportation, radio, television broadcasting, and Crown corporations. Under the emergency powers enumerated in section 91, the federal government may assume all legislative power over labour law during war or peacetime emergency.

Subsection 92(13) gives the provinces jurisdiction to pass laws concerning property and civil rights. This gives the provinces the power to pass laws regarding trade unions, hours of work, workers' compensation, paid vacations, industrial standards, and many other laws respecting employers and employees.

Section 9 of the *British North America Act* as amended in 1870 gives to the commissioner and territorial councils the powers that are bestowed upon the provincial legislatures by section 92 in the *Constitution Act (1867)*.

The Canada Labour Standards set forth minimum regulatory standards in respect of wages, hours of work, rest periods, holidays, statutory holidays, maternity or pregnancy leave, paternity leave, termination, termination notices, layoffs, employment equity, recourses for lost wages, and some employee responsibilities. Canada is divided into 14 jurisdictions for this purpose, and the standards may vary depending on the jurisdiction. The regulations do not apply to all employees. For example, domestic workers and research assistants receive relatively little protection from the legislation.

Human Resources Development Canada administers the Canada Labour Code, the *Fair Wages and Hours of Labour Act*, and the Fair Wages Policy Order. Although its role has expanded over the years, the number of workers that are affected by its legislation is well below the number covered by provincial labour legislation. Provincial labour laws are enforced by tribunals, commissions, and, in Quebec, by the labour court.

Provincial Labour Standards

Each province has enacted legislation to set minimum standards of employment applicable to all persons who perform work or supply services to an employer for wages. Excluded are owners, sole proprietors, and independent contractors. The standards are implied in every employment contract, oral or written, to which the legislation applies. No one may deviate from the standards set forth in the legislation, even by agreement between the parties. Every agreement that is contrary to the legislation is invalid. Provisions that constitute improvements for employees are allowed. The legislation deals with such matters as:

- Wages
- Hours of work, rest periods, statutory holidays, and paid nonworking days
- Annual vacation, family, and maternity leaves
- Notice of termination of employment
- Notice of layoff for six months or more
- Civil recourses
- Recourse for wrongful dismissal
- Recourse against forbidden practices

The employment standards of a province do not apply to all employees in the province. Employees who are not covered must fend for themselves and rely on general laws of contract and negligence for protection. Examples of employees who may not be covered include:

1. Employees of the federal government and any Crown corporation
2. Practitioners of architecture, chiropody, dentistry, law, medicine, optometry, pharmacy, professional engineering, psychology, public accounting, surveying, veterinary science
3. Students training for the professions noted in item 2
4. Registered practitioners of drugless medicine
5. Certain teachers
6. Persons engaged in commercial fishing
7. Domestic servants employed directly by a household for 24 hours or less a week
8. Babysitters or companions employed to attend primarily to the needs of a child

9. Registered real estate agents

10. Sellers other than commission sellers who sell away from the employer's establishment

11. Persons employed on a farm whose employment is directly related to the production of eggs, milk, and so on, or otherwise generally related to farm activities and the fur trade

Specific Requirements

An in-depth discussion of all the standards applicable in all the jurisdictions in Canada is beyond the scope of this book. They can be ascertained by obtaining legal advice and/or copies of the legislation and relevant government publications. In this section, we will discuss some standards of employment. The provisions are similar across Canada, but there are differences. Record keeping is a major responsibility of every business in Canada. An employer should know exactly what information is required, such as name, address, wages paid, employment contract, and social insurance number. Innkeepers must be aware of how long revenue, tax, and personnel records must be kept in their jurisdictions.

Personnel Records

With a few exceptions, employers are required to keep personnel records for several years. These records are not of the work performance but of such items as name, date of birth, occupation, telephone number, residential address, date of commencement of employment, wage rate, hours worked each day, benefits, gross and net wages for each pay period, each deduction made from the employee's wages and the reason for it, dates of statutory holidays taken by the employee and the amounts paid by the employer, dates of the annual vacation taken by the employee together with the amounts paid by the employer and the days and amounts owing, the amount of money taken by the employees from the employee's time bank, how much time remains, and the amounts paid and the dates taken.

The statement of wages must include the name, address, hours worked, wage rate and basis, and overtime wage rate and hours worked at this rate; any money, allowance, or other payment to which the employee is entitled; the amount and purposes of each deduction; how wages are calculated if other than hourly and salaried; gross and net wages; and how much money the employee has taken from the employee's time bank, and how much remains.

Minimum Wage

The federal government and each of the provinces and territories have established minimum wage provisions that set forth the minimum wage that must be paid per hour to adult employees and employees below a certain age. The minimum wage for the two groups need not be the same. The rules also restrict the amount an employer can deduct for room and board from the minimum wages paid to an employee. The jurisdiction may also require that an employer pay a certain minimum to an employee who is called into work but then is not required to work, or who works for less than the minimum number of call-in hours.

Minimum Age

For businesses under federal jurisdiction, persons under 17 may be employed in any office, plant, maintenance or repair service, transportation, communication, construction, or another federal work as long as there is no provincial requirement for the person to be in school at the time. The work involved must be within approved categories and not present health or safety dangers to the person. Persons under 17 cannot work between the hours of 11:00 p.m. and 6:00 a.m. under any circumstances.

The provinces and territories also have detailed requirements designed to protect young people while they gain work experience. For example, the Alberta Employment Standards Code prohibits the employment of children during normal school hours. No person under 16 years of age may be employed without the written permission of a parent or guardian and the approval of the Director of Employment Standards who may also impose conditions on the employment. Children in vocational training or employed in agriculture as specified in the Code are exempt. An adolescent is defined as someone over 12 but under 15. An adolescent may be employed in delivering small wares, newspapers, flyers, and handbills provided the employment is unlikely to be injurious to the life, health, welfare, or education of the adolescent. The written consent of a parent or guardian is required. The hours of employment are restricted to two on school days and eight on all other days. Employment is prohibited between 9:00 p.m. and 6:00 a.m. A young person is defined as a person over 15 but under 18. A young person cannot be employed between 12:01 a.m. and 6:00 a.m. Between 9:00 p.m. and 12:01 a.m., a young person may not be employed in connection with the following unless he or she is in the continuous presence of a least one person 18 years of age or older:

1. A retailer of any foods, beverages, commodities, goods, wares, or merchandise

2. Gasoline, diesel fuel, or any other petroleum or natural gas product

3. Any premises that require a visitor's accommodation business and licence

Hours of Work and Wage Rates

The standard workweek in Canada is 40–48 hours, beyond which the employee is entitled to increased compensation, typically 1.5 times the regular rate of pay. These provisions generally do not apply to management employees who receive salaries. Each jurisdiction limits the total number of hours that an employee must work, and establishes minimum wages, minimum call-in standards, and other requirements. For example, employees may be entitled to a half-hour lunch break after a certain number of hours have been worked. The hours of work provisions usually do not apply to a family business employing only family, travelling sellers, agricultural workers, domestics, volunteers, students, professionals, and independent contractors; minimum wage and other provisions do apply.

The Payment of Wages

Labour standards respecting the payment of wages cover the payment interval, method of payment, permissible deductions, priority of wages owing to workers, and summary proceedings for the recovery of unpaid wages. Some pay periods are set by collective agreement. Payment may be by cash, cheque, or direct deposit to the employee's account. Employers must deduct and remit statutory remittances. In some jurisdictions, an employer cannot deduct for property damage or missing cash and property unless the employee had exclusive control of the property. Any deductions for room and board cannot bring the wage below the legal minimum. Following the bankruptcy of an employer, employees are unsecured creditors, which means they will not receive their unpaid wages until the secured creditors have been paid. Most jurisdictions hold the directors of a corporate employer personally liable to the employees for wages that are unpaid for several months.

Vacations

Almost every Canadian employee is legally entitled to at least two or three weeks' paid annual vacation depending on the jurisdiction and triggering length of service—generally about 12 months of consecutive employment. Maternity and parental leaves do not interrupt the employment. If an employee is terminated before taking vacation or has vacation owing, the employer must pay the vacation entitlement for a previous year not taken and the portion earned in the current year. If a public holiday occurs during the vacation, the employee will be credited with an additional day. Some employees can make a written request to postpone or give up their vacation time and receive vacation pay instead. Employers may determine when an employee may take vacation, but must give notice of the start date in writing. The vacation may be taken as two one-week sessions or one two-week session, and must not be divided into less than a seven-day period except at the request of the employee.

Vacation Pay

Depending on the jurisdiction, vacation pay is 4 percent or 6 percent of gross wages earned in the 12-month period during which the vacation occurs. The employer must determine whether the calculation should include commission payments, tips and gratuities, vacation pay, discretionary bonuses, overtime, and allowances for the cash value of board and lodging. Expenses are not included because they are not remuneration.

Holidays and Statutory Holidays

Holiday pay is calculated as not less than the total of regular (i.e., not including overtime, holiday, or premium pay) wages and vacation pay payable to the employee in the four weeks before the workweek in which the holiday falls, divided by 20. Statutory holidays are legislated paid holidays. If a statutory holiday falls on a day when the employee is scheduled to work or is away on vacation, the employee may choose to have a replacement day off or to receive wages in lieu. For a statutory holiday, the employer must pay not only the holiday pay but also premium pay of at least 1.5 times the regular rate of pay for all hours worked on the statutory holiday. An employer need not pay an employee for a statutory holiday when the employee:

1. does not qualify for holiday pay;
2. fails to work the scheduled workday immediately preceding or following the statutory holiday;
3. has agreed to work the statutory holiday and fails to perform the work without reasonable explanation; or
4. is employed under an agreement that gives him or her the option to refuse work when asked.

The statutory holidays are:

1. New Year's Day
2. Good Friday (or Easter Monday in Quebec)
3. Victoria Day (except Quebec and the four Atlantic provinces)
4. St. Jean Baptiste Day (Quebec only)
5. Canada Day
6. August Civic Holiday (where applicable)
7. Labour Day
8. Thanksgiving (except the four Atlantic provinces)

9. Remembrance Day (except Newfoundland and Labrador, Prince Edward Island, New Brunswick, Quebec, and Ontario)

10. Christmas Day

11. Boxing Day (only federal and Ontario employees)

Jurisdictions may have their own unique holidays; e.g., Yukon observes Discovery Day on the third Monday in August and Alberta observes Family Day on the third Monday in February. Employers need not recognize civic holidays unless they have agreed to do so in a collective agreement.

Required Days of Rest

Employers must provide employees with rest periods of at least 24 consecutive hours in every workweek or 48 consecutive hours in every period of two consecutive workweeks. The maximum daily hours of work provisions also apply.

Leaves of Absence

Depending on the jurisdiction, employees may be entitled to leaves of absence of varying lengths and for varying reasons such as to recuperate from illness or injury; to vote in federal, provincial, or municipal elections; to perform jury duty or appear as a witness in court; or for bereavement over the death of defined family members.

Parental Leave

Maternity leave is recognized throughout Canada. Women have the right to maternity leave to ensure a healthy pregnancy and a bonding period with the newborn; however, the right to maternity leave is separate from the right to payment of benefits. Thus, women not covered by employment standards legislation are entitled to leave but not to payment from an employer unless an agreement provides otherwise. Most jurisdictions require a woman to have worked continuously for the employer for at least 13 weeks preceding the estimated delivery date in order to qualify. Payment during maternity leave normally falls under employment insurance benefits, which grant

Parental leave may be taken by either parent.

Chapter 14 / Employees and Employment Standards

15 weeks of benefits for maternity leave if the mother has accumulated 600 insured hours in the last 52 weeks or since the last employment insurance claim been employed for 20 weeks.

Two to four weeks' written notice of an intention to take maternity leave is usually required. In some cases, medical reasons may shorten the notice period. Maternity leave is generally about 17 weeks. Extensions may be given if a doctor certifies that the woman is unable to return to work. At their option, women may shorten the leave period. Parental leave can be taken by either parent. Employment insurance benefits for parental leave may be claimed by either parent or shared between them but must not exceed a combined maximum of 35 weeks. The eligibility requirements for parental leave are the same as those for maternity leave. The same rights exist for most adoptive parents. In most jurisdictions, parental leave is available at any time within the first year following the baby's birth.

Those returning from parental and maternity leave should be placed in their former jobs. If this is not possible, they should be placed in a position with equivalent wages and benefits. Vacation pay and seniority usually continue as though uninterrupted. When benefits accrue during the leave period, the employee is required to continue making his or her contributions. Federally regulated and Quebec employees who are pregnant or nursing are entitled to have their jobs modified or to be reassigned if the work is posing a risk to the mother, fetus, or child from the start of pregnancy to 24 weeks after birth.

Individual Termination

Generally speaking, no one in Canada is guaranteed a job and an employer can terminate an employee at will. An employer who terminates an employee without just cause is required to provide the employee with reasonable notice of termination, payment equal to the amount the employee would have made had he or she worked the notice period, and any other pay (e.g., vacation or severance pay) that is due to the employee.

Every jurisdiction has a statutory minimum notice period that varies according to the employee's length of service. Some interruptions of service such as some temporary layoffs may be ignored when calculating the length of service. Seasonal employees, employees hired for definite terms, and short-term employees (typically those with less than three months' service) may be terminated without notice. Most employees are entitled to notice or payment in lieu of notice, i.e., the amount the employee would have earned had he or she been allowed to work during the notice period. The payment in lieu of notice is based on the number of regular hours worked and does not include overtime. If the hours fluctuate, an average is taken.

The notice period may be extended beyond the statutory minimum by the common law according to such factors as the employee's level of responsibility, length of service, age, and job prospects. The notice period may also be extended if the job is not a common one such that finding similar alternative employment would be difficult.

If an employee works beyond the notice period with the employer's consent, the notice may become void such that the employer may have to start the process over again.

Group Termination

Group termination takes place when a business closes down or significantly downsizes. The issues are generally the same as those surrounding the termination of a single employee except that in some instances employees are given a longer notice period and the employer must notify the Minister of Labour. In some instances, an effort will be made to investigate methods of avoiding the termination or softening its effects. Each jurisdiction has rules as to what constitutes a group termination, e.g., termination of 50 employees within two months in British Columbia. An employer contemplating a group termination should consult a lawyer.

Severance Pay

Ontario, for example, requires an employer to pay severance when 50 or more employees are terminated within a period of six months or less as a result of the discontinuance of all or part of the employer's business. **Severance pay** is also required when one or more employees are terminated by a business with a payroll of $2.5 million or more. Severance pay is calculated by multiplying one week's regular pay by the number of years of employment and by the number of completed months of employment, and dividing that number by 12, to a maximum of 26 regular weeks of pay. An employee who elects to collect severance pay thereby abandons the right to be recalled to work.

Layoffs

When employees are laid off, they do not qualify immediately for their rights under termination. In the various jurisdictions, once a specified period of time has passed, the layoff is considered a termination. In Newfoundland and Labrador, a temporary layoff is less than 13 weeks in a period of 20 consecutive months; beyond that point, it is considered a termination. In some jurisdictions, the employee continues to be paid during the layoff.

Equal Pay and Pay Equity

On June 25, 1987, the Canadian Human Rights Commission issued an evaluation of **equal pay legislation** that expressed the following four principles (regarded as the four phases through which equal pay legislation tends to progress):

1. Equal pay for equal work. Male and female employees must be paid the same wages for doing the same job.

2. Equal pay for substantially similar work. Male and female employees who have different job titles but who perform substantially the same work must be paid the same wages. This type of legislation exists in every province and has been applied to equalize the pay of nurses' aides and orderlies.

3. Equal pay for work of equal value. This principle differs from the preceding ones in that it compares not the work per se but the value of the work, which is determined through the use of job evaluation techniques. Thus, comparisons may be made between jobs that are as dissimilar as apples and oranges. While it is impossible to compare an apple and an orange in terms of consumer tastes and preferences (factors that would largely affect the fruit's market value), an apple and an orange can be compared in terms of cost of production, storage, and nutritional value. Equal value laws reflect a political view that workers' wages should not be determined exclusively by market forces.

4. Pay equity. Pay equity legislation assumes that wage discrimination against women is endemic and requires a broad and systemic remedy. This type of equal pay legislation abandons the complaint system of enforcement in favour of a regulatory model; it does not simply prohibit wage discrimination but places positive obligations on employers to ensure that their pay practices comply with the legislation.

Phase 1 has been adopted throughout Canada. Phase 2 participants include Alberta, British Columbia, and the private sectors in Manitoba, New Brunswick, Newfoundland and Labrador, Nova Scotia, Prince Edward Island, and Saskatchewan. Phase 3 participants include the federal government, Quebec, and the Yukon's public sector. Phase 4 participants include Manitoba, New Brunswick, Newfoundland and Labrador, Nova Scotia, Prince Edward Island's public sector, and the public and private sectors in Quebec and Ontario.

The purpose of pay equity legislation is to redress systemic gender discrimination in compensation for work performed by employees in female job classes. Systemic discrimination consists of the historical under-evaluation of women's work merely because it has usually been performed by women. Where enacted, pay equity legislation generally applies to all employers in the private sector who employ a minimum number of employees, and all employers in the public sector. A practical guide to implementing a pay equity plan is *The Pay Equity Handbook* by Cheryl Elliott and Stewart Saxe (Canada Law Book Inc., 1987). An employer who institutes an equal pay or pay equity program may not reduce wages to the levels of other job classifications; wages may only be increased.

Employment Equity

The *Canadian Charter of Rights and Freedoms* and provincial human rights legislation prohibit discriminatory hiring and employment practices. Employment equity initiatives require employers not simply to avoid prohibited practices, but to take steps to remove historical or systemic barriers that certain groups have faced and thereby to improve the representation of those groups in the workforce. Affirmative action programs boost candidates from particular groups that have been traditionally underrepresented in certain job categories. Subsection 15(2) of the *Charter* expressly states that programs designed to improve the "conditions of disadvantaged individuals or groups" are allowable under the *Charter*.

Employment Insurance

The *Constitution Act (1867)* gives the federal government exclusive jurisdiction over employment insurance (EI). The *Employment Insurance Act*, which replaced the *Unemployment Insurance Act* enacted in 1940, came into force on June 30, 1996. Following a transition period, the provisions of the Act took full effect on January 1, 1997. The fund is self-funding through contributions made exclusively by employers and employees. Set forth below are some of the important features of the Act.

Premiums and Insurable Earnings. Employers must withhold EI premiums for all insurable earnings whether the employee is engaged in full-time or part-time work. Annual maximums replace weekly maximums. Employers must withhold EI premiums until they reach the annual maximum. If an employee works for more than one employer, each employer must withhold until the maximum is reached, at which point a refund will be issued to the employee by the Canada Customs and Revenue Agency.

Hours-based Claims. Hours of employment form the basis for the calculation of benefits. Every hour, including hours worked in part-time and casual work, is used. The minimum number of hours of work a person needs to be eligible for benefits is a floating number between 420 and 700 depending on the regional unemployment rate. For regions with an unemployment rate of less than 6 percent, the minimum number of hours of work is 700; for regions with an unemployment rate of over 13 percent, the requirement is only 420 hours of work. New entrants to the workforce require 910 hours to qualify. For employees claiming sickness, maternity, or paternity benefits, a minimum of 600 hours is required to qualify. Employers must keep a record of employment (ROE) that records the employee's first and last days of employment and the total hours worked. There are tough sanctions and penalties for claimants who fail to declare work-related earnings and for employers who knowingly issue false records. The eligibility requirements can be raised anywhere between 25 percent and 100 percent for dishonest claimants. Employers are penalized an equal amount, and corporate directors can be personally liable for the employee's penalty.

Benefits. The maximum weekly benefit is $413 or 55 percent of the claimant's average insured earnings, whichever is lower. Claimants whose benefits are less than $200 can earn up to $50 without any deductions from their benefits. Claimants whose benefits exceed $200 can earn up to 25 percent of their benefits without any deduction from their benefits. Benefits can be received for a period of time ranging from 14 to 45 weeks depending on the number of weeks of insurable employment. Families with children who earn less than $25,921 annually and who receive the Child Tax Benefit (CTB) will receive a supplement based on the CTB. The benefit can be increased to a maximum of 65 percent as long as the weekly benefit is not greater than $413.

Repayment of Benefits. Employees whose net income exceeds $48,750 must repay $30 for every $100 over the maximum. With some exceptions, employees may be required to repay up to 100 percent of the benefits. Effective in 2000, certain special benefits such as maternity/parental leave benefits do not have to be repaid regardless of net income.

Uninsurable Employment. All employment in Canada under a contract of service is insurable employment and, as such, is subject to employee and employer premiums. Forms of employment that are not insurable and not subject to the payment of premiums include:

1. Casual employment that is not for the purpose of a usual trade or business

2. Some employment in which the employer and employee are not at arm's length from each other, including persons connected by blood, marriage, or adoption

3. Employment involving a shareholder who controls more than 40 percent of the voting shares of the corporation

4. Employment that involves an exchange of work or service

5. Employment in agriculture or horticulture in which the person receives no cash remuneration and works fewer than seven days in the year

6. Employment in connection with a circus, fair, parade, carnival, or similar activity in which the person works fewer than seven days a year

7. Employment in rescue operations of persons who are not regular employees

8. Employment as a government census taker by persons who are not regular government employees

9. Employment in Canada by employees who are on an exchange program and who are not being paid by a Canadian employer

10. Employment in religious orders by persons who have taken a vow of perpetual poverty

11. Employment that requires unemployment premiums to be paid to the United States or other accepted countries

Employment Outside of Canada. Employment outside Canada is insurable if (1) the employer is a resident of Canada, (2) the insured person normally resides in Canada, (3) the employment is not insurable in the country of employment, or (4) the employment is not exempted.

Included Earnings. Most earnings that are paid to an employee are subject to premiums, including salaries, wages, bonuses, commissions, and the following:

- The value of board and lodging

- Retiring allowances

- Workers' compensation top-up paid by a regular employer

- Wage-loss indemnity top-up paid by an employer

- Supplemental unemployment benefit payments

- Payments by an employer during a waiting period for parents
- Maternity benefits paid by an employer
- Certain other incomes that are excluded by the *Income Tax Act*

Employer and Employee Premiums. In 2002, the employee's employment insurance premium was 2.2 percent of insurable earnings. The employer's premium rate was 1.4 times the employee's EI deduction.

Special Benefits. Maternity benefits are paid to a claimant who proves her pregnancy and who has accumulated 600 insurable hours in the last 52 weeks or since her last employment insurance claim. The benefits are payable during the period commencing eight weeks before the week in which her confinement is expected or the week in which her confinement occurs. Maternity benefits can be collected within 17 weeks of the actual or expected week of birth, whichever is later. The maximum number of weeks of benefits payable to the mother is 15. In the event that a child of the pregnancy is hospitalized, the 17-week limit can be extended for every week the child is hospitalized up to 52 weeks following the week of the child's birth.

Parental benefits are paid to a claimant who remains at home for one or more newborn children of the claimant or one or more adoptive children. The benefit can be taken by either parent or shared. The benefit is paid upon the arrival at home of the newborn or adoptive child or within 52 weeks after the arrival. Parental benefits may be claimed by either parent or shared between them but may not exceed a combined maximum of 35 weeks.

Sick leave benefits are payable to a claimant who has an interruption of earnings due to illness, injury, or quarantine and who has accumulated 600 hours of insurable earnings in the last 52 weeks or since the claimant's last claim. The maximum benefit period is 15 weeks.

More than one type of special benefit can be claimed within a period, to a maximum of 30 weeks.

Disqualifications. A claimant may be disqualified from receiving benefits if, without good cause, he or she (1) refuses to apply for or fails to accept suitable employment, (2) neglects to accept suitable job opportunities, (3) fails to carry out reasonable written directions from an officer of the Employment Insurance Commission, or (4) fails to attend a course of instruction to which he or she has been referred. Employment is not suitable if it arises out of a work stoppage because of a labour dispute; is employment in the claimant's usual occupation, but at a lower rate of earnings or under less favourable conditions; or is employment in other than the claimant's usual occupation and at lower earnings or in less favourable conditions than he or she might reasonably expect.

A claimant will be disqualified from receiving benefits if he or she voluntarily leaves the employment without just cause or loses the employment by reason of his or her own misconduct. Employees who quit a job within three weeks after the end of the term of employment or within three weeks after the layoff date will still receive benefits. An employee who leaves the job for just cause is entitled to benefits. Section 29 of the *Employment Insurance Act* defines just cause.

Claimants whose employment is lost due to a work stoppage resulting from a labour dispute at their place of employment, or who are inmates of a prison or a similar institution, or who are absent from Canada are not entitled to receive benefits. However, employees in approved work-sharing agreements are entitled to benefits, as are insured participants who meet the criteria established by the National Employment Services.

Appeals. A claimant or an employer may appeal to a board of referees any decision of the Employment Insurance Commission. Such an appeal must be made within 30 days after the commission's decision is received. If circumstances of sexual harassment are being considered in the appeal, the hearing may be held in camera at the request of the claimant.

Labour Relations

Under federal and provincial law, most employees may belong to a trade union. Management employees and independent contractors do not have this right. A detailed analysis of the laws that relate to the organization of employees into unions and labour relations is beyond the scope of this book. Suffice it to say that, in general, depending on the precise wording of the relevant legislation in the jurisdiction, employers in the hospitality industry:

1. must not unlawfully interfere with the employees' right to join a union;
2. must not discriminate against employees on the basis of their participation in a union or its activities;
3. must bargain in good faith with the union;
4. must act in accordance with any collective agreement to which they are parties;
5. must not threaten to call or call an illegal lockout;
6. must not use the services of professional strikebreakers to prevent a strike; and
7. must not unlawfully disrupt a legal strike.

For their part, unions:

1. must bargain in good faith with the employer;
2. must act in accordance with any collective agreement to which they are parties;
3. must not use unfair and unlawful tactics to intimidate employees into joining the union or participating in its activities;
4. must not threaten to call or call an illegal strike; and
5. must not interfere with the rights of another union.

If a union has been certified to represent the employees in a collective bargaining unit, the union and the employer may bargain between themselves or submit the matter, or merely the outstanding matters, to binding arbitration. Once the collective agreement has been entered into, disputes between the employer and an employee arising out of the collective agreement are first dealt with through the grievance process. Disputes between the employer and the union may also be settled directly by the parties or submitted to binding arbitration. The grievance and arbitration processes are governed by rules of procedure. Judicial review in the courts will occur only if the decision of the arbitrator or the arbitration board was outside their jurisdiction, or was clearly reached unfairly or unreasonably on the face of the evidence.

Health and Safety in the Workplace

In addition to relevant federal legislation, each province has enacted legislation that imposes on both employers and employees heavy obligations to adhere to minimum standards of safety in the workplace. The statutes and regulations set forth general rules applicable to almost all workplaces; specific rules applicable to certain—usually more hazardous—workplaces; rules that deal with specific hazards regardless of the workplace; and rules covering the identification, control, storage, and handling of toxic and other hazardous substances such as explosives and dangerous chemicals.

Employers have a general responsibility to ensure the health and safety of their employees in the workplace. This includes providing sufficient instruction and information as to the hazards of the job, proper training for the job requirements, proper emergency training, competent supervision, safe and well-maintained equipment, and safe working conditions. Employees have a responsibility to ensure the health and safety of themselves and others. They must accept and apply the training, follow proper directives, report hazards or breaches of the health and safety legislation to their supervisors or employers, and take all reasonable steps necessary to protect themselves and others from harm. Generally, no employee may be forced to perform unsafe work unless the failure to do so would endanger others. Once the danger to others has passed, the employee may immediately cease to perform the unsafe task. No employee may be disciplined or terminated over a proper refusal to work, even if it is later determined that there was no danger. In addition to government programs, the Canadian Restaurant and Foodservices Association also offers a national safety training program.

Workplace accidents must be reported to the supervisor or employer and subsequently by the employer to the provincial ministry responsible for workplace health and safety and, if applicable, the union. The detail and timing of the report vary depending on the nature of the accident and the injuries suffered.

The ministry has the right to inspect workplaces and to order the employer to comply with the legislation. Employers have a right of appeal. Penalties for contravening the legislation or a work order may include further orders, hefty fines, and, in extreme cases, incarceration. The penalty may be assessed against, among others, an individual or corporate employer; a supervisor, officer, director, or shareholder; or an employee. Generally, the guilty party will be strictly liable unless it can be established that every reasonable precaution was taken. If the danger of the activity was extreme, the guilty party may be strictly liable even if all reasonable precautions were taken. Any person who is charged or is likely to be charged with an offence under health and safety legislation should respond as one would respond to a charge under the *Criminal Code* and seek legal advice. A seemingly small matter can escalate into a major problem unless it is effectively managed.

Summary

Employers may engage the services of employees, agents, or independent contractors. It is the true nature of the relationship, not how the parties label themselves, that governs. The distinction is important because different rights arise depending on the nature of the relationship. Written contracts of employment are recommended. The duties of employees to their employers include proper performance, good faith and loyalty, confidentiality, noncompetition, and the giving of reasonable notice of termination. Termination of employment may occur by contractual dismissal, rightful dismissal (for cause), and wrongful dismissal. In the case of wrongful dismissal, the employee is entitled to notice or cash in lieu of notice and fair dealing in all other respects.

Employers must abide by all legislative obligations imposed on them under federal and provincial labour standards, including such requirements as keeping proper personnel records, and abiding by minimum requirements as to wages, age, hours of work, pay periods, vacation time, vacation pay, statutory holidays, days of rest, leaves of absence, parental leave, termination rights, group termination rights, severance pay, layoffs, employment insurance, and pay and employment equity under the *Canadian Charter of Rights and Freedoms* and provincial human rights legislation. Federal and provincial labour relations legislation applies to most employers and employees, and prohibits unfair labour practices, whether by management or by unions. Federal and provincial legislation regulates health and safety in the workplace in the interests of both the employers and the employees. Employers have a heavy responsibility to ensure that their workplaces meet or exceed the regulatory requirements.

1. What are the regulatory requirements for keeping personnel records in your jurisdiction?

2. What is the vacation pay calculation in your jurisdiction?

3. What are the minimum age and minimum wage requirements in your jurisdiction?

4. By statute, what leaves of absence, and for what purpose, duration, and remuneration, must an employer grant in your jurisdiction?

5. By statute, how much notice must an employer in your jurisdiction give to an employee whose length of employment is (a) two months, (b) two years, and (c) 10 years?

6. What are the regulatory requirements, in particular the reporting requirements, for workplace accidents in your jurisdiction?

7. What is the safety training program for the hospitality industry nearest you?

8. What pay should an employee earn on a statutory holiday? What would the pay be for four hours of overtime on a statutory holiday?

PART
FIVE

The Agency
Relationship

Chapter 15
The Travel Industry

5

15

Chapter 15

The Travel Industry

Learning Outcomes

1. List and describe international travel regulations.

2. List and describe federal travel regulations.

3. List and describe provincial travel regulations.

4. Define the agency relationship and describe how it is created.

5. Describe the duties of an agent to a principal.

6. Describe the duties of a principal to an agent.

7. Explain what duty of care is owed as a result of the common law.

8. Describe the protection offered travellers under the Quebec, Ontario, and British Columbia travel Acts.

Introduction

Never in history have so many people been able to travel so often and so far and for so long. The unprecedented demand for travel services has fostered an explosion in suppliers, bringing the cost within reach of most people. Even coast-to-coast air travel is now affordable for almost everyone. The allure of distant cities, churches, castles, shores, and mountains has always inspired people to travel. Broader advertising and the improving quality of artificially made attractions have further increased the desire to travel. Television has brought into our homes the farthest reaches of the globe, whetting an appetite to experience them in person.

Las Vegas (Spanish for "The Meadows") is an excellent example of how attractions have developed. Las Vegas was once only a gambling and adult entertainment centre. Today, Las Vegas caters not just to gamblers and thrill seekers, but also to families who desire more wholesome pursuits. Families are a vast source of revenue. It will be interesting to witness the priority that the casinos of Mississippi receive in the rebuilding of that state after Hurricane Katrina. Today, casinos are not limited to Las Vegas, Atlantic City, and locally licensed charity fairs. They are sprouting on Native reserves and in many cities across Canada.

In addition to pleasure trips, another boon to the travel industry has been business travel. Despite the proliferation of telephones, fax machines, and e-mail, business hops among Canada's cities and towns by air and rail are numerous. With the globalization of the world economy, Canadians must participate in order to survive. We must market our products, technologies, and skills while keeping abreast of the products, technologies, and skills of our foreign competitors—all of which necessitates a vast amount of business travel. The growth in tourism and business travel over the last 50 years can be attributed to many factors, including:

1. increased prosperity, disposable income, and leisure time;
2. increased education and awareness of the world;
3. improved travel safety and affordability;
4. the globalization of the world economy;
5. the improved quality of attractions; and
6. more effective marketing of the industry.

Tourism is one of the largest generators of socioeconomic activity in the world. Its importance to the Canadian economy is immense, accounting for over 500 000 jobs. According to the Canadian Tourism Commission (CTC), Canadians spent $33 billion travelling within Canada in 1997. In 1996, the World Tourism Organization identified Canada as the tenth-most-popular tourist destination in the world, behind the United States, Spain, France, Italy, the United Kingdom, Germany, Austria, Hong Kong, and China. Foreign visitors spent $13 billion in Canada that year. Of these, 63 percent were American leisure travellers. According to the CTC,

> Canada enjoys a certain mystique in the American market. Among the most noteworthy of its advantages is the loyalty of U.S. visitors. Nine of ten Americans who visit Canada have been here before. A survey ... showed that they rated Canada much better than the U.S. in terms of safety, cleanliness, beauty of its landscape, unspoiled wilderness, and friendliness of its people.

Tourist expenditures, both domestic and foreign, are expected to grow into the next century. The weakness of the Canadian dollar against other currencies, particularly the American dollar, makes Canada an attractive destination for foreign tourists. New regulations in the United States requiring its citizens to have a passport when returning to the U.S. will surely hurt travel between the two countries.

The international nature of the travel industry presents regulatory challenges.

Many people make their travel plans directly with the carrier or through the Internet, but a substantial number of travellers consult travel agents—the retail arm of the travel industry—who, in turn, engage the services of travel wholesalers (e.g., tour operators). Travel agencies are located in most communities in Canada. Although some agencies specialize, most handle both personal and commercial accounts. The range of agencies and their specialties is limited only by the range of human travel. Tourists are even voyaging into space.

The Impact of the Law on the Travel Sector

By virtue of the seamless web of the law, the travel industry is affected by the law in a myriad of ways. Primary among these are government regulation, the **agency relationship**, the **duty of care,** and other legal rights. Making up the travel industry are the following major players:

1. Transportation providers, such as airlines, railways, shipping lines, bus lines, car rental agencies; and excursion outfitters, such as whitewater rafters.

2. Travel wholesalers who create tour packages by linking transportation providers with attraction and accommodation providers. Wholesalers usually market to travel agents, but sometimes directly to the public through an in-house agency.

3. Travel retailers, commonly known as travel agents, who market a variety of travel services to the public, such as tour packages, business trip bookings, and general travel counselling. The term "travel agent" refers not only to the agency itself, but also to the employees of the agency who give the travel advice to the public. Travel agencies act as a central processing unit for the public, travel wholesalers, and providers of transportation, accommodation, and attractions.

4. Travel insurers who provide trip, cancellation, business, and liability insurance.

5. Tourism boards such as the World Tourism Organization and the Canadian Tourism Commission whose purpose is to promote tourism and to assist wholesalers and retailers in marketing destinations to citizens and foreigners.

6. Administrative boards that regulate the travel industry internationally, nationally, and provincially.

7. Trade associations such as the Alliance of Canadian Travel Associations (ACTA) that advance the interests of their members through lobbying, seminars, trade publications, and other support services.

The travel sector interacts with many other enterprises including hotels, resorts, museums, and theatrical and entertainment booking agencies. In this chapter, we shall be primarily concerned with travel wholesalers, travel agents, and regulatory bodies.

Government Regulation

International Travel Regulation and Security

International laws affecting travel include not only laws relating to tickets, landing rights, and so on, but also laws relating to terrorism, piracy, and other criminal acts. The air transportation industry is the most regulated of all the international transportation industries. Other modes of travel such as trains and ships are subject to fewer international regulations. International police cooperation is fostered through Interpol (<u>inter</u>national <u>pol</u>ice) and by fairly standardized airline boarding procedures. Pilots and crew can be assured that passengers embarking in Los Angeles, Tokyo, Brasilia, Athens, New Delhi, Montreal, or Cape Town will have gone through security checkpoints. It is a crime even to joke about sabotage when boarding or aboard an airplane. Buffoonery is taken very seriously at airports.

The Warsaw Convention of 1929 generated the first intergovernmental rules respecting international air travel. It codified the concept of a limitation on an airline's liability for deaths, personal injuries, and property losses or damages of passengers. The Chicago Convention of 1944 led to the formation of the International Civil Aviation Organization (ICAO) and the International Air Transport Association (IATA). ICAO provided a forum whereby national governments could negotiate international standards and cooperate in the development of the airline industry. IATA is an association of about 200 airlines offering scheduled international air services. Thus, some charter companies may not join. These organizations are responsible for many of the numerous agreements and protocols that now govern international air travel.

The 1946 Bermuda Agreement generated a template for countries negotiating landing and other rights and enunciated the following eight freedoms of air transportation:

1. The right of transit (i.e., to fly over other countries)

2. The right to land in other countries for refuelling, safety reasons, maintenance, and crew changes

3. The right to disembark passengers in another country

4. The right to embark passengers in another country and return them to the airline's country of registration

5. The right to embark and disembark passengers for further or return travel provided the flight originates or terminates in the airline's country of registration

6. The right to embark passengers in another country and disembark them in yet another, provided the flight makes a stop in the airline's country of registration

7. The right of an airline registered in one country to operate flights between two or more other countries without stops in the airline's country of registration

8. The right of **cabotage** (i.e., the right of an airline in one country to operate flights between two or more locations inside another country)

Each of these freedoms must be negotiated between the two countries; not all of them are necessarily included in the final agreement.

The Hague Protocol, adopted in 1955, amended many of the provisions of the Warsaw Convention, updating them and adapting them to the post–Second World War period. Since then, further adjustments have been negotiated as needed.

IATA was established to regulate scheduled international air services and to encourage safe and marketable international air services. IATA regulates airfare revenues, appoints travel agencies that wish to sell international airline tickets for commission, and governs

Chapter 15 / The Travel Industry

many aspects of the daily operations of the agencies. The travel agency must sign a contract (known as the Sales Agency Agreement) with IATA agreeing to its terms and conditions before it is allowed to earn commission on international air fares.

Section 6 of IATA Resolution 804, being the Sales Agency Agreement for Canada, sets forth the Billing and Settlement Plan (BSP), which functions as a clearing-house for the receipt of ticket proceeds for all member airlines and travel agencies in Canada. Travel agents are obliged to deposit in a trust account all payments earmarked for IATA, and to submit weekly reports to the BSP Processing Centre detailing ticket sales on behalf of the various airlines.

The system works as follows. The airlines supply the travel agents with blank tickets. According to the IATA Sales Agency Agreement, the documents remain the property of the airline until sold to the consumer. Upon a sale by the agent to the consumer, the proceeds become due from the travel agent to the airline. The money collected from the consumers is deposited in a trust account by the agent and reported to the BSP Processing Centre. The trust money is collected at regular intervals by IATA and redistributed to the airlines.

Federal Regulation

With a grant of $50 million in 1995, the federal government created the Canadian Tourism Commission. The CTC, whose purpose is to devise and implement tourism policy, acts in partnership with the private sector. The CTC has the authority to plan, direct, manage, and implement programs designed to generate and promote tourism both within and from outside Canada. The two main objectives of the CTC are to regulate the marketing of Canada as a tourist destination and to provide accurate tourism information to visitors. In the two years following the inception of the CTC, Canada's integrated marketing budget rose to $145 million in the context of a business worth over $40 billion.

The *Carriage by Air Act* contains many of the provisions of the Warsaw Convention for such matters as tickets, baggage checks, waybills, liabilities of carriers, and provisions relating to the death of a passenger. The *Aeronautics Act* regulates the performance standards and technical requirements of aircraft. The *National Transportation Act*, through the National Transportation Agency, regulates airlines, railways, and bus lines. The *National Passenger Transportation Act* was enacted partly to render passenger rail service more efficient and less costly to the taxpayers by allowing routes and services to be cut. The *Immigration Act* regulates entry into Canada by setting visa requirements such as maximum allowable stays and levels of health. Other statutes regulate what goods may be brought into Canada.

The *Competition Act* prohibits conspiracies to reduce competition. It also prohibits "bait and switch" and other unfair business practices. For example, it is illegal to entice a travel consumer to a destination by offering the use of an inexpensive hotel suite, later claim that it is no longer available (when it probably never was), and then switch the consumer to higher-priced accommodation. Note that such a scenario could happen for legitimate reasons (which explains the frequent success of bait-and-switch techniques). If the scenario happened legitimately, the agent would not be liable under the *Competition Act*. Complaints under the *Competition Act* are made to, and investigated by, the Competition Bureau of Industry Canada.

Provincial Regulation

The federal *Competition Act* is valid legislation under subsection 91(2) of the *Constitution Act (1867)* (Regulation of Trade and Commerce), while the provincial business practices Acts are valid under subsection 92(13) of the *Constitution Act (1867)* (Property and Civil Rights in the Province). Business practices legislation exists in every province to regulate, among other things, business advertising and selling techniques. Consumer protection legislation also exists in every province. The Acts apply to any transaction over a certain threshold—for example, $50. Thus, they apply to the vast majority of travel transactions. The legislation typically requires that a receipt describing the services purchased be issued for each transaction over the threshold. Failure to issue a receipt may result in the loss of legal recourse.

Formal travel Acts exist only in Quebec, Ontario, and British Columbia. In these provinces, only persons registered as travel agents or travel wholesalers may sell travel services. The registered members must maintain a compensation fund to compensate consumers who do not receive the services for which they have bargained. Bonding of travel agencies is required only in Quebec.

Municipal Regulation

Municipalities, which derive their power and authority from provincial legislation, require many businesses (including travel businesses) to obtain licences and to operate in areas zoned for the type of business. Licensing is discussed in Chapter 12.

The Agency Relationship

Actual and Apparent Authority

Agency is a legal relationship whereby one party (the principal) authorizes a second party (the **agent**) to enter into contractual agreements on behalf of the principal with a third party (the consumer). The principal delegates to the agent the authority to negotiate contracts on the principal's behalf with the consumer. Because the agent is authorized to act on behalf of the principal, the principal is bound by the agreement that the agent negotiates with the third party. If the principal wishes to be bound only in certain circumstances, the agency agreement must clearly define any limits on the authority of the agent. A principal will not ordinarily be bound by contracts negotiated outside the scope of the actual authority granted.

If an airline company has a written contract authorizing a travel agent to sell tickets on its flights, the airline must honour the tickets sold by the agent. The agency contract must specify any limits to the authority. For example, the airline's responsibility to honour tickets is limited by the agency contract to the destinations the airline serves. Thus, the agent cannot make the airline responsible for tickets to destinations it does not serve.

A third party is not required to ask whether the agent has the authority to act provided the agent is acting within the apparent range of authority of an agent in such circumstances. Thus, if an airline company that flies to Europe and to Asia has given an agent the authority to sell tickets to Europe but not to Asia, the agent will have actual authority to sell tickets to Europe; however, the agent will also have the apparent authority to sell tickets to Asia because that activity is within the normal range of travel agency activity. Thus, the consumer will enjoy the benefit of any tickets to Asia purchased from the agent, and the consumer need not inquire as to whether the airline has restricted the normal authority. To avoid liability to the consumer, the airline would have to take steps to notify the consumer of the restricted authority. Failing this, the airline company's only recourse would be against the agent.

Creation of an Agency Relationship

By Contract
An agency agreement may be oral or in writing, with consideration or **under seal**. When the relationship is for longer than one year, the agreement must be in writing to be enforceable. The formation of the contract may be express or implied from the conduct

of the parties. Whether a contract has been formed is a question of fact. Anyone with the capacity to contract may act as a principal or an agent. The requirements of contracts are discussed in Chapter 3.

By Ratification

A **principal** will not ordinarily be bound by a contract negotiated outside the authority granted. If someone purports to contract with a consumer as an agent without having received authorization from the principal, the principal will be bound by the contract only if the principal leads the consumer to believe that the agent does have the authority or if the principal adopts and ratifies the agreement that the agent has entered into. The ratification need not be done expressly, but may be implied from the conduct of the principal, such as the principal choosing to benefit from the agreement and acting in accordance with the terms of the agreement. Only disclosed principals may ratify.

If an unauthorized travel agent arranges a group tour that includes an Air Canada flight, Air Canada need not honour the arrangement. However, if the tour group arrives at the Air Canada airport counter, and if Air Canada chooses to board them (thereby honouring the arrangement), then Air Canada has ratified the agreement and the agent and carrier are in the same position as if they had entered into a formal agency contract. Similarly, if a person calling herself a travel agent books rooms with a hotel, there has been no official recognition of the agency relationship by the hotel. However, once the hotel accepts the guests who are the subject of the reservations, then the agency relationship crystallizes. Once the agency is established, the agent becomes entitled to the appropriate commissions.

By Estoppel

If a principal allows a consumer reasonably to think that someone is his agent, then the principal will be **estopped** from denying the agency relationship afterward. For example, a person may have in his business window a VIA Rail Canada sticker, with the tacit consent of the local VIA office. If the person sells the services of VIA to a consumer who has seen the sticker, the person becomes the agent of the carrier. VIA would be estopped from disavowing the agency. To avoid this result, VIA would need to take action (perhaps by a lawyer's letter or seeking a court injunction) to prevent the person from presenting himself as an agent of VIA.

By Necessity

On rare occasions, an agency relationship may be imposed on the parties without authority or ratification. Where a ship's captain is forced to sell perishable goods abroad in order not to lose the entire value of the cargo, the principal cannot later sue the captain or the buyer by claiming that the sale was unauthorized. Modern communications have largely removed the need for a captain to make such decisions without prior consultation.

Employees and Independent Agents

Agents may be employees of the principal or independent contractors. A **principal** is vicariously liable for the acts of employees in the course of their employment. Except for honouring the agreement negotiated by the independent agent, the principal will not normally be vicariously liable for the acts of independent agents unless there has been fraudulent misrepresentation.

The Duties of an Agent to the Principal

Obedience

An agent is expected to honour the express terms of the agency agreement. If the agreement restricts the authority of the agent, the principal will not ordinarily be liable to the agent for any actions taken outside the scope of the agent's authority. Depending on the circumstances, the principal may still be liable to an innocent third-party consumer. There are also implied terms in any travel agency agreement. For example, whether or not the agreement refers to them, the parties are bound by the IATA regulations.

Competence

In *Hedley, Byrne & Co. Ltd. v. Heller & Partners Ltd.*, [1963] 2 All E.R. 575, [1964] A.C. 465 (H. of L.), a banker gave negligent advice about a target business to a person who was not a client of the bank (or even known to the bank at the time the advice was given), but who was a potential investor in the target business. In finding liability, Lord Morris said, " [I]f someone possessed of a special skill undertakes, quite irrespective of contract, to apply that skill for the assistance of another person who relies on such skill, a duty of care arises." Professionals are held accountable for the advice they give and, in some circumstances, for the advice they fail to give. Failure to render fully a professional opinion can amount to negligence by omission, an aspect of tort liability that is discussed in Chapter 4.

Travel agents are experts in travel planning. While they are not expected to be conversant with all aspects of the travel industry, their recommendations have the force of professional opinion. Further, agents who know or ought to have known of a health problem at a certain destination are expected to advise their clients of the problem, and may be liable for any failure to do so. Small claims courts handle the majority of claims against travel agencies. Judge Pamela Sigurdson is a small claims court judge with extensive experience presiding over travel claims. She had this to say about standards of competence among travel agents:

> Clients have a right to expect professional advice and service from their travel agents. Retailers face the legal (and possibly costly, probably time-consuming) consequences if they don't provide it. ... Agents are professionals now. No one expects them to be perfect, but they have to act like professionals. Instead of an agent saying, "I don't know anything about this product," either know or find out. Just handing out a brochure isn't enough.

Volk v. Schreiber and Faraway Enterprise Limited, [1978] 18 O.R. (2d) 446 (Divisional Court)

The plaintiff purchased from the defendant's Ontario-based travel agency a package tour to India that would start in England. The defendant advised her that a visa would be necessary to enter India. He mailed her an application, which she completed and returned to the defendant. The defendant wrote back as follows: "[E]nclosed is [your] visa application for India together with unused passport photographs. I have checked with both Air India in Toronto and the Indian Consulate and am assured that providing the stay does not exceed 28 days, no visa will be required. This revision is apparently quite recent and only came to light when checking with the above two offices. If you still feel you would like to get your visa ahead of time, this could of course be handled by you in person in London at the Indian Embassy or at Capital Cities on route."

The plaintiff took the letter at face value and left for London without the visa. Once in India, she was informed that a visa was necessary. She managed to obtain one, but at a cost of $250. On a claim for reimbursement, she lost at trial and appealed. At the trial, the defendant relied on section 2(8) of the IATA Sales Agency Agreement, which states that visas are required, "except for ... [t]ourists continuing their onward or return journey by air within 28 days from any town in India, provided they are holding tickets and other documents required for their onward return journey. Transferring from air to sea or from sea to air transportation is also allowed. This facility can only be used once within 6 months. However, re-entry into India within the 6-month period is permitted to tourists returning from visits to the neighbouring countries of Nepal, Sri Lanka and Bangladesh, provided a landing permit has been obtained for this purpose."

The trial judge refused to admit the evidence concerning the calls to Air India and the Indian Consulate on the basis that the advice given during the calls was hearsay. He denied the claim. The appeal judge found that the defendant was in doubt as to whether the visa was required and continued to be in doubt right up to the trial. At the trial, the defendant had described the question as a "grey area" and as a "matter of interpretation." The appeal judge found that Section 2(8) was not grey or ambiguous, and that it clearly provided that any traveller proceeding overland to India needed a visa. The appeal judge stated that:

> ... the obligation of a travel agent or anyone holding himself out as having special knowledge and ability is to exercise the appropriate degree of skill and diligence in the matter. So far as his skill is concerned, it is my conclusion that he was unable properly to interpret what he described as the bible of his trade. So far as his diligence is concerned, he was in doubt on the matter and informed his customer that there was no doubt. He also failed to obtain the visa for her when, in my view, he could readily and should have done so. For these reasons I would find that the defendant was in breach of his contractual obligations as the travel agent for the plaintiff and, accordingly, the appeal should be allowed and the judgment should go for the plaintiff against both defendants.

Personal Performance

An agency agreement usually calls for performance by the agent who is the party to the agreement, not for performance by the agent's delegate. Delegation in breach of contract may absolve the principal of liability. Where a subagent has the authority to perform the duties of the agent, there is privity of contract only (1) between the principal and the agent, and (2) between the agent and the subagent. While there is no privity of contract between the principal and the subagent, the agent is liable to the principal for any defaults of the subagent. The principal cannot directly sue the subagent in contract (although there may be an avenue via the tort law bypass). Instead, the principal would have to sue the agent who, in turn, would have to sue the subagent by means of a third-party claim.

The contract may expressly allow the contract agent to employ outside or part-time agents to represent the agency. If so, the contract agent is responsible for their actions under the theory of vicarious liability. Contract agents should check the professional background and qualifications of any outside agents they intend to engage as diligently as they would scrutinize the résumés of in-house agents.

Honesty Toward the Public

If an agent behaves dishonestly or makes fraudulent statements to, or fraudulent arrangements with, a consumer, the consumer may sue the agent for any losses that result. In some circumstances, the consumer may also sue the principal. If the innocent principal also becomes saddled with the judgment, the principal may claim indemnity from the agent.

Good Faith Toward the Principal

The agency relationship is one of trust. A high degree of good faith and professionalism is imposed on the parties to the relationship. In many circumstances, principals are able to engage numerous agents without engendering a conflict of interest. On the other hand, an agent who serves two principals may more easily be caught in a conflict of interest. If Hotel A pays higher commissions than Hotel B, the agent may be inclined to recommend Hotel B only when Hotel A is no longer accepting reservations, even though Hotel B may be better suited to the consumer's needs. In reality, travel agents frequently represent several principals such that potential conflicts abound. Agents should demonstrate evenhandedness and integrity at all times. Agents must consider the best interests of the consumers as a first priority and recommend the accommodation best suited to their needs regardless of commission rates and other self-serving considerations.

Any money held by an agent on behalf of the principal must be kept in bank accounts that are separate from those of the agency. Payments on behalf of the consumer are made from the trust account. Only after the agent has earned the right to payment for commission or disbursement reimbursement may the agent transfer funds from the trust account into the agency's general business account. Trust monies do not belong to the trustee, and thus cannot be attached (i.e., attacked and grabbed) by any creditors of the trustee. In the case of a bankruptcy of an agent, monies in trust belonging to the principals and the consumers will not be subject to claims by the agency's creditors. If those funds have been improperly placed in the agency's general account, the creditors or the trustee in bankruptcy may be able to attach them to the prejudice of the rightful owners.

The Duties of a Principal to the Agent

Generally

Like the agent, the principal is expected to honour the agency agreement, to be competent, to respect the privity of the relationship, to be honest, and to act in good faith.

Commissions

As with any commercial enterprise, the raison d'être of a travel agency is to generate a profit for the owner. The income of a travel agency is derived from the commissions earned on the sales of travel services. The commission rates are set forth in the sales agency agreements. Where no rate is set forth, a reasonable rate is implied. Some hotels mistakenly believe that they do not have to pay commissions on reservations they receive from unauthorized travel agencies. In fact, once the hotel accepts a reservation, the agency has a legal right to the commission even if there is no formal agreement with the hotel. The right to the commission arises *quantum meruit* the moment the hotel takes advantage of the reservation. According to trade practice, the commission on a hotel reservation is 10 percent of the room rate. Perhaps unfairly, few hotels pay commission for any nights the guest stays past the original reservation.

Costs

Unless the agency agreement provides otherwise, the agent is entitled to be reimbursed for reasonable costs incurred on behalf of the principal. Reimbursement may be made either by direct repayment or by deduction from amounts owing by the agent to the principal. Proper documentation is essential to avoid disagreements. If the agency agreement is silent on the issue of costs, a term may be implied into the agency contract requiring the principal to pay the reasonable costs necessarily incurred to give effect to the agreement. Unauthorized costs are not the responsibility of the principal but must be borne by the agent.

Liability of the Agent and the Principal

The agency relationship both exposes travel agents to **liability** and protects them from the defaults of their principals. The key to the protection lies in the agent duly informing the consumer that the relationship is one of agency. Provided the agent has performed her part of the contract as intended, she is not liable for any lack of performance by the principal. The principal alone is liable for any lack of performance on his part.

After a travel agent makes a room reservation for a client, the agent has no liability if the hotel fails to honour the reservation. Agents should retain all relevant documentation of such transactions for future reference and protection. A hotel may deny that a reservation was made in order to avoid honouring the guest's claim. Hotel reservations systems that do not issue confirmation records present problems for agencies and make good record keeping even more important. If an agent knows that a particular hotel has a reputation for dishonouring reservations, the agent may be liable to the consumer for negligently making the reservation.

Undisclosed Principals

The agent may still be liable for the failure of the principal if the agent fails to reveal the existence of the principal to the consumer. A consumer who is led to believe that the agent is the principal is entitled to sue the agent as a bearer of primary responsibility. The only recourse for the agent would be to sue the principal and hope for indemnity.

Stringer et al. v. Domhar Travel Agencies Inc.; Sunquest Vacations Ltd., Third Party (1983), 20 A.C.W.S. (2d) 42 (Ont. Co. Ct.)

The Stringers bought a Sunquest holiday package through a Domhar travel agency. On arrival at the hotel, they were told by the clerk that the hotel was overbooked. The Stringers were accommodated, but at a lower-quality hotel. Rather than suing Sunquest, they sued Domhar Travel. In their suit, they contended that they had never been advised that Sunquest Tours was the principal, and that they had not been given a Sunquest brochure. The judge stated:

> I find, as a fact, that the plaintiffs were not provided with the Sunquest brochure or alerted by [the counsellor] about the involvement of Sunquest in the travelling arrangements. ... I do not see why a customer sitting in the office of a travel agent should concern himself as to the agent's relationship with the party called in arranging the accommodation, unless this is brought home to the customer. ... The law is clear that if an agent, acting as an agent, does not clearly make known to the other party that he is so acting and leaves it open to himself to act as principal or agent, he is personally liable.

> The judge ordered the agency to repay the Stringers the cost of their vacation (namely, $6,120 plus $3,000 for other damages). The agency had a claim against the principal, but that issue could not prejudice the plaintiffs. The agency delivered a third-party claim against Sunquest and recovered against them.

An agent who presents himself as an agent when he is not authorized to do so is liable if the principal does not ratify the contract. During Grey Cup week, an agent may attempt to sell hotel accommodation to fans without being an authorized agent of the hotel. If the hotel refuses to ratify the reservation contract on the basis that the hotel is full or deals only with authorized travel agents, the agent will be personally liable to the fans. If the hotel does ratify the contract, the fan will normally be bound because the fan intended to enter into the contract. Generally, it does not matter that the contract is with a now-disclosed principal and not the agent. On the other hand, if the personal identity of the principal is a key consideration, the courts may excuse the consumer from the contract upon disclosure of the principal.

> **Said v. Butt, [1923] K.B. 497**
>
> The plaintiff tried to buy a theatre ticket but was refused because he had caused trouble there in the past. He had a friend buy the ticket for him, but when he arrived for the show, the theatre would not admit him. The court held that the identity of the principal purchaser of the ticket was a vital consideration and refused to enforce the contract.

Liability to Nonclients

If an agent negligently advises a nonclient who reasonably relies on the advice and suffers damage as a result of the reliance, the agent will be liable even though no contractual relationship exists. Travel agents render professional opinions within the meaning of *Hedley, Byrne & Co. Ltd. v. Heller & Partners Ltd.* cited earlier in this chapter.

Termination of the Agency Relationship

The agency relationship may be terminated automatically pursuant to the terms of the contract, upon giving proper notice, upon the insanity or death of an individual party, upon the dissolution of a corporate agent or principal, or upon the occurrence of any matter that may properly terminate a contract, such as frustration (i.e., a supervening event that makes it impossible to perform the contract).

The Duty of Care

Duty of care is discussed in detail in Chapter 4. Generally speaking, the duty of care imposed on travel agencies, retailers, and wholesalers is to provide complete and accurate information to each other and to consumers, and to ensure, as far as possible within the limits of foreseeability and reasonableness, that all aspects of the tour will satisfy a reasonable person. Travel agents should interview the client and, based on the information elicited, make recommendations that reflect the circumstances of the client and the destination. The agent should, where warranted, canvass such issues as health conditions of the client, medical conditions at the destination, sunburn, vaccinations, exotic foods, crime rates, political stability, border crossing requirements, and so on. Agents should disclose or disclaim possible dangers and recommend precautions and travel and medical insurance. For example, an agent may recommend that a person with a serious heart condition not fly high in unpressurized aircraft. Someone wishing to backpack alone should be apprised of the risks; it should not be assumed that the backpacker is aware of them. In the case of cruise ships, which are in essence floating hotels, the International Council of Cruise Lines (ICCL) reports that as many as one passenger a week disembarks because of a medical emergency. Even cruise lines catering to younger and presumably healthier passengers handle one or two emergencies a month. An agent has a duty to be satisfied that cruise ships have adequate medical facilities unless the agent clearly and effectively disclaims knowledge to the client. Meeting the duty of care may even include, where warranted, investigating other travel service providers and visiting recommended sites. In short, travel agents and wholesalers may be liable in contract for breach of contract or in negligence for breach of the duty of care whenever the consumer does not receive the services bargained for or the duty of care reasonably expected.

Keks v. Esquire Pleasure Tours Limited and Pleasure Tours (Canada) Ltd., [1974] 3 W.W.R. Manitoba County Court, Hewak Co. Ct. J.

The defendants, wholesalers of vacation tour packages, made accommodation arrangements with the Hilton Hawaiian Village in Hawaii, which they then sold as part of tour packages to travel agencies, including the Winnipeg-based Travel Centre. To promote the tours, the defendants printed brochures that described the packages and provided such information as prices, type of accommodation, and length of stay.

In 1972, the plaintiff decided to take his family to Hawaii for Christmas. His wife made the arrangements through the Travel Centre. The agency provided verbal information and the defendants' brochure. The Keks decided to stay at the Hilton Hawaiian Village and specifically in the Diamond Head Apartments, which offered kitchen facilities. In order to avoid restaurant food, the Keks planned to bring along their housekeeper to cook their meals; they advised the Travel Centre of their intention to do so.

The Keks and their housekeeper travelled to Honolulu on December 23, 1972, arriving at midnight. The clerk at the hotel registration desk informed them that the accommodation they had booked was not available. The hotel made arrangements to accommodate them in the Rainbow Towers. Although the Rainbow Towers was superior to the Diamond Head in most respects, the new accommodations were on separate floors and did not contain the desired kitchen facilities. The next day, the plaintiff was told that the original accommodation was still not available. However, the Rainbow Towers moved the family into adjoining rooms so that they could at least be together.

The plaintiff made daily inquiries about the original reservation. On December 28th, the original accommodation was finally available, and the Keks moved into the Diamond Head Apartments. Unfortunately, the kitchen stove was inoperable and there were no utensils. The family was moved back to the Rainbow Towers to a penthouse suite that had a small refrigerator but no other kitchen or cooking amenities.

The Keks and their housekeeper completed their vacation in the penthouse. Upon returning to Winnipeg, the plaintiff filed a special damages claim for the extra cost of the meals, the air fare for the housekeeper, the extra gratuities paid to porters and waiters, and the cost of the drugs prescribed by a doctor to relieve anxiety suffered by the plaintiff as a result of his experience in Hawaii. In addition, he claimed general damages for nervous strain, anxiety, and distress. The plaintiff had requested and paid for a certain type of accommodation that the defendants, through their brochures, had assured him was available. Based on the representations, the plaintiff decided to bring the family housekeeper. Had the Keks known that they would be required to eat in restaurants, they would not have brought the housekeeper.

The defendants admitted that at no time did they make any special inquiries of the Hilton Hawaiian Village management with respect to the availability of the plaintiff's desired accommodation. Their position was that since they had heard nothing to the contrary from the management, everything was fine. The defendants submitted that the plaintiff had not acted reasonably and had made no attempt to mitigate his damages. However, the court found that the plaintiff had done what any reasonable, prudent, and patient person would have done. Although the quality of accommodation was higher then expected, it lacked the facilities specifically requested. If a person has reserved a half-ton truck and is given a Cadillac, the Cadillac may be a better vehicle, but it cannot perform the tasks required. The plaintiff was awarded the following:

- $615 for meals eaten in outside restaurants;
- $25 for additional tips and gratuities;
- $34.95 for tranquilizers prescribed by a doctor;
- $461 for the housekeeper's air fare;
- $800 for general damages; and
- $300 for court costs.

The next case examined (1) whether a tour operator is responsible for ensuring that transportation provided by a subcontractor is safe, and (2) the effect of a disclaimer clause.

Craven et al. v. Strand Holidays (Canada) Ltd. et al. (1982), 142 D.L.R. (3d) (Ont. C. of A.)

The Cravens arranged a holiday through Strand, a tour operator, and booked it through an Ontario travel agency against whom the action was dismissed. The bus driver and Expresso Brasilia, the Colombian bus company, were not joined as parties to the action. Strand's brochure, entitled *Winter Sunshine Strand Holidays*, described a travel package to Colombia's Costa del Caribe. Included was this feature: "Private transfers by road between Barranquilla airport and Cartagena, and between Santa Marta and the airport, including baggage handling." Prominently displayed at the top of the back page of the brochure was the following: "Important Notice: Your booking for these vacations involves an agreement between you and those who provide the services. Please read all the information on this page since it sets out the conditions covering the travel and other services offered." Strand's brochure also contained the following disclaimer:

> The Strand Companies make arrangements with airlines, cruise lines, coach companies, transfer operators, shore excursion operators, hotels, and other independent parties to provide you with the travel services and other services you purchase. Although the Strand Companies take great care in selecting these suppliers, the Strand Companies are unable and do not have any control over them and therefore cannot be responsible for their acts or omissions. The travel services and other services provided are subject to the conditions imposed by these suppliers and their liability is limited by their tariffs, conditions of carriage, tickets and vouchers and international conventions and agreements.

Under Colombian law, Strand was not allowed to deal directly with local transportation companies, but had to engage an appointed government travel agent. Strand selected Tropical Tours as its Colombian agent, which in turn engaged the transportation company. Approximately two months before the incident that gave rise to this case, the Strand representative in Colombia, Jean Robinson, became dissatisfied with the safety and services of the bus company then used by Tropical Tours. Robinson conveyed her concerns to Mr. Lewis, Strand's vice-president responsible for tour packages. Mr. Lewis travelled to Colombia and requested that Tropical Tours engage another bus company. Colombia's Director of Tourism advised Mr. Lewis that Expresso Brasilia was the best bus company available. Mr. Lewis asked Tropical Tours to engage Expresso Brasilia. There was evidence that Strand had requested that mechanical inspections of the buses be performed, but no evidence that Strand had ensured that they had been done.

Mr. and Mrs. Craven were elderly, experienced travellers who had dealt with the travel agency before. They had selected the Strand tour after perusing a variety of brochures, and had received a confirmation folder from the travel agency. The brochure and the folder contained the disclaimer statements set forth above. After arriving in Barranquilla, the Cravens and other members of the tour were met at the airport by Jean Robinson. She and the tour members boarded the bus for the drive to Cartagena. While driving down the main coastal highway at speeds that witnesses described as moderate to excessive, the bus burst a tire and overturned, landing in a ditch. The Cravens suffered physical injuries and recovered damages at trial. The jury found the following:

1. The defendant was negligent in its selection of the bus company, and that Mr. Lewis and Ms. Robinson had negligently assumed that the inspections would take place without seeking any proof or records of the inspections.

2. The bus company and driver were negligent because of the speed of the bus and the unnecessary and unsafe passing that occurred.

3. The plaintiffs were unaware of the disclaimer that limited Strand's liability.

Strand appealed the finding of liability, and the Cravens cross-appealed the damage award (meaning that the Cravens thought the damage award was too low while Strand did not think it should be asked to pay anything). Strand appealed partly on the basis that the issue of the disclaimer had not been properly framed to the jury. The jury had found that the Cravens were unaware of the disclaimer; however, the question of the limitation clause had been put to the jury too narrowly. The jury should have been asked whether Strand had taken reasonable measures to draw the disclaimer to the Cravens' attention. The limitation was not buried in dense wording or in discouragingly tiny print, but was prominently positioned in the brochure and set in a readable typeface. The Cravens were seasoned travellers who had ample opportunity to read the brochure and confirmation folder in full. The jury had also found the defendant negligent with respect to the bus inspections; however, there was no evidence before them that a mechanical inspection would have detected the likelihood of a tire blowout. There was no evidence of a causal connection between the failure to inspect and the accident. The Court of Appeal quoted favourably from the American case of *Dorkin et al. v. American Express Co.*, (1973) 345 N.Y.S. (2d) 891, affirmed in 351 N.Y.S. (2d) 190:

> The crucial issue is the relationship between the defendant and the foreign bus company on whose bus plaintiff was injured. While the allegations of the complaint, if proved, are sufficient to hold the defendant liable, an examination of the papers submitted on the motion reveals that the tour bus was owned and operated by an independent contractor. Such relationship, therefore, precludes any liability on the part of the defendant, either on a theory of negligence or

breach of contract. Defendant agreed to supply plaintiffs with a planned European tour with meals, lodging and transportation. It did not, however, insure the safety of plaintiff. The disclaimer in the tour contract negates any intent of the defendant to assume a contractual obligation for such safety.

Mr. Justice Lacourcière of the Ontario Court of Appeal stated, "[this] appeal illustrates the difficulty in formulating appropriate questions for a jury where it is unclear whether the damages suffered arise from a breach of contract or from the breach of an obligation or duty fixed by tort law." A new trial was ordered, but the parties settled.

Vicarious Liability

Travel agents may be liable for the negligence of tour operators if the agent knew or ought to have known of deficiencies in the tour operator's management or tour packages. Tour operators are not generally liable to the consumer for the negligence of independent travel agents. When a travel agent gives wrong information or advice to a consumer, the negligence usually occurs prior to the effective involvement of the tour operator. In the next case, a poorly informed travel agent caused a consumer to cancel his plans and lose his deposit. Despite winning at trial, the consumer was ultimately unsuccessful in recovering his deposit when he sued the tour operator instead of the travel agent.

Regent Holidays Ltd. v. Cooper, [1989] O.J. No. 1778 (Ont. Div. Ct.)

In January 1986, Mr. and Mrs. Cooper purchased a package from Discount Travel through Mr. Slade. Mrs. Cooper was a nervous flyer, especially during landings and takeoffs. Mr. Cooper expressed to the agent a strong desire to fly from Toronto and land at Gatwick Airport in England, with no other stops. After paying for the package, Mr. Cooper noted that the flight they were booked on seemed to be 90 minutes longer than other flights. Mr. Cooper questioned Mr. Slade about the longer flight time, and again stated their desire to take off in Toronto and make no stops until Gatwick. Mr. Slade phoned the tour operator, Regent Holidays, in Montreal to clear up the matter.

The trial transcripts revealed that Mr. Slade, despite being a licensed travel agent, did not know the difference between a nonstop flight and a direct flight. A nonstop flight does not stop until it reaches its intended final destination. By contrast, a direct flight may make several stops on the way to the final destination, although the passengers heading to the final destination do not have to change planes. The difference between the two flights is considerable, and fundamental to the knowledge of a competent travel agent. Mr. Slade used the word "direct" in his discussions with Regent. He did mention Mrs. Cooper's nervous condition to the Regent representative. The Regent representative informed Mr. Slade that the flight was a direct flight; however, Mr. Slade conveyed the information to Mr. Cooper in such a way that Mr. Cooper left the agency reasonably believing that he and his wife were booked on a nonstop flight.

As advised by Mr. Slade, Mr. Cooper had bought flight insurance, but when he learned that the flight was (or so he thought) a nonstop flight, he cancelled the insurance. When Mr. Cooper learned that the flight was direct with stops, he made other arrangements and sued to recover his deposit on the basis that he had been misinformed about the flight. He had not been told that a direct flight is not necessarily nonstop or that this flight included at least one stop. The trial judge held Regent liable. Regent appealed.

The error in this case was by the travel agent who did not know the difference between direct and nonstop flights. In speaking to the Regent representative, Mr. Slade had consistently referred to a direct flight. There was no evidence that the Regent representative had referred to the flight as anything but a direct flight. Because Regent had done nothing wrong, the appeal was allowed and the judgment set aside. The Coopers' cause of action was against Discount Travel and its employee, Slade.

Mental Distress

In cases of breach of contract as opposed to breach of duty of care, damages for mental distress were once difficult to obtain. The courts are more inclined today to entertain such claims in contract. To establish a claim for mental distress, a plaintiff must prove that the parties contemplated at the time they entered into the contract that its breach might entail mental distress such as shock, frustration, annoyance, or disappointment. The following are two cases in which a plaintiff successfully sued for mental distress.

Destinations should meet the traveller's expectations.

Jarvis v. Swan Tours Ltd., [1973] 1 All E.R. 71 (C.A.)

Jarvis booked a two-week ski holiday in Switzerland through Swan Tours. The brochure led Jarvis to believe that he would be in the midst of a winter wonderland among many other party-minded guests. Upon arrival, he discovered that the ski hill was much farther away than expected, that the rental equipment was substandard, and that there were few other guests and in fact none during the second week. Jarvis spent the holiday he had so looked forward to in a state of boredom and annoyance. He sued successfully for various special damages and general damages for the mental distress of his loss of enjoyment, disappointment, upset, and frustration caused by the breach of contract.

In the *Jarvis* case, because there were no issues involving the carrier, only the tour operator was liable. In the following case, only the carrier was liable. There were no issues about the holiday arrangements, and so the travel agency and tour operator were not liable.

Newell et al. v. Canadian Pacific Airlines, Ltd. (1976), 14 O.R. (2d) 752

Mrs. Newell used a wheelchair. Mr. Newell was recovering from a heart attack. To recuperate, they bought two tickets from Toronto to Mexico City on Canadian Pacific, a reputable airline. They wished to take their two pet dogs with them. Prior to the flight, the dogs had been examined by a doctor and found to be in excellent health. When the Newells arrived at the airport, employees of the defendant advised them that the dogs could not join them in the passenger section of the aircraft. Indicating their concern for the welfare of the dogs, the Newells offered to reserve the entire first-class section so that they could keep their dogs with them. The defendant refused, as was its right.

Before the plaintiffs boarded the plane, representatives of the defendant informed them that the dogs had been stowed safely in a cargo compartment and would be "in first class condition when the aircraft arrive[d] in Mexico City." When the defendant accepted the dogs, it issued the plaintiffs an Excess Baggage Ticket that referred to "live dogs" weighing 28 kilograms and an excess baggage fee of $56.56. On the front of the Ticket was the instruction, "For conditions of contract, see passenger ticket and baggage check."

Upon arrival, one dog was dead and the other comatose from carbon dioxide poisoning. With the help of the defendant's agent in Mexico City, medical aid was obtained for the sick dog. The plaintiffs took turns for 48 hours administering oxygen to it to save its life. The Newells, who had loved the dogs as family, were greatly distressed. Mrs. Newell became very concerned about the effect of the incident on her husband's health. On the return flight to Toronto, the defendant agreed to allow the dog in the passenger section provided the plaintiffs purchased the six seats behind the bulkhead at a cost of $450.

The plaintiffs sued for general damages for "anguish, loss of enjoyment of life and sadness" and for special damages in the amount of $1,058.27. The defendant disputed the claim for general damages, admitted liability for special damages, but submitted that its liability was limited under the *Carriage by Air Act*. Counsel for both parties agreed that, if the court found a limitation on the amount of special damages, $560 would be the amount. They further agreed that the defendant's liability arose under Article 18(1) (a) of the Warsaw Convention, which states:

> [a] carrier is liable for damage sustained in the event of the destruction or loss of, or of damage to, any registered baggage or any cargo, if the occurrence which caused the damage so sustained took place during the carriage by air.

The Article of the Warsaw Convention limiting liability was 22(2)(a). It was replaced by The Hague Protocol of 1955, which states:

> (a) In the carriage of registered baggage and of cargo, the liability of the carrier is limited to a sum of two hundred and fifty francs per kilogram, unless the passenger of consignor has made, at the time when the package was handed over to the carrier, a special declaration of interest in delivery at destination and has paid a supplementary sum if the case so requires.

The plaintiffs submitted that the defendant could not rely on Article 22(2)(a) as replaced because the defendant had acted "recklessly and with knowledge that damage would probably result" under Article 25 of The Hague Protocol, which states:

> The limits of liability specified in Article 22 (of the Warsaw Convention) shall not apply if it is proved that the damage resulted from an act or omission of the

carrier, his servants or agents, done with intent to cause damage or recklessly and with knowledge the damage would probably result; provided that, in the case of such act or omission of a servant or agent, it is also proved that he was acting within the scope of his employment.

In the alternative, the plaintiffs claimed that the dogs were "cargo" such that if no waybill was issued, the defendant could not rely on the limitation. The court found that the defendant had demonstrated its intention to treat the dogs as baggage, not cargo, when it issued the Excess Baggage Ticket. The plaintiffs then claimed that the defendant could not rely on the limitation because the Excess Baggage Ticket gave no notice of the limitation as required by Article 22(2)(a) as replaced. However, Article 4 of the Hague Protocol relieves the carrier from printing on a baggage check the information required with respect to limitation of liability if the baggage check is combined with, or incorporated into, the passenger ticket. The court found that the plaintiffs' tickets contained all the required information.

The court then considered the application of Article 25 of The Hague Protocol. Counsel for the plaintiffs submitted that his clients were entitled to rely on its provisions to recover the entire amount of their special and general damages because they had satisfied the onus contained in the Article, in that the damages had resulted from the reckless act or omission of the defendant with knowledge that damage would probably result, and that the act or omission was that of a servant or agent of the defendant acting within the scope of his employment.

Ronald Hoffman, the ramp service manager of the defendant, testified that the dogs had been placed in a cargo compartment designated for the carriage of live animals, but near a shipment of vaccine packed in dry ice. Dry ice is solid carbon dioxide. When thawing, it emits carbon dioxide in a gaseous state, sufficient quantities of which are deadly. Mr. Hoffman explained that three different departments of the defendant were responsible for loading the aircraft—Cargo Services, Passenger Services, and Ramp Services. Cargo Services had accepted the vaccine shipment and was aware that it was packed in dry ice. Passenger Services had registered the plaintiffs and accepted their dogs. Ramp Services had loaded the aircraft. One of the duties owed by the defendant was to ensure that animals and dry ice were not placed in the same compartment. However, Cargo Services had failed to inform Ramp Services that the vaccine had already been loaded into the compartment.

Mr. Hoffman made the following statement: "The personnel at the aircraft saw the containers and vaccine going on the aircraft with the indication of dry ice. And this did not register on them because at the time they didn't have the animals. ... When the animals showed up to be loaded, it still did not register on them that there was a dangerous condition in relation to the animals. ... But basically what happened is that the individual responsible for planning the loading of that aircraft was not aware of these two conditions, the existence of the dogs or the existence of the dry ice. ... We had a communication failure." Mr. Hoffman added that the cargo manual indicated that "live animals should not be carried in the same compartment as ... dry ice." It was the responsibility of Cargo Services to notify Ramp Services that a shipment of dry ice was to be loaded on the aircraft so that Ramp Services could take the necessary precautions. The notification did not take place.

The court found (1) that the employees in Cargo Services had known that if live animals and dry ice were placed in the same compartment, there was a risk to the animals, and (2) that they had failed to notify Ramp Services. The court found that the employees in Cargo Services had been grossly careless. The court ruled that the defendant could not rely on the limitation of liability. The defendant contested the $450 claimed by the plaintiffs for transporting the remaining dog back to Toronto. The court found that, in the circumstances, that was a reasonable way for the plaintiffs to transport the sick dog. The plaintiffs recovered their special damages.

Further, the evidence made it clear that the parties had contemplated at the time they entered into the contract that its breach might result in mental distress. The defendant was aware of the plaintiffs' deep concern for the welfare of their pets. It acknowledged that concern when its employees assured the plaintiffs that their dogs would be safe in the cargo compartment. The defendant had enough information to realize that if injury or death were to befall the dogs, it would likely cause the plaintiffs mental distress. The Newells recovered general damages of $500.

Verbal Contracts

Many contracts or terms of contracts in the travel industry are verbal. Disputes are inevitable. The burden of proof necessary to tip the scales beyond 50 percent lies with the plaintiff. (For a discussion of the formation and enforceability of contracts, see Chapter 3.)

In an unreported case, the traveller claimed to have been quoted $349 for a trip. The travel agent claimed that the quote was $399. The judge heard the witnesses and concluded that he could not establish which version was the truth. The judge found that both parties were telling the truth as they saw it and that it was likely that there had been a misunderstanding between two honest people over what the quote had been. Where a judge cannot find that one party is the greater cause of the misunderstanding, the evidence will be in balance, leaving the plaintiff without a remedy. In other words, when there is no presumption favouring either party, the parties are in balance, and the plaintiff will fail to tip the scales in his favour.

Notwithstanding this case, travel agencies should not rely on a finding of honesty to save them from liability. In a contest between an honest traveller and an honest agent, the courts have a tendency to consider that it is more likely that the traveller's memory of the terms is more accurate than the agent's, on the basis that the traveller has to remember only one arrangement, while the agent must juggle the arrangements of scores of clients. Courts tend to find that the agent is honest but mistaken. For example, in another unreported case, the travel agency had agreed to remind the customer by telephone of the departure time of his flight. The customer had been assisted by two agents. The agency's written checklist indicated that one of the agents had telephoned the customer the day before departure, but he missed the flight anyway. Under oath, the customer contradicted several of the statements contained in his pleadings. The judge found both agents honest and trustworthy, yet found for the customer.

Disclaimers

Disclaimers are statements that attempt to limit the liability of the party relying on them. Often appearing in travel brochures, documents, and contracts, they advise the consumer of limitations on the issuer's liability. **Disclaimers** have met with mixed success in the courts. For a more detailed discussion on disclaimers and waivers, see Chapter 3.

Tilden Rent-A-Car Co. v. Clendenning (1978), 18 O.R. (2d) 601

C argued that he was not bound by a provision in a car rental agreement that he had signed. The provision was printed on the reverse side of the contract in such small print that all but the most cautious consumers were discouraged from reading it. The rental clerk had made no attempt to draw C's attention to the provision. The court found that "[t]he clerk could not help but have known that C had not in fact read the contract before signing it." In these circumstances, Tilden could not rely on the clause.

Disclaimers will generally not avail their issuers if they are not brought reasonably to the attention of consumers, especially if the consumers are practically discouraged from reading them. However, the outcomes of cases involving disclaimers will vary depending on the facts. In *Craven et al. v. Strand Holiday (Canada) Ltd., supra*, the Cravens tried to avoid the impact of the disclaimer on the back of a travel brochure. The Court of Appeal stated:

> This is not a case where the passengers accepted a standard form contract containing onerous provisions in small type in circumstances where no one could be reasonably expected to read it. This was not a transaction carried out in a hurried manner where speed could be said to be one of the attractive features of the services provided. ... Before entering into the contract, the passengers, who were professional people as well as experienced travellers, discussed the proposed travel package with an employee of the agency. They had ample and extended opportunity to examine the brochure and familiarize themselves with the conditions. Their failure to do so ... does not, in my view, exonerate them from the effect of the conditions.

Thus, a disclaimer that is well written and clearly and fairly presented to the consumer will tend to be found effective in limiting liability in the manner set forth in the disclaimer.

Court Actions

Litigation is expensive. Often the cost of the action outstrips the amount of the claim. For claims below a threshold, all provinces have provided a small claims court that dispenses with many of the costly trappings of the formal litigation machinery. The simplicity and economy of bringing an action in a small claims court make it a very busy hive. Although the participants may retain lawyers or paralegals to represent them, the system is designed to allow the participants to represent themselves. Because the participants tend to be unfamiliar with the process and misled by what they see on television, the judge takes a much more involved and inquisitorial approach. Although claim limits vary by jurisdiction (e.g., $10,000 in Ontario), they are high enough to allow the small claims courts to hear the vast majority of travel cases.

Rules of procedure allow a large number of small claimants to band together to bring a class action against a common defendant where there are substantially common grounds. The greater resources of the class allow the lawyers for the group to pursue the defendant vigorously, a pursuit that often results in larger returns to the individual claimants.

Insurance

During the 1990s, the number of claims against travel agents in the United States rose about 30 percent. The costs are eventually borne by travel suppliers and consumers. While Canadians are not as litigious as Americans, they appear to be headed in the same direction. Residents of other countries are also able to seek recourse against travel agents in their home countries in such a way that the costs are eventually passed onto Canadian suppliers. The true number of claims is impossible to calculate because many of the cases settle without court action. Many claims are frivolous, but some are well founded. Excellent operating procedures within the agency reduce the potential for claims. The risk cannot be eliminated because agencies may be sued for innocent errors **vicariously** or as conduits to the truly blameworthy. An agency should consider insurance as protection against potentially ruinous claims.

Other Legal Rights

Ticket Refunds

Travellers are not entitled to ticket refunds as of right. It depends on the circumstances and the policies of the transportation provider. If the provider fails to honour its obligation (e.g., by cancelling a leg of a flight without right), then the provider must refund the ticket. If the traveller through no fault of the provider fails to make use of the ticket, the provider is under no obligation to refund the cost of the ticket. Depending on the type and price of the ticket, VIA Rail and many airlines routinely alter tickets for business travellers whose plans have changed. For example, there are flights between Ottawa and Toronto almost every hour except overnight. Travellers may change or even cancel their tickets and receive a substantial refund. The airlines ignore their strict contractual rights in the interest of good public relations.

Baggage Claims

Failure to deliver or return baggage is a breach of contract entitling the traveller to damages. Less than .05 percent of all luggage handled by the transportation industry goes missing each year. Of that luggage, 80 percent is returned to its owners within one day and 15 percent within the first week. The remaining 5 percent represents about 20 000 pieces of luggage, most of which are lost.

For international flights, the Warsaw Convention limits the liability of the airline for lost, damaged, or stolen baggage to $20 (U.S.) per kilogram up to 32 kilograms or $640 (U.S.) per bag. A traveller has a right to declare a greater value and buy additional coverage. If so, the airline is bound by the declaration. The traveller may also purchase separate travel insurance. The airlines lose their right to limited liability if they have engaged in willful misconduct or if they fail to follow the notice, tagging, and other requirements set forth in the Warsaw Convention. If a flight attendant takes control of a passenger's carry-on luggage without issuing a baggage check, the notice and tagging requirements of the Convention have not been met. The airline would be liable for the full value of the carry-on luggage and its contents. In return for the limitation of liability, the airlines are presumed liable unless they can show that they took all reasonable precautions to avoid the loss or damage.

The Warsaw Convention does not apply to domestic flights. The limitation of liability for such losses on domestic flights is found in tariffs applicable to the domestic airline industry.

Human Rights Issues

With respect to employment practices and dealing with the public, all travel industries are subject to applicable human rights legislation. For discussion of these topics, see Chapter 2.

Travellers with Disabilities

Airlines and other carriers must take reasonable steps to accommodate travellers who have disabilities. If, on **bona fide** considerations, it would truly be dangerous or impractical to carry the passenger with a disability, the carrier may refuse to do so. Mere inconvenience or additional expense will not excuse the carrier. A carrier may not refuse a traveller on the grounds that the wheelchair will be bulky because a wheelchair can be stowed and tied down. However, an airline could refuse to board a passenger with a sufficiently serious heart problem.

Right to Cancel Transportation

A carrier may cancel transportation with impunity if on reasonable grounds it believes that the weather conditions are dangerous or if it has received a bomb threat. To avoid becoming liable for breach of contract on other grounds, the carrier must assist the passengers in making alternative travel arrangements.

Right to Refuse or Eject Troublesome Travellers

The captains of planes and ships, the conductors of trains, and their delegates have the right on behalf of their employers to refuse entry and to eject travellers who are unreasonably boisterous, belligerent, drunken, disruptive, or threatening. Such actions must be taken upon a bona fide and prudent analysis of the situation. If the carrier reasonably believes that a failure to refuse or eject such a person would result in liability to innocent passengers, it is very unlikely that the carrier would be liable to the refused or ejected person.

Right to Refuse Illegal Ticket Holders

A carrier has the right to refuse carriage to any person who has acquired a ticket in violation of applicable law or carrier's tariffs, rules, or regulations. It is a violation for one person to use a ticket that has been issued in the name of someone else. In addition to reasons of security and identification, the right to refuse arises from the fact that no true contract has been created between the carrier and the traveller. In the absence of simple inadvertence on the part of the traveller, the carrier may reasonably conclude that the traveller's violation of the law and rules is an indication of untrustworthiness amounting to a greater and unacceptable risk.

Right to Refuse Pets

Carriers may refuse to carry animals (except seeing-eye dogs) in the main passenger sections of the transport. Animals are treated as pieces of luggage; thus, they may be carried in the cargo areas. As demonstrated in the *Newell* case, *supra*, the carrier has a duty to ensure that the conditions in the cargo hold are conducive to the proper and healthy transportation of live animals.

Overbooking

For the same reasons that hotels overbook, carriers overbook their carriage capacity. If they overestimate the number of no-shows, they face the unhappy prospect of bumping annoyed travellers. They are subject to the same duties as hotels to take all reasonable steps to assist the inconvenienced passengers. If the carrier is unable to eliminate the special and general damages of the passenger, the carrier will be liable for them. If the carrier fails to attempt to make alternative travel arrangements, a court might well be moved to assess exemplary damages to prod all carriers into more considerate conduct.

Many travellers are aware that the cost of travelling would rise if carriers could not over-book. They may even be willing to accept some short-term inconvenience for the greater good of all, but they do require a fair and courteous attempt by the carrier to minimize the inconvenience.

Trust Money

The money received by travel agents from their customers may be used only (1) to purchase the travel services contracted for by the customer, (2) to reimburse the customer, or (3) to pay the agent the commission once it has been earned. Until the commission is earned, the customer's money is trust money (whether or not it is in a designated trust account) and does not belong to the agent. Deposits made pending the commencement of the travel service are also trust monies. Quebec, Ontario, and British Columbia have passed travel Acts that include provisions relating to trust accounts (see "The Provincial Travel Acts," page 347). Where there is no statutory trust account requirement, the protection of the money may be found in other legislation (e.g., misuse of trust funds may be theft under the *Criminal Code of Canada*), contract law, or the common law. For example, the IATA Sales Agency Agreement requires that airline ticket receipts be deposited in a trust account pending remittance to IATA. Under common law, cheques issued on a general account containing customers' money should never in the aggregate result in there being less money in the account than is necessary to reimburse every customer. Cheques issued on a trust account are restricted to:

1. a refund to the customer;
2. the purchase of travel services on behalf of the customer; and
3. the transfer of the profit portion of the sale of the travel services to the agent's general account.

Lowden v. The Queen (1982), 139 D.L.R. (3d) 257

Mr. Lowden was the president and principal shareholder of a corporate travel agency. The agency accepted customer deposits and deposited them in the agency's general account. For eight years, the agency operated in this manner, using customer deposit money and a line of credit to meet expenses. The bank eventually called the loan and the agency went out of business. Mr. Lowden was convicted of theft.

Canadian Pacific Airlines, Ltd. v. Canadian Imperial Bank of Commerce, 61 O.R. (2d) 233 (H.C.)

Two actions were tried together. The actions arose from the affairs of two travel agents, Vittore's Travel Agency and Uniglobe Markham Travel Limited. Section F of the Passenger Sales Agency Agreement (now section 6 of IATA Resolution 804, being the Sales Agency Agreement for Canada and Bermuda) required all travel agents to deposit in a trust account all payments earmarked for IATA, and to submit to the BSP Processing Centre weekly reports detailing ticket sales made on behalf of the airlines. The Passenger Sales Agency Agreement in force at the time stated in part:

> [A]ll money collected by the Agent for transportation and ancillary services sold under this Agreement, including applicable commissions which the Agent is

entitled to claim thereunder, shall be the property of the Carrier and shall be held by the Agent in trust for the Carrier or on behalf of the Carrier, until satisfactorily accounted for to the Carrier, and settlement made.

The travel agents were authorized to sell "travel documents" for Canadian Pacific and other carriers. IATA duly collected the proceeds and distributed them to the proper parties. Vittore's maintained both a trust account and a general account. Vittore's wrongly deposited its customer receipts in the general account. The money was transferred by the bank from the general account into the trust account only when the IATA preauthorized payment forms were presented. In the case of Uniglobe, there was no trust account, but only a general account in which all monies were deposited and from which the IATA payments were made. Both agencies had a revolving line of credit with the bank that allowed overdrafts up to a specified limit. Deposits made were used to reduce the overdraft. Thus, funds that should have been held in trust were used to reduce the agencies' debts and interest charges.

From January to April 1981, Vittore's sold 22 Canadian Pacific tickets for $13,166. The funds were deposited in Vittore's general account. The bank applied the funds to Vittore's line of credit. When IATA presented its preauthorized payment form, the bank refused to honour it. In November and December 1984, Uniglobe received from Kubota Tractor two payments of $24,000 and $80,510 for a group trip to Japan. The cheques were deposited in Uniglobe's general account. The bank applied $65,000 to the line of credit. Canadian Pacific received partial payment but could not collect $71,169. The remaining $6,169 was never traced.

The court found that all the characteristics of a trust were present and that a trust relationship existed between Canadian Pacific and the two agencies. The issue was whether or not the defendant bank knew, or should have known, that the funds in the travel agency accounts were impressed with a trust and therefore were not available to the bank for the purpose of reducing corporate indebtedness.

A corporation is deemed to have the knowledge of its officers. A former owner and officer of Vittore's testified that he had shown the IATA agreement to the late Mr. Batler, a manager at the bank. Mr. Batler could not testify from the grave. The judge commented that he "listened to [the owner] on this point and observed his demeanour in the witness stand, and was uneasy and unable to believe that testimony." The owner's evidence was rejected. However, another official of the bank with knowledge of the circumstances testified that he was aware that Vittore's had two accounts and that the bank was honouring the preauthorized payments to IATA by transferring the appropriate amount from the general account to the trust account.

The court found it rather strange that there should be a trust account at all, if all the money was deposited to the general account only to be transferred to the trust account when demand by IATA was made. This arrangement, which took place under the bank's nose, appeared to be a mishandling of the trust account by Vittore's. None of the evidence showed any attempt by the bank to determine the reason for the odd processing of funds. The court concluded that the bank knew, or ought to have known, that the money was the proceeds of ticket sales sold by Vittore's as agent for the airline as principal. A bank is deemed to have a reasonable knowledge of the nature of its customer's business. The court went on to find that a reasonable person would conclude that, when a consumer purchases airline tickets through an agent, the bulk of the money surely belongs to the airline. The court held that the bank's standard procedure of transferring funds from Vittore's general account to the trust account proved that the bank was aware of the nature of the relationship between its account holder and Canadian Pacific. In the case of Uniglobe, the bank knew that the money had come directly from the sale of tickets to Kubota Tractor.

In both cases, the bank was aware, through its officers and employees, that at least part of the money was not the property of the agents and could not be used to reduce its debts. The bank was found to be a constructive trustee of the funds. Canadian Pacific obtained judgment for $78,166.75 plus interest and costs. Canadian Pacific did not bother to sue the agencies because they were in financial distress and unlikely to honour any judgments entered against them.

It is risky to deal with sloppy or dishonest agencies. Ticket revenues may be lost, innocent principals may suffer damage to their goodwill, and customers may be left with invalid tickets or suffer miserable holidays for which financial compensation is insufficient comfort.

The Provincial Travel Acts

Consumers frequently make their travel plans on faith. The purchaser of a holiday vacation usually does not have the opportunity to inspect the premises prior to booking. Too often in the past, vacationers arrived at destinations only to find that the amenities were not as advertised, that the hotels were substandard (and sometimes not even built), and that the small airlines were unavailable for the return trip. Too often, the travel agencies and wholesalers went out of business, taking the tour deposits with them. The three provinces with the greatest number of travel agencies and agents— Quebec, Ontario, and British Columbia—responded to the need to protect the public from poorly managed operations and unscrupulous agents by each passing a travel Act and introducing a compensation fund. The travel Acts restrict and control persons engaged or wishing to be engaged in the travel business. Recent changes to the Act in Ontario places no liability on the travel agent for the failure of an end supplier. Agents are no longer responsible for funds passed in good faith in arm's-length transactions. Every licensed travel agent and travel wholesaler contributes to the fund. The main purpose of the Acts is to ensure that:

1. all travel agencies and wholesalers are registered and subject to regulation;

2. all travel agencies and wholesalers use proper business practices;

3. money deposited with the travel agency or wholesaler is kept in trust, if so required by the Act, and used for the intended purpose; and

4. customers who suffer losses as a result of the actions of an agent or wholesaler are compensated.

The travel Acts contain the power to revoke the registration of a registrant under certain conditions. Revocations can be for violations of the statutory requirements or for reasons in the public interest—a very broad latitude. The registrant has a right to notice of the intention to revoke (and the reasons for it) and to a hearing.

Most licence revocations are for financial offences. However, such was not the case when the registration of Outdoor Adventures Ltd. of Mississauga, operated by L. Nyuli (also known as Rod Hunter), was suspended by the registrar for carrying on its business from premises that were a residence. The company was not open to the public during normal hours, did not always make available complete books and records, was unreasonably slow in filing financial reports, and failed to file changes in address. The tribunal upheld the suspension, stating, "[We] take a very serious attitude to all violations, particularly when repeated."

The travel Acts were effective and drove many substandard operations out of business. The Acts may also be used to help travel agents and wholesalers who are in financial difficulty as a result of having honoured customer travel arrangements without receiving payment.

When in Rome

Travellers should always bear in mind local differences and be courteous and adaptable. Tourism is one of the world's most important economic activities. Most hosts are eager to please. Fortunately for English speakers, it is almost always possible to find someone who speaks some English at or near most non-English travel destinations. However bad the host's English, it is usually better than the Canadian traveller's grasp of the local language. Therefore, the following examples of notices are offered good-naturedly and with the rueful realization that our attempts to write notices in other languages must be equally comical.

- Hotel in Mexico: "The manager has personally passed all the water served here."
- Italian clinic: "Specialist in Women and Other Diseases."
- Norwegian bar: "Women are requested not to have children in the bar."
- Austrian inn: "In case of fire, do your utmost to alarm the hotel porter."
- Austrian ski resort: "Not to perambulate late the corridors in the hours of repose in the boots of ascension."
- Swiss restaurant: "Our wines leave you nothing to hope for."
- Swiss hotel: "Because of the impropriety of entertaining guests of the opposite sex in the bedroom, it is suggested that the lobby be used for this purpose."
- Hong Kong clothing store: "Ladies may have a fit upstairs."
- Hungarian hotel: "The lift is being fixed for the next day. During that time we regret that you will be unbearable."
- Polish hotel dining room: "Salad a firm own make. Limpid red beet soup with cheesy dumplings in the form of a finger. Roasted duck let loose. Beef rashers beaten up in country people's fashion."
- Tokyo car rental brochure: "When passengers of foot heave in sight, tootle the horn. Trumpet him melodiously at first, but if he still obstacles your passage, then tootle him with vigour."

In China, "Finger-lickin' good" was translated as "Eat your fingers off," and a cola ad was translated as either "Female horse stuffed with wax" or "Bite the wax tadpole." Lastly, from England, in English, at a laundromat, "Automatic Washing Machines. Please remove all your clothes when the light goes out," and in a London office, "Toilet out of order. Please use floor below," and in a department store, "Bargain Basement Upstairs."

Recommendations

1. Disclose the principal to the client at or before the time of contracting.
2. Fulfill all undertakings. Undertake no obligations that cannot be fulfilled.
3. Avoid generalities that may not be true, e.g., "Everyone on the tour will speak English."

4. Be certain of all statements of fact or opinion.

5. Do not promise good weather, good fishing, a good time, or other subjective matters.

6. Be certain of government requirements and restrictions before commenting on them.

7. Be truthful, forthright, and courteous at all times.

8. Meet high professional standards. Agents are liable for negligent advice to clients or anyone else who may reasonably rely on the advice.

9. Bring to the client's attention any disclaimers and explain them clearly.

10. Document that travel insurance was explained and offered to the customer.

11. Read all visa information carefully.

12. Recommend the best product for the customer's needs.

13. Inform the customer of any weaknesses of the product known to the agency.

14. Inform the customer of any relevant information that arises after the sale.

15. Maintain trust accounts wholly within the requirements of the law. If a separate trust account is not required, treat all funds received from customers as trust funds and sacrosanct. Correct all inadvertent banking errors without delay.

16. Maintain all other required business records. Submit the governmental filings on time.

Summary

Travel and tourism constitute one of Canada's largest industries. The tourism and travel sector is heavily regulated in the public interest by federal, provincial, and international regulation.

Many travel wholesalers and consumers engage travel agents to assist with travel plans. Agency is a legal relationship whereby one party, the principal, authorizes a second party, the agent, to enter into a contractual agreement on behalf of the principal with a third party, the consumer. The principal delegates to the agent the authority to negotiate contracts on the principal's behalf with the consumer. Provided the agent acts within the real or apparent authority of the principal, the principal will be bound by the contract entered into by the agent. The principal is not ordinarily bound by contracts entered into outside the scope of the actual or apparent authority granted. The agency relationship may be created by contract, ratification, estoppel, or necessity. Agents may be employees of the principal or independent contractors.

The duties that an agent owes the principal include obedience, competence, personal performance, honesty toward the public, and good faith toward the principal. The duties that a principal owes the agent include honouring the agency agreement, competence, honesty, good faith, the payment of earned commissions, and reimbursement for proper costs. An agent may be liable for the failure of the principal to honour the contract if the agent has failed to reveal the existence of the principal to the consumer. In such a case, the agent would have to sue the principal for indemnity. Agents are also liable when presenting themselves as agents when they are not authorized to do so, provided the principal does not ratify the contract.

Agents and principals may also be liable to each other, and to others who are parties to their contractual arrangements, for any breaches of contract in line with general contract law. Agents and principals owe each other and the public a duty of care in line with general negligence law. An agent, like any professional adviser, may also be liable in tort to a nonclient who reasonably relies on the advice and suffers damages as a result of the reliance even though there was no contractual relationship between the agent and the nonclient. As with other persons relying on disclaimers, principals and agents may not rely on them unless they are clear and reasonable and have been brought reasonably to the attention of the consumer.

Quebec, Ontario, and British Columbia have enacted travel Acts, which restrict and control persons engaged in the travel business.

Discussion Questions

1. What are the main objectives of the Canadian Tourism Commission?

2. Which provinces have a travel Act and what are the main purposes of the travel Acts?

3. What is the name of the legal relationship between a travel retailer and an airline?

4. When does a principal have to honour sales made on its behalf?

5. Does the agency agreement have to be in writing to be binding on all parties?

6. Describe an instance of estoppel in the principal–agent relationship.

7. Are the agreements made by a subagent of an agency binding on the principal?

8. Is a principal bound to reimburse an agent for unauthorized costs? Discuss.

9. When is an agent liable for the actions of a principal?

10. What, if any, is an agent's responsibility for the safety of vehicles used for transportation at the holiday destination by the holiday provider?

11. What is the responsibility of an airline in the case of over-booking?

Appendix: Sample Airline Ticket Disclaimer

Notice of Notice and Conditions (on front)

Passenger Ticket and Baggage Check—IATA—Subject to conditions of contract in this ticket. This ticket is not valid and will not be accepted for carriage unless purchased from the issuing carrier or its authorized travel agent.

Notice (on back)

If the passenger's journey involves an ultimate destination or stop in a country other than the country of departure, the Warsaw Convention may be applicable, and the Convention governs and in most cases limits the liability of carriers for death or personal injury and in respect of loss of or damage to baggage. See also notices headed "Advice to International Passengers on Limitation of Liability" and "Notice of Baggage Liability Limitations."

Conditions of Contract

1. As used in this contract, "ticket" means this passenger ticket and baggage check; or this itinerary/receipt, if applicable, in the case of an electronic ticket; of which these conditions and the notices form part, "carriage" is equivalent to "transportation," "carrier" means all air carriers that carry or undertake to carry the passenger or his baggage hereunder or perform any other service incidental to such air carriage, "electronic ticket" means the itinerary/receipt issued by or on

behalf of carrier, the electronic coupons and, if applicable, a boarding document. "Warsaw Convention" means the Convention for the Unification of Certain Rules Relating to International Carriage by Air signed at Warsaw, 12th October 1929, or that Convention as amended at The Hague, 28th September 1955, whichever may be applicable.

2. Carriage hereunder is subject to the rules and limitations relating to liability established by the Warsaw Convention unless such carriage is not "international carriage" as defined by that Convention.

3. To the extent not in conflict with the foregoing, carriage and other services performed by each carrier are subject to (i) provisions contained in this ticket, (ii) applicable tariffs, (iii) carrier's conditions of carriage and related regulations which are made part hereof (and are available on application at the offices of carrier), except in transportation between a place in the United States or Canada and any place outside thereof to which tariffs in force in those countries apply.

4. Carrier's name may be abbreviated in the ticket, the full name and its abbreviation being set forth in carrier's tariffs, conditions of carriage, regulations or timetables; carrier's address shall be the airport of departure shown opposite the first abbreviation of carrier's name in the ticket; the agreed stopping places are those places set forth in this ticket or as shown in carrier's timetables as scheduled stopping places on the passenger's route; carriage to be performed hereunder by several successive carriers is regarded as a single operation.

5. An air carrier issuing a ticket for carriage over the lines of another air carrier does so only as its agent.

6. Any exclusion or limitation of liability of carrier shall apply to and be for the benefit of agents, servants and representatives of carrier and any person whose aircraft is used by carrier for carriage and its agents, servants and representatives.

7. Checked baggage will be delivered to bearer of the baggage check. In case of damage to baggage moving in international transportation, complaint must be made in writing to carrier forthwith after discovery of damage and, at the latest, within 7 days from receipt; in case of delay, complaint must be made within 21 days from date the baggage was delivered. See tariffs or conditions of carriage regarding non-international transportation.

8. This ticket is good for carriage for one year from date of issue, except as otherwise provided in this ticket, in carrier's tariffs, conditions of carriage, or related regulations. The fare for carriage hereunder is subject to change prior to commencement of carriage. Carrier may refuse transportation if the applicable fare has not been paid.

9. Carrier undertakes to use its best efforts to carry the passenger and baggage with reasonable dispatch. Times shown in timetables or elsewhere are not guaranteed and form no part of this contract. Carrier may without notice substitute alternate carriers or aircraft, and may alter or omit stopping places shown on the ticket in case of necessity. Schedules are subject to change without notice. Carrier assumes no responsibility for making connections.

10. Passenger shall comply with government travel requirements, present exit, entry and other required documents, and arrive at airport by time fixed by carrier or, if no time is fixed, early enough to complete departure procedures.

11. No agent, servant or representative of carrier has authority to alter, modify or waive any provision of this contract.

Carrier reserves the right to refuse carriage to any person who has acquired a ticket in violation of applicable law or carrier's tariffs, rules, or regulations. Issued by the Carrier whose name is in the "Issued By" section on the face of the Passenger Ticket and Baggage Check. Subject to Tariff Regulations. The price of this ticket may include taxes and fees that are imposed on air transportation by government authorities. These taxes and fees, which may represent a significant portion of the cost of air travel, are either included in the fare, or shown separately in the "TAX" box(es) of this ticket. You may also be required to pay taxes or fees not already collected, such as departure taxes or Local Airport Improvement Fees.

Appendix 1

Table of Statutes
(C + number refers to chapter; e.g., **C3** means Chapter 3, The Law of Contracts)

Table of Cases

(C + number refers to chapter)

Cempel v. Harrison Hot Springs Hotel Ltd.
(March 18, 1996), Doc. Vancouver
C936351 (B.C.S.C.) **C5**

City of Saint John v. 5. N.B. Ltd. (June 27,
1996, Doc. No. S/M/44/96 Jud. Dist.
Saint John, Turnbull J. (N.B.Q.B.)) **C12**

Clark v. Canada (1994), 3 C.C.E.L. (2d)
172 (Fed. T.D.) **C2**

Craven et al. v. Strand Holidays (Canada)
Ltd. et al. (1982), 142 D.L.R. (3d)
(Ont. C. of A.) **C15**

Crocker v. Sundance Northwest Resorts Ltd.,
[1988] 1 S.C.R. 1186 **C7**

D. v. 5 Ont. Ltd. (Jan. 28, 1991, Gibson J.
(Ont. Gen. Div.)) **C4**

D. v. H.H.L. (May 12, 1989,
B.C.H.R.C.) **C2**

Dewolf v. Ford, 86 N.E. 527 (N.Y.,
1908) **C10**

Dino's Place Ltd. v. Corfu Restaurant Ltd.,
Geordino Restaurant Ltd. et al. (1991),
36 C.P.R. (3d) 146 (B.C.S.C.) **C13**

Doherty and Meehan v. Lodger's
International Ltd. (1981), 3 C.H.R.R.
D/628 (N.B. Bd. of Inq.) **C2**

Donoghue v. Stevenson, [1932] A.C. 562
(H.L.) **C4, C6, C7, C9**

Dorkin et al. v. American Express Co.
(1973), 345 N.Y.S. (2d) 891, affirmed
in 351 N.Y.S. (2d) 190 **C15**

Doyle v. Walker, [1867] 26 Upper Canada
Queen's Bench Rep. 502 **C9, C10**

Drodge v. St. John's Young Men's and
Young Women's Christian Association
(1987), 67 Nfld. & P.E.I.R. 57 (Nfld.
T.D.) **C5**

Dulieu v. White and Sons, [1901] 2 K.B.
669, p. 679 **C4**

Edwards v. Tracy Starr's Shows (Edmonton)
Ltd. (1984), 33 Alta. L.R. (2d) 115, 56
A.R. 285, 13 D.L.R. (4th) 129 (Q.B.),
varied (1987), 61 Alta. L.R. (2d) 233
(C.A.) **C5**

Elsley v. J.G. Collins Insurance (1976), 13
O.R. (2d) 177 (C.A.), [1978] 2 S.C.R.
916 **C13, C14**

Emmke v. Desilva, 293 Fed. 17 (1923) **C10**

Faltus v. Bazel (1990), 73 Alta. L. R. (2d)
75 (Q.B.) **C10**

Fehr v. O.T. Karz Kafe Ltd. (1993), 110
Sask. R. 207 (Q.B.) **C5**

Fink v. Greeniaus (1973), 2 O.R. (2d) 541
(H.C.) **C5**

Fog Cutter Inc. v. New Brunswick (Liquor
Licensing Board) (1989), 99 N.B.R.
(2d) 392 (Q.B.) **C12**

Ford v. Seligman, [1954] O.R. 957, [1955]
1 D.L.R. 796 (C.A.) **C11**

Foster v. Lewkowicz et al. (1993), 14 O.R.
(3d) 339 **C8**

Francescucci v. Gilker (February 12,
1996), Doc. CA C10259, C8229
(Ont. C.A.) **C7**

Frank v. Berryman, [1894] 3 B.C.R. 506
(C.A.) **C11**

Fraser v. McGibbon (1907), 10 O.W.R. 54
(Co. Ct.) **C8, C11**

Fraser River Pile & Dredge Ltd. v. Can-
Dive Services Ltd., [1999] 3 S.C.R.
108 **C3**

Gal-Cab Investments Ltd. v. North West
Territories (Liquor Licensing Board),
[1986] N.W.T.R. 90 (S.C.), affirmed
[1987] N.W.T.R. 100, 34 D.L.R. (4th)
363 (N.W.T.C.A.) **C12**

Garnet Angeconeb v. 517152 Ontario Ltd.
and Ruby Cullen (1993), 19 C.H.R.R.
D/452 (Ont. Bd. Inq.) **C2, C9**

Gee v. White Spot Ltd. (1986), 7 B.C.L.R.
(2d) 235, 32 D.L.R. (4th) 238 **C6**

George v. Williams, [1956] O.R. 871, 5
D.L.R. (2d) 21 (C.A.) **C11**

Gordon v. Blakely, [1931] 2 W.W.R. 902
(B.C.S.C.) **C5**

Greeven v. Blackcomb Skiing Enterprises Ltd.,
22 C.C.L.T. (2d) 265 (B.C.S.C.) **C5**

Gutek v. Sunshine Village Corp. (1990), 65
D.L.R. (4th) 406 (Alta. Q.B.) **C4**

Gwynn v. Ochapawace Indian Band
(1987), Vol. 6, No. 43, T.L.W. 644-016
(Sask. Q.B.) **C5**

H. v. K. (July 15, 1996, Doc. No. C954322,
Vancouver, Lowry J. (B.C.)) **C3**

Hague v. Billings (1989), 48 C.C.L.T. 192, reversed in part 13 O.R. (3d) 298 (C.A.) **C7**

Hamm Estate v. Wellington Hotels Ltd. (1990), 65 Man. R. (2d) 133 (Q.B.) **C4**

Harwood v. Westview Holding Ltd. (1991), 61 B.C.L.R. (2d) 115 (C.A.), affirmed (July 13, 1989), Doc. Powell River 86 060 (B.C. Co. Ct.) **C4, C5**

Hedley, Byrne & Co. Ltd. v. Heller & Partners Ltd., [1963] 2 All E.R. 575, [1964] A.C. 465 (H. of L.) **C4, C15**

Heimler v. Calvert Caterers Ltd. (1974), 4 O.R. (2d) 667 (H.C.J.), affirmed (1975), 8 O.R. (2d) 1 (C.A.) **C4, C6**

Holiday Inns, Inc. v. Holiday Inn, 364 F. Supp. 775 (S.C. 1973) **C13**

Horsley v. MacLaren (1972), 22 D.L.R. (3d) 545 (S.C.C.) **C4**

Howells v. Southland Canada, Inc. (February 28, 1995), Doc. New Westminster S013266 (B.C.S.C.) **C5**

Hurd v. Hotel Astor Co., 169 N.Y.S. 359 (1918) **C10**

Hurley v. Mustoe, [1981] 1 R.L.R. 208 (Employment. Appeal Tribunal) **C2**

J. v. W.S.L. (June 21,1988, Doc. No. C862739, Lander J. (B.C.S.C.)) **C6**

Jacobsen v. Nike Canada Ltd. (1996), 133 D.L.R. (4th) 377, [1996] 6 W.W.R. 488 (B.C.S.C.) **C7**

Jacobson v. Kinsmen Club of Nanaimo (1976), 71 D.L.R. (3d) 227 (B.C.S.C.) **C7**

Janzen v. Platy Enterprises, [1989] 1 S.C.R. 1252 **C2**

Jarvis v. Swan Tours Ltd., [1973] 1 All E.R. 71 (C.A.) **C15**

Joyce v. Canadian Pacific Hotels Corp. (1994), 26 Alta. L.R. (3d) 72, 161 A.R. 53 (Q.B.) **C5**

Juengle v. City of Glendale, 164 S.W. (2d) 610 (Mo., 1942) **C8**

Karalekas v. Canada Trustco (unreported, 1998) Ottawa Small Claims Court **C3**

Keks v. Esquire Pleasure Tours Limited and Pleasure Tours (Canada) Ltd., [1974] 3 W.W.R. Manitoba County Court, Hewak Co. Ct. J. **C15**

Knight v. G.T.P. Development Co., [1926] S.C.R. 674 **C8**

Krohn v. United Enterprises Ltd. (May 16, 1994, Sask. Bd. of Inq.) **C2**

L.E.C. v. N.Y. (February 7, 1996, Rosenberg J. (Ont. Gen. Div.)) **C12**

Laing v. Allied Innkeepers Ltd. (1969), [1970] 1 O.R. 502, 8 D.L.R. (3d) 708 (Div. Ct.) **C11**

Lambert v. Lastoplex Chemicals Ltd. (1972), 25 D.L.R. (3d) 121 (S.C.C.) **C4**

Lee v. Jacobson; Weber v. Jacobson (1992), 87 D.L.R. 4th **C10**

Little Plume v. Weir, Marco Polo Pub Ltd., et al. (1998, 220 A.R. 332) **C7**

Lockett v. A. & M. Charles, Ltd. et al., [1938] 4 All E.R. 170 (K.B.) **C6**

Love v. New Fairview Corp. (1904), 10 B.C.R. 330 (C.A.) **C5**

Lowden v. The Queen (1982), 139 D.L.R. (3d) 257 **C15**

Lynar v. Mossop (1875), 36 U.C.Q.B. 230 (Ont. C.A.) **C11**

M. v. B. Ltd. (March 15, 1997, Doc. No. 26627 Kelowna, Bauman J. (B.C.S.C.)) **C5**

Mackniack v. Brown (1967), 62 W.W.R. 633 (Sask. Q.B.) **C5**

Major Mack Hotel v. Ontario Liquor Licence Board (1994), 76 O.A.C. 326 (Div. Ct.), affirmed April 30, 1999, Doc. CA C21043 (Ont. C.A.) **C12**

Marshall v. British Columbia (1988), 23 B.C.L.R. (2d) 320 (C.A.) **C5**

McCarthy v. Pupus Enterprises Ltd., [1996] B.C.J. No. 967 (Q.L.) **C4**

McChesnie v. Tourond (1995), 99 Man. R. (2d) 209 (Q.B.) **C5**

McDonald's Corp. v. C.H. Stores Ltd. (June 5, 1996, Doc. No. A-278-94 Ottawa, Marceau, Hugessen and Decary JJ. (Fed. C.A.)) **C13**

McGeough v. Don Enterprises Ltd., [1984] 1 W.W.R. 256, 28 Sask. R. 126 (Q.B.) **C7**

McKenna v. Greco (1981), 33 O.R. (2d) 595 (C.A.) **C10**

McLean v. University Club, 97 N.E. (2d) 174 (Mass., 1951) **C9**

McNab v. Calyniuk Restaurants Inc. (1995), 24 C.H.R.R. D/22 **C2**

McNeil v. Airport Hotel (Halifax) Ltd. (1980), 76 A.P.R. 490 (T.D.), 41 N.S.R. (2d) 490 (S.C.) **C6**

McPhail v. T & L Club (Brantford), [1968] 2 O.R. 840, 1 D.L.R. (3d) 43 (C.A.) **C5**

Menow v. Jordan House Hotel Ltd. and Honsberger (1973), 38 D.L.R. (3d) 105, [1974] S.C.R. 239 **C4, C7**

Mohammed v. British Columbia (Liquor Control and Licensing Branch) (1994), 51 B.C.A.C. 62, 84 W.A.C. 62 (C.A.) **C12**

Montgomery v. Black, [1989] B.C.J. No. 1800 (Q.L.) **C4**

Murphy v. Little Memphis Cabaret Inc., [1996] O.J. No. 4600 (Q.L.) (December 9, 1996, Doc. No. 94-GD-28654, Windsor, Zuber J. (Ont. Gen. Div.)) **C4**

N. v. W.S.L. (April 11, 1988, Spencer J. (B.C.S.C.)) **C6**

Nelles v. The Queen in Right of Ontario, [1989] 2 S.C.R. 170 **C1**

Nelson v. Ritz Carleton Restaurant and Hotel Co., 157A 133 (N. J. 1931) **C5**

Newell et al. v. Canadian Pacific Airlines, Ltd. (1976), 14 O.R. (2d) 752 **C15**

Niblock v. Pacific National Exhibitions and the City of Vancouver (1981), 30 B.C.L.R. 20 (S.C.) **C7**

Nieto v. Bison Properties Ltd. (1995), 56 B.C.C.A. 303, 92 W.A.C.S. 303 (C.A.) **C4, C5**

Nixon v. Greensides, [1993] 11 Sask. R. 75 (Q.B.) **C2**

Noddin v. Laskey, [1956] S.C.R. 577, 3 D.L.R. (2d) 577, reversing in part [1955] 5 D.L.R. 442 (N.B.C.A.) **C5**

Ouelette v. Kinsmen Club of Ladysmith (March 20, 1990, Doc. No. V00885 (B.C.C.A.), affirming (October 18, 1988), Doc. No. Nanaimo CC7451 (B.C.S.C.)) **C5**

P. v. G. (May 15, 1990, Sask. Bd. of Inq.) **C2**

P. v. H., [1988] 3 W.W.R. 119 (Man. Q.B.) **C2, C9**

P.P.H. v. N.F. (June 29, 1995, Doc. No.166/91, Fleury J. (Ont. Gen. Div.)) **C13**

Pajot v. Commonwealth Holiday Inns of Canada Ltd. (1978), 20 O.R. (2d) 76 (H.C.), 86 D.L.R. (3d) 729 (H.C.) **C5**

Philp v. Hunts Limited, [1947] O.W.N. 529 **C11**

Picka v. Porter and the Royal Canadian Legion (1980), 2 A.C.W.S. (2d) 428 (Ont. C.A.) **C7**

Ponson v. Premier Hotel Ltd. (1957), 21 W.W.R. 664 (B.C.S.C.) **C11**

R. v. Coté (1974), 51 D.L.R. (3d) 244, 252 **C4**

R. v. D. (Oct. 5, 1995, Lamkin, Prov. Div. J. (Ont. Prov. Div.)) **C6**

R. v. Levy Bros. Co., [1961] S.C.R. 189 **C4**

R. v. Rymer, [1877] 2 Q.B.D. 136, 46 L.J.M.C. 108 **C9**

R. v. S.R.L. (April 29, 1991, Ont. H.R. Bd. of Inq.) **C2**

Ram v. McDonald's Restaurant of Canada Ltd. (1991), 16 C.H.R.R. D10 **C2**

Ramsay v. Hesselman (1983), 148 D.L.R. (3d) 764, 42 O.R. (2d) 255 (Div. Ct.) **C8**

Re Adult Entertainment Bar Association and Metropolitan Toronto (Municipality) (1997); Thomas-Johns, Goldberg et al., interveners, 35 O.R. (3d) 161 **C12**

Re Blainey and Ontario Hockey Association et al. (1986), 54 O.R. (2d) 513 (C.A.), leave to appeal to the Supreme Court of Canada refused (1986), 58 O.R. (2d) 274 **C2**

Re Calye, 77 Eng. Rep. 520, 521 (K.B. 1584) **C5, C8**

Re M. (July 29, 1988, Ont. H.R.C.) **C2**

Rees v. B.C. Place Ltd. (November 25, 1986) (B.C.S.C.) 3 A.C.W.S. (3d) 313) **C5**

Reference re Amendment of Constitution of Canada (Nos. 1, 2, 3), [1981] 1 S.C.R. 753 **C1**

Regent Holidays Ltd. v. Cooper, [1989] O.J. No. 1778 (Ont. Div. Ct.) **C15**

Reibl v. Hughes (1980), 114 D.L.R. (3d) 1 (S.C.C.) **C4**

Repushka v. Perentes Enterprises Ltd. (1996), 140 Sask. R. 55 (Q.B.), additional reasons at [1996] 9 W.W.R. 734 (Sask. Q.B.) **C5**

Restaurant & Food Association of British Columbia and the Yukon et al. v. The City of Vancouver (October 30, 1996, Doc. No. A961963 Vancouver, Cohen J. (B.C.S.C.)) **C6**

Rex v. Ivens, 173 Eng. Rep. 94 [1835] **C8**

Rivtow Marine Ltd. v. Washington Iron Works (1940), 40 D.L.R. (3d) 530 (S.C.C.) **C4**

Robertson v. Marleau, [1989] B.C.J. No. 1915 (Q.L.) **C4**

Robertson v. Red Robin Restaurants of Canada Ltd. (1998), B.C.J. No. 884 Vancouver Registry No. 96-29769 **C14**

Robinson v. Madison (November 9, 1987) (B.C.S.C.), 7 A.C.W.S. (3d) 166 **C5**

Rudy's Enterprises Ltd. v. New Brunswick (Liquor Licensing Board) (1993), 139 N.B.R. (2d) 307 (Q.B.) **C12**

S. v. E.P. Ltd. (November 21, 1996, Doc. No. 4340, St. John's (Nfld. S.C. Trial Div.)) **C4**

S. v. F.S.H.L. (December 13, 1994, Doc. No. 282T/93, Platana J. (Ont. Gen. Div.)) **C4**

S. v. J.M.I. (1992), 106 Sask. R. 71 (Prov. Ct.) **C4**

Saari v. Sunshine Riding Academy Ltd. (1967), 65 D.L.R. (2d) 92 (Man. Q.B.) **C5**

Said v. Butt, [1923] K.B. 497 **C15**

Sawler v. Franklyn Enterprises Ltd. (1992), 117 N.S.R. (2d) 316, 324 A.P.R. 316 (T.D.) **C5**

Schmidt v. Sharpe and the Arlington House Hotel (1983), 27 C.C.L.T. 1 (Ont. H.C.) **C7**

Shandloff v. City Dairy Ltd. et al., [1936] O.R. 579 **C6**

Shepherd v. Bama Artisans Inc. (1988), 9 C.H.R.R. D/5049 (Ont. Bd. of Inq.) **C2**

Sherrill v. King Edward Hotel Co. (1929), 63 O.L.R. 528, [1929] 2 D.L.R. 612 (H.C.) **C11**

Shooter Sports Inc. v. Nova Scotia (Liquor Licence Board), (May 24, 1996, Doc. No. S.H. No.127717 Halifax, Gruchy J. (N.S. S.C.)) **C12**

Simpson v. Consumers' Association of Canada et al. (2002), 57 O.R. (3d) 351 (C.A.) **C2**

Skinner v. Baker Estate (1991), 34 M.V.R. (2d) 157, [1992] I.L.R. 1-2809 (Ont. Gen. Div.) **C7**

Smart v. McCarty (1980), 33 N.B.R. (2d) 27 (Q.B.) **C4**

Stanton v. Twack et al. (1982), 14 A.C.W.S. (2d) 447 (B.C.S.C.) **C7**

Stewart v. Pettie (1993), 13 Alta. L.R. (3d) 142, [1995] 1 S.C.R. 131, 121 D.L.R. (4th) 222 **C7**

Stringer et al. v. Domhar Travel Agencies Inc.; Sunquest Vacations Ltd., Third Party (1983), 20 A.C.W.S. (2d) 42 (Ont. Co. Ct.) **C15**

Targett v. Magic Mountain Water Park Ltd. (1991), 120 N.B.R. (2d) 95, 302 A.P.R. 95 (Q.B.) **C5**

Thomas v. Duquesne Light Co., 545 A. (2d) 289 (Penn., 1988) **C7**

Tilden Rent-A-Car Co. v. Clendenning (1978), 18 O.R. (2d) 601 **C15**

Tiro v. Old Country Smoked Meats, [1988] B.C.J. No. 168 (Q.L.), affirmed [1989] B.C.J. No. 304 (Q.L.) **C6**

Vannan v. Kamloops (City) (1991), 63 B.C.L.R. (2d) 307, [1992] 2 W.W.R. 759 (S.C.) **C5**

Veinot v. Kerr-Addison Mines Ltd., [1975] 2 S.C.R. 311 **C4**

Vicars v. Arnold (1914), 7 W.W.R. 676, 7 Sask. L.R. 298, 20 D.L.R. 838 (C.A.) **C11**

Volk v. Schreiber and Faraway Enterprise Limited, [1978] 18 O.R. (2d) 446 (Divisional Court) **C15**

Wallace v. Shoreham, 49 A. (2d) 81 (D.C. 1946) **C10**

Waters v. Beau Site Co., 114 Misc. 65, 68, 186 N.Y.S. 731, 732 (N.Y. City Ct. 1920) **C10**

W.E.M.L. v. M.R.C.L. (December 4, 1995, Alta. C.A.) **C3**

Whitehouse v. Pickett, [1908] A.C. 357 (H.L.) **C11**

White's Case, [1558] 2 Dyer 158b **C10**

Williams v. Linnit, [1951] 1 K.B. 565 **C11**

Young v. Hubbards Food Services Ltd. (1995), 145 N.S.R. (2d) 13, 418 A.P.R. 13 (S.C.), additional reasons at (1995), 41 C.P.C. (3d) 349, 146 N.S.R. (2d) 70, 442 A.P.R. 70 (S.C.) **C5**

Zabner v. Howard Johnson's, Inc., 201 So.(2d) 824 (Fla., 1967) **C6**

Appendix 3

Hotel Forms and Sample Contracts

Guest Registration Form
Deposit Box Agreement
Reservation Contract Reply Form
Special Event Contract

Appendix: Sample Guest Registration Form

WALKRITE INN, A DIVISION OF COMFYBED HOTELS INC.

123 Main Street, Newtown, Nunavut Z1P 3P6
Tel: 555–555–5555   GST No. 123456789

Last name: _____   First name: _____

Address: _____   City/Town: _____

Prov/State: _____   Postal/Zip: _____

Number of adults: _____   Number of children: _____

Make of car: _____   Plate no.: _____

Prov/State: _____   Travel agent: _____

Company: _____   Group code: _____

Arrival date: _____   Payment method: _____

Departure date: _____   Departure time: _____

Room number: _____   Room rate: _____

Other info: _____

Special Needs: ☐ COT   ☐ CRIB   ☐ PETS   ☐ NONSMOKING   ☐ PARKING
☐ GUARANTEED ROOM

I hereby register as a guest in accordance with law. I am jointly and severally liable to pay all proper bills arising in connection with my stay. I agree to vacate the premises by the departure date and time indicated above. I agree to save the innkeeper harmless from any and all claims for loss, damage, public liability, or otherwise arising from my acts or omissions or the acts or omissions of anyone under my charge while a guest or entrant on the premises. I acknowledge that safety deposit boxes are available for property. Payment shall be by cash or credit card or, with the consent of the innkeeper, by cheque. Returned payments are subject to a $50 fee.

Signature _____   Clerk _____   Date _____

[NAME OF INN]

[ADDRESS OF INN]

I, the undersigned Guest, acknowledge receipt of the key to deposit box number _____, and agree to abide by all the rules and regulations printed on the reverse of this Agreement.

Date	Room	Guest's Signature	Clerk's Signature
_____	_____	_____	_____

I, the undersigned Guest, acknowledge that I have had access to the deposit box as follows:

Date	Time	Guest's Signature	Clerk's Signature
_____	_____	_____	_____
_____	_____	_____	_____
_____	_____	_____	_____
_____	_____	_____	_____

I, the undersigned Guest, acknowledge that all property placed in the deposit box has been returned to me, and the key has been returned to the innkeeper. If the property was not returned in satisfactory condition, a statement of damage has been completed and signed.

Date	Room	Guest's Signature	Clerk's Signature
_____	_____	_____	_____

DEPOSIT BOX USE: RULES AND REGULATIONS

I agree that the inn has furnished me with a deposit box which I have inspected and approved. I understand that I am subject to the laws of this province and to all the regulations of the inn. I agree that the inn shall not be liable whatsoever in the case of loss or damage to any property I may place in the deposit box irrespective of the cause of such loss or damage, unless it is proven that the loss or damage was caused by the willful act, default, or negligence of the inn.

I have been advised by the inn that the deposit box is equipped with one key only, and I agree that should it be lost or stolen, I will pay the cost of opening the box and fitting it with a new lock and key. I agree not to hold the inn responsible for any loss or damage should I authorize someone other than myself to open the deposit box. Any such authorization shall be in writing.

Should I leave the hotel and fail to remove the contents of the deposit box and surrender the key, the inn shall continue not to be responsible for its contents, and shall, after my departure, be at liberty to make a charge for its continued use. The inn will retain the contents of my deposit box for a period of 90 days after my checkout. I understand that I must make my claim for the contents of the safety deposit box within this period of time, after which the inn will be at liberty to dispose of the said contents as it deems fit with no further responsibility to me.

I agree that this document constitutes notice under the *Innkeepers/Hotel Keepers Act*.

▴ LORD ELGIN HOTEL ▴

A HISTORY OF HOSPITALITY IN THE HEART OF OTTAWA

To: _____   Fax No: (_____) _____

Attention: _____   No. of Pages: _____

From: _____   Date: _____

(Reservations Department Representative)   D   M   Y

As requested, the Lord Elgin Hotel is pleased to confirm the following reservation(s):

Guest Name(s): _____   No. of People: _____

Guest Name(s): _____   Room Type: _____

Arrival Date: _____   Room Rate: _____

Departure Date: _____   Conf. No: _____

6:00 p.m.: _____   (The room will be held only until 6:00 p.m. unless guaranteed.)

Guaranteed: _____   (The guest must cancel the room by 6:00 p.m. to avoid being charged.)

Remarks:

_____

_____

360 Guest Rooms
13,000 sq. ft. of Meeting Space
Upgraded Services and Amenities
Internet and Business Connections
Heated, Underground Parking Garage

Indoor Swimming Pool
Expanded Health Facility
New Full Service Restaurant
Honeymoon/VIP Executive Suite
Regular and Group Airport Shuttle

▴ LORD ELGIN HOTEL ▴

100 Elgin Street, Ottawa, Ontario, Canada K1P 5K8
(613) 235-3333 Fax (613) 235-3223 Toll Free Canada & U.S 1-800-267-4298

NAME OF SPECIAL EVENT PROVIDER ("Provider")

Provider Contact Person: _____

Address: _____

Phone: (_____) _____ Fax: (_____) _____

E-mail: _____ Web site: _____

NAME OF SPECIAL EVENT CUSTOMER ("Customer")

Customer Contact Person: _____

Address: _____

Phone: (_____) _____ Fax: (_____) _____

E-mail: _____

1. AGREEMENT FOR A SPECIAL EVENT

In consideration of the mutual covenants herein and subject to the due performance by the Customer hereunder, the Provider and the Customer hereby agree that the Customer may use those premises and facilities described in Schedule A for the purpose and upon the terms and conditions hereinafter set forth, based upon the number of participants and requirements described in Schedule A. Should any of the terms of Schedule A change to the detriment of the Provider, the Provider may amend the terms of this Agreement. This Agreement shall not constitute a commitment by either party until 15:00 hours on _____ pending delivery of written notice of commitment by the Customer to the Provider. Should the Provider receive a bona fide offer from another person for a booking which conflicts with the Event, the Provider shall give the Customer _____ hours' written notice. If the Customer fails to confirm this Agreement during the notice period, the Provider may accept the second offer without liability to the Customer and shall forthwith return the Customer's deposit without interest or penalty.

2. PURPOSE OF THE EVENT

The special event (the "Event") contemplated by this Agreement is for the sole purpose of:

2006 SYMPOSIUM ON THE REGULATION OF SYMPOSIUM ORGANIZERS

3. DURATION OF THE EVENT
The Start Date of the Event is:

The End Date of the Event is:

4. BOOKING INFORMATION
One-Bed Rooms Room Rate $ _____
Two-Bed Rooms Room Rate $ _____
Suites Room Rate $ _____
Meeting Rooms _____   Meeting Room Rate $ _____
Banquet Rooms _____   Banquet Room Rate $ _____
Other Rooms _____   Other Rooms Rate $ _____
NUMBER TOTAL $ _____

5. PAYMENT
The Customer shall pay a non-refundable deposit of _____ % of the TOTAL upon acceptance of this Agreement, and a further deposit of _____ % of the TOTAL on or before _____. The deposits shall be applied to the billing for the Event or to any cancellation fee if the Event is cancelled. The balance of the TOTAL plus any other fees and charges as may be applicable are payable upon delivery of billings by the Provider to the Customer as set forth in Schedule B.

6. RESERVATION POLICIES
Authority
Reservations may be made by the Customer Contact Person or directly by members of the Customer who will be attending the Event. The Customer confirms that the Customer Contact Person has the authority to bind the Customer and its members.

Cut-Off Date
Reservations for the Event must be finalized by _____ ("Cut-Off Date"). Any rooms not reserved by the Cut-Off Date may be resold at current rates to the public or the Customer.

Rooming List and Reservation Cards
Prior to the Cut-Off Date, the Customer shall provide the Provider with a rooming list of all persons who will be attending the Event ("Guest"). All reservations made pursuant to the rooming list are guaranteed by the Customer. The Provider shall provide to the Customer reservation cards for each name on the rooming list. The Customer shall distribute the cards to the persons on the rooming list for completion and return by no later than check-in. Should the Customer prefer to use its own registration forms, any such forms must be pre-approved by the Provider.

Guaranteed Reservations
All reservations where the Guest will be arriving after 16:00 hours must be guaranteed by a recognized major credit card or cash deposit for the first night.

7. CHECKING IN AND CHECKING OUT
Guests may check in after 15:00 hours. Guests may pre-register prior to 15:00 hours. If the reservation is not guaranteed, the reservation may be cancelled at 17:00 hours and the room resold. If the reservation is guaranteed, the reservation shall not be cancelled, and the Guest shall be responsible to pay the room rate for each reserved night unless the reservation is cancelled in accordance with the Cancellation Policies set forth below. Guests must check out by 13:00 hours to allow the Provider to prepare for new arrivals. The Provider will reasonably accommodate Guests who wish to check in early or check out late.

8. CANCELLATION POLICIES
Room Blocks
The Customer may cancel blocks of rooms, without a cancellation fee, as follows:

180 or more days before Start Date __% of original room block
179 to 90 days before Start Date __% of original room block
89 to 30 days before Start Date __% of original room block
Thereafter, the following provisions apply.

Full Cancellation of the Event
Should the Customer cancel the Event and the Provider succeed in booking a comparable event over the same dates without being obliged to reschedule an existing event, the Provider shall waive any cancellation charges as are covered by the comparable event, and shall charge the Customer only for any net loss.

Partial Cancellation of the Event
Should the Customer not cancel the Event but cancel some of the rooms, the Provider shall make reasonable attempts to resell the rooms after other vacancies for that night have been filled, and shall charge the Customer only for rooms not resold. Upon request, the Provider shall provide proof of occupancy for such night(s).

Definition of Total Gross Revenue
Total gross revenue includes all reasonably anticipated revenues from guest room sales, meeting room sales, food and beverage sales, and from any other services specified herein.

Room Reservations
The Provider may charge a fee for cancelled rooms as follows:

365 or more days before Start Date __% of total gross revenue
364 to 180 days before Start Date __% of total gross revenue
179 to 120 days before Start Date __% of total gross revenue
119 to 90 days before Start Date __% of total gross revenue
89 to 60 days before Start Date __% of total gross revenue
59 to 30 days before Start Date __% of total gross revenue
29 to 15 days before Start Date __% of total gross revenue
14 or fewer days before Start Date __% of total gross revenue

Food and Beverage Functions
The Provider may charge a fee for cancelled food and beverage orders as follows:

180 or more days before Start Date __% of total gross revenue
179 to 120 days before Start Date __% of total gross revenue
119 to 90 days before Start Date __% of total gross revenue
89 to 30 days before Start Date __% of total gross revenue
29 or fewer days before Start Date __% of total gross revenue

9. MEETING ROOM PROVISIONS
Meeting rooms are reserved in accordance with Schedule A. Any set-up and tear-down times must be indicated in Schedule A.

10. BANQUET (FOOD AND BEVERAGE) PROVISIONS
A minimum of _____ diners is required for banquets. The Provider may charge a labour cost of $_____ if fewer than the minimum attend. Payment is based on the number of dinners reserved or

on the number of diners who attend, whichever is the greater. The Provider may charge a fee for any extraordinary banquet services. The Customer shall advise the Provider of the final number of diners at least five days before the Start Date. All other banquet details including the menu, wine list, tableware, number of staff, and so on must be finalized at least 15 days before the Start Date. No changes may be made after five days before the Start Date. The Provider shall advise the Customer of the final per-diner banquet price on or before _____ or at a reasonable time prior to the Start Date. All applicable sales and other taxes and a 15 percent gratuity shall be added to the banquet price. No food or beverages may be brought into the premises of the Provider without the prior written consent of the Provider, and subject to reasonable labour and service charges.

11. SCHEDULES
This Agreement includes the following schedules:
SCHEDULE A as to number of participants, facilities required, and other information.
SCHEDULE B as to other terms and conditions applicable hereto.

12. ACKNOWLEDGMENT
The parties acknowledge each receiving one true copy of this Agreement including all schedules. Each signatory below has the authority to bind the party.
IN WITNESS WHEREOF the Provider has hereunto set its hand and seal.

PROVIDER

Per:

_____

I have authority to bind the Corporation.

IN WITNESS WHEREOF the Customer has hereunto set its hand and seal.
WITNESS

_____

CUSTOMER

SCHEDULE A

PREMISES
OTHER FACILITIES
NUMBER OF PARTICIPANTS
NUMBER OF ROOMS
SET-UP REQUIREMENTS
TEAR-DOWN REQUIREMENTS
SCHEDULE OF EVENTS
OTHER INFORMATION

SCHEDULE B
OTHER TERMS AND CONDITIONS

1. RELATIONSHIP BETWEEN THE PARTIES

Each party is an independent business entity and, except as expressly provided for herein, neither has any power, right, or authority to represent or bind the other, expressly or impliedly, directly or indirectly. Nothing herein shall be construed as creating any of the relationships of partner, principal and agent, employer and employee, or master and servant. Except for the times, premises, and facilities expressly and exclusively reserved to the Customer hereunder, the Provider may use and occupy its premises. Should the Customer vacate any part of the premises before the expiry of this Agreement, the Provider may re-let the part vacated.

2. USE OF PREMISES

The Customer shall have access to and the use of the premises and facilities of the Provider for the times and purposes of the Event all as designated in Schedule A.

3. BILLING POLICIES
Delivery and Liability

The Customer agrees to pay all room rates and incidental charges forthwith upon delivery of the billing. Delivery occurs whenever a billing is delivered to the Customer, or on the fourth day after it is mailed with correct prepaid postage. The Customer is jointly and severally liable with each member of the Customer for all billings applicable to the member's room.

Room Rates

Room rates are in Canadian dollars per room, per night, subject to Canadian goods and services tax, provincial sales tax, and municipal lodging tax in effect at the time of the Event.

Incidental Charges

Incidental charges are in addition to room rates and consist of all charges relating to the use of the telephone, other in-room equipment, movies, minibar, and other goods and services offered by the Provider, which are not included in the room rate.

Interest

Interest shall accrue to any billing beginning ten days after delivery at a rate equal to the Royal Bank of Canada Prime Rate in effect on the date of delivery plus six percent.

Commissions

Should the Customer make bookings through an agent, the Provider shall pay a _____ % commission on actual revenue received for such bookings to the agent. The Provider is not responsible for any other fees, rebates, commissions, or charges paid or payable by the Customer to any agent for any aspect of the Event. Should the Provider become liable for same, the Provider may add them to the room rate and the Customer shall pay them forthwith.

4. MASTER ACCOUNTS

The Customer may, upon written notice to the Provider and credit approval satisfactory to the Provider, charge any of the following to a Master Account in the Customer's name:

a) Room rates for the members of the Customer
b) Incidental charges for the members of the Customer
c) Food and beverage charges

d) Business room and equipment usage charges

e) Other charges as agreed by the Provider and the Customer

5. OVERHOLDING

Unless the Customer is prevented by a reason beyond its control such as act of God, emergency, or strike by a third party, the Customer shall vacate the premises at the end of the Event. Overholding shall be charged at the rates specified in this Agreement pro rated hourly plus a bonus of _____ % of such rates plus any other costs or charges suffered by the Provider as a result of the Customer's failure to vacate, payable forthwith.

Neither overholding nor payment for overholding extends the term of this Agreement. Overholding charges are liquidated damages for overholding and do not preclude the Provider from exercising any other rights against the Customer.

6. OVERDUE ACCOUNTS

The Customer shall be liable for all reasonable costs incurred in collecting payment of overdue accounts including without limitation legal costs on a solicitor and client basis.

7. EVENT INFORMATION

The Customer shall provide in a timely fashion all information about the Event and the Customer reasonably required by the Provider including without limitation:

a) evidence of compliance with any government licensing and approval requirements;

b) a plan indicating the floor space needed and details of any alterations requested;

c) the proposed nature, design, and location of all displays, equipment, booths, and the like;

d) any aspects of the Event which may affect the balance of the facilities of the Provider;

e) any other information reasonably required.

8. TICKET SALES

Should the Provider allow the Customer to sell tickets for the Event to the general public excluding the members of the Customer who are on the rooming list, the methods and procedures of such sales shall be subject to the approval of the Provider in its sole discretion. The Customer shall set aside _____ complimentary tickets for the exclusive use of the Provider.

The Provider shall have a first lien on all ticket sales receipts up to the amount owing by the Customer to the Provider. The Customer shall inform any ticket or other agents it employs of the existence of the lien and shall direct such agents to remit all ticket receipts to the Provider without deduction which are the subject of the lien.

9. CONCESSIONS

Unless otherwise provided in this Agreement, the Provider shall operate all concessions on the premises including without limitation for the sale or other distribution of all goods, refreshments, snacks, beverages, gifts, souvenirs, sundries, tobacco products, vending-machine products, and the use of arcade machines.

10. BROADCASTING

The Customer shall not permit any Internet, radio, television, or broadcasting operations on the premises without the prior written consent of the Provider.

11. PERFORMERS

Where the Event is intended to feature the appearance or performance of one or more well-known acts or personalities, the Customer shall not permit the substitution of any such acts or personalities without the prior written consent of the Provider. In the sole discretion of the Provider, where the Customer seeks to substitute an act or personality or where an act or personality cancels, the Provider may cancel the performance and retain any deposits.

12. INSPECTIONS

The Provider reserves the right to inspect and limit all private functions held on its premises. The Provider is not responsible for any damages, losses, or injuries to property or to persons of the Customer or its members or guests of the member or Customer, unless such damages, losses, or injuries are the result of the gross negligence or willful misconduct of the Provider including its directors, officers, staff, employees, and independent contractors.

13. INSURANCE

From the Start Date of the Event and for one year thereafter, the Customer shall maintain in full force and effect comprehensive valid insurance that meets the following requirements:

a) The insurance shall be obtained from an insurer licensed to sell insurance in Province acceptable to the Provider.

b) The policy shall name the Provider as a co-insured and contain a cross-liability provision.

c) The insurance shall include comprehensive general liability coverage of not less than $5,000,000.00 for property damage, personal injury, death, and loss of use.

d) The insurance shall include coverage for

  i) personal injury liability for wrongful entry or eviction, defamation, false arrest or detention, malicious prosecution, invasion of privacy, and human rights violations;

  ii) blanket written contractual liability;

  iii) broad form tenant's legal liability;

  iv) contingent employer's liability;

  v) non-owned automobile liability; and

  vi) products liability.

e) The Customer shall provide proof of such insurance to the Provider, and failure to provide such proof shall constitute breach of this Agreement.

14. INDEMNIFICATION

The Customer shall indemnify and save harmless the Provider, its directors, officers, employees, independent contractors, guests, entrants, and other members of the public from any and all claims, demands, injuries, liabilities, costs, legal costs, and other expenses for any damages or losses incurred by any person whatsoever arising out of the use and enjoyment of the premises, facilities, or services by the Customer or any member of the Customer or any other person who has the expressed or implied permission of the Customer to such use and enjoyment, with respect to any one or more without limitation of the following:

a) personal injury including death;

b) property loss or damage including without limitation losses to personal effects, trademarks, copyright, patents, equipment, or devices;

c) infringement under any consumer protection law, laws relating to false or misleading advertising, other regulatory provisions, or human rights code; and

d) the failure by the Customer to vacate the premises at the end of the Event and to leave the premises in the same or better state of cleanliness, safety, and repair as at the Start Date.

15. COVENANTS OF PROVIDER

The Provider covenants with the Customer:

a) To allow the Customer reasonable access to and from the premises for the purposes of the Event.

b) To maintain a reasonable temperature in the premises.

c) To supply utilities deemed by the Provider sufficient for the ordinary requirements of the Customer, provided that the Provider is not obliged to provide utilities in excess of its capacity, nor is the Provider liable for any interruption or failure of the utility supply or accident to the fixtures and chattels of the Provider. Should the Customer require extra utility services that the Provider is able to obtain, the Customer shall pay to the Provider the extra costs thereof.

d) To provide normal cleaning of aisles and corridors in exhibit areas and general housekeeping in areas permitted for meetings and public performances, and in all other public areas.

16. COVENANTS OF CUSTOMER

The Customer covenants with the Provider:

a) To pay the rental charges and any overholding charges to the Provider promptly when due.

b) To abide by all rules and regulations of the Provider.

c) To procure at the Customer's expense all regulatory licences, permits, and approvals from governmental authorities required for the Customer's use of the premises.

d) To abide by all laws, bylaws, and codes applicable to the Customer's use of the premises including without limitation as to fire, labour, and safety.

e) Not to allow the premises to be used for any other purpose other than provided herein.

f) Not to allow any activity on the premises deemed by the Provider to be a nuisance or detrimental to the Provider, or to be improper, immoral, or objectionable, or which espouses or promotes false views and ideas which promote or are likely to promote discrimination, contempt, hatred, or violence to any person or group on any basis.

g) Not to admit to the premises a larger number of persons than the seating capacity or a larger number of persons than can safely move about the premises, and to accept the Provider's decision in this regard as final.

h) Not to allow disorderly conduct in the premises, and to permit the Provider or its agents to eject any disorderly person from the premises and facilities.

i) To provide at the Customer's expense such security services and number of security personnel deemed necessary by the Provider.

j) Not to allow any part of the premises or any furnishings or fixtures therein to have applied to them any permanent or temporary paint or other covering without the prior written consent of the Provider.

k) To ensure that all exhibits, displays, and other supplies are freestanding and not affixed to any walls, ceilings, floors, or fixtures without the prior written consent of the Provider.

l) Not to allow any obstruction of the sidewalks, entries, halls, passages, vestibules, elevators, or stairways other than for ingress and egress from the premises.

m) Not to allow any covering, obstruction, or removal of any doors, windows, radiators, and house lighting attachments.

n) Not to operate any motors or machinery or use any fuels or other dangerous substances in the premises.

o) Not to use for any decorative purposes flammable materials such as tissue or crepe paper, and to ensure that all decorative materials shall be treated with flame-proofing and approval by the Fire Department for the Municipality before installation.

p) Not to allow anything within the premises which may conflict with the conditions of any insurance policy upon the premises or in any way increase the rate of insurance upon the premises or any property kept therein.

q) At the end of the Event, to surrender the premises, facilities, and chattels all in the same condition and repair as originally furnished to the Customer, normal wear and tear only excepted.

r) To provide cleaning and janitorial services for exhibit booths and other areas.

17. OTHER ARRANGEMENTS

a) The Provider shall provide to the Customer one free room night for every _____ fully paid room nights.

b) The Provider shall, at no charge, supply a podium microphone and loudspeaker for the head table in the banquet room and a standing microphone for questions from the floor.

c) During the Event, the Provider shall supply one easel in the main lobby displaying the name, locations, and times of the functions scheduled for the Event.

d) The Customer shall make its own parking arrangements.

e) Should the Provider be unable to fulfill or be delayed or restricted in the fulfilling of any of its obligations under this Agreement due to causes beyond its control, the Provider may not fulfill such obligations for the period during which such obligations cannot be performed, and may refund a pro rata share of applicable fees to the Customer.

f) If the premises or facilities occupied by the Customer shall be destroyed or damaged by fire or the elements or causes beyond the control of the Provider, or if the premises shall in the Provider's opinion be so badly damaged or destroyed as to be unfit for occupancy during the term of this Agreement, the Event shall terminate from the date of such damage or destruction, and the Customer shall immediately surrender possession of the premises and facilities to the Provider and, provided such damage or destruction was not caused by the negligence or willful act or omission of the Customer, pay a fee only up to the time of such surrender of possession, and damages will be paid to the Customer equivalent to the cost incurred by the Customer for relocation.

g) The Provider may take possession of any items left on the premises after the Event by the Customer or its members and other attendees, and if such items are not claimed within a reasonable time, may dispose of them as the Provider deems appropriate. Upon request, the Provider shall provide a list of such items to the Customer.

h) Should the Customer require any special or extraordinary utilities, materials, or services which the Provider has agreed in writing to supply, the Customer shall pay to the Provider such additional fees and charges as are reasonable for the costs of same.

18. BREACH OF AGREEMENT

Without limitation, the following occurrences shall constitute a breach of this Agreement:

a) A default made or threatened by the Customer or its Subcustomers, agents, directors, officers, or employees of any material aspect of the performance of the Customer under this Agreement, materiality being determined in the sole discretion of the Provider;

b) Any damage or waste caused, permitted, or threatened by the Customer or its Subcustomers, agents, directors, officers, or employees against the Provider or its premises, equipment, furnishings, or personnel; and

c) A filing by or against the Customer for bankruptcy or insolvency or the appointment of a receiver or a trustee for the Customer or its assets.

19. REMEDIES

Upon any actual or pending violation of this Agreement and in addition to any other remedies, the parties agree to the issuance by a competent court of an appropriate restraining order or other injunctive relief or other relief. The rights and remedies of the parties are cumulative and in addition to any rights or remedies provided by law. Any single or partial exercise of any right or remedy for default of breach hereof shall not waive, alter, affect, or prejudice any other right or remedy to which such party may be entitled. A minor or purely technical breach of this Agreement shall be insufficient cause to terminate this Agreement. Remedies available to the Provider include without limitation the following:

a) Requiring the Customer to provide additional financial security for its obligations;
b) Without notice, terminating this Agreement;
c) Retaining all sums received into the control of the Provider;
d) Without notice, entering and taking possession of the premises and, in the Provider's sole and unfettered discretion, removing any and all persons and things therein; and
e) Bringing an action or application for court relief against the Customer.

20. WAIVER

No waiver of any provision in this Agreement is effective unless in writing and signed by the Provider. No waiver of any provision shall constitute a waiver of any other provision.

21. ASSIGNMENT

This Agreement may not be assigned or transferred by the Customer to any other person without the prior written consent of the Provider, which consent may be arbitrarily withheld.

22. ENTIRE AGREEMENT

This Agreement constitutes the entire agreement between the parties except as may otherwise be expressly sanctioned herein. No modification or amendment of this Agreement is valid unless agreed to in writing by the parties. Any previous oral or written agreements between the parties are hereby superseded.

23. SEVERABILITY

Should any provision in this Agreement be held by a court to be invalid or unenforceable, such provision shall be severed from this Agreement and the Contract shall be binding and enforceable as if the severed provision had not existed.

24. SURVIVAL OF OBLIGATIONS

The obligation and covenants of the Customer under this Agreement and its schedules shall survive any termination of this Agreement, notwithstanding any agreement to the contrary.

25. TIME

Time is of the essence in this Agreement.

26. NOTICE

Notices under this Agreement shall be in writing and delivered by hand, fax, or post to the address of the party listed above.

27. GOVERNING LAW

This Agreement shall be construed in accordance with the laws of _____, whose courts shall have exclusive jurisdiction to resolve any disputes and claims arising between the parties.

Comprehensive Case Studies

Negligence

These fictional cases will give you the opportunity to discuss various aspects of negligence. The facts have purposely been presented to leave room for numerous interpretations. You may even want to add details to expand your discussion of the cases. Use tort law to find the hotel guilty or innocent. Is there a case for breach of contract?

1. Ms. Laura Doyle, an 87-year-old retired school teacher, was attending the annual convention and banquet for her sorority. The organizing committee for the sorority had met with the hotel to approve all the details and plans for the event. The banquet started with cocktails served from 5:00 p.m. to 6:30 p.m. After the cocktails the guests went into the large banquet room. The room was set up with large rectangular tables, each set for 20 guests. The chairs were placed so tight such that each was back to back and touching the chair behind and adjacent. Two bottles of red wine and white wine were placed strategically on each table. Laura took a seat in the middle of the table. The servers could not serve each guest individually but rather the meal plates were passed down the table by the guests themselves. At about 9:00 p.m. the tables were cleared of the dinner plates and the lights were dimmed for the speeches and presentations. After about 15 minutes Laura rose to meet her nephew, Donnie, in the lobby. She got past the first two guests and then she fell awkwardly to the ground.

2. Michael Wallace was graduating from Algonquin College's two-year Hotel and Restaurant Management program. It had been a challenging three-and-a-half years of school but he had finally met all the requirements. His parents had promised him a party "not to forget" upon graduation. Accompanied by his parents, he met with the banquet and party planners for a local hotel. The event was planned for the second weekend in May. The hotel would cater the party. The hotel could not promise that the pool in the court yard would be ready for a gathering that early in the season. The big day came and the weather was glorious. The party was held in a pool-side suite. The guests started to assemble just after noon. That evening, at about 10:30, Mimi, Michael's girlfriend for the last seven years, called him to join her in the pool. Mimi was crouched in the shallow end of the pool attempting to keep her shoulders out of the cold night air. Michael ran to the pool and dived in without looking, hitting his head on the bottom of the pool, rendering him a quadriplegic. The depth markers for the pool were not evident. Michael testified that he did not see the markers nor did he look for them.

Responsibilities of Innkeepers and the Rights of Guests

Analyze the following cases. These cases will test your knowledge of the responsibilities of innkeepers and the rights of guests.

1. Mr. Roger James, a travel agent, arrived at Ottawa International Airport. Ottawa was a regular stopover for him. He gathered his luggage and headed for the area where all the cabs and limos for the various hotels were parked. He gave his luggage to the limo for The Chateau. Once the luggage was safely in the trunk, he took a cab to a local restaurant for lunch. After a wonderful lunch but one that took too long because of slow service, he went on to The Chateau. When he arrived at the front desk, he was informed that the hotel was overbooked but that it had made a reservation for

him across the street at the Western Hotel. He was informed that his luggage would be forwarded to the Western Hotel. Later that afternoon, Mr. James checked into the Western Hotel. His luggage never arrived at his room. His luggage contained personal effects valued at $1,200, a laptop computer valued at $925, and a Rolex watch valued at $6,000. He is suing The Chateau, the limo, The Western Hotel, and the restaurant where he had lunch.

2. Mr. Cormack was a travelling sales representative for Beck's Jewellery Company. His sales territory was Canada. He was on a regular trip to Vancouver and planning on staying at The Impress Hotel. When he arrived at the front desk, he was greeted like a lost friend by the front office manager. He explained to the manager that he did not have time to check in but that he would do so later. This was acceptable to the hotel. Rather than carry his luggage with him, he left it in the care of the front office staff. He then went out to make some calls. When he returned to the hotel, there was a message awaiting him, requesting that he return immediately to Montreal. He asked for his luggage. It could not be found. Mr. Cormack is suing for recovery. He indicates that his loss was personal luggage valued at $2,000, a laptop valued at $925, and a jewellery sample case containing $24,000 in diamonds.

3. Claude was staying at the Ajax Hotel. He was employed by Air Canada and was in Toronto for a six-month training program. His friend Ben was also staying in the same hotel while on business in Toronto. The two friends thought it would be fun to invite another friend, Julian, from Cornwall to visit and party with them over the weekend. They met up in the hotel lobby, had a couple of drinks, and headed out to the Casino for a night's fun. They gambled all night and Julian was fortunate enough to win over $800. They returned to the hotel and put the winnings in the hotel vault. This was a big weekend for the boys; they changed, had a light lunch, and took off for a baseball game. After the game, they hit a couple of bars. Some young ladies from Toronto made the acquaintance of the three men. They all continued to party and spent the night together in one of the girl's apartments. When the three men returned to the hotel, the lobby was full of police. The entire hotel had been robbed. The men are suing for recovery. Claude lists his losses as $3,000 personal, a stereo, and books valued at $400. Ben lists his losses as $1,200 personal and $50 for his cell phone. Julian is attempting to recover for $600 personal and the $800 he put in the safe.

4. Harvey, a senior citizen travelling across Canada, was staying over in Edmonton. He checked in and went to his room. The night auditor for the hotel called him about 3 a.m. to let him know that his credit card was on a hot list for American Express and that he should come down to the desk. The clerk informed him that he could not leave and that security was at the door at this very minute. Harvey could not stand the stress. He suffered a heart attack. He is now suing for damages.

Appendix 4 / Comprehensive Case Studies

Glossary

abandoned property   property that the owner has given his or her title to

ab initio   from the beginning

absolute liability   total responsibility or total liability

acceptance   the unqualified willingness to enter into a contract on the terms of the offer

accommodate   the duty of an employer to modify work rules, practices, and requirements to meet the needs of individuals who would otherwise be subjected to unlawful discrimination

actus reus   guilty act

addendum   something added to the main document

adjudicate   decide, often in a judicial or quasi-judicial setting

affidavit   a written statement made under oath

agency relationship   a relationship that exists when one party represents another party in the formation of legal relations

agent   a person who acts on behalf of a principal

appeal   the process of arguing to a higher court that a court decision is wrong

arraignment   the reading of the criminal charge in open court

bailee   the person who is entrusted the property for care

bailor   the person who is depositing the property

Bill of Rights   the first national listing of human rights in Canada

board of directors   one or more individuals elected by the shareholders to manage the corporation

bona fide   in good faith; genuine

building codes   the minimum building standards

bylaws   laws made by the municipal level of government

cabotage   the right of an airline in one country to operate flights between two or more locations inside another country

Canada Labour Standards   laws that set minimum standards in the Canadian workplace

Canadian Charter of Rights and Freedoms   a guarantee of specific rights and frreedoms enshrined in the Constitution and enforced by the judiciary

capacity   the ability to make binding contracts

chattels   moveable, tangible items of personal property

common law   rules that are formulated in judgments

consideration   the price paid for a promise

contract   an agreement between two parties that is enforceable in a court of law

contributory negligence   a defence claiming that the plaintiff is at least partially responsible for the harm that has occurred

counteroffer   the rejection of one offer and the proposal of a new one

damages   an award to the plaintiff to punish the defendant for malicious, oppressive, and high-handed conduct

deceit   fraudulent misrepresentation

defamation   the public utterance or dissemination of a false statement of fact or opinion that harms another's reputation

defendant   a person defending a lawsuit or criminal charge

disclaimer   a provision intended to protect oneself against liability

discovery   the process of disclosing evidence to support the claims in lawsuit

discrimination   the treating of someone differently on the basis of a prohibited ground

duty of care   the responsibility owed to avoid careless acts that cause harm to others

easement   the right to use the land of another for a particular purpose

enjoin   obtain an injunction against; prevent

equal pay legislation   provisions designed to ensure that female and male employees receive the same compensation for performing similar or substantially similar work

equitable fair, honest, according to conscience

estop prevent

eviction lawful removal of a guest from the property

exemplary damages damages awarded to make an example of the wrongdoer

false arrest unlawful detention or physical restraint of a person

fiduciary relating to the holding of something in trust for another

franchise a right or set of rights granted by the owner of the rights permitting another person to use the rights in exchange for consideration

good faith acting honestly, without fraud, collusion, or participation in wrong doing

gratuitous without payment; without compulsion

gratuitous promises a promise for which no consideration is given

guest a person temporarily housed, fed, or entertained by another

hospitality law a set of established rules governing hospitality relationships, including the enforcement of rights

hotel a public house offering overnight rest and accommodation

house rules regulations that govern the behaviour of people while on the property

human rights in Canada the fundamental rights of a person in Canada

ill-repute bad reputation

independent contractors a person who is in a working relationship that does not meet the criteria of employment

infra hospitium within the walls of the inn

injunction a court order preventing something

injurious falsehood the public utterance or dissemination of a false statement about another's business, goods, or services that is harmful to the reputation of the business, goods, or services

inn a public house offering overnight rest and accommodation

innkeeper someone who offers temporary lodging to the public

intangibles personal property, the value of which comes from legal rights

invitation to treat an expression of willingness to do business

invitees any person who comes onto the property, with the occupier's expressed or tacit consent, to provide the occupier with a benefit

irrevocable cannot be revoked

judgment-proof a protected state in which one's assets cannot be seized

jurisdictions the power that a given level of government has to enact laws

just cause employee conduct that amounts to a fundamental breach of the employment contract

land lien the right to encumber land owned by another as security for the performance of the land owner's obligation

landlord a person who leases land to a tenant

law the set of rules and principles guiding conduct in society

legality a contract must not be contrary to legislation or public policy

liability legal responsibility for the event or loss that has occurred

licence the right to do something that only the holder can do

licensee any person whose presence on the property is not a benefit to the occupier but to which the occupier has objection

lien the right to retain possession of personal property until payment for service is received

liquidated fixed or able to be calculated with certainty

litigant a participant in a civil lawsuit

litigation the process involved when one person sues another

lost property property that has been separated from its owner and the owner is unaware of its location

mens rea guilty mind or criminal intent

mislaid property property that the owner has forgotten the location of

mitigate take steps to lessen one's damages and losses

mortgage a loan contract whereby real estate is given as security

mortgagee a person receiving real estate as security for a loan

mortgagor a person giving real estate as security for a loan

negligence   a civil wrong arising from a failure to take proper care

negligence per se   the failure to meet a government regulation

negligent misrepresentation   an incorrect statement made carelessly that causes harm to another

nepotism   favouritism shown to family members

nonguests   these include: invitees, trespassers, licensees

occupier   any person with a legal right to occupy premises

occupiers' liability   occupiers owe a reasonable duty to persons who enter upon their premises

offeree   the person to whom the offer is made

offeror   the person making the offer

option   a choice; a right of first refusal

paramountcy   the constitutional superiority of some laws over other laws

parol evidence rule   a rule that limits the evidence that a party can introduce concerning the contents of a contract

passing off   presenting one's own goods or services as those of others

plaintiff   a person commencing a lawsuit

pleadings   the formal documents concerning the basis for a lawsuit

principal   a person who contracts with other parties through an agent

private nuisance   any activity on a occupier's property that unreasonably and substantially interferes with a neighbour's rights to enjoyment of her property

privity   the legal principle that only those who are parties to a contract can enforce the rights and obligations it contains

privity of contract   the obligations and benefits arising under a contract are confined to the parties to the contract

promissee   the person to whom the promise is made

promissory   the person making the promise

provincial fire codes   the minimum fire standards for construction and operation of premises

punitive damages   awards above actual financial losses to punish tortfeasors

Quebec Civil Code   the rules of private law that govern Quebec

racism   discrimination on the basis of race

real property   immovable property including land, buildings, and fixtures

reasonable person   the standard used to judge whether a person's conduct in a particular situation is negligent

received   the transient is accepted by the innkeeper as a guest

rejection   the refusal to accept an offer

repudiate   deny the application of a contract or agreement

rescission   cancellation of a contract by an innocent party

res ipsa loquitur   the thing speaks for itself

revoked   the offer is withdrawn

royal prerogatives   historical rights and privileges of the Crown, including the right to conduct foreign affairs and to declare war

severance pay   an amount owed to a terminated employee under employment standards legislation

shareholder   a person who has an ownership interest in a corporation

statutory   of statutes, formal laws enacted by the legislative branch of the federal or provincial government

strict liability   liability is imposed regardless of how innocent the tortfeasor was or how much care was taken to avoid causing the injury

Supreme Court of Canada   the final court for appeals in the country

tenant   a person who leases land from a landlord

thin skull rule   the principle that a defendant is liable for the full extent of a plaintiff's loss even where a prior vulnerability makes the harm more serious than it otherwise might be

tort   a harm, usually other than by a criminal act caused by one person to another, other than through breach of contract, for which the law provides a remedy

tortfeasor   person committing a tort

trademark   a symbol, word, name, or device adopted to identify a company or its product

transient   a person who passes through or stays for a very short time

trespasser   any person who is neither an invitee nor a licensee and whose presence on the property is either unknown or is objected to by the occupier

trial   a formal hearing before a judge that results in a binding decision

under seal   promises made under the promissor's seal are binding even in the absence of consideration

vexatious   not in good faith or for proper reasons

vicarious   substituted for another person or thing

vicarious liability   the liability that an employer has for the tortious acts committed by an employee in the ordinary or usual course of employment

voluntary assumption of risk   the defence that no liability exists as the plaintiff agreed to the risk inherent in the activity

walking the guest   finding alternative accommodation for guests with room reservation

zoning   allowed activities in the area

Selected Bibliography

Amirault, Ernest, and Maurice Archer. *Canada's Hospitality Law*. Toronto: Macmillan, 1978.

Cournoyer, Norman G., Anthony G. Marshall, and Karen L. Morris. *Hotel, Restaurant and Travel Law*. 4th ed. Albany, New York: Delmar, 1993.

DuPlessis, Dorothy, Steven Enman, Shannon O'Byrne, and Sally Gunz. *Canadian Business & the Law*. 2nd ed. Toronto: Thomson Nelson, 2005.

Echlin, R., and C. Thomlinson. *For Better or For Worse: A Practical Guide to Canadian Employment Law*. Aurora, Ont.: Canada Law Book Inc., 1996.

Elliott, Cheryl, and Stewart Saxe. *The Pay Equity Handbook*. Aurora, Ont.: Canada Law Book Inc., 1987.

Gibson, D.L., T.A. Murphy, F.E. Jarman, and D. Grant. *All About Law*. Scarborough, Ont.: ITP Nelson, 1996.

Grosman, Brian A., and John R. Martin. *Discrimination in Employment in Ontario*. Aurora, Ont.: Canada Law Book Inc., 1994.

Harvey, Cameron. *The Liability of Canadian Innkeepers for the Goods or Property of Guests or Travellers*. Peterborough, Ont.: Chitty's Law Journal, 1969.

James, Phillip. *Introduction to English Law*. 12th ed. Markham, Ont.: Butterworths, 1989.

Keene, Judith. *Human Rights in Ontario*. 2nd ed. Scarborough, Ont.: Carswell, 1992.

Sherry, John H. *The Laws of Innkeepers*. Ithaca, N.Y.: Cornell University Press, 1973.

Walker, James W. St. G. *Race, Rights and the Law in the Supreme Court of Canada: Historical Case Studies*. North York, Ont.: The Osgoode Society, 1997.

Wright, David. *Professional Travel Counselling*. 3rd ed. Toronto: Canadian Institute of Travel Counsellors of Ontario, 1997.

Yates, Richard. *Business Law in Canada*. 4th ed. Scarborough, Ont.: Prentice-Hall Canada, 1995.

Zablocki, Christine. *Hospitality Law in Ontario: A Practical Guide*. Aurora, Ont.: Canada Law Book Inc., 1997.

Zwarensteyn, Hendrik. *Legal Aspects of Hotel Administration*. East Lansing, Mich.: Bureau of Business and Economic Research, Graduate School of Business Administration, 1962.

Copyright
Acknowledgments

Grateful acknowledgment is made to the copyright holders who granted the publisher permission to use the following materials.

Cover image and, in modified form, pages i, iii, xxx, 114, 176, 238, and 320: Todd Pearson/Photodisc Red/Getty Images

Chapter 1, page 10: © KING FEATURES SYNDICATE

Chapter 2, page 39: Photodisc/Getty Images

Chapter 3, page 58: Sheraton Center Toronto Hotel/Starwood Hotels & Resorts Canada; page 59: PEANUTS: © United Feature Syndicate, Inc.; page 81: Sheraton Center Toronto Hotel/Starwood Hotels & Resorts Canada

Chapter 4, page 100: Sheraton Center Toronto Hotel/Starwood Hotels & Resorts Canada; page 107: WeatherPine Inn (B&B)

Chapter 5, page 122: Four Seasons Hotel Toronto; page 128: Sheraton Center Toronto Hotel/Starwood Hotels & Resorts Canada; page 143: Corel

Chapter 6, page 154: Corel; page 159: Corel

Chapter 7, page 163: Photodisc/Getty Images

Chapter 8, page 181: Sheraton Center Toronto Hotel/Starwood Hotels & Resorts Canada

Chapter 9, page 192: Reprinted by permission of Lions Foundation of Canada Dog Guides

Chapter 10, page 205: Sheraton Center Toronto Hotel/Starwood Hotels & Resorts Canada

Chapter 11, page 223: Photodisc/Getty Images

Chapter 12, page 264: Photodisc/Getty Images; page 267: Photodisc/Getty Images

Chapter 13, page 276: Reprinted by permission of Choice Hotels Canada

Chapter 14, page 311: Photodisc/Getty Images

Chapter 15, page 324: Corel; page 338: Corel

Appendix 3, page 365: Reprinted by permission of Lord Elgin Hotel

Index

Cases in boldface type are discussed in some detail in the text. Other indexed cases are merely mentioned.

EMily Dare